CONQUERING THE OCEAN

Ancient Warfare and Civilization

SERIES EDITORS:

RICHARD ALSTON ROBIN WATERFIELD

In this series, leading historians offer compelling new narratives of the armed conflicts that shaped and reshaped the classical world, from the wars of Archaic Greece to the fall of the Roman Empire and the Arab conquests.

By the Spear
Philip II, Alexander the Great, and the Rise and Fall of the Macedonian Empire
Ian Worthington

Taken at the Flood
The Roman Conquest of Greece
Robin Waterfield

In God's Path
The Arab Conquests and the Creation of an Islamic Empire
Robert G. Hoyland

Mastering the West
Rome and Carthage at War
Dexter Hoyos

Rome's Revolution
Death of the Republic and Birth of the Empire
Richard Alston

The Plague of War
Athens, Sparta, and the Struggle for Ancient Greece
Jennifer T. Roberts

Rome Resurgent
War and Empire in the Age of Justinian
Peter Heather

Conquering the Ocean
The Roman Invasion of Britain
Richard Hingley

CONQUERING THE OCEAN

The Roman Invasion of Britain

Richard Hingley

OXFORD
UNIVERSITY PRESS

OXFORD
UNIVERSITY PRESS

Oxford University Press is a department of the University of Oxford. It furthers the University's objective of excellence in research, scholarship, and education by publishing worldwide. Oxford is a registered trade mark of Oxford University Press in the UK and certain other countries.

Published in the United States of America by Oxford University Press
198 Madison Avenue, New York, NY 10016, United States of America.

Library of Congress Cataloging-in-Publication Data
Names: Hingley, Richard, author.
Title: Conquering the ocean : the Roman invasion of Britain / Richard Hingley.
Description: New York, NY : Oxford University Press, [2022] |
Series: Ancient warfare and civilization | Includes bibliographical references and index.
Identifiers: LCCN 2021037374 (print) | LCCN 2021037375 (ebook) |
ISBN 9780190937416 (hardback) | ISBN 9780197555002 |
ISBN 9780190937430 (epub) | ISBN 9780190937423
Subjects: LCSH: Romans—Great Britain. | Great Britain—History—Roman period,
55 B.C.–449 A.D. | Great Britain—History, Military—55 B.C.–449 A.D. |
Great Britain—History—Invasions. | Rome—History,
Military—265–30 B.C. | Rome—History, Military—30 B.C.–476 A.D. |
Great Britain—Antiquities.
Classification: LCC DA145 .H497 2022 (print) | LCC DA145 (ebook) |
DDC 936.1/04—dc23
LC record available at https://lccn.loc.gov/2021037374
LC ebook record available at https://lccn.loc.gov/2021037375

DOI: 10.1093/oso/9780190937416.001.0001

1 3 5 7 9 8 6 4 2

Printed by LSC communications, United States of America

Dedicated to Anthony (Tony) Birley (1937–2020), in memory of his scholarship and a precious friendship.

PREFACE

I VIVIDLY RECALL THE COPY of Sheppard Frere's *Britannia* (1967) that my mother lent to me when I was a child. Reading this book at an early age inspired me to take an interest in the Iron Age and Roman periods of the British past, and this eventually led to my career in academic research. Frere's influential volume was one of the first of numerous published works focusing on the Roman military conquest of Britain and the assimilation (also termed 'Romanisation') of its peoples.[1] This well-established academic tradition was challenged by my generation of researchers in Roman studies as we turned our attention to the complex identities of the peoples of ancient Britain, the mobility of their populations, and the highly variable ways in which individuals and communities responded to the Roman conquest and to the assimilation of these lands. Meanwhile, ancient historians lost confidence in the value of the classical texts as a source of historical knowledge, and began to focus on their role as literary products. The new research in both fields has achieved considerable successes; for archaeology this is demonstrated by the individual contributions to the *Oxford Handbook of Roman Britain* (2016).[2]

There is, however, no detailed discussion of the chronology of the Roman conquest of Britain in this *Handbook*; and none of the essays it contains consider the motivations of the emperors and commanders who led the invasion of Britain—these topics are usually left to the ancient historians. In this sense, the approach taken in this book, which focuses on the Roman conquest, echoes a tradition of the study of the Roman elite that many archaeologists of my generation have long been determined to critique. Research in archaeology has now progressed to the point that we are much better able to appreciate the lives of people in the past who were not particularly privileged, and although I draw attention to this information here wherever possible, my main aim is to return attention to the military acts and political decisions that led to the conquest itself.

Because the amount of information provided by the surviving classical texts is limited, recent work on Roman Britain has been dominated by archaeologists. Despite this, however, a fresh seam of research in classical literature has emerged to shed new light on how the Roman elite viewed Britain and its peoples.[3] Archaeologists tend not to make much use of such research, with the result that studies of Roman Britain have increasingly been divided into two distinct fields with different approaches and interests. Of particular importance for the narrative of my account of the conquest of Roman Britain are two synthetic volumes by ancient historians, Anthony Birley's work *The Roman Government of Britain* (2005), and Roger Tomlin's *Britannia Romana* (2018).[4] The first contains a very detailed and scholarly synthesis of the literary texts and inscriptions which elucidate the history of the Roman conquest and occupation. Tomlin's book, meanwhile, includes information about many of the inscriptions discussed in the chapters here. Roman Inscriptions of Britain (*RIB*) online, which includes the Bloomberg writing tablets (London) and those from Vindolanda, as well as the inscriptions from Britain on stone, has also served as a vital resource.[5] The archaeological information drawn upon here is published in many different books and journals.

This book seeks to navigate the division between accounts of classical literature and studies of archaeological materials. It also aims to cross another intellectual boundary hampering research, that between the studies of Iron Age and of Roman Britain. While researching and writing this work, I have also been encouraged and inspired by the publication of an impressive body of research on the Roman conquests of Iberia, Gaul, and Germany.[6] Although I have needed to gloss over various disagreements in the interpretation of the events narrated here, I have included references in the notes to works that complicate my simplified narrative.

I am particularly grateful to Stefan Vranka at Oxford University Press (New York) for the invitation to write this book. My research has been assisted by the Arts and Humanities Research Council funding for the 'Ancient Identities' project (2016–19; project number AH/N006151/1).[7] Durham University provided two terms of research leave during 2019–20, which enabled me to complete an early draft of this book. I am also extremely grateful to friends and colleagues for help and advice with my research. My greatest debt, as with my earlier books, is to my partner, Christina Unwin, for her work on preparing the illustrations, and for her thoughtful and intellectual approach to interacting with the themes and topics discussed. Martha Stewart worked tirelessly to improve the narrative and provided additional insights. I am also most grateful to the Newgen production team and, in particular, to Martha Ramsey for the thorough and careful editing and preparation of this book. Colin Haselgrove provided important commentary on the contents of chapters 1–5, while Matthew Symonds commented on the entire text. I am also most grateful to Paul Bidwell, Andrew Birley, David Breeze, Barry Burnham, John Creighton, Philip Crummy, Manuel Fernández-Götz, Andrew Fitzpatrick, Adam Gwilt, William Hanson, Nick Hodgson, Lynn Pitts, Kurt Raaflaub, Duane W. Roller, Chris Rudd, Michael Shanks, Robert Strassler, Ilkka Syvanne, the series editors, and the anonymous reviewer for their help and advice with the text and images.

Richard Hingley
Holly Tree Lodge, Shincliffe, Durham, UK
10 June 2021

CONTENTS

INTRODUCTION

SETTING THE SCENE

AN OCEANIC ISLAND

Why should a distant island beyond the north-western edge of the Roman Empire have become the target of Roman ambitions for conquest? Julius Caesar was the first Roman to campaign in Britain. He tells us that little was known about the land or its people before this, and that his desire to know more motivated both his landing in south-east Britain in 55 BCE and his return with a larger army the following year. With these campaigns Caesar intended to extend his conquest of the vast lands of Gaul, already achieved over the previous three campaigning seasons. Members of the Roman elite were particularly attracted to the mysterious land of Britain, as they thought of the world as a large island surrounded by the waters of 'Ocean' (fig. I.1). Ocean had a special attraction.

The Romans inherited the worship of Oceanus from the Greeks, and believed that the waters surrounding the inhabited world were endless.[1] According to ancient legend, the Titan Oceanus was one of the first gods, and father of all the water deities, who inhabited sea foam, rivers, rainwater, and wells (fig. I.2). Travel by sea beyond the waters of the Mediterranean was dangerous and daring, and risked divine disfavour. Almost three centuries before Caesar travelled to Britain, the Macedonian general Alexander won fame by his campaigns across the lands of Mesopotamia and to India beyond. A contemporary of Caesar recorded that Alexander

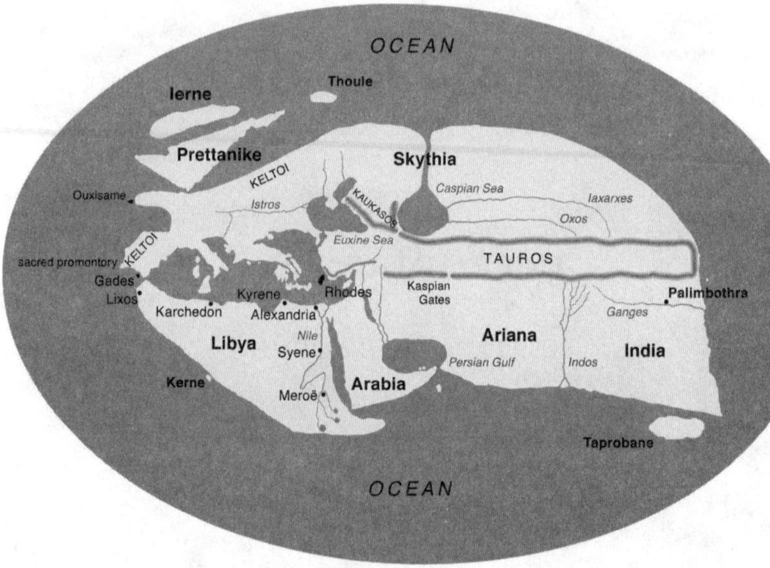

FIG I.1.
The world according to Strabo, showing the location of Prettankie (Britain) and Ierne (Ireland) (after Roller 2018, fig. 1)

FIG I.2.
Floor mosaic showing Oceanus and his wife Tethys from the ancient city of Zeugma (Turkey) (Shutterstock, image ID: 641982193).

had sacrificed to Oceanus before sailing back west from India, across the Arabian Sea.[2] Alexander, in his own exploits, was emulating the widespread travels of the mythical Heracles, from whom he claimed descent.[3] Known to the Romans as Hercules, Heracles was the son of Zeus and a mortal woman, and was reported to have sailed far across Ocean to an island of the Hesperides in the far western Mediterranean, in order to steal the cattle of the giant Geryon. Some believed that Heracles had sailed into the Atlantic Ocean through the Straits of Gibraltar, known in antiquity as the 'Pillars of Hercules' (fig. I.3); but even so great a hero as this half-god did not reach the islands of Britain.

At about the same time Alexander was campaigning in India, however, the Greek traveller Pytheas had sailed to Britain, and beyond, to the mythical island of *Thule* (Shetland or Iceland). In Caesar's time, Roman knowledge of the western seas beyond their Mediterranean world was limited, although there were tales of sailors who had navigated these waters. Phoenician and Carthaginian traders had been attracted by the

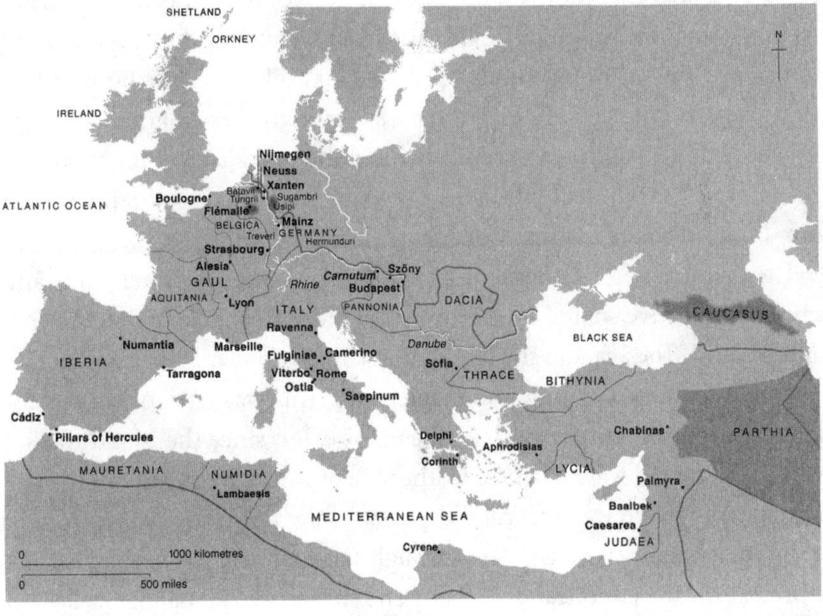

FIG I.3.
The Roman Empire, showing its frontiers around 120 CE, showing places and regions mentioned in the text.

mineral resources to be found in Britain, particularly tin, for several centuries before Caesar travelled to the island.[4] Pytheas' account of Britain was one of the few available to Caesar's contemporaries at Rome, but many doubted his observations. When Caesar saw the statue of Alexander at the temple of Hercules Gaditanus at Cadiz (*Gades*, Spain),[5] he was inspired to emulate the great commander by seeking glorious conquests.[6] By invading Gaul and Germany, and then by voyaging across Ocean to Britain, Caesar was emulating Alexander's reputation for campaigning in unknown and distant lands (fig. I.4). To travel to Britain was to seek the subjection not only of the peoples living beyond the limit of the inhabited world but also of the divine power of Ocean.

Some of Caesar's contemporaries expressed disappointment with the wealth and slaves he brought back to Rome after the surrender of several British kings. Despite this, his campaigns heightened the Roman elite's awareness of Britain, creating the idea that the conquest of this land (and Ocean) would contribute considerably to the reputation of an ambitious emperor in search of military success. After Caesar's death Rome was ruled by a succession of emperors; the first two, Augustus and Tiberius, secured peace in Britain by diplomatic means. Caligula, however, in a bid to acquire military credentials, decided to emulate Caesar by invading Germany and Britain. He failed to carry through these plans, and it was his successor, Claudius, who commanded the first successful invasion of Britain in 43 CE. Indeed, the propaganda of this emperor's reign placed him in the elevated company of Alexander and Caesar.

The conquest and settlement of Britain by Rome was a religious and military objective shared by senior commanders from Caesar to Hadrian and beyond. The sea and the land lying within it had a numinous quality that elevated campaigning to a magical act. This was true, of course, for all campaigns across the lands of the empire, but since the island was set within the sacred waters of Ocean, the idea of commanding the successful invasion of Britain was accorded a special quality. As the emperors sought to increase their personal power through self-deification, religion became a pretext for the conquest of Britain. The success of campaigns in Britain helped secure the divinity of several emperors, including Claudius, Vespasian, and Hadrian. Conversely, failures in Britain contributed to the

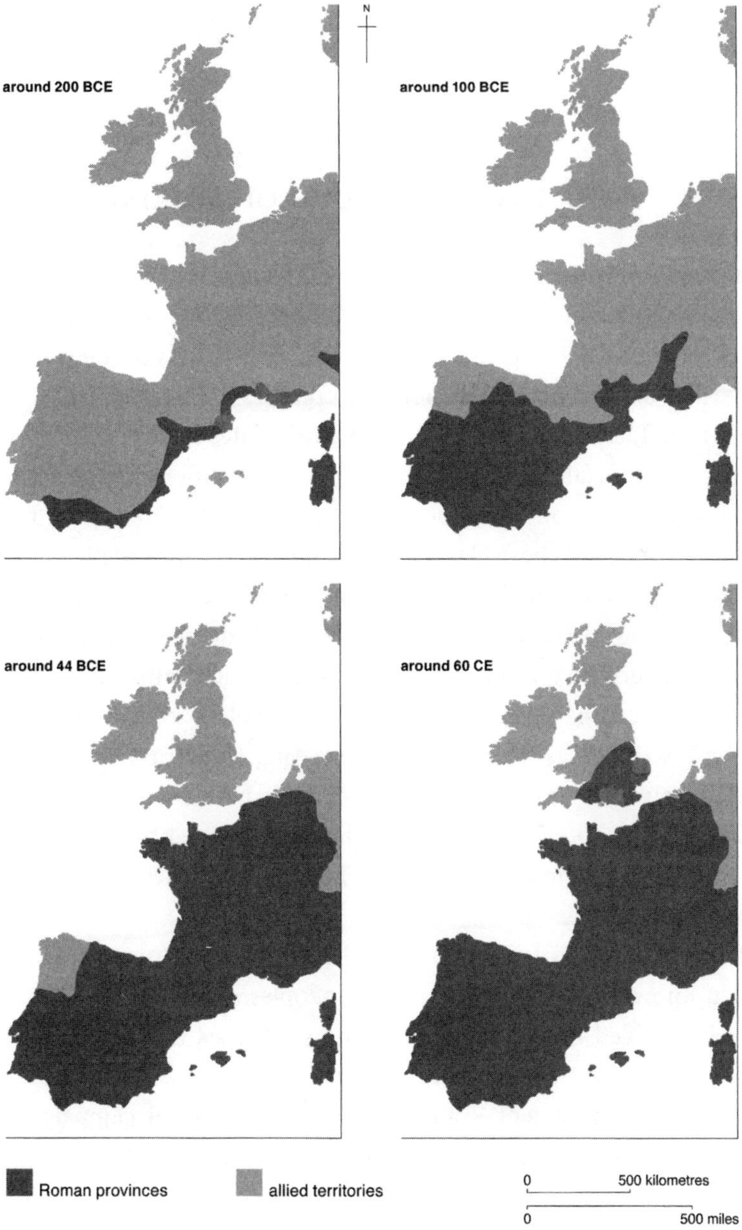

FIG I.4.
Roman imperial expansion, 200 BCE–60 CE, showing the significance of Caesar's conquest of Gaul (after Millett 1990, fig. 1, with additions)

poor reputation of the emperors Caligula, Nero, and Domitian, who were damned at death by order of the Roman Senate.

HOW DO WE KNOW ABOUT THE ROMAN CONQUEST OF BRITAIN?

Much of our knowledge of the motives of the generals and emperors who oversaw the conquest of Britain has been derived from the writings of classical authors. These also give us dates, and details of the geographical extent of the Roman invasion and conquest of Britain. The accounts in Caesar, Tacitus, and Cassius Dio provide dates for its decisive events, names of important Romans and Britons, and opinions on the actions of prominent people on both sides of the conflict. There are gaps in the historical coverage of these classical texts, however, with little recorded for the entire period from 84 to 138 CE apart from a few comments. Ancient historians and archaeologists have long considered these accounts as 'sources', a term that implies that they contain factual information about events that can be taken on trust. Today, scholars instead usually refer to these writings as 'literary texts', reflecting the idea that they tell us at least as much about the attitudes of their authors as the events that they describe. To evaluate the information provided by these writings, we therefore need to know about the lives and attitudes of the men who wrote them.

Two of the key authors writing on the conquest of Roman Britain possessed knowledge of the land and its peoples. Caesar's two campaigns, indeed, enabled him to experience the south-east of the island at first hand. By the time he led his legions across the English Channel to Kent, this scion of an ancient Roman family had also been campaigning in nearby Gaul for the previous three years. Tacitus (c. 56–120 CE) was born into a wealthy family probably living in the prosperous territory of Cisalpine Gaul, the northern part of modern Italy. He was also a prominent member of the Roman senatorial elite. It is possible that Tacitus had direct experience of campaigning across the west and central region of the island, or at least derived his information from conversations with his father-in-law Agricola, the province's governor. The writings of Tacitus provide crucial information for the military campaigns in Britain of the mid to late first century CE.

Although they were well-informed authors, Caesar and Tacitus had their own motives for writing about Britain. Caesar's account was designed to glorify his own achievements, and although his work *The Gallic War* was written to be read as a descriptive account of the eight years' conflict, it is important to consider his comments in this context. In book 5, for example, he described the population of Kent as the most civilized in Britain, and the peoples of the 'inlands' (the lands north of the River Thames) as nomadic barbarians. There was a long classical tradition of referring to non-Romans who lived beyond the Mediterranean as nomadic pastoralists, addicted to fighting. As I will show, however, a century of archaeological research has demonstrated that these Iron Age peoples had their own cultures, and for the most part lived at peace, in a settled agricultural landscape (fig. I.5). Caesar's own actions seriously disrupted their lives, bringing warfare to north-western Gaul and Britain on an unprecedented scale. He wrote that the Britons fought alongside

FIG I.5.
A reconstructed Iron Age roundhouse at Butser Ancient Farm (Hampshire); houses of this type were very common across southern Britain and help to indicate that Caesar exaggerated the Britons' bellicose character (Photograph by Richard Hingley)

the Gauls during the early years of the Gallic War, which, if true, suggests that the peoples of south-eastern Britain would have been fully aware of the slaughter Rome could inflict on its enemies. Caesar used such violent resistance to Roman incursions as the justification for further attacks against neighbouring peoples, the 'free barbarians' inhabiting territory beyond the immediate area of conflict. Other commanders employed this same line of Roman imperial propaganda on many occasions during the conquest of Britain.

Despite the limitations of his account, Caesar was an important eyewitness to Iron Age society in Britain, and many of his observations have been supported by subsequent archaeological research. Caesar directly exploited the lack of unity he encountered among those who resisted his campaigns. Britain, like Gaul, was inhabited by many different peoples, often designated 'tribes' by modern authors.[7] Caesar referred to several peoples and their leaders by name; the most powerful of them sought friendship with Rome and were called 'kings'. Other leaders chose to lead their people against Caesar, supported by their kin and by friends from neighbouring territories. During his second invasion, although the Britons had mustered in numbers large enough to constitute an effective opposition to his legions—including, we are told, four thousand warriors in chariots—Caesar was always ready to exploit rivalry between the peoples of Britain. At the time of the Roman invasions, there was no concept in the minds of the inhabitants of a united 'Britain'. Instead, they operated as local and regional groupings with loose affiliations to friends and enemies alike. Britannia was a Roman concept of an island on which successive Roman generals and emperors focused their ambitions of conquest.

The name used for Britain varies in the classical texts.[8] The earliest name for the main island is thought to have been *Albion* (Mainland?), although Britannia (*Prettanike*, *Brettania*) was more commonly used from the first century BCE. This name has no direct origin in the Celtic languages and is probably a Latin version of an ethnic term, or even a poetic creation. The term was coined by the Romans as a name for the island during the time of Caesar. The people he encountered had no unity that would have required them to express their identities as

Britons. References to the 'Britannic islands' normally meant Britain and Ireland. Ireland was known by several terms, including *Ierne* and *Hibernia*, by the Romans.

Tacitus made observations about Britannia in both his accounts of the history of the Roman empire, the *Annals* and the *Histories*.[9] Passages in both works describe the military campaigns, the resistance of the Britons to the Roman invasion, and the important actors in the conflict, both Roman and British. Tacitus was fascinated by the idea of female rule. He remarked that it was not unusual for women to lead the Britons in war, a famous example being Boudica, who led her forces against Rome in 60 CE. Another significant female leader was Cartimandua, queen of a people called the Brigantes, although there is no indication that she led her people into battle. Tacitus' motivation for writing about Britain was most clearly expressed in the *Agricola*, a biography of his recently deceased relative. Agricola enjoyed great success during his extended term as provincial governor in Britain, almost completing the conquest of the mainland with the victory at *Mons Graupius* in 84 CE. By portraying Agricola's career as exemplary, Tacitus was also condemning the dictatorial rule of the late emperor Domitian and supporting the damning of his memory by the Senate.

Although Caesar and Claudius led invasions of Britain in person, other emperors appointed provincial governors such as Agricola to act on their behalf. These governors conducted military campaigns in the province, usually serving for three or four years before they were either recalled to Rome or assigned elsewhere in the empire and replaced by a new commander. In the *Agricola* Tacitus wrote about the campaigns led by his father-in-law, exaggerating his success in northern Britain to suggest that the conquest was almost complete. As we learn in the opening paragraph, this is not intended primarily to be a descriptive historical account but a literary work in praise of Agricola. Archaeological research into the distribution of Roman fortifications across northern Scotland has demonstrated that Roman forces did not, in fact, subdue the extensive and mountainous Scottish highlands and that consequently the conquest of Britain remained incomplete.

The third classical author known to have written a significant amount about the Roman conquest of Britain was Cassius Dio (c. 164–229 CE), a member of the Roman senatorial elite from Bithynia (modern Turkey).[10] His *Roman History*, in eighty books, was written in Greek and gives an account of Rome and its empire from the foundation of the city, traditionally 753 BCE, to 229 CE. Dio himself had no personal experience of Britain or its people. He gathered information, however, from earlier writings, summarized many accounts no longer surviving, and described events not recorded elsewhere. His account of the first few years after the invasion of Claudius, for example, is vitally important because the chapters of Tacitus' *Annals* in which these events would have been described have not survived. The manuscripts of many texts have not survived in full, and consequently the history of the conquest must be reconstructed from often fragmentary accounts. Dio's famous description of Boudica having tawny hair, a cloak of many colours, and a torc around her neck has inspired many depictions of this British ruler since the sixteenth century (fig. I.6). As this is the only physical description of a Briton in surviving classical texts, we are uncertain whether this was based on the observations of a Roman who had met Boudica or was a literary invention on the part of Dio, or of one of the texts on which he drew, intending to enliven his account.

Archaeological discoveries and interpretations have the potential to nuance the perspectives of these elite male authors, who tended to focus on the powerful men on both sides of the conflict. Accounts of Boudica and Cartimandua are the exception, although it is also clear that Tacitus and Dio wrote about Boudica partly to emphasize the 'otherness' of the ancient Britons in not living according to Roman concepts of society, including accepted gender divisions. The inscribed stone grave-markers of legionary and auxiliary soldiers found throughout Roman Britain have provided insights into the lives of men who were too lowly in status to be of interest to classical authors. For example, Longinus Sdapeze, an auxiliary cavalry soldier from Sofia (Bulgaria), was buried at Camulodunum (Colchester, Essex) during the first decade of the Claudian invasion. His tombstone depicts him riding down a naked barbarian (fig. I.7). Inscriptions from burial monuments sometimes also include information

FIG I.6.
Woodcut print of 'Boadicea' from the 1632 edition of John Speed, *The History of Great Britaine*; Cassius Dio's descriptions of Boudica/Boadicea have inspired many images from the late sixteenth century to the present day (Reproduced by permission of Durham University Library)

about freed slaves and women. From South Shields (*Arbeia*; Tyne and Wear), for instance, comes the memorial to a British woman called Regina, a freed slave married to a Syrian trader, who died during the late second century (fig. I.8). The Vindolanda 'letters', small fragments of bark on which Latin messages are written in ink, have provided considerable information about the military community on the northern

FIG I.7.
The tombstone of Longinus Sdapeze from Camulodunum (Copyright: Colchester Museum)

frontier during the late first and early second century, including women and slaves.

Britons are generally difficult to locate in these local written sources. This is despite the fact that the leaders of the peoples living in the south-east had used Latin script before Claudius' invasion, as shown by the legends of late Iron Age coins, which, in imitation of Roman types, included the names of kings and royal centres. Latin became the main language

FIG I.8.
The Roman tombstone of Regina from South Shields (from J. C. Bruce 1907, p. 242)

used by many inhabitants of the province during the Roman occupation, and occasionally it has been possible to identify Britons such as Regina from surviving inscriptions. Another example, on a commemorative stone from the temple to Neptune and Minerva at Chichester (*Noviomagus*, West Sussex), records the name of Togidubnus, a British king friendly to Rome in the years immediately following Claudius' invasion. Since there were close links between south-eastern Britain and

Gaul throughout the conquest period, it may be that this great ruler was actually a Gaul.

The discipline of archaeology has also contributed to our understanding of the events and personalities addressed in this book. By providing detailed information about the settlements and landscapes occupied by ancient Britons, the forts established by the Roman forces, and the urban centres subsequently developing across southern and central Britain, it sets the classical writings in context. Archaeological research has shown that Iron Age society was highly sophisticated, and very different from the classical authors' portrayal of it. Iron Age Britons had their own social and cultural ways of life, building substantial houses and settlements within a landscape developed for agricultural production millennia before the arrival of Julius Caesar. Excavations at Roman forts have uncovered significant information about how the soldiers who invaded Britain were living. The character of the strongholds of the Late Iron Age and the towns of early Roman Britain has also been revealed though excavation, challenging the assumptions derived from the classical texts. Information emerging from archaeological excavations has also helped us to understand more of both the chronology and the strategy of the Roman conquest.[11]

A NOTE ABOUT THE GEOGRAPHY OF THE CONQUEST, PLACE NAMES, AND TERMS

Claudius' invasion campaign in 43 CE succeeded partly because he was able to call upon the support of several rulers friendly to Rome.[12] By the time of his death and deification in 54 CE, the new province had been extended across much of southern Britain. These relatively low-lying lands, fertile for cultivation, provided much of the food required by the troops as they campaigned further into Britain. The Roman forces advanced swiftly from the south-east, abandoning forts as they drove westwards into Wales and northwards into northern England and southern Scotland. From around 50 CE, these western and central lands of Britain became the focus of Roman campaigning, including the hilly and mountainous landscapes which proved far more difficult for Rome to conquer. The inhabitants had far less experience of Rome than people further south and east, and as the progress of the conquest slowed, many were determined to resist the Roman military forces. Despite these difficulties, after more than forty years of Roman campaigning in Britain Agricola won a famous victory at the battle of *Mons Graupius,* an unknown location in the eastern lands of Caledonia in the far north.

Since Rome needed to maintain its garrison across northern Wales and central Britain throughout the period of its rule, these northern conquests quickly proved to be unsustainable. The wetter climate and poorer soils made it difficult for the Romans to establish settled conditions across their frontier lands. The geography of the province was therefore already established by the late first century, with the Roman forces advancing from a civil zone of developing urban centres in the south into lands of military occupation across the western and northern frontiers. This military zone of north Wales and central Britain retained its garrison throughout the period of Roman rule, until the late fourth and early fifth centuries. The lands of northern Britain and the island of Ireland to the west, meanwhile, remained beyond direct Roman control.

The names of the present-day countries of England, Scotland, and Wales are used in this book as a convenient way of mapping the gradual extension of Roman control over the lands of their province. These countries, first formed in the medieval period as independent kingdoms, have now long been combined as the United Kingdom.[13] Some Roman-period names for particular places and peoples throughout Britain are also known from classical texts and inscriptions (see appendix 2). Place names from the classical texts which have become common currency today include Camulodunum (Colchester), Verulamium (St Albans), and Vindolanda (Chesterholm).

For all the other places where the Roman-period name is not in common use today, the modern name is used with the Roman name (where known), which is shown in italics, for example 'London (*Londinium*)' and 'Silchester (*Calleva*)'.

We also know the names of many of the different peoples inhabiting southern, western, and central Britain during the time of the Roman conquest. Information for the period of the invasions of Caesar and Claudius, however, is limited.

By the second century CE, however, many of the territories of the peoples of the province of Britannia had been transformed into *civitates* (citizen communities); we call their urban centres '*civitas* capitals' (the centres of citizen communities).

The lands beyond direct Roman control in northern Britain also contained many distinct peoples; our understanding of these groups is far less detailed.

1

JULIUS CAESAR IN BRITAIN

> For he [Caesar] was the first man to sail the western Ocean with a fleet, and convey an army into battle through the waters of the Atlantic; and the island itself was said to have been so large that no one could believe it existed at all. Writer after writer had entered the bitter controversy. Britain was just a name and a legend they said; the island did not exist and never had existed. Now Caesar attempted to conquer it, and advanced the Roman Empire beyond the bounds of the human world.
>
> —Plutarch, *Caesar*[1]

BY THE TIME HE led his invasions of Britain, Julius Caesar (100–44 BCE) was already an experienced politician and successful military commander. As a member of a patrician family which claimed a pedigree reaching back even earlier than the foundation of the city of Rome, Caesar seemed destined to climb the political career ladder. In 63 he was elected praetor, a senior role in Roman politics which also qualified him for a military command there. After a year in that post at Rome, he began a term as governor of the Roman province of Spain and won his first military campaign. Provincial governors, who managed military and civil affairs in Roman provinces, were often appointed for around three or four years. Returning to Rome in 60 he was made consul; following his year in this senior office he was appointed governor of Cisalpine Gaul and Illyricum. Transalpine Gaul was later added to his command. In 58 he travelled to Gaul and led Rome into a major eight-year war, enabling him to demonstrate his considerable prowess as a general.

During the first three years of this campaign Caesar made extensive conquests across central and northern Gaul. The Gauls were subdivided into many independent peoples who did not form politically unified groups but were loose associations united under a single leader. Some of these peoples fought Caesar while others submitted, and indeed the division of the Gallic opposition was a significant reason for Caesar's swift successes. He led campaigns against those who opposed him, defeating and subduing them individually and driving back some Germanic groups to their lands to the north of the Rhine. Then, late in the fourth season of campaigning, he decided to invade Britain.

The dispatches Caesar sent back to Rome conveyed news of these campaigns to his peers and were later summarized in the eight books of his famous work *The Gallic War* (*De Bello Gallico*). Each book addressed the campaigns of a single year, and his account of his two invasions of Britain, which I draw upon here, is included in books 4 and 5.[2]

THE MOTIVES FOR INVADING

Sailing over the Channel to Britain was the most challenging undertaking Caesar and his legions had attempted. Why did he wish to campaign in Britain? As mentioned earlier, he was attracted by the idea of emulating the deeds of Hercules and Alexander, but he had already defeated many peoples in Gaul. Why was travelling to Britain so important to him? The attraction of invasion arose from the very lack of information about Britain available at Rome.[3] Caesar provided a practical reason for wishing to force the submission of the Britons, observing that his enemies had received reinforcements from the island in almost all of the wars he had fought in Gaul. He described one of these occasions, observing that the Britons, together with Gallic allies, had provided assistance to the Veneti, a coastal people of north-western Gaul, with their resistance to Rome in the winter of 57–56 (fig. 1.1).[4] Indeed,

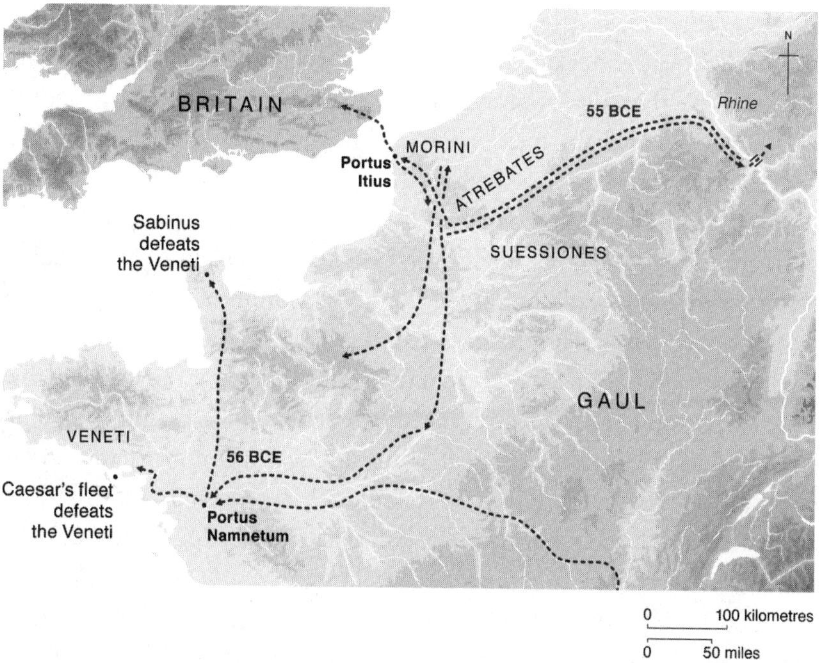

FIG 1.1.
Julius Caesar's campaigns in northwest Gaul in 56–55 BCE, showing the location of the Atrebates, Suessiones, and Veneti (after Raaflaub 2017a, maps 3.12, 3.28, and 4.1, with additions)

Caesar's naval campaign against the Veneti may provide a clue to the motivation that drove him to invade Britain the following year. The Veneti, Caesar explained, excelled in the nautical skills they had learned by living beside a 'fierce and open sea' with only a few 'exposed landing places'. They used their large fleet to dominate this coast by exacting tolls on those who travelled on the sea and traded with Britain.[5] Rome had long been renowned for its land-based legionary forces, which had been the core of the successes that had built the empire. In contrast to the Veneti, as Caesar remarked, his soldiers had little skill with ships, while their knowledge of the waters, landing places, and islands of this coast was very limited. These comments were somewhat disingenuous, however, in view of the experience that Roman troops had gained as a result of earlier naval campaigns, including Pompey's defeat of the pirates in the Mediterranean ten years before.

Caesar titled these Atlantic waters 'the great unbounded Ocean', observing that sailing them was a distinctly different experience from navigating the landlocked Mediterranean Sea. The name 'Mediterranean' is derived from the Latin *mediterraneus*, meaning 'in land' or 'in (the middle of the) land', but the Romans, like the Greeks before them, called it simply *mare nostrum*, 'our sea', for Roman commanders had defeated the peoples who lived around it. A naval campaign on the fierce open waters of the Atlantic was a far more challenging undertaking than sailing the Mediterranean. Caesar's observations on the nature of the 'unbounded Ocean' described the practical difficulties he faced in mounting a naval campaign. He may have been aware of the accounts of Phoenician and Carthaginian explorers, and that of Pytheas the Greek, who, in previous centuries, was said to have sailed through the Pillars of Hercules. These writings addressed the extreme difficulty of navigating the Atlantic, with its dense fogs, difficult waters, severe storms, and giant sea creatures.[6]

Caesar ordered the construction of a substantial fleet for campaigning against the Veneti and laid siege to their coastal strongholds (*oppida*), while the Roman ships, commanded by Decimus Brutus, won a battle at sea in 56. This maritime victory may have emboldened Caesar to undertake the challenging task of crossing Ocean to campaign in Britain. He thought the voyage would also provide an opportunity to reconnoitre the island and its people: he observed that it would be 'a great advantage' to land on the island and to observe what kind of people lived there and the nature of their territories, harbours, and approaches. The Gauls he had interviewed apparently had claimed to know little about Britain. Even the traders refused to provide any detailed knowledge of the lands and peoples that lay beyond the coastline opposite Gaul. Caesar intended to supplement Roman knowledge by obtaining information about the island and its people and by forcing their leaders to submit to him. He profited from the bribes he received and the booty he collected from the peoples he conquered: his campaigns were partly motivated by avarice. He must have wondered about the potential for plunder in these otherworldly lands. Moreover, the sons of other elite families at Rome flocked to serve on Caesar's staff, and booty forfeited from defeated enemies made fortunes for many.

THE FIRST INVASION

Late in the fourth campaigning season of the Gallic War, having constructed a substantial bridge over the Rhine and crossed into Germany for a short campaign, Caesar turned his attention to Britain. Before setting sail, he dispatched a warship under the charge of Gaius Volusenus, a military tribune and cavalry commander, with instructions to conduct reconnaissance of the coast of Kent and find the best place to land. Caesar then assembled his military forces in the territory of the Morini, a Gallic people whose land offered the shortest crossing to the south-eastern coast of Britain.

The many peoples of Britain did not unite into one force to oppose Caesar, and while the Roman fleet was being prepared for the invasion, envoys from several of their leaders approached him to promise their loyalty and offered to send hostages. Caesar sent them home to Britain with a Gallic nobleman called Commius, whom he had previously established as king of the Atrebates, a people of northern (Belgic) Gaul. In the belief that Commius had influence across the Channel, Caesar charged him with persuading more British leaders to pledge their loyalty to Rome.

To understand why Commius was sent to Britain, we must consider the organisation of Iron Age society in Gaul, together with the strategies Caesar used to manipulate these peoples for political and military gain. Each of the Iron Age peoples living in Gaul and Britain was formed from a community that was loosely held together by the authority of its elite families.[7] This people occupied a territory which they farmed and, from time to time when necessary, defended against the aggressive acts of others. Power within this community was not consolidated in the hands of a single male leader. Instead, senior individuals competed as patrons to attract the largest number of clients. In return for armed service and supplies of food, clients gave their loyalty to a senior patron who could offer security from danger and the rewards of gifts and generous feasts.

It was difficult for ambitious leaders to maintain personal power over their people in this decentralized political system, but one method of providing the wealth to reward clients and to retain their loyalty was to achieve success in war. This had led to serious conflicts between the peoples of Gaul in the centuries before Caesar invaded.[8] Caesar's Gallic War also impelled many warrior-leaders in Gaul to take up arms, which proved a dangerous strategy. We are told that 'The campaigns in Gaul lasted for less than ten years, and in that time he took over 800 cities by force of arms, he conquered 300 nations, he faced a total of three million enemy in successive battles, and he killed one million of these in action and took the same number again as prisoners'.[9] The prisoners taken by Caesar were enslaved.

An alternative strategy for a Gallic leader was to seek the friendship of Rome, a policy many of them adopted. The Germanic leader Ariovistus of the Suebi, for example, had been declared king and friend by the Senate, and gifts had been bestowed upon him.[10] When Caesar made Commius king of the Atrebates, he followed this policy of favoritism by making the Gallic leader his client and providing him with support. Commius repaid Caesar with practical assistance in the form of supplies for the troops and of cavalry to serve in the Roman campaigns. Commius was one of a number of powerful war-leaders in Gaul whom Caesar titled 'king'. This indicated that such leading men were exercising increased power over their people, in a way that challenged the traditionally decentralized character of Gallic society.[11]

The networks of patronage maintained by these kings extended well beyond the territories occupied by the individual people they ruled over and included the leaders of communities at some distance from their lands. In the case of Commius, this may have involved clients who lived in Britain. Caesar mentioned one Diviacus, a leader of the Suessiones in northern Gaul, who had also controlled a large part of Britain.[12] Commius may even have had Caesar's support in a bid to increase his own influence over the leaders of south-eastern Britain. In the short term this was to backfire since, having crossed the Channel to deliver Caesar's demand that the British leaders should submit to Rome, he was thrown into chains.

After sending Commius to Britain, Caesar assembled his military forces to cross the Channel. He had ordered ships to be assembled from the surrounding areas of Gaul, and his fleet also included the ships he had constructed to fight the Veneti. Eighty ships were mustered to ferry the

Seventh and Tenth Legions to Britain, with supplies of food and equipment, probably setting sail from Boulogne (*Portus Itius*) in Gaul (fig. 1.2). The individual legions, the core of Caesar's fighting forces, had a 'paper strength' of around 5,000 strong, which suggests an invading force of around 10,000 men distributed among eighty ships. The actual number of soldiers may have been rather lower.[13] This was something less than half the legionaries Caesar had available in Gaul, as the first campaign in Britain was intended as a scouting expedition and he also needed to guard his supply lines. Eighteen other ships, which carried the cavalry soldiers, failed to make land despite several attempts.

The Roman legion had originated several centuries earlier as an infantry unit with a small contingent of cavalry. Legionaries in the time of Caesar wore chain mail and a bronze or iron helmet. Each carried a shield, and their main offensive weapons were the *pilum* (javelin) and the *gladius* (short sword).[14] Much of the cavalry available to Caesar was provided by his Gallic allies. Commius, for example, had a retinue of thirty loyal cavalry soldiers, the sons of his most senior clients, who accompanied him to Britain. The failure of the cavalry to land in Britain limited the tactical advantage provided by Caesar's well-drilled legionary soldiers.

Caesar crossed the Channel, probably on 12 September 55.[15] The Britons were drawn up along the cliff tops and, using slingshots, caused Caesar to abandon his first attempt to land, instead forcing him to sail another 10 kilometres (6.5 miles) up the coast in search of an open shore on which to disembark his troops.[16] His landing site has not been established. He may have initially attempted to land at Dover (*Dubris*) in Kent, and he would probably then have sailed up the coast to Deal or Walmer.[17] The Britons had anticipated Caesar's tactics, however, and sent chariots, horsemen, and men armed with slings to prevent the Romans' second attempt to land. This was the first of several occasions on which Caesar was to comment on the effective use of chariots, which the Britons customarily used in battle. Chariots had ceased to be used in warfare in Gaul by this time, and their use in Britain would have added to Britain's allure as a fabulous place.[18]

As a result of the difficulty Caesar faced in landing the troops, he brought the Roman warships forward to face the Britons, attacking

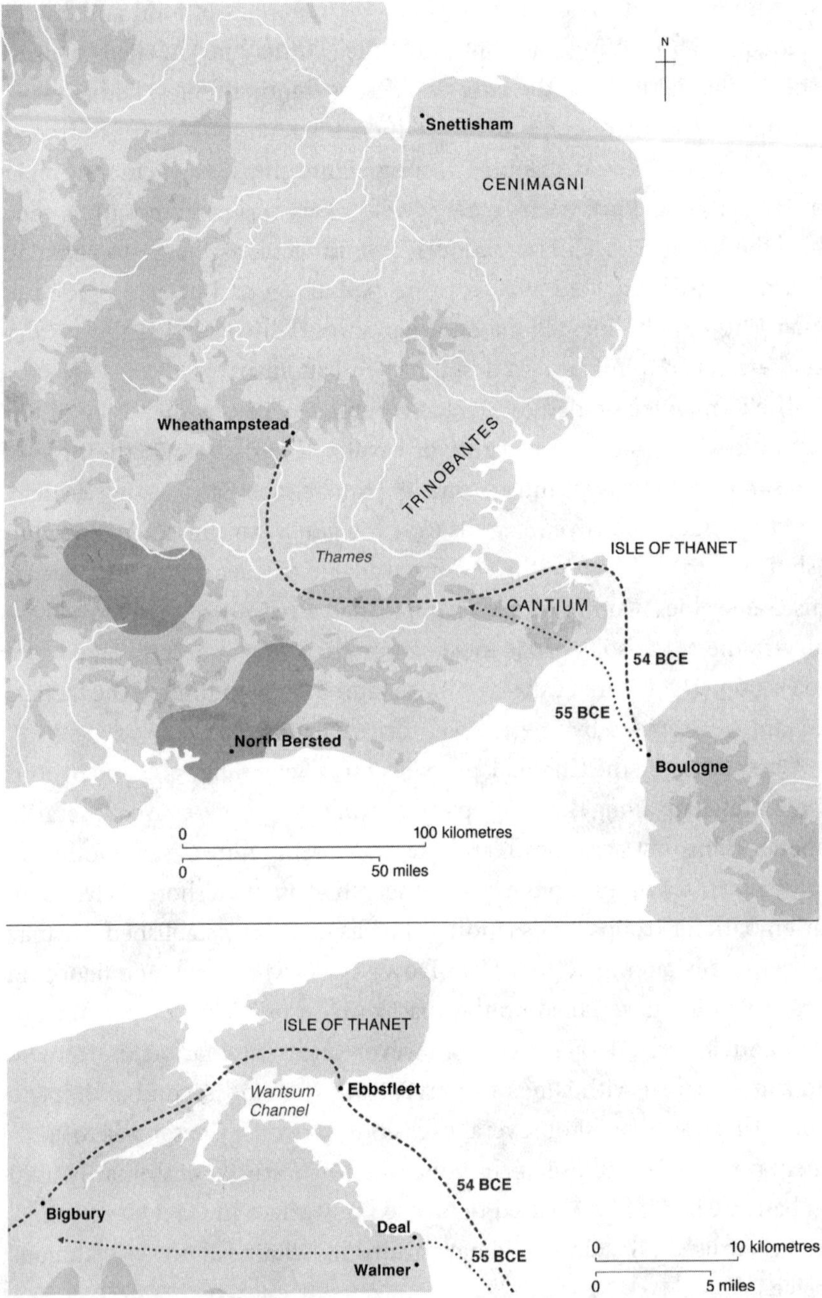

FIG 1.2.

Caesar's invasions of Britain in 55 and 54 BCE, showing the extent of the distribution of the coins of Commius (in darker tone), who ruled in southern Britain immediately after Caesar's second invasion their enemy's flank and repelling them with slings, arrows, and artillery machines. This enabled the legions to land, although not without considerable difficulty, and many of the Britons were able to withdraw without serious losses. The cavalry meanwhile had failed to make a landing at all, and in consequence Caesar had no horsemen to pursue the Britons in retreat. He encamped close to the landing site, establishing a base for his soldiers according to the usual Roman practice while campaigning in enemy territory.

Following their defeat on the coast, the Britons sent envoys to discuss peace terms, accompanied by Commius, who had been captured on his arrival in Britain. Caesar pardoned the Britons in exchange for hostages, who were provided. The leaders of the Britons now began to assemble at the coast to pledge their loyalty to Caesar and avoid becoming the targets of his military campaign. The dangers of sailing Ocean now caught up with the Romans, as a number of transport ships anchored off the coast were wrecked or damaged by a storm lasting several days. This was the cause of great concern among the troops, who, according to Caesar, feared that they might not be able to return to Gaul and did not have sufficient supplies to overwinter in Britain. For only a swift campaign in Britain had been planned. The Britons also reassessed the Roman position and, perceiving the storm damage to the ships and the lack of grain in the camp, decided to renew hostilities.

Caesar's men had been able to mend most of the ships, but the soldiers of the Seventh Legion, who had been sent out to harvest grain, were surrounded and attacked by British horsemen and chariots. The Romans were thrown into confusion by their enemies' unfamiliar use of chariots, although Caesar's arrival with additional soldiers enabled his troops to repel the Britons. After driving off their enemy, the Romans were nevertheless confined to camp by bad weather. The Britons sent out messengers and mustered a huge force of infantry and horsemen, intending to drive the Romans away from Britain for ever. Once more, Caesar's forces managed to defeat this attack; they then pursued the Britons, setting fire to buildings far and wide.

The detailed account Caesar provided of the bellicose 'barbarians' portrays them as worthy adversaries. The emphasis on Britain as 'other', a place distant from and different from Rome, established an effective contrast to the 'civilized' culture of the Roman elite. In battle, the Britons massed in a large number, supported by their artillery, sling-throwers, and archers and the flexible use of many chariots. Archaeological research has backed up these observations. The Iron Age 'warrior burials' found across much of Britain have included the interred remains of members of the Iron Age elite, accompanied in death by the weapons they had used in life, including swords, shields, spears, and the occasional helmet (fig. 1.3).[19] Such weapons were used in displays of fighting prowess, and although most warrior burials are male, some burials of women with weapons have also been found. Women may even have fought against Caesar in Britain, although he did not mention it. The chariots were used in a flexible way that seems to have created panic in Roman ranks on a number of occasions, while also enabling a speedy retreat if the charioteers were hard pressed. The remains of Iron Age chariots, which were built to carry several people, have been found across much of Britain. Riding in a chariot would have conveyed prestige on the riders, and the chariot remains are an indication of the dominant role played by the Iron Age elite in the staging of conflicts.[20] These warriors were members of a privileged cadre amongst their own people, whereas the majority of those fighting against Caesar would not have possessed impressive metal weapons or chariots. The slingers, mentioned by Caesar several times, used a weapon that would have been far more widely available to many Britons. The value of slings in ancient warfare was that nothing, not even a bow, could send a missile as far.

Caesar's account of the Britons he faced in 55 mentioned little else about these people, referring only to the crops seized by the Seventh Legion in the fields and the buildings close to his camp, which were burnt by his troops. Until the 1960s, archaeologists tended to emphasize the warring nature of Iron Age peoples, drawing upon Caesar's account, and quoting the widespread recovery of weapons and hillforts throughout much of Britain.[21] Caesar was to describe two British fortifications in his account of the second invasion. More recent archaeological work has conveyed a very different image, that of a relatively peaceful and settled Iron Age (discussed later).

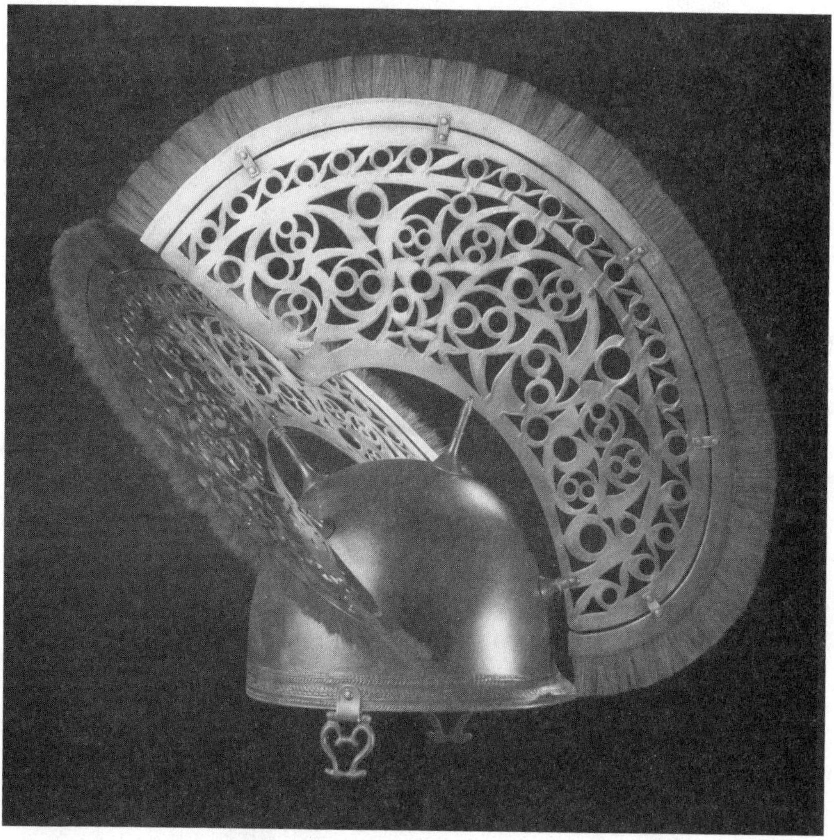

FIG 1.3.
A reconstruction of the helmet from the Iron Age burial at North Bersted; helmets were in common use in Gaul but are rare finds in Britain (Copyright: the Novium, a service provided by Chichester District Council) (© FionaMillsArts. All rights reserved)

When the envoys of the Britons returned to surrender, Caesar requested double the number of hostages and sailed for Gaul, probably at the beginning of October. His campaign in Britain had lasted for around three weeks, and he cannot have progressed very far beyond his camp. Messengers were sent to Rome with news of the submission of the Britons, and the Senate decreed a period of thanksgiving of twenty days. This reflected how warmly the news was received in Rome. A summary of Caesar's achievements, written almost two centuries later, observed: 'having penetrated everywhere [in Gaul and into Germany] by land and sea, he [Caesar] turned his gaze toward Ocean, and as if this world were not enough for the Romans, set his thoughts on another'.[22] Caesar's voyage over Ocean and his campaign in Britain were portrayed as the achievements of a truly supreme commander.

THE SECOND INVASION

After the Roman fleet returned to Gaul, only two of the peoples of Britain sent hostages as promised, and Caesar tells us that he was motivated to renew his campaign in Britain the following year (see fig. 1.2). Before this second invasion, moreover, a young man called Mandubracius approached Caesar to seek his support. Mandubracius had been forced to flee from Britain after his father, king of the Trinobantes (Trinovantes), had been killed by Cassivellaunus, another powerful leader. This is the first time Caesar provides names for any of the Britons, either individuals or peoples, and he describes the Trinovantes as one of the most powerful peoples in Britain. At the time of Claudius' invasion in 43 CE, the Trinovantes were living in the more southerly part of present-day East Anglia, to the north of the River Thames.

The killing of the leader of the Trinovantes suggests that Cassivellaunus had overwhelmed this people and Mandubracius had been forced to flee across the Channel to seek protection for them. Mandubracius hoped that Caesar would lead a campaign to restore him as leader of the Trinovantes by driving Cassivellaunus away from his lands. He must have been aware of the campaign Caesar had undertaken in south-eastern Britain the previous year. Since Caesar had been in Britain for less than a month, his invasion had not progressed very far from his camp in Kent, and his troops would not have reached the Thames or beyond into the territory ruled by Mandubracius' father. Evidently Mandubracius, or his father, had been in contact with Caesar before Cassivellaunus attacked the Trinovantes. It is possible that these leaders of the Trinovantes had been amongst the leading Britons who had assembled the previous autumn on the Kent coast to pledge their loyalty to Rome. By fleeing to Caesar to seek his support against a rival, Mandubracius was setting a precedent which was followed by a succession of deposed British leaders who fled to the emperors Augustus, Caligula, and Claudius in the course of the next century.

Caesar used Mandubracius as an excuse for targeting Cassivellaunus directly during his second invasion. Over the winter in Gaul, he made preparations for a very substantial expedition. His forces were drawn up at Boulogne, where he now received the leaders of pacified Gallic peoples from all over Gaul, who had assembled with 4,000 cavalry. Quintus Atius Labienus, in command of three legions and 2,000 cavalry, was left in Gaul to guard the harbour, manage the supply of grain to the military, and maintain control. At the end of July 54 BCE, Caesar set sail for Britain with five legions, a force of as many as 20,000 infantry and 2,000 cavalry. To carry the soldiers across the Channel he assembled an immense fleet of 800 ships, almost ten times the number used in the first invasion. Many of these ships had been constructed during the winter, and preparations for a naval campaign on this scale will have required very careful planning.

The Roman soldiers were in Britain for around two months during this second season. It is unlikely that the ships carried enough supplies to feed the 22,000 soldiers for the 1.3 million person-days they spent in Britain, and the legions must once again have foraged for food. Caesar also clearly intended to use the ships to seize and carry back to Gaul large numbers of hostages and booty, particularly slaves. He had a particular talent for making money through warfare, and he was especially determined to profit from this campaign because the small size of his fleet on the first occasion had served to restrict the amount of booty he could take home. He noted that the fleet of his second expedition included privately owned vessels built by individuals who hoped to profit from the invasion. These ships were manned by traders who were supplying the military and had been attracted to Caesar's expedition to Britain by rumours of wealth there.

The main profit from this invasion would be obtained from the slaves captured in war, who would be taken back to Gaul and transported on to the Mediterranean to be sold. Cicero, whose brother was serving with Caesar in Britain, observed in a letter written to his friend Atticus during the summer of 54: 'it is now ascertained that there is not a single grain of silver on the island nor any prospect of booty except for captives, and I am sure that you will not expect any of them to be highly qualified in writing or music.'[23] Cicero did not expect the Britons to be skilled in a range of spheres including the artistic, as Roman slaves from the Greek East often were. They were sold to wealthy Romans across the Mediterranean and were destined to work in poverty as agricultural slaves or to be trained to work in industry.

Despite adverse weather conditions, the fleet reached the place on the coast of south-eastern Britain which, according to the information Caesar had obtained the previous summer, would be best for disembarkation. A large force of Britons had advanced to meet the Romans, but having observed the number of ships decided not to engage in battle and instead hid themselves on higher ground. Caesar's forces disembarked on the sandy, low-lying beach and selected a suitable site for a camp. Caesar's account observed that he immediately set off in pursuit of the Britons, leaving Quintus Atius Varus in command of a substantial garrison to guard the ships. The information he provided has made it possible to consider exactly where his forces landed in 54. The favoured location is close to the modern town of Ebbsfleet in east Kent, on the Isle of Thanet. This would have enabled Caesar to exploit the Wantsum Channel, which was formerly a substantial arm of the sea that separated the Isle of Thanet from the mainland of Kent.

It has recently been suggested that the remains of the ditched enclosure that has been located at Ebbsfleet formed Caesar's camp.[24] The gently sloping sandy beach immediately to the east of this camp would have provided an excellent location for Caesar's ships to land to disembark 20,000 soldiers and their supplies, as this large area was well protected from storms. This interesting and well-informed suggestion would in fact mean that Caesar chose to land his substantial forces on an island off the coast of Britain. If Roman forces disembarked on the Isle of Thanet, they would have had to cross the Wantsum Channel before they could pursue the Britons. Caesar's military forces were evidently fully capable of crossing substantial waterways, since they managed to cross the Rhine and the Thames in pursuit of enemies.

After marching for around 18 kilometres (11 miles), the Romans caught sight of the Britons, who had brought their horsemen and chariots forward from higher ground, as far as a river. The Roman troops forced the Britons back, and they concealed themselves in a forest, occupying a structure Caesar described as fortified both by 'nature and defences', previously constructed by the Britons 'to serve in their domestic wars', with all its entrances blocked by felled trees. The Britons came out of the forest in small detachments, preventing the Romans from entering the fortification; eventually, however, the Seventh Legion built a ramp against the structure and took the stronghold, driving the Britons away.

It has long been suspected that this British fortification was the hillfort known as Bigbury Camp, just east of present-day Canterbury (Kent).[25] By the time of Caesar's invasions, many of the hillforts, a predominant type of site during the Iron Age in southern Britain, had been abandoned, although some remained in use as meeting places (fig. 1.4).[26] They were defended hilltop fortifications designed to provide strongholds at times of conflict, although they were often also important settlements and meeting places. Bigbury Camp is one of only two known Iron Age hillforts in eastern Kent. Archaeological excavations have indicated that it was occupied from the second century BCE to the first century CE. A number of iron slave chains have been recovered from Bigbury Camp and from other Iron Age sites in Britain, which suggests that the Romans were not alone in their practice of enslaving captives.

The next morning, Caesar sent infantry and cavalry to pursue the Britons, although he had to delay his campaigning after receiving information that a storm had again damaged some of the Roman ships, with around forty lost and the remainder requiring repairs. Caesar remarked that he had not ordered the ships to be beached on arrival, notwithstanding the storm that had destroyed part of his fleet the previous year. He arranged for all the ships to be safely beached and for a single line of defences to be built around the vessels and the camp, work that took the soldiers ten days to complete. This substantial fortification protected the ships within a single enclosure that was connected to the camp. Once the building of the camp was completed, Caesar took his forces back to the place where the Britons had last been observed before the news of the storm had arrived. He was leading a campaign into the interior of Britain, using the excuse of Mandubracius' plea for assistance to make Cassivellaunus his main military target.

FIG 1.4.
The Iron Age hillfort of Maiden Castle (Dorset) from the air
(Crown copyright: Historic England, aerial image nmr_15853_02)

A larger British force had meanwhile elected Cassivellaunus, whose name meant 'handsome and good', as their leader and had gathered to confront the Romans. It has long been thought that Cassivellaunus was the leader of a people called the Catuvellauni, meaning 'men good in battle'.[27] Caesar observed that there had previously been continuous war between Cassivellaunus and the other British peoples. Although Cassivellaunus was already a famous war-leader, it was only the crisis of the arrival of the Roman forces that led the British peoples who opposed them to appoint him to command their forces of resistance, increasing his power over a number of such peoples as a result. Caesar wrote that

Cassivellaunus had territories—separated from the 'coastal states' by the River Thames—located 80 Roman miles (120 kilometres; 75 miles) from the sea. This distance refers to Caesar's march from the sea to the place where he was to cross the Thames.

Caesar provided a summary of his knowledge of the people of Britain, drawing a stark contrast between those living in coastal Britain, who were relatively civilized and grew crops, and the inland peoples, who did not plant crops but apparently lived on milk and meat and clothed themselves in animal skins. Caesar described these inland peoples as nomadic pastoralists, a reflection of the classical conception that the barbarians living furthest beyond the reaches of Rome had not developed agriculture or established permanent settlements.[28] He regularly mentioned forests and marshes as hiding places for Britons who wished to ambush Roman legionaries and as places to which his enemies retreated when hard-pressed in battle. The imagery of dense forest infested with barbarians was a literary device he used on several occasions to describe the barbaric territories that lay furthest from the 'civilisation' of the Mediterranean lands.

Archaeological research has enabled a very different understanding of the Iron Age as a settled agricultural society. Peoples across mainland Britain had in fact cleared much of the supposed woodland Caesar claimed was there, and they had been domesticating animals and growing crops for millennia by this time.[29] There would still have been woods and areas of thick forest across southern Britain at this time, although all the natural resources of the landscape were fully exploited by Iron Age communities. Many families lived in substantial roundhouses in established settlements, some of which were not defended by enclosing earthworks (see fig. I.5). These people created artefacts that included fine items of metalwork, such as the gold torcs from Snettisham (Norfolk), which do not fit particularly well with Caesar's use of the word 'barbarians' (fig. 1.5).[30] The regular warfare he described as a British addiction would have threatened the production of the crops on which Iron Age communities depended. The extreme military aggression his invasion brought to Britain caused considerable loss of life and would also have severely disrupted the lives of many people in south-eastern Britain. He seized on the violent reaction of

FIG 1.5.
The four gold torcs from the Blair Drummond Hoard (Stirling, Scotland) (image © National Museums Scotland)

many Britons to his invasion to illustrate their barbarity. While the Iron Age peoples of Britain were not always at peace, the scale of conflict Caesar directed against them was out of all proportion with the traditions of warfare evident in the archaeological record.

Comments Caesar made at this point in his narrative portrayed the people of Britain as otherworldly, in the sense that they transgressed Roman codes of dress and marital relations.[31] According to his account, all the Britons painted themselves a dark blue colour with woad, to appear more frightening in battle. They had long hair and shaved their bodies, except for the upper lip and head. Groups of ten or twelve men shared their wives in common. It is certainly possible that Caesar observed some such practices amongst the Britons. Iron Age society was deeply imbued with religious beliefs, and peoples of Britain and Gaul often dedicated offerings of weapons, animals, and other items to their gods. Many of these items were deposited, for instance, in rivers and wetlands, which Iron Age peoples evidently considered sacred.[32] Yet Caesar had little more to say about these matters in his account of Britain, apart from remarking that it was considered wrong to eat hare, chicken, or goose. In an account of the activities of the Druids in Gaul, he mentioned that this religious institution was believed to have originated in Britain and that those who wanted to understand these matters usually travelled to this island.[33] The Druids were involved in matters of religion and, according to Caesar, managed public and private sacrifices in Gaul. The idea that these powerful religious specialists had originated in Britain once again added to the island's allure as an otherworldly land.

While Caesar's forces marched to confront the Britons of the interior, there was an attack on the Roman camp on the coast. The Britons suddenly rushed out of the wood, setting off another fierce battle, with the Romans eventually driving their enemy away, despite losses. The following day the Romans also defeated a substantial British attack on three legions that were foraging for food at some distance from the camp. Caesar meanwhile marched to the River Thames and into the territory of Cassivellaunus. He noted that the river could only be forded at a single location on foot, which may have been inland from the point at which the river became tidal, upstream of where the modern city of London is located. He provided no further information on how his soldiers crossed the Thames, and the use of a ford would suggest that the water in the river must have been relatively low. A large assembly of Britons on the far bank was unable to withstand the assault of the Roman legionaries and cavalry, despite having reinforced the bank and bottom of the river with sharpened wooden stakes. Cassivellaunus had disbanded much of his force but retained 4,000 charioteers to harry the Roman soldiers while they were foraging for food.

The Trinovantes again requested assistance to protect their leader, Mandubracius, from Cassivellaunus. Caesar sent Mandubracius back to them and ordered the Trinovantes to send him forty hostages and grain for the troops. At this point six British peoples surrendered to Caesar: the Trinovantes, Cenimagni, Segontiaci, Ancalites, Bibroci, and Cassi. The Cenimagni were probably the people living in northern East Anglia, later called Iceni by the Romans. The territories of the remaining four cannot be identified, and indeed all we know about them is contained in this single mention in *The Gallic War*. This suggests that these peoples may have formed temporary groups based on the loyalty of clients to a powerful leader. The survival of the Trinovantes and Iceni into the Claudian period, however, suggests that some of the peoples of Late Iron Age Britain had a greater degree of political stability. Caesar's actions against Cassivellaunus ensured that Mandubracius inherited his father's role as leader of the Trinovantes.

The peoples who surrendered to Caesar informed him that the *oppidum* of Cassivellaunus was located nearby and was situated not far from the Thames. A substantial group of people and cattle had been assembled there. Some of the *oppida* mentioned by Caesar in Gaul were urbanized settlements and important economic and trading centres.[34] The Latin term *oppidum* is usually translated as 'walled town' but could also mean 'stronghold'. Caesar observed that the Britons 'apply the word *oppidum* to a dense wood which they have fortified with a rampart and ditch, and where they often assemble to avoid the attacks of enemies'. He also commented that Cassivellaunus' *oppidum* was 'protected by woods and marshes'.[35] This description is characteristic of a new type of site that appeared in Britain during the first century BCE but was to become more common after Caesar's invasions (discussed later). In keeping with the image of the inland Britons as nomadic, the description of Cassivellaunus' *oppidum* demonstrated that it was not an urbanized centre.

Caesar's legions attacked from two sides and overwhelmed Cassivellaunus' *oppidum*, seizing large numbers of cattle and capturing many of their enemy's contingent, who were then put to death. The large-scale killing of defeated enemies was a common practice adopted by Caesar to create fear among potential adversaries.[36] Cassivellaunus meanwhile had sent messengers to the four kings of Kent—Cingetorix, Carvilius, Taximagulus, and Segovax—ordering them to attack the Roman camp. No other reference to these kings is known to us, and it is not clear whether they ruled one people together or four separate groups. The fact that Cassivellaunus had the authority to command these kings to attack the Romans demonstrates that his power as the leader of the resistance to Caesar extended over a substantial area of southern Britain. This rearguard action failed, and Cassivellaunus then sought Commius' support in surrendering himself to Caesar. That Cassivellaunus could appeal to Commius to argue his case is an indication of the extensive network of contacts existing between the leaders of peoples in Britain and Gaul at this time.

Caesar decided at this point to return to Gaul, as it was late in the summer and the hostilities seemed likely to continue if he remained in Britain. He demanded hostages, set an annual tribute to be paid to Rome, and instructed Cassivellaunus to leave Mandubracius and the Trinovantes alone. The defeat of Cassivellaunus presumably ensured that he would not cause any further problems for his neighbouring rulers. Once the hostages had arrived, Caesar journeyed back to his fleet, finding that the ships had been repaired. Because the number of prisoners was so large and some of his ships had been destroyed in the storm, he decided to ferry the troops back to Gaul in two crossings during late September 54.

Caesar's prisoners included not only hostages but also a large number of captured Britons. The fate of Britons who had been taken as hostages is unknown; they may have been taken to Rome or transported to other more distant locations in the empire. Since they probably included the sons of British leaders, some of them may have been taken to Rome by Caesar to secure the loyalty of their fathers. There was a long tradition of the sons of friendly kings on the eastern frontiers of the empire being taken to the city of Rome.[37] Here they served as hostages, while being treated as friends and clients of their patron. The act of handing over a son and heir for safekeeping expressed the loyalty of a king to his Roman patron. It also provided the young man with an education likely to encourage him to maintain friendly relations with Rome once he returned to take up the leadership of his own people. That Caesar set an annual tribute suggests that he intended to intervene in Britain again, since any failure to pay the sums he imposed would have provided the excuse for another invasion.

COMMIUS IN BRITAIN

We do not know how long the annual tribute set by Caesar continued to be paid as the threat of further Roman interference diminished. We hear nothing further about Mandubracius and Cassivellaunus. The career of Commius suggests, however, that Caesar continued to manipulate the leaders of the southern Britons. Commius had played a significant role in Caesar's invasions. In advance of the first landing, Caesar had sent him to Britain to negotiate with its leaders, and during the second invasion, Commius had intervened on behalf of Cassivellaunus following the sacking of his *oppidum*. Commius also assisted Caesar on several occasions during the campaigns in Gaul, although Caesar noted that in 52 Commius changed his allegiance and took up joint command of the Gallic forces at a major confrontation with the Romans at *Alesia* (Burgundy) in central Gaul.[38] After Caesar had defeated this substantial Gallic army, Commius used his cavalry to raid the Roman supplies and to encourage further revolt. Roman soldiers were sent to assassinate him on two occasions, but he survived, and he made peace with Mark Antony, who was serving with Caesar in Gaul.[39] Commius surrendered hostages but asked for one concession, that he should 'not be required to come within sight of any Roman because of the attempts to kill him'. Antony pardoned him and accepted the hostages, actions that suggest that Antony had sympathy with Commius. As a result of Antony's clemency, during the eighth year of the Gallic War (51 BCE) it appears that Commius was sent across Ocean to rule in Britain.[40] Either Caesar may indeed have left southern Britain in a condition receptive to this ruler imposed by Rome, or Commius may have retained sufficient influence to move the main theatre of his interest there.

Nothing further is recorded of Commius in the surviving classical texts, although some inscribed Iron Age coins from southern Britain bear the inscription 'COMMIOS', which has been assumed to represent him.[41] These coins drew upon a long tradition of Iron Age coin-making, although the inclusion of a personal name was a striking innovation in Britain and indicates that Latin literacy had spread to the leaders of Iron Age peoples from the Continent. Coins made in Gaul had been imported, and these were soon copied, as a series of regional British coin types emerged. These coins, which were made from gold, silver, and bronze, included abstract designs derived originally from the gold staters of Philip II of Macedon (r. 359–36 BCE) and included depictions of a head of Apollo on the obverse and a two-horse chariot on the reverse. Commius' coins followed this iconographic tradition but also included his name. Iron Age coins did not serve as currency in a modern sense but were used as valuable artefacts to discharge social obligations, as gifts, and as tribute. The gold and silver from which the coins were made came into Britain in the form of gifts from patrons in Gaul, either in the form of bullion or as Roman coins that were melted down. Some coins may also have been produced from British gold and silver. Many coins were passed on from leading Britons to their clients.[42]

The coins bearing the name Commius have mainly been found in the area of modern Hampshire (see fig. 1.2); coins inscribed with the same name have been found in Gaul, clustered in the territory of the Atrebates.[43] That Commius was king of the Atrebates of Gaul before he sailed to Britain may suggest that he ruled peoples with the same name on either side of the Channel. Until recently, little more could be added to the tale of Commius, but a recent archaeological discovery provides additional insight. A warrior burial from North Bersted (Bognor Regis, West Sussex) contained a helmet, shield, sword, and spearhead of Iron Age type, besides the remains of a man who may have been a follower of Commius (see fig. 1.3).[44] The helmet was worn by a mounted warrior and was of a type used by Gallic cavalry soldiers around the time of Caesar's Gallic War. Helmets were a common type of armour in Gaul, whereas they have very rarely been found in Britain, which tends to suggest that British cavalry soldiers rarely wore them. The North Bersted helmet was embellished with a remarkably ornate metal crest, supplemented with hair or feathers possibly representing a fighting bird. Roman cavalry soldiers certainly paraded with weapons and light armour which were not necessarily protective, and this warrior may also have adopted the Roman fashion.

The man buried at North Bersted may have been one of Commius' retinue of cavalry soldiers who fought in Gaul and Britain under Caesar's overall command. When Commius moved his centre of operations to Britain, the North Bersted warrior may have followed him before dying and being interred in this well-furnished burial close to the southern coast. Commius and his clients may well then have aimed to keep peace with Rome when they crossed the Channel to live in southern Britain, given the possibility that the Roman legions might return.

CIVIL WAR IN ROME

Caesar's governorship of Gaul ended in 50. His opponents were concerned about his increasing military and political power, afraid that it was damaging the control the Roman aristocrats in the Senate attempted to exercise over Roman society. Caesar crossed the Rubicon in 49, leading to a lasting conflict that divided the Roman elite. By 46, he had effectively won this civil war, and when he celebrated his fourth triumph in Rome, his Gallic victories were illustrated with depictions of the Rhine and the Rhône rivers and of Ocean in gold.[45] Serious political divisions persisted, however, and Caesar was murdered in 44. One of the assassins, Decimus Brutus, had commanded Caesar's fleet in the victory against the Veneti twelve years earlier.

THE LEGACY OF CAESAR'S INVASION

Caesar's dispatches had increased knowledge about Britain among his peers in Rome. The information he recorded and sent back also reflected the limited area of Britain he and his scouts had been able to reach by land and sea. His campaign had been restricted to Kent, along with a swathe of country his forces marched through on the way to the *oppidum* of Cassivellaunus, just north of the Thames. Caesar described Britain as a triangular island with several islands lying off the western coast, including *Hibernia* (Ireland) and *Mona* (Anglesey or the Isle of Man). His scouting ships clearly sailed along the south coast, but additional information about the east and west coasts of Britain was derived from talking to the Britons or the Gauls. He underestimated the size of the island. The first recorded circumnavigation of northern Britain by a Roman fleet did not occur until 83 CE.

Caesar described the Britons as innately aggressive, barbaric, and incapable of uniting to oppose Roman invasion. These peoples were decentralized and with no permanent and stable social hierarchies; they provided a direct contrast to the class-based power structure of Rome. The large number of horsemen and chariots which rode out to confront

Caesar demonstrated that Britons could mount serious resistance to Rome, although the tendency for some leaders, including Mandubracius, to seek alliances with Caesar demonstrated the fragility of their resistance. Diplomacy had been used effectively to divide the British opposition. Caesar had come into contact with a number of influential leaders in southern Britain, drawing them into Rome's sphere of patronage. The extent of his contacts in Britain was not restricted to the area where he had campaigned, since the rulers of these peoples, or their envoys, had on several occasions travelled to meet him and pledge their loyalty. This may have included powerful individuals from some distance away who were seeking his support.

Caesar and the senior officers who had served with him in Britain may have continued to maintain contact with these friendly leaders through emissaries. They would have been aware that the friendship of Rome could help them extend their powers over their own peoples. British leaders could use gifts from patrons overseas, such as gold and silver coins and bullion, to reward their own clients in a bid to secure their loyalty. Mandubracius and Commius were the first friendly rulers in Britain who can be identified. The other leaders in Britain who may have wished to oppose Roman domination, including Cassivellaunus, had been made aware of the extreme violence Roman commanders could direct against their enemies, and this would have kept them in order for a while.

The Romans did not find the riches many had expected, and some commentators argued that the invasions had been a failure; Caesar had achieved nothing significant and had not penetrated very far into the island.[46] Slaves were one important resource acquired in large number in Britain, and an indication of the wealth the Romans were expecting to find in the island is indicated by the corselet made from pearls grown in Britain that Caesar dedicated to Venus Genetrix at her temple in Rome.[47] There is some uncertainty about whether the British pearls were from molluscs living in rivers or in the sea. Classical authors remarked upon them as being small and of poor colour, in contrast to the pearls from the East, which were very popular in Rome. Since Britain was set in Ocean, Caesar evidently considered its pearls an appropriate gift to the goddess Venus who, according to myth, was born of sea foam. The suggestion in

Rome that the invasions were a failure misinterpreted his main motivation, which was to undertake a fabulous adventure that would increase his status and power in Rome. His actions drew the attention of the Roman elite to Britain. Many members of Rome's ruling classes took part in his campaigns as members of his staff, while his dispatches helped to establish a tradition in literature that portrayed Britain as an otherworldly place open to further conquest and adventure.

A later classical writer provided an adroit summary of Caesar's achievement in Britain: 'Ocean became calmer and more settled, as though it confessed itself unequal to opposing him.'[48] The submission of British leaders was one thing. The conquest of this exotic island, however, was a challenge that even Caesar, despite his political and military brilliance, had been unable to achieve.

2

EMPERORS AND KINGS

Why do our oars violate seas
That are not ours,
Waters that are holy?
Why should we disturb the Gods' quiet home?

—Albinovanus Pedo[1]

AUGUSTUS AND BRITAIN

Julius Caesar's adopted son Octavian rose to power as the victor in the conflicts following Caesar's assassination in Rome. He consolidated his authority and in 27 BCE was awarded the title 'Augustus', meaning 'Revered One', by the Senate. He ruled the Roman Empire for forty years (27 BCE–14 CE) and, as Caesar's heir, contemplated whether to follow his example by invading Britain. It was recorded that Augustus considered the possibility on three separate occasions when visiting Gaul in 34, 27, and 26.[2] When he returned to Gaul in 16–13, he may yet again have been planning an invasion of Britain, although he evidently chose to maintain order through diplomacy instead. Roman diplomacy at the outer reaches of the empire included the practice of rewarding friendly kings, a strategy that helped to retain their loyalty.[3] Caesar and Augustus followed this precedent in their dealings with British kings.

Envoys from the dominant rulers of southern Britain would have travelled to meet Augustus when he visited northern Gaul, and the authority he exercised helped to maintain Roman domination over the southern part of the island. We hear of the British rulers as living mainly in peace amongst themselves under Augustus and being of no particular concern to Rome as a result.[4] The maintaining of peace with Britain, which Augustus modelled on Caesar's diplomatic and military actions there, was part of his claim to wide-ranging power over his empire. Throughout this time, Britain continued to feature in the Roman view of the world as an otherworldly and barbaric place located in Ocean and beyond the edge of civilization.

A classical account included a key observation providing insight into the policy pursued by Augustus: 'some of their leaders [of Britain], have sent ambassadors and favours to Caesar Sebastos [Augustus], established friendship and making dedicatory offerings on the Capitolium. This has virtually made the whole island all but one with the Romans'.[5] Since the approval of the Senate was required by those wishing to make such offerings on the Capitoline, these dedications must have been the result of formal treaties agreed between Augustus and at least two of the kings of southern Britain. The Capitoline, one of the seven hills of Rome, had long been associated with the extensive power exercised by the Roman people. A temple to the Capitoline Triad of Jupiter Optimus Maximus, Juno, and Minerva stood there, behind an open space filled with trophies, statues, and smaller temples.

Since the second century BCE, dedicatory offerings had been made on the Capitoline by foreign rulers from eastern lands. These included marble statues and monuments bearing inscriptions which pledged these leaders' loyalty to the people of Rome.[6] Strabo provides no detailed information about the British dedications, although it is possible that the British envoys had commissioned statues or monuments from sculptors during their visits to the city. Although inscriptions in Latin were not erected in Britain itself until after the Claudian conquest, from around 50 BCE coins began to include legends in Latin, as mentioned in chapter 1, and images portraying classical statues and monuments came to be included.

The same classical author produced a description of Britons in the city of Rome that emphasized their barbarity: 'the [British] men are taller than the Celts [Gauls], their hair is less yellow, and they are less graceful.

This is because of their size: I saw in Rome young men who were taller than the tallest here by as much as half a foot, but they were bandy-legged and not elegant in appearance. Some of their customs are like those of the Celts, but others are simpler and more barbarous'.[7] These Britons might have been slaves, emissaries, or even the sons of kings taken to Rome by Caesar or Augustus. It has been suggested that Augustus may have taken the sons of two of the leading kings of southern Britain to Rome as children, only returning them to their peoples when their fathers died.[8] The Latin legends and classical images included on the coinage issued by Tincomarus and Tasciovanus, two British rulers who rose to prominence around 20 BCE, have been taken to indicate that they spent time in Rome during their youth.

Tincomarus and Tasciovanus each ruled a kingdom in southern Britain, which I shall call the southern and the eastern kingdoms (fig. 2.1). It is probable, although not certain, that Tincomarus ruled a people known as the Atrebates, while Tasciovanus is thought to have been king of the Catuvellauni. In both cases, their kingdoms included several additional peoples, who were kept tied to the dominant group through patronage and the threat of violence. British society when Caesar invaded consisted of small groups of loosely coordinated peoples, united by and under a powerful leader.[9] Each people had a number of elite families that vied for power. The kingdoms ruled by Tincomarus and Tasciovanus developed from this decentralized tradition as kings took power over larger groups of elite clients and the southern and eastern kingdoms incorporated the territories of several subservient peoples, each with its own leader who was a client of the king. These were dynastic kingdoms, since the kings of each claimed descent from an earlier ruler. The king of each realm built his power on his descent from the ancestral founder of his dynasty, as well as the authority of treaties defining the terms of his friendship with the Roman emperor. Patronage was fundamental to these experiments in kingship, as these kings used precious gifts, including gold and silver coins and regular feasts, to extend their power over clients across and beyond the territories they controlled. The gifts Augustus provided to these kings formed a key element in their ability to extend their networks of influence.

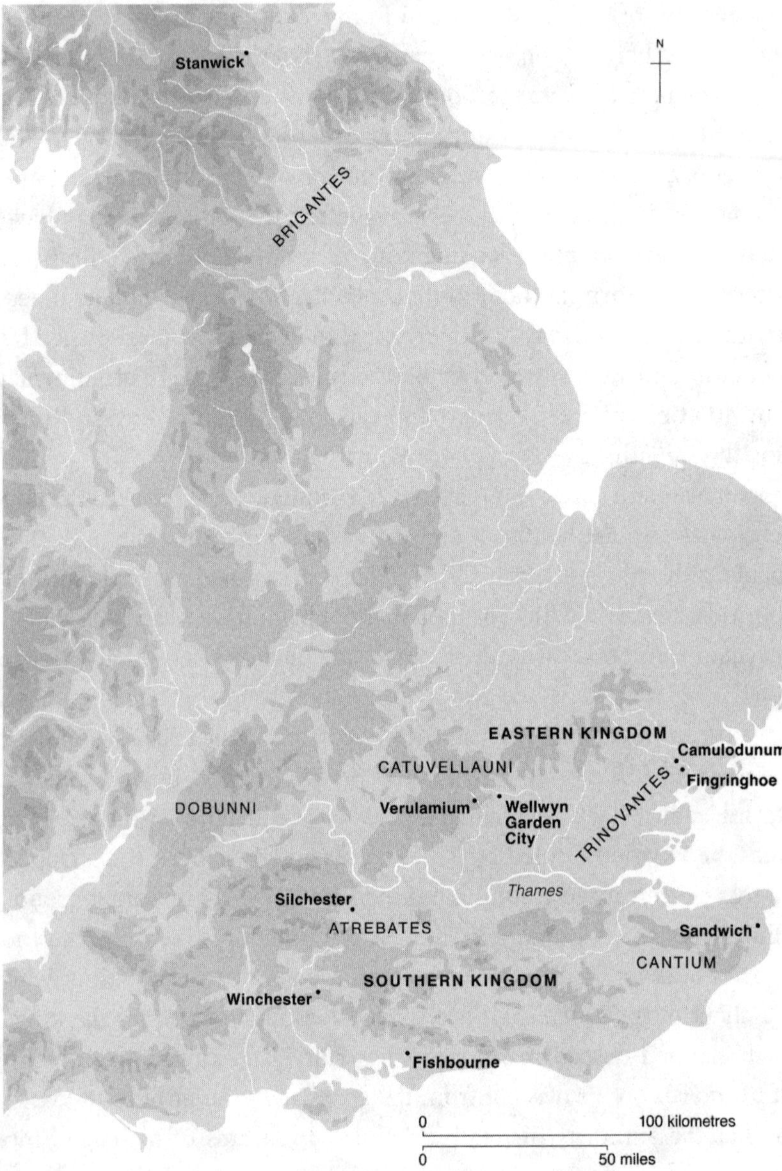

FIG 2.1.
Late Iron Age Britain, showing places and peoples

Augustus aimed to keep these rulers loyal to Rome, and the treaties independently agreed by Tincomarus and Tasciovanus would have required them to remain at peace with each other. Caesar had likewise required Cassivellaunus to leave Mandubracius in peace, and Augustan policy followed a comparable logic, with the object of keeping order between the leaders of the southern and eastern kingdoms in Britain. The stream of British supplicants to Rome demonstrates the instability of these two kingdoms. By the early first century CE, the most powerful of all these Iron Age kings, Cunobelin of the eastern kingdom, had taken control of much of southern Britain.[10]

Tincomarus of the Southern Kingdom

The coins that feature the name Tincomarus have been found across a large area to the south of the Thames, the territory of the southern kingdom.[11] Commius had been the first leading king in Britain to issue coins under his own name, a practice followed by Tincomarus (fig. 2.2). Indeed,

FIG 2.2.
Gold coins from the Alton Hoard (Hampshire), which contains coins inscribed 'TINC', for Tincomarus (Copyright: Tony Baggett)

some of his coins are inscribed 'COMMIOS F', indicating that he was Commius' son. Whether Tincomarus was actually the biological son of this earlier ruler is uncertain. A later ruler named Verica also claimed the same descent and was almost certainly not Commius' son (discussed later). The power held by Tincomarus over his clients partly relied on this dynastic link, in much the same way that Augustus drew on his status as Caesar's heir and adopted son. Commius, and Tincomarus after him, are thought to have ruled over a people called the Atrebates, who, rather than being a single people under the secure rule of a powerful monarch, represented a loose association of elite families held together through the patronage of their king.

These coins, along with those issued by Tasciovanus, were the first made in Britain to draw directly on Roman imagery, including classical-style temples, altars, and human figures wearing wreaths and drinking wine from cups.[12] Earlier Iron Age coins had featured designs derived from classical types, including a head of Apollo on the obverse and a two-horse chariot on the reverse, but the motifs on the new coins were copied more directly from Roman coins. In emphasizing his political connections with Rome, Tincomarus may well have been influenced by his own experience of the buildings, traditions, and religious festivals of the city of Rome.

Emperors used gold and silver bullion to bribe these rulers in Britain. Although there were deposits of these metals in western and northern Britain, there is no indication that they were exploited on a large enough scale to be exported to the Continent.[13] The quantity of these precious metals circulating in Britain increased substantially in the time of Augustus, presumably as a result of the gifts or bribes he made to British kings. It is thought that Tincomarus redistributed some of this bullion to senior clients across the southern kingdom in the form of coins, whose distribution, uncovered by archaeological finds, indicates the extent of his networks of patronage. The leaders of neighbouring peoples were drawn into Tincomarus' network of clients because of his power to protect them from common enemies, although the distribution of coins indicates that his kingdom was rather smaller than that of Tasciovanus. In addition to providing gifts of coins to these senior clients, Tincomarus would have held regular feasts to which these leaders came to pay their respects. It is not known, however, how many such peoples were incorporated into Tincomarus' sphere of power. At the time of the Roman conquest of Britain, we know that the southern kingdom included three peoples, but we should not assume that the political situation had remained static during the Late Iron Age.

In 2000, a metal detectorist made a fabulous discovery of gold artefacts on a low hill about 16 kilometres (10 miles) south-east of Winchester (Hampshire), comprising two torcs, two bracelets, and two pairs of brooches.[14] The torcs, or gold necklaces, were of a design unparalleled in north-western Europe, as they were made from a large number of small gold rings, bent into loops and threaded together to form a gold rope with a considerable degree of flexibility. This construction method differed distinctly from that of other gold torcs found in Britain. Those in the famous Iron Age hoard at Snettisham (Norfolk), for example, were made from gold wire twisted together and would have been difficult to wear. The Winchester torcs not only would have been far more comfortable as adornments but also had an unusually high gold content. Details of the way they were made suggest that they were the work of a goldsmith who lived in Italy. As they are of different sizes, the torcs may have been intended to be worn by a woman and a man. As these fine and unique torcs display noticeable signs of wear, they were evidently highly prized and worn over a long time.

Torcs were fairly common in Britain during the Iron Age and were symbolic of barbarian splendour in Roman eyes. The suggestion that the objects from Winchester were a gift from Augustus to a friendly king derives in part from the torcs worn by two children portrayed on the Altar of the Augustan Peace (*Ara Pacis*) in Rome.[15] This monumental marble altar, which was dedicated by the Senate in 9 BCE, included carvings depicting members of the imperial family engaged in an elaborate sacrifice. The clothing and appearance of the two boys with torcs served to indicate their differing geographical origins, from the Bosporus and Gaul, and the inclusion on the relief of these barbarian princes, from opposite ends of the empire, symbolized the political reach of the Augustan peace. It is likely that this remarkable hoard from Winchester was a lavish gift

Augustus presented to an important friendly king of the southern kingdom. He could easily have been Tincomarus.

Tincomarus is even named in the self-serving account Augustus produced of the highlights of his reign (the famous *Res Gestae Divi Augusti*).[16] Inscribed in bronze and displayed, after his death, in front of his mausoleum in the Field of Mars at Rome, this account described his rise to power as emperor and the gifts he had made to the Roman people, including a list of military conquests achieved under his command, together with an account of the situations in which diplomacy had precluded the need for armed intervention. The list named leaders of several peoples who had fled to Augustus as supplicants, including Parthians, Medes, and two Britons named Dumnobellaunus and Tincomarus. This mention of these British supplicants is an indication of the competition among the Late Iron Age elites in southern Britain. Rival leaders could emerge among the descendants of the founders of each kingdom, who could then seek to extend their own power by challenging the dominant king. The identity of the first of these kings is uncertain, whilst the inclusion of the name Tincomarus indicates that the leader of the southern kingdom was driven out of Britain by a rival around 10 BCE and fled to Rome. If the Winchester torcs were gifted to Tincomarus, he must have left them behind when he was driven out of Britain.

Tasciovanus of the Eastern Kingdom

To the north of the Thames another series of Iron Age coins has been discovered, also dating from around 20 BCE, which employs classical imagery. These coins bear the name Tasciovanus, the ruler of the eastern kingdom.[17] Tasciovanus was one of the earliest rulers to have coins issued with his name in the area beyond the Thames. He may originally have been from the Catuvellauni but, like Tincomarus, came to rule over several peoples.[18]

The inscriptions on Tasciovanus' coins included abbreviated names for two royal centres: the *oppida* at Verulamium and Camulodunum.[19] One possibility is that Tasciovanus was king of the Catuvellauni who ruled from Verulamium and subsequently conquered the Trinovantes and their *oppidum* at Camulodunum.[20] This is, however, merely speculative. Tasciovanus might equally well have come to rule the Catuvellauni and the Trinovantes as a result of a dynastic marriage. It has often been assumed that a change in the rule of an *oppidum* or a people was the result of a successful military campaigning of conquest, but dynastic marriage and diplomatic agreements between kin may also have led to such transitions of power. The distribution of Tasciovanus' coins also indicates that he controlled several other peoples in the Thames Valley and south-eastern and eastern England. The territories of the eastern kingdom were extended as a result of the growing power of a dynasty of leaders which included Tasciovanus and the three kings who claimed on their coinage to be his sons (discussed later).

The *oppida* at Verulamium and Camulodunum had several features in common, some of them reminiscent of Cassivallaunus' *oppidum* as represented by Caesar, who described a fortification set in dense woodland, in which a large group of people and cattle had been gathered. These *oppida* are also characteristic of archaeological sites that typify the Late Iron Age across parts of southern and eastern Britain (fig. 2.3). Each *oppidum* was defined by discontinuous lengths of ramparts and ditches, marking out territory which included scattered areas of occupation. Extensive open spaces served as places of assembly where people and animals could be gathered together, the ceremonies of the community were staged, and decisions affecting the community were made. These gatherings at *oppida* were central to the power of the kings of Late Iron Age Britain, as the relationships that created and sustained their power were cemented through regular feasting. The peoples who fell under the authority of the kings of the southern and eastern kingdoms each had their own *oppida*. Although their leaders were clients of the dominant king, they themselves also had clients, who met regularly for festivals.

The *oppida* of Tasciovanus therefore played a vital role in the systems of patronage that established the rule of this king over his extensive kingdom. The regular feasts were venues where Tasciovanus' power was displayed to his senior clients, who visited to take part in these events. There is little to indicate the nature of these ceremonies, apart from the common

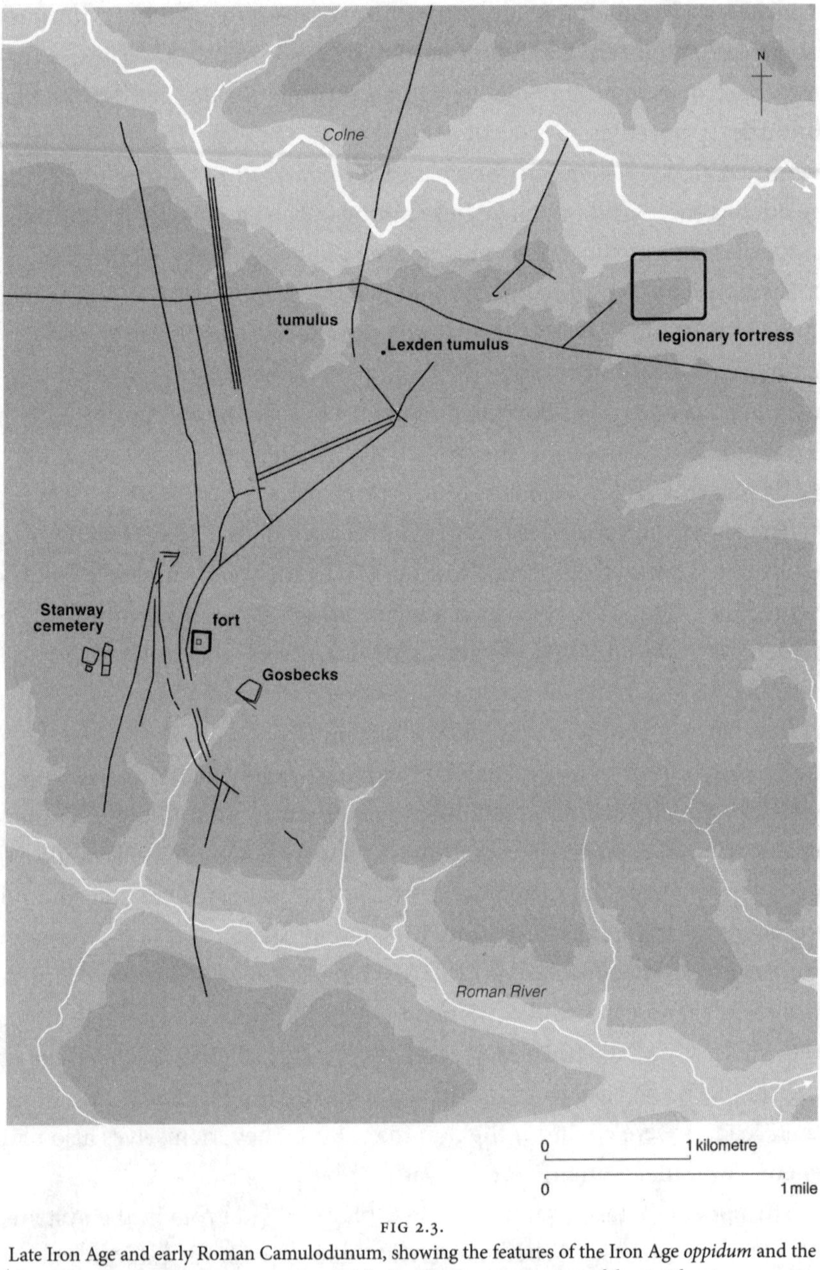

FIG 2.3.
Late Iron Age and early Roman Camulodunum, showing the features of the Iron Age *oppidum* and the location of the Roman fortress constructed during the Roman conquest of the *oppidum* in 43–44 CE (after Hingley and Unwin 2005, fig. 8; Creighton 2006, fig 7.2)

discovery of evidence for feasting at Camulodunum and Verulamium. High-status burials at both *oppida* contained artefacts deposited as offerings to accompany the deceased into the afterlife, including high-quality works such as silver and fine pottery dining ware and amphorae that had contained wine and olive oil imported from the Mediterranean. The wealthy elite families of the eastern kingdom treated their senior clients to fine food and wine to secure their loyalty at festivals, and the most important ones were held at the *oppida*. Tasciovanus may also have lived at one or both of the *oppida* named on his coins, although Iron Age kings did not build elaborate Roman-style houses.

At Verulamium (St Albans, Hertfordshire), the dykes marked out a marshy river valley which contained several small farms and cemeteries.[21] People were living and were buried there, although the significance of Verulamium was as a meeting place rather than an urban centre. The Iron Age buildings uncovered during excavations were not particularly substantial, and the roundhouses which typified the earlier phases of the Iron Age are not common at these *oppida*. The 'Central Enclosure' in the valley floor at Verulamium has been interpreted as a ritual and administrative space and a site of coin production.

The *oppidum* at Camulodunum (Colchester, Essex) was defined by an even more extensive set of earthworks, acting as the focus for areas of farmland, dispersed settlement, and high-status burial, across an extensive plateau between two rivers (see fig. 2.3).[22] The name 'Camulodunum' signified 'fortress of Camulos', an Iron Age god of war. Camulodunum became the most important of the Iron Age *oppida* in Britain, reflecting the power of Tasciovanus and his son and successor Cunobelin. Significantly, two nearby burial grounds, at Lexden and Stanway, have been found to contain the cremated remains of people of great consequence. The Lexden Tumulus, a barrow 30 metres in diameter, is the more remarkable of these burial sites. It was formed from a large mound of earth that was constructed over the buried remains of a decesed individual, and the burial it covered provides a clear indication of a growing differentiation of status within Late Iron Age society. Barrows were rarely constructed in Britain at this time, and the tumulus at Lexden is most comparable to burial mounds built to commemorate important rulers in

Late Iron Age Gaul. The deceased individual at Lexden was accompanied by a remarkable collection of offerings displaying his wealth, including at least sixteen amphorae which would have contained 450 litres of Italian wine, fragments of gold thread, silver-alloy mounts, statuettes, and the remains of an iron mail shirt. Several of these items were of Mediterranean origin and included a silver medallion of the emperor Augustus, a gift from him to a friendly ruler. The bust of Augustus on the medallion is of the same type that was used on coins issued around 18–16 BCE, which suggests that the friendly king buried under the Lexden Tumulus died during the late first century BCE. Judging from the lack of characteristically later imports from the grave, the Lexden Tumulus is unlikely to have contained the remains of Tasciovanus, who did not die for another decade or two, and the identity of the powerful king buried at Lexden has not been established.

The Lexden Tumulus is a particularly lavish example of a type of burial that became common in the area of the eastern kingdom during the second half of the first century BCE.[23] A slightly less lavish burial of the same date has, for instance, been uncovered at Welwyn Garden City (Hertfordshire). Among the accompanying grave goods are five amphorae, an Italian silver cup, a bronze bowl and strainer for wine, many pottery vessels, including some imported from central Gaul, and numerous gaming counters. The silver cup may have been a gift from an Italian patron, and the grave goods symbolize the important role of the deceased as a provider of feasts for clients. The man or woman buried at Welwyn was a member of the local elite and may have been a client of a king, perhaps Tasciovanus or his predecessor. The items associated with feasting from wealthy Late Iron Age burials, including Lexden and Welwyn, indicate the central role patronage played in the creation of power in the eastern kingdom.

Eppillus of the Southern Kingdom

Tincomarus appears to have had brothers, since two kings named Eppillus and Verica also implied on their coins that Commius was their father.[24] All three of these rulers were laying claim to a direct paternal relationship with Commius, the famous founder of the southern kingdom. Eppillus probably drove his brother Tincomarus to seek sanctuary with Augustus in Rome. Verica must have ruled later (discussed later). The distribution of coins bearing the name Eppillus suggests that he ruled two territories, one around Silchester and the other in Kent.[25] Some of his coins included the abbreviated legend 'CALLEV', indicating that he controlled the *oppidum* at Silchester (*Calleva*, Hampshire). The main phase of occupation at Silchester did indeed begin around the time of Eppillus, although the site may have originated earlier as a meeting place under Tincomarus.[26] Silchester was very different in character from Tasciovanus' *oppida* at Verulamium and Camulodunum. It was densely settled, with substantial rectangular timber houses, and the enclosing earthworks contained an area of land far smaller than the twin *oppida* of the eastern kingdom. Silchester was more directly comparable, in fact, to some of the *oppida* of Gaul. After the Roman conquest, this *oppidum* became the urban centre of the people known as the Atrebates, linking Silchester with Commius and Tincomarus, the earlier rulers of the southern kingdom (see fig. 4.3).

There was, however, a second *oppidum* within the territory of the southern kingdom, at Chichester, with more features in common with Verulamium and Camulodunum. A series of ramparts, the Chichester Dykes, defined an extensive area of land that included the coastal headland of Selsey Bill (West Sussex). Excavations within the area defined by the dykes have indicated that occupation close to the port at Fishbourne began at about the time Eppillus was ruling.[27] We do not know the name attributed to this *oppidum* during the Iron Age, and coins were not issued that named this centre. After the Roman conquest, the people in this area were referred to as 'Regnenses', which meant simply 'the people of the kingdom', but we do not know what they called themselves during the Iron Age. They were one of several peoples gifted to the friendly king Togidubnus by Claudius (discussed later), and the association of Togidubnus with Chichester indicates that the *oppidum* at Chichester played a significant role in events during the Roman conquest.

Stanwick and a Kingdom in Central Britain

The developing contacts with Rome during the Late Iron Age were restricted mainly to the peoples of southern Britain, and indeed, *oppida* have not been found across south-western, western, or central Britain. The *oppidum* at Stanwick (North Yorkshire) is a dramatic exception to this rule, and archaeological research has suggested that the people living there had contacts with far-distant patrons (see fig. 2.1).[28] Stanwick had a very extensive system of dykes enclosing a high-status settlement with large open spaces, in an arrangement comparable to the *oppida* at Camulodunum, Verulamium, and Chichester. From around 20 BCE, the resident community imported high-quality tableware and amphorae originating from the western provinces of the Roman Empire and the Mediterranean. Excavations at Scotch Corner, around 7 kilometres (5 miles) south-east of Stanwick, have uncovered another large settlement with equally high-quality goods, which began to be supplied a few decades later than at Stanwick.[29]

Initially imported in far smaller quantities than at the southern centres, these goods arrived as a result of diplomatic contacts, which were not, nevertheless, directly with the emperor or patrons from the Mediterranean. It is more likely that these items came to Stanwick through gift exchange with patrons in Gaul or southern Britain. The exchange of gifts formed one of the means through which dominant Iron Age leaders created power over others living at some distance away, and the *oppidum* at Stanwick was the royal centre of a high-ranking leader with widespread contacts. We know from accounts in the classical texts that Stanwick lay within the territory of the Brigantes. Cartimandua was a queen friendly to Rome who ruled the Brigantes after the Claudian invasion, and her capital was probably at Stanwick. Cartimandua's power was evidently built on the networks of friendships cultivated by her predecessors before the Roman invasion. Across most of the British Isles, however, contact with patrons in Gaul and Rome would appear not to have had as significant an impact. It is not known exactly why an *oppidum* developed at Stanwick, so far from the centre of Roman influence; presumably it was the result of the widespread contacts of the powerful leaders based there.

TIBERIUS AND BRITAIN

Tiberius rose to power and influence during the latter part of the reign of Augustus and was adopted as his son in 4 CE. Five years later, the security of the empire was threatened by the catastrophic defeat, suffered at the hands of the Germanic leader Arminius, of three legions under their commander, Varus, in the Teutoburg Forest beyond the River Rhine.[30] The remarkable discovery of the remains of these Roman legions at Kalkriese (Lower Saxony, Germany) has provided vital insights to the events of this notable Roman defeat.[31] Tiberius, already a highly successful military commander, then won several battles against the Germans and restored order on the frontier with the Germanic peoples. When Augustus died in 14, Tiberius took power as emperor in Rome, reigning until his death in 37. This succession established the first of Rome's imperial dynasties, the Julio-Claudians, consisting of the first five emperors.

Tiberius sent his nephew and heir Germanicus to continue the campaign to reestablish security on the Rhine frontier, and an expedition in 15 led to the recovery of the legionary standards lost during the defeat of Varus six years earlier. The fate suffered by a Roman fleet in the North Sea the following year provides an insight into the potential hazards of navigating Ocean (fig. 2.4). The dangers faced by this fleet may have been seen as further justification for Augustus' policy of controlling the kings of British peoples through diplomacy.

The Infinity of Ocean

Germanicus assembled an immense fleet of 1,000 ships to continue the German campaigns, and having disembarked his soldiers in territory beyond the Rhine, he defeated Arminius in two battles. But after leaving the River Ems, his fleet suffered considerable damage in the North Sea during its return journey. We are told that Ocean, which was 'more violent than the sea in general', 'swallowed up' some ships and threw others onto faraway islands.[32] The soldiers who returned from these distant places had stories to tell 'of the wonders of whirlwinds, unheard-of beasts, marine monsters, and creatures that were neither man nor beast'. Some

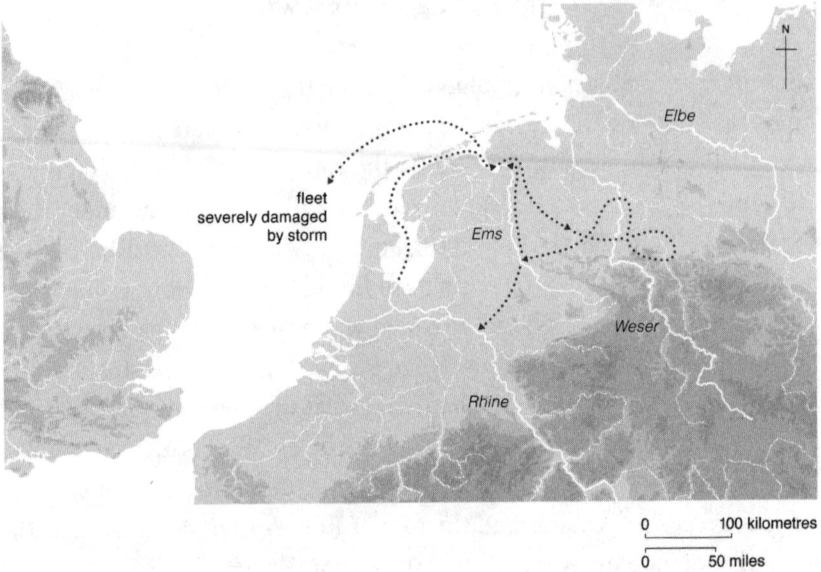

FIG 2.4.
The campaign of Germanicus in Germany in 16 CE and the loss of the Roman fleet (after information provided by Dr Ilkka Syvanne)

of the soldiers were washed up on the coast in Britain, whose 'kinglets' returned them to Rome.

An eyewitness account of this disaster is provided by the poet Albinovanus Pedo, who served in Germanicus' forces.[33] Drawing upon earlier works which addressed the dangers of sea travel, including Homer's *Odyssey*, he mused upon the numinous quality of Ocean. He described the serious hazards faced by soldiers sailing in the fleet, including vicious whales and sea hounds lying beneath the surface. He used experiences that Germanicus' soldiers had faced to ask why the Romans should want to sail such seas at all:

> Day itself is in flight and
> the end of nature closes the abandoned world with endless shadows.
> Are we looking for peoples
> who are beyond, in another clime,

another world untouched by breezes?
The gods call us back, forbidding us to know the end of creation
with mortal eyes. Why do our oars violate seas
that are not ours,
waters that are holy?
Why should we disturb the gods' quiet home?

The fleet had challenged the limits imposed on men by the gods, and the wrecking of the ships was the direct result. Pedo's comment about seas that were 'not ours' drew the same distinction between Ocean and the waters of the Mediterranean that Caesar had used in his description of the campaign against the Veneti.

If nothing lay beyond Ocean, what would be the purpose of taking a military force across its waters to invade Britain? Caesar had faced difficulties during his invasions, including the wrecking of substantial numbers of ships on two occasions. The British kinglets' return of the soldiers illustrated the success of Augustan diplomacy. To take more direct action and invade Britain might challenge the wrath of the gods. As a result, under Tiberius the relationship between Rome and Britain remained mostly peaceful and restricted to trade.

Trading across the Channel

A considerable quantity of trading between south-east Britain and the Continent is indicated by archaeological finds, and the writings of Strabo helps to explain why the conquest of Britain was not a priority for Rome at this time. Commenting on the heavy duties the Britons paid on both imports from and exports to Gaul, Strabo observed that for Rome to garrison the island would not be worth the expense.[34] He portrayed the unconquered territories on the margins of Rome's empire, including Britain, as unprofitable and undesirable targets for conquest.[35] He listed exports from Britain as grain, livestock, gold, silver, iron, hides, slaves, and dogs suitable for hunting, noting that imports from the Continent included ivory chains, necklaces, amber, glassware, and 'other trinkets'.

The large quantities of goods that have been uncovered during archaeological excavations throughout south-eastern Britain include fine pottery tableware, glass, and amphorae that had contained wine and olive oil imported from Gaul and the Mediterranean.[36] These new foodstuffs and pottery vessels were important for local rulers, since they were used to assert the authority of their owners at feasts with clients who customarily ate in more traditional ways. A few of the highest-status items were gifts the emperor had sent to friendly kings, as in the case of the gold torcs from Winchester and the medallion of Augustus from the Lexden Tumulus. Other imported goods, including the silver cup from the Welwyn burial, amphorae with wine and olive oil, and high-quality pottery produced in Gaul, may have been passed on to British clients by patrons who lived either in Rome or in Gaul. Once they had been gifted to kings and high-ranking clients in Britain, some of these objects would then be handed on to more junior clients as rewards for loyalty.

Imported pottery and amphorae have been recovered in south-eastern Britain in such large quantities that this material cannot all have represented gifts from patrons overseas to clients in Britain. Much of this would have arrived there via trade arranged through the ties between the coastal peoples of Gaul and Britain.[37] Trade itself was managed as gift exchange, whereby Gallic traders provided wine, olive oil, and high-quality pottery vessels in return for goods produced in Britain, particularly livestock, crops, and slaves. In addition, the diplomatic agreements Roman emperors made with the kings of Britain quite possibly included arrangements to allow safe passage for Roman traders within their territories.[38] Several 'ports' were located on the southern and eastern coasts of Britain, at Sandwich (Kent), Fishbourne (West Sussex), and Fingringhoe (Essex).[39] These were not established landing places with wharves but sheltered beaches where goods could be unloaded and shipped inland up the rivers. The Gallic ships Caesar encountered had flatter bases to their hulls than their Roman counterparts, enabling them to negotiate shallow waters and land on sandy beaches.[40] Ships coming from the Mediterranean would have had to drop anchor out at sea and use smaller vessels to bring goods to and from land.

Cunobelin and the Expansion of the Eastern Kingdom

With the rise to power of the most influential Late Iron Age British kings, the uncertainty that characterizes our understanding of the political history of southern Britain during this period lifts slightly. One classical writer referred to Cunobelin as 'the British king', suggesting the extent of his influence and that he was well-known in Rome.[41] Cunobelin's coins are common finds across southern Britain, and they provide information about his reign which helps to supplement the classical writings that mention him. These coins record his claim to be the son of Tasciovanus. One notable series featured his name alongside a likeness of Tiberius, indicating that Cunobelin was seeking to place himself in direct association with Tiberius as ruler of an empire. Many of Cunobelin's coins were made from gold, derived from subsidies Tiberius paid him to secure his loyalty.

These coins also included the abbreviated name Camulodunum, confirming that this *oppidum* was Cunobelin's capital.[42] Assemblies at Camulodunum would have featured ceremonies in which rival leaders negotiated their positions within the loosely organized dynastic kingdom Cunobelin ruled. An unexcavated site at Gosbecks, within the dykes of this *oppidum*, is thought to be a high-status burial enclosure which may have been the focus for cult worship of Cunobelin after his death (see fig. 2.3).[43] The distribution of his coins indicates that he had control over an extensive territory which included several subservient peoples. His coins have been found over an area comparable to the one where the coins of his father, Tasciovanus, occur, although the coins of Cunobelin extend further into Kent and west along the Thames Valley. In an extensive area of Britain, from Dorset and the Severn-Cotswold region to Lincolnshire and East Anglia, Roman contact with the leaders of the eastern kingdom was transforming the lifestyles of the local elites. As a result of the networks of patronage dominated by Cunobelin, imported wine and fine continental pottery was finding its way into their homes.[44]

Cunobelin's territory may have been expanded through fighting, although apart from the names of kings who fled to Rome seeking sanctuary, there is little to indicate that conflicts occurred in the Late Iron Age.

Cunobelin exerted much of his influence over more distant peoples by acting as patron to their leaders or through the manipulation of peoples to receive his sons as rulers.[45] One indication that his control extended over 200 kilometres (130 miles) to the west of Camulodunum is that we hear from Dio that his sons, Caratacus and Togodumnus, were dominating the 'Bodunni', probably the Iron Age people known as the Dobunni, at the time of the Claudian invasion (discussed later).

Verica of the Southern Kingdom

Verica may have succeeded Eppillus as king of the southern kingdom and claimed, like Tasciovanus and Eppillus, to be a son of Commius.[46] Dio mentions that just before 43 CE, a king called Berikos, probably Verica, sought sanctuary with Claudius (discussed later). As Commius probably died around 20 BCE, if Verica was actually his biological son, he would have to have been approaching his seventies by the time Claudius took power in Rome. This suggests that at least some of the Late Iron Age rulers' claims to be the sons of powerful dynastic rulers may have actually been based on more distant family relationships. Both Julius Caesar and Augustus arranged dynastic succession through adoption, since neither had a living son to inherit his power. Late Iron Age rulers in Britain may well have followed a comparable tradition. Verica's coins show that he placed considerable emphasis upon the cult of his 'father', Commius, the founder of the southern kingdom.

Many of Verica's coins have been found in the area around the *oppidum* of Silchester, which was presumably his political centre. Coins bearing the name Epaticcus have also been found concentrated around Silchester, some of which identify him as son of Tasciovanus of the eastern kingdom.[47] Conventionally it was thought that Epaticcus drove Verica out of this region before the invasion of Claudius, adding this territory to the eastern kingdom. Joint rule may not, however, have been uncommon during the Iron Age. Four kings ruled in Kent at the time of Caesar's second invasion, while Prasutagus, king of the Iceni, bequeathed his kingdom to the emperor Nero and his two daughters in 60 CE. Epaticcus may have taken over part of the southern kingdom through dynastic marriage or by a diplomatic agreement, leaving Verica in control of the lands to the south, perhaps with his royal centre at the *oppidum* within the Chichester Dykes. Verica may then have been driven out of this territory around the time Claudius became emperor in Rome.

CALIGULA AND THE PLANNED INVASION

When Caligula (Gaius) came to power at the death of Tiberius in 37, he decided to invade Germany and Britain.[48] This was a direct change of policy after almost a century of Roman diplomatic control of Britain. Caligula, the son of Germanicus by Augustus' granddaughter Agrippina, lacked the military pedigree of his predecessors Augustus and Tiberius and chose to lead the campaigns in person to enhance his prestige. A hint about the motive behind Caligula's decision to invade Germany and Britain is provided by his obsession with the idea of sailing on Ocean. To demonstrate his desire to control the seas, he built a fleet of pleasure ships in Italy, while the substantial bridge of boats he commanded to be constructed across the Bay of Naples, between Baiae and Puteoli, allowed him to claim to have bridged the sea.[49] Caligula evidently though that he could challenge the reputation of Julius Caesar, who had invaded Germany and Britain only to withdraw.

In 39 Caligula assembled a massive military expedition and marched to the Rhine. While Caligula was planning to cross the river into Germany, Adminius, son of Cunobelin, who had been exiled from Britain by his father, arrived with a few followers and surrendered to Caligula.[50] Adminius was probably the 'Amminius' who had issued coins in Kent, suggesting that he had ruled a people at some distance from the centre of Cunobelin's territories before fleeing over the Channel. Cunobelin, before they fell out, had presumably positioned his son as ruler of this people or may have married him into their ruling dynasty. Caligula then reportedly sent a grandiose message to Rome, recounting this surrender as though the entire island had submitted to him. Julius Caesar and Augustus had also made much of the significance of the kings of Britain who surrendered to them. Caligula then marched his forces from the Rhine through

Gaul to the English Channel. He had presumably arranged for a substantial fleet to be assembled for the planned crossing of the Channel, perhaps aiming to surpass the 800 ships involved in Caesar's second invasion. Caligula moved catapults and other artillery into position, and we are told that he ordered his soldiers to collect seashells as 'spoils from Ocean' to be displayed on the Capitoline and Palatine Hills in Rome. The emperor commanded a high tower to be constructed from which fires were to shine at night to guide ships, just like the lighthouse at Alexandria, and announced a bonus to his troops. But then no invasion took place, and indeed nothing survives to indicate that the lighthouse was constructed.

Caligula may actually have developed a practical plan to lead Rome to victory, and the collection of shells and the building of a lighthouse may have been intended to symbolize the subjection of Ocean as a prelude to an invasion which, for whatever reason, was never carried through. The destruction of his father's fleet by a storm on the North Sea twenty-three years earlier may have been on Caligula's mind by the time he reached the Channel. He had been only four years old at the time of the disaster and may have been surprised to find stories of whirlwinds on Ocean, marine monsters, and creatures that were neither man nor beast circulating amongst his soldiers, probably causing general concern about the emperor's plans.

Caligula wished to be granted a triumph in Rome as a result of his sham victories in Germany and Britain, although he eventually accepted the lesser honour of an ovation. His planned invasion was the fourth time in eight decades that an emperor considered invading Britain only to abandon the idea. The crisis of confidence that developed during Caligula's short reign, which lasted less than four years, was partly a result of his failure to lead a successful military campaign in either Germany or Britain. When he was assassinated in 41, it was imperative that his successor, Claudius, achieve an impressive military victory, and this exigency would lead to a new, more practical plan for an invasion of Britain.

3

SUBDUING OCEAN

CLAUDIUS AND BRITAIN

> there is nothing that helps us more against such very powerful peoples [of Britain] than their lack of unity.
>
> —Tacitus, *Agricola*[1]

THE MOTIVES FOR INVADING

When Claudius became emperor in January 41 CE, in succession to Caligula, his political position in Rome was precarious. He may almost immediately have decided to invade Britain, thinking that a great war of conquest beyond Ocean would help establish his reputation as ruler of the known world. Poets had celebrated Caesar's two invasions of Britain, after all, while Augustus had emphasised the diplomacy with which he had kept the barbarian Britons pacified. On the other hand Caligula's failure to lead a successful invasion had contributed to the political instability that had resulted in his murder. At the time of Claudius' accession, Britain was prominent in the minds of the senatorial elite at Rome, and he chose to capitalise on this. He intended with the British campaign to subdue not just the peoples at the empire's north-western edge but also his critics in Rome.[2] An unstable political situation in Britain, meanwhile, provided him with his excuse to invade.

Berikos, presumably Verica of the southern kingdom, had been driven out of Britain and had persuaded Claudius to intercede on his behalf.[3]

Cunobelin had died by this time, and we are told that his sons, Caratacus and Togodumnus, had succeeded him.[4] It is presumed that they had driven Verica to flee to Rome. This aggressive action would have contravened the terms of the treaty of friendship agreed between Tiberius and Cunobelin, stipulating that he was to leave neighbouring kings to live in peace. By breaking the terms of their father's treaty, Caratacus and Togodumnus presented Claudius with an excuse to intervene. Another classical author records that Britain was in a state of unrest at this time, as the Romans had not returned some deserters of their peoples to them.[5] Adminius, who had fled to Caligula four years earlier, was presumably another of these. Verica and Adminius may even have helped Claudius to plan the strategy for the invasion, with the initial aims of defeating Caratacus and Togodumnus and conquering Camulodunum.

THE INVASION BEGINS

Claudius, like Caligula before him, lacked direct military experience. That being the case, he and his advisors planned to force the submission of the kings of Britain without having to face the dangers of leading troops into battle. He selected Aulus Plautius to lead the initial phases of the invasion. Plautius had previously governed Pannonia and was a kinsman of the emperor's first wife.[6] The province of Pannonia included much of present-day eastern Austria, western Hungary, northern Croatia, north-western Serbia, northern Slovenia, and northern Bosnia and Herzegovina. The journey from Rome to Britain took at least a month, and Claudius, having learned from Caligula's errors, planned his own role in the campaign to maximize the impact of a short visit there. He trusted Plautius to win the initial victory and then summon him when conditions were secure for him to arrive in Britain.

During the spring of 43, the Roman forces were assembled under Plautius' command on the coast of Gaul but, according to Dio, were unwilling to campaign outside the limits of the known world, afraid to cross Ocean. Perhaps tales about the inhuman beasts that infested Ocean and the lands beyond were still circulating. Nevertheless, the troops were eventually persuaded to sail and were organised into three divisions, to lessen the possibility of being hindered during landing. Disembarking all soldiers and supplies at one location on a single occasion might have presented difficulties.

These divisions probably comprised three legions: the Second Augusta, the Ninth Hispania, and the Twentieth.[7] The Fourteenth Legion Gemina, may also have crossed the Channel in 43, or might instead have arrived in Britain six years later, when a new campaign was planned for Wales. The legionary commander Flavius Vespasianus (the future emperor Vespasian) had been placed in command of the Second before he joined the invasion and would play a significant role in the conquest of southern Britain. The Ninth, meanwhile, sailed to Britain from Pannonia with Plautius.[8] The identity of the commander of the Twentieth is not known, which serves to illustrate the gaps in our knowledge of the invasion. Three legions provided manpower of 15,000 heavy infantry and military engineers. In addition, a similar number of auxiliaries—cavalry and light infantry—would have formed part of the invasion force, representing a total of 30,000 men. This was comparable in size to the forces that had accompanied Caesar during his second invasion; Plautius' troops must have sailed to Britain in several hundred vessels. It is possible that Claudius was able to call upon ships and soldiers designated for Britain by Caligula three years previously, before he abandoned the idea.

Plautius and these divisions may all have landed over several days at Pegwell Bay in the Wantsum Channel (Kent), probably making use of the wide sandy beach where Caesar had disembarked in 54 BCE (see fig. 1.2).[9] The earlier Roman camp at Ebbsfleet may have been reused, and another camp was established at Richborough (*Rutupiae*) on a raised area of land that formed an island in the Wantsum Channel.[10] This island was connected to the mainland of Kent by an artificial causeway and was to become the main port where all the supplies for the Roman military forces in Britain arrived. From the main point of disembarkation in the Wantsum Channel, a detachment of Roman ships ferried military units along the south coast to the harbours on the English mainland facing the Isle of Wight (fig. 3.1).[11] A Roman base was established at a harbour at Fishbourne which lay within the dykes of the Iron Age *oppidum* at

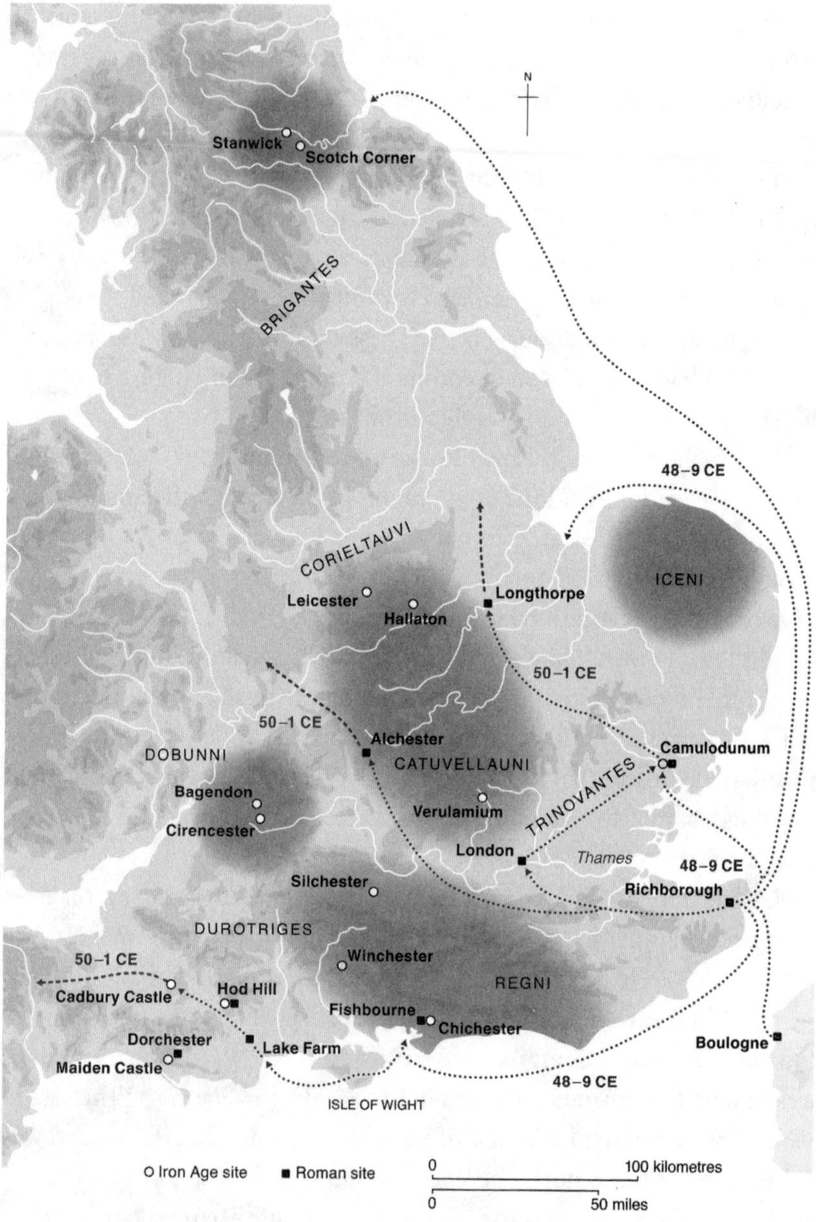

FIG 3.1.

The invasion under Claudius and Plautius, showing places, peoples, and Roman campaign routes on land and sea; the darker areas may all have been friendly kingdoms in the Claudian period

Chichester. From there, campaigns could be conducted into the south-west of Britain against the peoples beyond the western boundaries of the southern kingdom.

A Two-Pronged Attack

The Britons did not attempt to prevent the Romans from landing in Kent, and Plautius met with no resistance as he marched west. He initially found it difficult to locate the British fighters, although when he did find them, he defeated first Caratacus and then Togodumnus. The sequence of events indicates that this Roman victory occurred at an unknown location to the south of the Thames, probably in the territory of the southern kingdom. A handful of Iron Age coins that name 'CARA' have been found in this territory, indicating that Caratacus was ruling the southern kingdom in the vicinity of the Silchester *oppidum*. Although these coins are very rare, one important recent discovery is a gold coin that bears the letters 'CARAT', for Caratacus, with the figure of a cavalry soldier on the reverse and an ear of corn with the letters 'CUNO', for Cunobelin, on the obverse.[12] These coins indicate that Caratacus was ruling the southern kingdom, probably initially under the overall authority of Cunobelin before he died. Caratacus appears to have replaced Epaticcus during the early 40s.

It appears that Plautius then divided his military forces to undertake a two-pronged attack upon Camulodunum and the eastern kingdom (see fig. 3.1).[13] The main force, under the leadership of Plautius himself, marched toward the River Thames to seek further engagement with Caratacus and Togodumnus, while another force, perhaps a legion, marched further to the north-west. Concerning this second force, it is recorded that Plautius secured the capitulation of a section of the 'Bodunni' formerly dominated by Caratacus and Togodumnus and then established a garrison.[14] This action probably aimed to free the Dobunni, a people whose capital town in the Roman period was at Cirencester (*Corinium*, Gloucestershire).[15] The garrison (discussed later) may have been a temporary camp at Alchester (Oxfordshire), strategically located in the hinterland between the Dobunni and Catuvellauni.

Meanwhile, the main Roman force, which would have included at least two legions and supporting auxiliaries, marched toward the Thames. Two successive battles fought at rivers are described as Plautius marched onward toward Camulodunum.[16] At the first location, a river which is not named, the Britons had (apparently) anticipated that the Romans would not be able to cross the water without a bridge. Plautius sent across some auxiliaries, however, who were accustomed to swimming in armour, followed by the Second Legion under Vespasian's command. The victory appears to have been indecisive, although the Britons were then pursued to the Thames, 'where the river nears the Ocean, and a lake is formed at high tide'. Here the Romans were able to cross the river by making use of fords and firm ground. Plautius once again dispatched his auxiliary forces to swim across, while the other troops used a bridge slightly upstream. Between them, in this way, they attacked the Britons on several sides, and killed many. Roman losses notwithstanding, on this occasion Plautius had won a second and more decisive victory.

Dio's text provides a topographical clue to the Thames-side location of the battle, as the tidal head of this river was in the vicinity of the modern city of London, and the Britons may have exploited the islands at Southwark to cross the river.[17] Modern commentators have long viewed the bridge over the Thames as a Roman construction, assuming that the Britons lacked the technological knowledge required for building such structures. While it is certainly possible that Plautius ordered the construction of a temporary bridge, it is also fair to say that classical writers regularly underestimated the abilities of 'barbarians', and recent archaeological discoveries indicate that Iron Age peoples were fully capable of building bridges, as a number of substantial timber structures have been found in the Thames. The Roman urban settlement at London (*Londinium*) was established close to this crossing point a few years later.

It appears either that Togodumnus had been killed by this time or, perhaps, had been 'turned' from his anti-Roman actions and surrendered to Plautius.[18] The interpretation of the Greek phrase Dio used to describe this event is unclear. As the spelling of the name 'Togodumnus' in this account is very similar to that of the friendly king 'Togidubnus', who was mentioned in another context by Tacitus, these individuals were probably one and the same. It is possible that a king whom I shall call Togidubnus was persuaded to change sides as a result of the defeats he had suffered at the hands of Plautius and had surrendered. This would explain why Claudius then rewarded him with the gift of the extensive lands of the southern kingdom. After the desertion (or death) of his brother, Caratacus survived the battle and fled west, into lands beyond Rome's control, to continue his determined resistance to Rome. The fragmentary character of surviving classical texts means that we know nothing about Caratacus' acts of resistance until 51, when he fought against Rome in Wales. It appears strange that a king of the Catuvellauni might have power over people living well over 300 kilometres (190 miles) further west in Wales, although this is an indication of the extensive networks of patronage that characterised Iron Age societies in Britain.

Plautius halted his advance at the Thames and sent messengers to summon Claudius to Britain. Dio suggested that Plautius decided to wait for Claudius and his entourage because the Britons had stiffened their resistance, causing him to become afraid and to wish to defend what he had already won before the emperor's arrival. Plautius being afraid to campaign further into Britain, however, appears highly improbable; indeed, subsequent events indicate that by the time he summoned Claudius, the eastern kingdom had already collapsed. Another author provides a succinct summary of Claudius' contribution to the conquest of Britain: 'Without a battle or a drop of blood being shed, part of the island submitted within a few days'.[19]

CLAUDIUS IN BRITAIN

Preparations had been made for an expedition of reinforcements led by the emperor himself, substantially equipped, and including elephants to impress and terrify the enemy. Claudius' entourage included members of the Senate and a detachment of the praetorian guard. We know the names of a dozen of these companions, all high-ranking men from the Italian peninsula and the provinces.[20] Claudius sailed from Ostia to Marseilles and then travelled across Gaul, partly on land and partly by river. It would have taken at least a month for him and his entourage to reach Britain, and meanwhile Plautius was making preparations to ensure Claudius' security and stage-manage his visit.

The brief narrative of Claudius' activities makes it clear that he landed in Kent, probably at Richborough. This island of raised ground, close to the landing point of Julius Caesar, would have provided a suitable and secure location for the grand arrival of the first Roman emperor to cross Ocean to land in Britain. Once safely disembarked, 'he joined the legions that were waiting for him near the Thames. Taking over command, he crossed the watercourse, and engaging with the barbarians who had gathered at his approach, he defeated them in battle and captured Camulodunum, the [former] capital of Cunobelin. Thereupon, he won over many peoples, some through diplomacy and others by force'.[21] Although this suggests that the emperor led his legions into battle with the Britons after crossing the Thames, in reality he cannot have overseen any significant military engagement. He spent only sixteen days in Britain, and the distance by land from Richborough to Camulodunum via Southwark is 220 kilometres (140 miles). His itinerary itself would have taken several days to complete, especially if he also sailed back via Richborough, leaving him little time in which to join battle. Having met the legions at the Thames, he simply led them north-east through pacified territory to Camulodunum. Rather than as the result of military conquest, Camulodunum was evidently surrendered to him peacefully.

That Claudius won over 'many peoples' at Camulodunum refers to a meeting at which he received the surrender of several British kings. The Arch of Claudius, later erected in Rome to commemorate his victory, provides some details of this event: 'to Tiberius Claudius Caesar Augustus Germanicus, son of Drusus, pontifex maximus, in the eleventh year of his tribunical power, consul five times, *imperator* twenty-two times, censor, Father of his Country, from the Roman Senate and People, because he received in surrender [eleven?] kings of the Britons conquered without loss and first brought the barbarian peoples across the Ocean under the authority of the Roman people' (fig. 3.2).[22] The titles designating Claudius on this inscription indicate that the arch was not finally erected until eight years after the events it commemorates. Unfortunately, the section

FIG 3.2.
A reconstruction of the Arch of Claudius in Rome (by Christina Unwin)

of the inscription giving the number of kings who surrendered has not survived.

It is likely that Plautius spent some time before Claudius arrived orchestrating the gathering of British kings at Camulodunum, perhaps pursuing a strategy he had determined during the planning of the invasion before he even set sail for Britain. Before the *oppidum* was surrendered, it had formed the capital of the eastern kingdom under Cunobelin. The kings of the Catuvellauni had ruled several peoples through subkings, including the Trinovantes, Dobunni, and Cantiaci. Camulodunum had been the location where Tasciovanus and Cunobelin had met their client rulers for the regular celebrations that helped to unite the eastern kingdom under the rule of its great kings. This made the *oppidum* the logical location for Claudius to receive the submission of these senior clients. By submitting to him, the former clients of Cunobelin and his sons could also ensure that their peoples would not become the next targets of Roman aggression.

This gathering of kings might not have been restricted to the rulers of the subject peoples of the eastern kingdom. Since it is known that they became rulers friendly to Rome, Prasutagus of the Iceni and Cartimandua of the Brigantes might well have travelled to Camulodunum. The rulers of the Dobunni and Corieltavi may also have submitted. It is even possible that a ruler of peoples living in the islands of Orkney travelled to Camulodunum. Two authors who wrote more than three centuries after this event noted that Claudius brought Orkney into the empire (see fig. I.3).[23] Situated off the northern coast of Scotland and hundreds of kilometres from Roman territory, the Orkney Islands were nevertheless already known to some Romans in the mid-first century CE.[24]

Establishing Friendly Kingdoms

The swift conquest of southern Britain was probably the result of effective planning of the invasion. The formal agreements of surrender, or treaties, Claudius made with peoples of Britain included the establishing of several, perhaps six, friendly kingdoms (see fig. 3.1).[25] Friendly territories were not subjected to military campaigning, and their rulers were permitted to continue to lead their people. It is likely that all friendly rulers supplied the invading forces with food and recruits to the auxiliaries, while receiving gifts in return. One central feature of the treaty establishing any particular kingdom was that when its ruler died, the territory would be absorbed into the Roman province. Across much of southern Britain, this practice facilitated a peaceful transition to Roman rule during the three decades after Claudius' invasion.

After the Roman conquest, certain territories were granted to Togidubnus as a friendly king.[26] We hear from Tacitus that using kings as 'instruments of their own enslavement' was a long-established custom of the Roman people. As already mentioned, Togidubnus may have formerly been an enemy of Rome whom Plautius 'turned'. An impressive monumental inscription from Chichester names him Tiberius Claudius Togidubnus. This combination of three names (*tria nomina*) suggests that he was granted Roman citizenship by Claudius, perhaps at Camulodunum. The text of the inscription is thought to describe Togidubnus as the 'great king' who ruled over three peoples, the Regnenses, Atrebates, and Belgae. The name 'Regnenses' means 'the people of the kingdom' and was probably first adopted after Claudius gifted the territory around the *oppidum* at Chichester to Togidubnus. Before this, this Iron Age people must have been known by another name which has not survived. Since Tacitus was born in 56, his comment that Togidubnus remained loyal until the time Tacitus himself could remember suggests that Togidubnus continued to rule into the 70s.

The territory of the Iceni, to the north of Camulodunum, formed a second friendly kingdom. We hear with regard to events in Britain during 60 that Prasutagus was famed for his long-lasting prosperity.[27] This is the only reference to this ruler in classical literature; Iron Age coins issued in East Anglia bear a name which may possibly have referred to him.[28] The allusion to Prasutagus' enduring wealth suggests that he was made a friendly king in 43, when he may also have been granted Roman citizenship. Despite this wealth, a royal centre in the territory of the Iceni comparable to Silchester, Verulamium, or Camulodunum has yet to be found.[29] And although wine and high-quality tableware were both imported there from the Continent, the scale of this trade was far more limited than in other parts of southern Britain.

The Brigantes occupied a very extensive area across central Britain, far beyond the lands controlled by Rome in the early years of the conquest. Although Cartimandua is first recorded as queen of the Brigantes in an account of events of 51, she probably also travelled to Camulodunum to surrender to Claudius several years earlier.[30] We hear of her illustrious birth, indicating that her power and status were primarily inherited rather than acquired under Roman rule. Her royal status also tells us that women could lead Iron Age peoples in Britain, although she is the only 'queen' named in the Roman texts. Boudica, for instance, the wife of Prasutagus, was his consort rather than a queen in her own right.

The leaders of three other peoples of southern Britain might also have been granted the status of friends of Rome at this time. The burial at

Folly Lane, on a hill close to the *oppidum* of Verulamium, may have been that of a friendly king.[31] During the mid-50s, the remains of this wealthy king were cremated together with an assortment of rich offerings before being buried in a pit and covered with a tumulus. Included on the pyre with the remains of this king were imported silver, ceramic tableware, amphorae, and items of military equipment, including some indicating that he had served as an auxiliary officer in the Roman cavalry as a young man. Although the name of this king is unknown, he is likely to have been related to Cunobelin.[32] Might he have been Adminius, the son of Cunobelin, who had fled as a supplicant to Caligula? Claudius may have restored Adminius as ruler of part of his father's former kingdom during the first few weeks of the conquest, following the defeat of Caratacus and Togodumnus.

The leader of the Dobunni is also likely to have been made a friendly king after his people were liberated from the eastern kingdom. The Iron Age *oppidum* at Bagendon (Gloucestershire) was gradually abandoned during the first two decades of the conquest in favour of a neighbouring site at Cirencester (*Corinium*, Gloucestershire).[33] This became the capital town of the Dobunni. The gravestone of a Roman cavalry soldier found at Cirencester has been taken as evidence of an early fort at the site, from which the Roman town developed. It is also possible, however, that the governor sent a small detachment of auxiliary soldiers to support the friendly king of the Dobunni as this new centre at Cirencester began to be established.[34]

Our knowledge of the existence of the sixth friendly kingdom, the Corieltavi, is based upon a remarkable archaeological discovery. Included in a substantial Iron Age hoard, from a shrine at a hilltop location at Hallaton (Leicestershire), was an elaborate Roman cavalry helmet made from iron and plated with silver and gold foil.[35] The historical circumstances under which this helmet came to be deposited on a hill in midland England, along with a vast number of Iron Age and Roman coins, is unclear. This helmet is a particularly prestigious example of an item of military equipment closely associated with the military power of Rome. The brow guard is dominated by a female bust, perhaps representing the goddess Cybele, flanked by two lions. The cheekpieces depict a male soldier, spurred on by a winged figure of Victory, riding down a barbarian enemy of Rome. This ornate headgear probably belonged to a prince of the Corieltavi who had served as an officer in the Roman auxiliaries during the early decades of the first century.[36] He may then have taken over the rule of his people around the time of the invasion. Perhaps his body was cremated on a pyre on the hilltop at Hallaton before being left exposed to the elements, with some of his burial goods hoarded close by. Archaeological discoveries at Leicester (*Ratae*, Leicestershire), 20 kilometres (14 miles) to the west of Hallaton, suggest that this was the *oppidum* of the Corieltavi.

The cavalry equipment from Folly Lane and Hallaton indicates that during the decades before Claudius' forces invaded, several scions of the friendly rulers of Britain may have travelled overseas to serve as Roman auxiliary officers. These princes would have been accompanied by retinues of young men drawn from the leading families of their communities.[37] The fragments of four additional cavalry helmets from Hallaton might be what remains of those used by members of this prince's retinue. Some young nobles from British peoples may even have accompanied Claudius' forces and served in his campaigns to conquer Britain.

Victory Celebrations

After his brief visit to Britain, Claudius set out on the return to Rome, sending his sons-in-law, Magnus and Silanus, on ahead with news of the victory. The emperor's return journey lasted months, and he visited several places on the way, including the important naval harbour facilities at the mouth of the River Po at Ravenna. From there, he sailed out into the Adriatic aboard an impressive ship, in ceremonial commemoration of his audacious exploits in crossing over Ocean to Britain.[38] The Senate awarded him the honorary title 'Britannicus' and granted him the right to hold a triumph. An annual festival in Rome was proclaimed and the construction of two triumphal arches commissioned: one in Rome, which was eventually completed in 51–52, and the other in Gaul, at the place of his embarkation for Britain. It is not known whether the arch at Boulogne was ever actually constructed, since its remains have yet to be found.

The triumph staged in Rome in 44 CE was the first to celebrate the achievements of a ruling emperor since the time of Augustus. Claudius 'held a triumph of great splendour. To witness the spectacle, he permitted not only the provincial governors but even some people who had been exiled to stay in Rome. Among the enemy spoils was a naval crown which he fixed to the gable of the imperial palace alongside the civic crown, to show that he had traversed and, as it were, conquered Ocean. His wife, Messalina, followed his chariot in a carriage. Also following him in the triumphal procession were those who had won triumphal ornaments in the same war'.[39] The naval crown was a circular ornament of precious metal, a type of reward that had long been presented to victorious generals. This gift was presumably bestowed on Claudius by the Senate. Claudius himself had rewarded the senators who had travelled with him to Britain with triumphal regalia, probably togas with a special ornamentation.[40] It may also have been around this time that Claudius, dressed in a general's cloak, staged the spectacle of the conquest of Camulodunum and the surrender of the kings of the Britons.[41] This reenactment portrayed the operation as a military victory that Claudius commanded.

THE EXPANSION OF THE PROVINCE UNDER AULUS PLAUTIUS

Claudius' final acts in Britain had been to require the disarming of the peoples who had surrendered to him, and to transfer responsibility to Plautius for the conquest of others who resisted Rome. Through this action, Claudius appointed as governor the man who had commanded the successes of the first few months of the invasion and provided him with a set of instructions for the following few years. Plautius served in his role as the first provincial governor of Britain for four years, a typical period of appointment.[42] Provincial governors led campaigns and managed the administration of their provinces. As was usual, Plautius was accompanied by a small staff of officers drawn from the military forces serving in the province. The other senior Roman official in Britain was the provincial procurator, who acted independently from the governor and was responsible for soldiers' pay and the taxation of provincials. The governor and the procurator ruled the province on behalf of the emperor and usually liaised very closely.

Plautius also worked very closely with the commanders (legates) of the legions in Britain, including Vespasian, who led the Second. Legionary commanders, like governors, were regularly moved to new posts in different provinces or on to new military or administrative roles elsewhere in the empire. The three legions forming the backbone of the army of invasion were to remain in Britain during the early phases of the conquest. A fourth legion, the Fourteenth, may well have arrived in 49 (discussed later).

Securing Camulodunum

Plautius commanded the legionaries to construct a large temporary camp, in a strategic location within the dykes of the *oppidum*. This served as the base for those legions and auxiliary units who marched to Camulodunum with Claudius. Roman soldiers on campaign regularly constructed temporary camps, usually rectangular enclosures defined by ditches and ramparts or stockades, within which they pitched their tents.[43] These camps were used as bases for periods ranging from several days to a few months. In territories that had been entirely subdued, ramparts and ditches were not always dug, and indeed, few Roman camps at all have been found across the south-east of Britain. It is probable, however, that the camp at Camulodunum was fortified.

The troops would have begun to construct a more permanent base, or fortress, early in the autumn following the invasion (see fig. 2.3).[44] Extensive excavations have uncovered substantial defences and some of the internal buildings of this fortress, such as the barracks, which housed around 5,000 soldiers. The fortress later established in eastern Scotland at Inchtuthill forty years later provides a clear idea of the ground plan and main buildings of this type of archaeological site (see fig. 6.1). Fortresses were the winter quarters of the legions; they typically spent the summer months on campaign at some distance from their base. The fortress at Camulodunum, like all those the Romans built in Britain during the early decades of the conquest, was constructed from timber and earth.

Two military tombstones from the cemetery alongside this fortress indicate the diversity of the soldiers based at Camulodunum. The burial place of Marcus Favonius Facilis, a centurion of the Twentieth Legion, was marked with a carved tombstone depicting his weapons, armour, and clothing.[45] It was set up as a testament to him by two freedmen, slaves whom he had freed. Although we do not know where Facilis grew up, his tombstone was carved from stone brought from the legion's earlier base at Neuss on the Rhine, suggesting that the Twentieth retained connections with its former home. A second finely carved tombstone in the same cemetery commemorated Longinus Sdapeze, a *duplicarius* of the First Cavalry Regiment of Thracians (see fig. I.7). The Twentieth Legion and the First Cavalry Regiment of Thracians, which would have numbered some 500 men, formed the core of the strong military garrison at Camulodunum during the first six years of the conquest.

Longinus was an auxiliary soldier; his rank placed him second in command of a troop of thirty Thracian cavalrymen. He died at the age of 40, after fifteen years' service, and his tombstone was set up by his heirs. Born in Sofia (Bulgaria), he probably adopted his Latin name of Longinus only when he was recruited into the unit. The stone depicts a Roman soldier on horseback riding down a naked barbarian enemy of Rome, an image which helped to distance Longinus from his own people's recent history of violent defeat at the hands of the Roman military: we know, for instance, that an uprising in Thrace in 26, when he would have been a child, was violently suppressed by Rome.[46] Auxiliary soldiers such as Longinus were regularly recruited from the subject peoples of the empire and then used in Rome's wars against other 'barbarians'. If they survived twenty-five years' service to Rome, they could retire and were often rewarded with Roman citizenship. Longinus had not survived this long, clearly, although we do not know whether he died of natural causes or was killed in battle.

Extending the Province

During the second winter of the occupation, in 44, another fortress was constructed, at Alchester.[47] It would also have been preceded by a temporary camp, which may have been the site of the garrison which was established during the summer of 43 when the Dobunni were freed from Caratacus and Togodumnus (discussed earlier). The discovery of the tombstone of a veteran soldier of the Second Legion, Lucius Valerius Geminus, suggests that Alchester was the legion's base during the conquest period.[48] This fortress was located in neutral territory, in the hinterlands of three of the friendly kingdoms Claudius established at Camulodunum: the Dobunni, Catuvellauni, and Corieltavi.

The location of a third legionary fortress, to the north-west of Camulodunum at Longthorpe (near Peterborough, Northamptonshire), exploited a comparable location in the hinterlands of the friendly kingdoms of the Iceni and Corieltavi. Using the pottery found during the excavation of the site as a dating tool, archaeologists think that the Longthorpe fortress was occupied from about 45 and may have been the base of the Ninth Legion.[49] For the Ninth and Second Legions, the fortresses at Longthorpe and Alchester were convenient positions for overseeing the stability of the newly established friendly kingdoms. Although these legions were campaigning away from their bases during the summer months, their commanders would have left behind sufficient troops to keep an eye on any attempts to undermine the authority of the kings, and swift military action would have nipped any unrest in the bud. Small detachments of Roman troops would also often have been stationed with friendly kings at their political centres to provide support, as in the case of the cavalry soldier buried at Cirencester.

After the security of the lands already subdued had been assured, the next priority for Plautius was to direct campaigns against the peoples of southern Britain who were yet to surrender. Little is known of the activities of the Ninth and Twentieth Legions, although they were presumably campaigning from their legionary bases against resistant peoples in the vicinity of Camulodunum and Longthorpe. A single classical reference provides important information about the campaigns undertaken by the Second Legion in the south-west.[50] Vespasian 'fought thirty times against the enemy. He forced two very strong peoples to submit, as well as twenty *oppida* and the Isle of Wight [*Vectis*], close to Britain, partly under the command of Aulus Plautius the provincial governor, partly under the control of Claudius himself'. The reference to the Isle of Wight indicates that

Vespasian was campaigning across southern Britain and must have been using the Roman fleet to explore the south coast from several harbours, including Fishbourne. There is no indication of military campaigning on the Isle of Wight, and it is likely that its people surrendered voluntarily.

Another early fortress has recently been confirmed by archaeological geophysical survey at Lake Farm (Wimbourne Minster, Dorset).[51] For the Second Legion this was an additional base from which to subdue the resistant populations of the area to the west of Togidubnus' friendly kingdom. This fortress was well sited to be supplied by sea and to direct campaigns against the Durotriges while a garrison remained at Alchester. The large number of *oppida* that Vespasian subjugated presumably refers to the campaigns he directed against the hillforts of the Durotriges. Archaeologists generally apply the term *oppidum* to extensive Late Iron Age sites such as Camulodunum, Silchester, and Verulamium, whereas Suetonius was using the term in its alternative sense of 'stronghold'. The 'twenty *oppida*' were the communities amongst the Durotriges, who used hillforts as their political centres.

Although many of the Iron Age hillforts across southern Britain had been abandoned by this time, the territory of the Durotriges was an exception, since some of their very substantial hillforts, which had been constructed earlier in the Iron Age, continued to provide important centres drawing communities together from the surrounding landscape for important festivals.[52] There were many such communities in the territory of the Durotriges, and so Vespasian had to lead campaigns against several hillforts in order to force their submission. No single ruler had any form of centralised control over this people, and the communities making up the Durotriges did not band together to fight the Romans.

Archaeological excavation has demonstrated that Vespasian attacked three of the most impressive hillforts of south-western Britain, employing the same tactics earlier commanders had used to force the submission of peoples in Gaul and Iberia.[53] Human remains and weapons found around the eastern entrance of one of these, the hillfort of Maiden Castle (Dorset; see fig. 1.4) suggest that its Iron Age inhabitants were involved in armed combat with Roman soldiers.[54] Dozens of iron spearheads and bolt-heads indicate a Roman attack, although the dead were not buried where they had fallen, and some survived long enough for their injuries to begin to heal. A high percentage, including women and children, received violent injuries, and the presence of their remains indicates that women fought in armed conflicts alongside men. Although Vespasian made an example of this community, Dorchester eventually became the urban capital of the Durotriges during the succeeding decades. The development of Dorchester as the *civitas* capital of the Durotrigues also demonstrates that the Maiden Castle hillfort had a special status among this people.

A second very substantial hillfort at Hod Hill (Dorset) was also subjected to a Roman siege.[55] Ballista bolts were found amongst the many Iron Age houses occupying the area within the ramparts. Human remains were not found during the excavations; nonetheless, a large Roman fort was constructed inside the ramparts of this hillfort. Forts were usually built by legionary soldiers and occupied by auxiliary units of some 500 men. As a result, forts were far smaller in area than fortresses. The Roman fort at Hod Hill, as it was larger than most, may have housed a double auxiliary unit or may have been constructed for a mixed group of legionaries and auxiliaries. Since Vespasian campaigned against the communities that made up the Durotriges on an individual basis, much of the campaigning was presumably undertaken by single auxiliary units, or detachments of 500 legionaries. Several units would have been combined when attacks were directed at particularly important hillforts, including Maiden Castle and Hod Hill.

That only a few other Roman forts have been found in the territory of the Durotriges suggests that military units often repurposed the hillforts they had overwhelmed as temporary bases. Excavations uncovered Roman military timber buildings in the interior of the Iron Age hillfort at Cadbury Castle (Somerset), which seems to have been besieged before the Roman troops occupied it. A substantial deposit of earth, broken artefacts and human remains that had filled the lower part of the passageway formed by the south-western gateway of this hillfort included the scattered remains of bodies and weapons resulting from a battle between Roman troops and local people.[56] Marks on the bones indicated that these people, like those at Maiden Castle, had been subjected to considerable violence. At the hillforts of Maiden Castle, Hod Hill, and Cadbury Castle, military units had overwhelmed their opponents before constructing bases, either within the hillfort or close by, from which they could dominate these traditional meeting places while a new Roman order was being imposed.

The military campaigns which formed part of the conquest of southern Britain used considerable violence against the communities that resisted, resulting in heavy casualties, particularly to the Britons. The human remains from these hillforts represent a small sample of the many victims of the sustained military violence that was directed against people who resisted Rome. Roman soldiers had a particularly dismissive attitude toward the barbarians they fought. The tombstone of Longinius Sdapeze from Camulodunum depicts a cavalry soldier's rampaging horse trampling a naked barbarian beneath its feet. Roman sculptures on display at the imperial frontiers regularly portrayed this scene. Such images helped to project the dismissive views that soldiers fighting for Rome held of their resistant opponents. Otherwise, scant further trace of the remains of peoples caught up in these conflicts has been found across southern Britain, as the Roman military habitually cleared the battlefield of human remains. Two skulls were found in the ditch surrounding the fortress at Camulodunum which may have been the heads of defeated enemies displayed at one of the gates.[57] A later auxiliary tombstone from Lancaster depicts a cavalry soldier who has cut off the head of a barbarian enemy (discussed later). Indeed, the discovery of human skulls at Roman military sites across Britain suggests that auxiliaries regularly engaged in headhunting during the many conflicts characterizing the decades of the conquest.

The Extent of the Province in 47

Plautius was recalled to Rome in 47, and Claudius awarded him an ovation, or 'lesser triumph'.[58] After the reign of Augustus, no commander outside the imperial family was allowed to celebrate a triumph in Rome, and the reward Plautius received probably consisted of no more than the toga of a magistrate. Such togas had a decorative border signifying the enhanced status of magistrates and triumphant generals among their fellow Roman citizens and were displayed when these powerful men met in general assemblies in Rome. By this time, the Roman forces had established control of an area of southern Britain extending approximately to the line of the Fosse Way (fig. 3.3). Diplomatic and military activities were already under way to weaken the resistance of peoples living in the lands beyond.

The roads the military constructed across the lands under Roman control were just as instrumental as forts and fortresses in imposing Roman authority. The main arterial roads in southern Britain were laid out under Plautius and would have followed established Iron Age routes

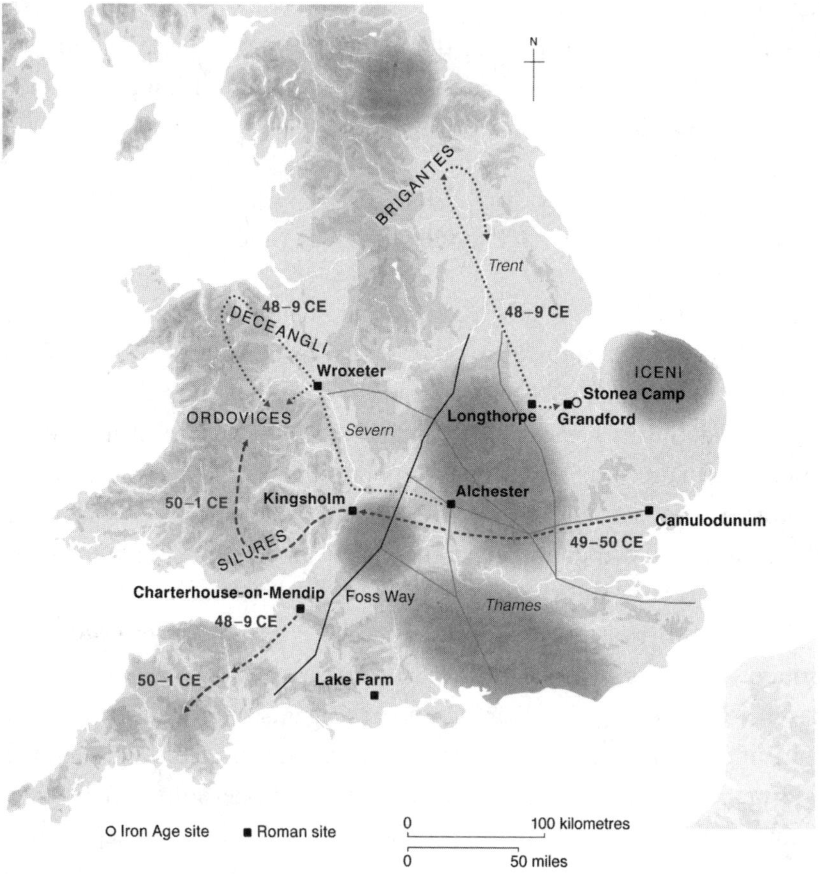

FIG 3.3.
Campaigns under Scapula, showing places and peoples

wherever possible.[59] The landscape of Britain was intersected by numerous tracks that Iron Age peoples used to travel between settlements; some of these would have run for long distances. Little is known about these routes since they were not as solidly built as the highly engineered and metalled roads laid by Roman military units on campaign. These metalled roads, which were carefully surveyed and paved with stones, often followed straight alignments across the landscape. Many of the Roman roads continued to be used in later times and remain in use as highways today. Although the friendly rulers may also have been encouraged, or actively supported, in constructing better-made roads in their own territories, the well-engineered, cambered roads with rammed gravel surfaces, hallmarks of Roman construction techniques, would have taken several more decades to complete. Forts would also have been built at strategic points in the road system, although few such sites have been located and excavated.[60]

THE CAMPAIGNS OF OSTORIUS SCAPULA

With the arrival of the new governor the conquest extended to new parts of Britain, and our knowledge of the distribution of Roman forts increases dramatically. After the winter of 47 began, Scapula arrived to replace Plautius as governor in Britain.[61] Little is known of his earlier career; his main contribution to the conquest of Britain was to begin the protracted process of subduing the highly resistant peoples of Wales. He also sent military units to defeat enemies who were threatening Rome's friendly rulers (see fig. 3.3).

Although there is no record of any military action in south-western Britain after Vespasian was recalled to Rome in 47, the Second Legion nevertheless continued their campaigns against the Durotriges and neighbouring peoples. Little is known of these actions, although stamped inscriptions on lead ingots (or pigs) from Charterhouse-on-Mendip (Somerset) indicate that one small detachment of the Second Legion was overseeing the mining of lead and silver deposits at this location by 49.[62] Rome considered the minerals in Britain prizes of victory.[63] The lead was used for pipes carrying the water supply in the forts and fortresses, while silver, which was of significant financial value to the Romans, was shipped back to Italy. The workforces at Roman mines were usually slaves, and captured Britons probably worked the minerals at Charterhouse under the direct supervision of legionaries.

Armed Support for Two Friendly Rulers

Although Scapula appears to have encountered some armed unrest in Wales soon after his arrival, the first more significant military situation he faced was in eastern Britain. Early in 48, he attempted to broker the disarming of all the people who lived to the south and east of the Severn and the Trent Rivers, a move which sparked resistance among the Iceni.[64] Described as a strong people who had not been crushed in battle, the Iceni by this time were probably already under the rule of Prasutagus. In challenging the Roman governor, some of the king's senior clients may have rebelled against his rule. Following the initiative of the Iceni, neighbouring peoples chose a place defended by a rampart as the site for battle. Tacitus relates that they were overwhelmed by the Roman force. This stronghold has been identified as possibly Stonea Camp (Cambridgeshire), an Iron Age fort constructed on slightly elevated land in the waterlogged region of the Fenlands.[65] The Iceni's disastrous defeat had the effect, we are told, of pacifying thereafter all those peoples who were considering opposition to Rome.

In 49, Scapula then led his forces against the Deceangli of northern Wales, ravaging and plundering their territory. This campaign took him well beyond the limits of Roman military control, and it appears likely that he was seeking out mineral deposits, as northern Wales was a source of both lead and silver (discussed later). His forces had almost reached the sea that faces Ireland when dissension among the Brigantes of central Britain caused him to withdraw from north-west Wales. After killing of a few Brigantes who had taken up arms and pardoning the rest, the Romans apparently settled the matter. Cartimandua is not mentioned in the very brief summary of this uprising, but she is known to have been ruling the Brigantes in 51 and was presumably already in charge at the time of the unrest. The first years of Scapula's governorship witnessed two insurrections against rulers who were friends of Rome, indicating that considerable work was still required to secure the lands that Rome was gradually drawing into its control.

A Major Campaign in Wales

The Silures (of southern Wales) had continued to engage in war with the Romans, and it was necessary to build a legionary garrison to subdue them.[66] Archaeological research indicates that a new fortress was constructed around this time at Kingsholm (Gloucester, Gloucestershire) to form the winter base of the Twentieth Legion, which advanced from its earlier base at Camulodunum. Two men who died while serving at Kingsholm, a soldier of the Twentieth Legion and a Thracian cavalryman, are commemorated on tombstones from the cemetery that accompanied the new fortress. This suggests that Kingsholm, like Camulodunum, was manned by a mixed garrison of legionary and auxiliary soldiers. The colony at Camulodunum (discussed later) was founded at this time to replace the earlier fortress and to provide a permanent home for retired veterans from the three legions serving in Britain.

The resistance of the Silures in 51 was supplemented by 'the strength of Caratacus, who[se reputation] had been elevated by many indecisive battles and many successful encounters, so that he towered over the other commanders of the Britons. On this occasion, with the advantage of a tricky locality but disadvantaged by the inferiority of his soldiers, by a strategem he transferred the war from the territory of the Silures to the land of the Ordovices; and, with the addition of those who dreaded peace with us'.[67] The Ordovices were neighbours of the Silures and lived across central Wales. This statement in Tacitus is very significant for our understanding of the situation in Britain, since Caratacus had formerly been the joint leader of the southern kingdom when they had fought against Plautius to the south of the Thames in 43. That Caratacus was able to lead the resistance against Rome in Wales indicates his considerable reputation as a war-leader as well as the strength of the alliances connecting

Iron Age peoples over extensive areas. Tacitus must have provided details of Caratacus' actions during the intervening years in the chapters of *Annals* that were lost in antiquity.

The Twentieth Legion spearheaded the attack on the Silures from their base at Kingsholm. The campaign against the Ordovices, meanwhile, was led by the Fourteenth Legion Gemina, which may have been transferred to Britain in 49. The fortress at Wroxeter (*Viroconium*, Shropshire), which was later to serve as the base of the Fourteenth, could have been constructed at this time.[68] These Roman legions were supported in their campaigns by auxiliary units of cavalry and infantry. The combined forces constructed temporary camps while campaigning against the Ordovices and Silures, and a large number of such sites have been located across Wales.[69] It took Rome almost thirty years to complete the conquest of this part of Britain, and because of the way the Iron Age peoples there organized their resistance, the empire experienced great difficulties during this campaign.

These peoples did not possess *oppida* of the type found across southern Britain and did not produce coins.[70] Imports of amphorae and fine wares from Gaul and the Mediterranean were also far less common in Wales, although some trading did occur. The peoples there lived in numerous small enclosed settlements, and some of the earlier hillforts were still in use as communal centres. But in fact, the decentralisation of these Iron Age societies was one of the factors that slowed the speed of the Roman forces' advance as they reached the Welsh Marches. Much of Wales is dominated by uplands and large valleys, which divided Iron Age communities into small areas of territory, in contrast to the lowland plains in southern Britain, which had been conquered swiftly. There is nothing to indicate that the Romans besieged hillforts in Wales, which suggests that local communities did not use them as strongholds and places of retreat when the Roman forces arrived. Perhaps they had learnt a lesson from Vespasian's attacks on the hillforts of their neighbours, the Durotriges.

One tactic that Roman commanders in both Gaul and southern Britain used with considerable success had been to march into hostile territory with the intention of forcing their enemies to unite under a single war-leader and then to fight a pitched battle. The decentralized peoples of western and northern Britain did not usually unite in this way; as a result, decisive battles were rare. Instead, the Britons practised what military historians have termed 'low-intensity warfare' or 'guerrilla warfare', using hit-and-run tactics to attack Roman troops.[71] In order to campaign successfully against the peoples of Wales, therefore, Scapula and his successors had to adopt a flexible strategy. This involved splitting their forces into smaller campaigning units. These units constructed roads and forts strategically, dividing communities into small parcels of territory which could be controlled while resistance was subdued. A particularly dense distribution of forts and fortlets (small forts) built across Wales during the thirty years it took to conquer these peoples illustrates the difficulties successive Roman commanders experienced.[72] The Roman forts in Wales have been very well studied by generations of archaeologists: several have been extensively excavated, and the locations of many more are known. The earliest of these forts, across the Welsh Marches, date to the campaigns of Scapula, while their gradual spread over a wider area helps to illustrate the process of conquest over time, until Agricola claimed the defeat of the final part of north-west Wales in 79.[73]

The only known occasion on which the peoples of Wales united in a large force to fight for their freedom was when Caratacus 'resorted to the ultimate hazard' of a pitched battle with Scapula in the mountains of central Wales in 51. This battle occurred at a location that Caratacus carefully selected: 'adopting a place for battle so that the entry, exit, everyting would be unfavourable to us and for the better of his own men, with steep mountains all around, and wherever a gentle access was possible, he strew rocks in front in he manner of a rampart. And in front too there flowed a stream with an unsure ford, and companies of armed men had taken up position along the defences.'[74] Caratacus flew hither and thither, proclaiming that today the battle would be the start of either his warriors' freedom or their permanent slavery. There would have been no Roman witnesses to hear his speech, and Tacitus used his imagination to write these words.

Scapula was stunned, we are told, by the eagerness of the Britons to fight and the strength of the location chosen for the battle, although the Roman soldiery demanded to meet them. He led the Roman forces across the river and stormed the rampart, losing a considerable number of his troops as a result of the Britons' effective use of slingshots. Fighting at close quarters, however, the Romans overwhelmed their enemies and drove them into the mountains, where the slaughter continued. It is remarked that the Britons had no breastplates or helmets to protect them and were in consequence vulnerable to the swords and javelins of the legionaries. Although Iron Age weapons have indeed been found in many places across Wales, well-armed warriors were very much in the minority among the forces facing the Romans. Only members of the Iron Age elite would have had access to swords, while shields, spears, and helmets were always rare among Iron Age communities in Britain.

The location of the battle has not been determined, and the description would fit many of the mountainous valleys of central Wales equally well. The recent discovery of battle sites where Roman commanders fought against Germanic peoples, however, has offered the prospect that the location of Caratacus' defeat in 51 may yet be found.[75] The Britons appear to have used very effectively the rampart Tacitus described to resist the force of the Roman attack, and this detail of the conflict might one day assist archaeologists to locate the battle site. Tacitus described the tactics of the Britons in several battles with the Romans, and the use of the rampart is an interesting insight, particularly as the discovery of a comparable rampart at another battle site in Germany—the location of the defeat in 9 CE of the Roman commander Varus at the hands of the Germanic war-leader Arminius—may confirm it.

The wife, daughters, and brothers of Caratacus were captured at the battle, while he, according to Tacitus, fled to seek sanctuary with Cartimandua and the Brigantes. It is entirely unclear why Caratacus would have sought sanctuary with Cartimandua, since, as a friendly ruler, she was required to surrender him to Rome. Although Tacitus, in his account of subsequent events, presents the actions of Cartimandua in a poor light, the brief description of the handing over of Caratacus in chains to the Romans may, in reality, have masked a more complex set of negotiations. Cartimandua might have acted as a go-between to enable Caratacus to surrender to Scapula, just as, a century before, Commius had assisted Cassivellaunus to surrender to Caesar.

Celebrations in Rome

The deeds of Caratacus had captured the imagination of people in neighbouring provinces, and his fame had spread as far as Rome itself.[76] The senior Roman officers who had served in Britain may also have carried home tales of his nine years of armed resistance to Rome. Claudius displayed his captive barbarian king in a victory parade held in Rome in 52. The ranks of the praetorian guard were drawn up in front of their barracks by the Porta Viminalis, and Caratacus' retainers, followed by his brothers, his wife, his daughters, and then finally Caratacus himself, were paraded past them.

The speech Tacitus gave to Caratacus developed the theme of native nobility in the face of adversity and contrasted royal barbarian morality with imperial degeneracy: 'if the degree of my nobility and fortune had been matched by moderation in successes, I would have come to this City as friend rather than captive, nor would you have disdained to receive with a treaty of peace one sprung from brilliant ancestors and commanding a great many peoples. But my present lot, hideous as it is for me, is magnificient for you. I had horses, men, arms, and wealth: what wonder if I was unwilling to loose them? If you wish to command everyone, does it really follow that everyone should accept your slavery?'[77] This is the first of three famous speeches that Tacitus placed in the mouths of British resistance leaders, all couched in similar terms. He used Caratacus to moralize about the former emperor Claudius' failings. Claudius subsequently pardoned Caratacus and his wife, surely the prearranged outcome of the celebrations, and Scapula was voted 'triumphal insignia' to celebrate his achievements. Presumably, like the previous governor Plautius, Scapula was presented with a magistrate's toga.

The Arch of Claudius (discussed earlier), was completed in 51–52, possibly as part of the celebration of the capture of Caratacus (fig. 3.2). Although the inscription on the arch made reference to the peaceful surrender of the king, the focus of the sculpted imagery decorating the arch, by contrast, emphasised the triumph of Rome's military might over the barbarian Britons. One of the few fragments of sculpture from the arch to survive from antiquity was recorded in a drawing by Pierre Jacques, a French artist of the sixteenth century.[78] One of a number of images of Roman victory which would have ornamented this arch, this one depicted Roman troops overwhelming their barbarian foe. One Briton, seminaked, appears in an upright stance in valiant hand-to-hand combat with a Roman soldier. This image forms a striking contrast with the downtrodden barbarians on Longinus' tombstone at Camulodunum. To emphasise to a Roman audience Claudius' great success in Britain, it was important to depict the Britons' valour on his triumphal arch.

Another interesting feature of the Arch of Claudius concerns its relationship to water. The Aqua Virgo, one of eleven aqueducts supplying Rome, carried water into the city by a channel that ran over the top of this arch.[79] Its inscription proclaimed Claudius' victory over Ocean, while the aqueduct provided a direct example of the control he exercised over water closer to home. Numerous other public works in Rome and Italy during Claudius' reign built upon the idea that he was master of water in all its forms, including the construction of harbours, the draining of lakes, and the completion of two further aqueducts.[80]

A SETBACK IN WALES

While Rome was celebrating the capture of the barbarian king, the military situation in western Britain was deteriorating. A detachment of legionaries who had been instructed to build a camp in the territory of the Silures found themselves surrounded and would have perished had troops encamped nearby not been summoned to relieve the legionary soldiers.[81] The Silures had apparently been infuriated by a speech Scapula delivered in which he announced that they ought to be exterminated just as the Sugambri (a people of the Lower Rhine) had once been, or that they should be transported to the Gallic provinces. Evidently, the defeat and capture of Caratacus had not entirely subdued this people.

The unstable situation may well have contributed to Scapula's death in 52, as Tacitus describes how he became exhausted by his responsibilities in Britain. Claudius appointed a new governor, Aulus Didius Gallus, a trusted and experienced military commander who came from an Italian family.[82] On his arrival in Britain, Gallus was greeted with the news that the Silures had defeated a legion. This must have represented a serious threat to Roman control of Britain. We know of only one, perhaps two, other occasions when Britons defeated a legion during the first century of the Roman conquest of Britain. Tacitus provides no additional information, however, and does not even name the legion but notes that until Gallus drove the Silures back they were scouring 'far and wide'. Claudius himself died in 54. He was succeeded by his adopted son, Nero, who would continue his stepfather's policy toward Britain.

SUBDUING OCEAN

As mentioned earlier, the conquests in Britain were the most notable achievement of Claudius' reign.[83] During a speech to the Senate in 48, on whether senators from the new provinces of Gaul should be admitted, he observed that he had extended the empire beyond Ocean. He had followed in Caesar's footsteps by challenging the gods and crossing Ocean to receive, in person, the submission of many kings. Britain was of particular significance because Claudius' campaign had extended the limits of the 'civilized' world and added new lands to the empire, an achievement that surpassed even the actions of the deified Julius. Tacitus observed that an ancient custom allowed Roman commanders who had conquered new territories to extend the area within the *pomerium*, the sacred boundary that surrounded the city of Rome, and that Claudius had extended the boundary in 49.[84] The incorporation for the first time of the lands beyond the edges of the civilised world into the empire warranted the extension of the city of Rome's own sacred boundary.

Despite all this, there is some evidence that the British campaigns were not entirely well received by the senatorial elite at Rome, as Claudius was still generally held to be a fool.[85] The personal foibles of the ruling emperor were of no concern, however, to many of the less wealthy people in the city. The triumph in 44 and events connected with the parading of Caratacus in 52 provided free entertainment, as spectacles glorified the conquest of an exotic new Oceanic territory.[86] Roman officers who had served in Britain also gained significant honours for their military service during Claudius' campaign. His semifabulous campaign clearly appealed to wealthy provincials at the other end of the empire, since the conquest of Britain was celebrated by the ruling elite of the cites of Corinth (Greece), Caesarea (Cappadocia, central Turkey) and Aphrodisias (Asia Minor, Turkey). At Aphrodisias, buildings dedicated to Aphrodite were constructed between 20 and 60 CE.[87] Sculpted friezes portrayed several Roman emperors in the guise of Greek heroes, including a naked Claudius in heroic pose, poised to deliver the final blow to the defeated figure of Britannia (fig. 3.4). The otherness of this conquered territory is shown in an image of the province of Britain as a female barbarian. Another sculpture from Aphrodisias depicts the naked Claudius as a divine hero receiving gifts from female divinities representing the land and sea (fig. 3.5).

While the conquest of Britain was a bold attempt to build Claudius' reputation, the troops who conducted these violent campaigns to enforce order and peace did so at the cost of many Roman and British lives. The few pieces of monumental sculpture representing the defeat of Britons include the tombstone of Longinus from Camulodunum, the frieze from the Arch of Claudius in Rome, and the Britannia sculpture from Aphrodisias. These images help to illustrate nuance in the Romans' attitude toward the people of Britain, who were seen either as valiant upholders of a desire to remain free of Roman tyranny or primitive barbarians entirely unable to contend with Roman military force. Despite the speech Tacitus wrote for Caratacus, we can only speculate on how Britons interpreted the invasion of Claudius, and clearly these people did not all react in the same manner. Friendly rulers cooperated with Rome through necessity and because the emperor's support increased their own power and wealth. Many other people chose to fight for their freedom from Roman control, especially as the military campaign extended to the south-west and Wales. The remains of victims at Camulodunum, Maiden Castle, and South Cadbury represent only a minute fraction of those who died as a result of Roman aggression in the course of the conquest. Many more who survived the battles were enslaved and shipped to the Mediterranean.

FIG 3.4.
Claudius and Britannia; marble relief from the Sebasteion at Aphrodisias (Turkey)
(Copyright: New York Excavations at Aphrodisias)

By the end of Claudius' reign, a substantial area of southern and eastern Britain had been conquered. A Roman colony had been imposed within the territory of the *oppidum* that had been Cunobelin's capital, and fortresses and forts had been constructed in the lands on the western and northern margins of Roman territory. Across the south, friendly rulers held extensive kingdoms, while the Brigantes, who lived well beyond the

FIG 3.5.
Claudius receiving gifts from the spirits of land (left) and sea (right); marble relief from the Sebasteion at Aphrodisias (Turkey) (Copyright: New York Excavations at Aphrodisias)

limits of the Roman province, also had a treaty that designated Queen Cartimandua a friend of Rome. The lands of the friendly peoples would be absorbed into the province as their rulers died, as was already the case at Verulamium, while the unconquered lands beyond the province offered successive emperors new horizons for military glory.

4

REBELLION

> [Nero] ... was never moved by the slightest desire or hope to extend or add to the empire, and even considered withdrawing the army from Britain but was disuaded by the shame which he would have incurred in seeming to detract from the glory won by his own parent.
>
> —Suetonius, *Nero*[1]

THE CONQUEST OF BRITAIN had been the most notable achievement of Claudius' reign. When he died in 54, he was succeeded by his sixteen-year-old adopted son, Nero; the Senate granted him authority to declare his stepfather a god. Since Tiberius had not been deified, Nero was the first emperor since Augustus to possess a deified father. Writers in Rome viewed the initial years of the young Nero's rule very favourably, as he left much of the government to his advisors. This favourable impression was not, however, to last.

THE TEMPLE OF CLAUDIUS AT CAMULODUNUM

Nero may swiftly have issued a command to the provincial governor of Britain, Aulus Didius Gallus, to establish a centre for the cult of Claudius at the colony at Camulodunum. The formal Roman title of this colony was Colonia Victricensis, a name which commemorated its foundation during the reign of Claudius (fig. 4.1).[2] Constituted in 49, this colony was

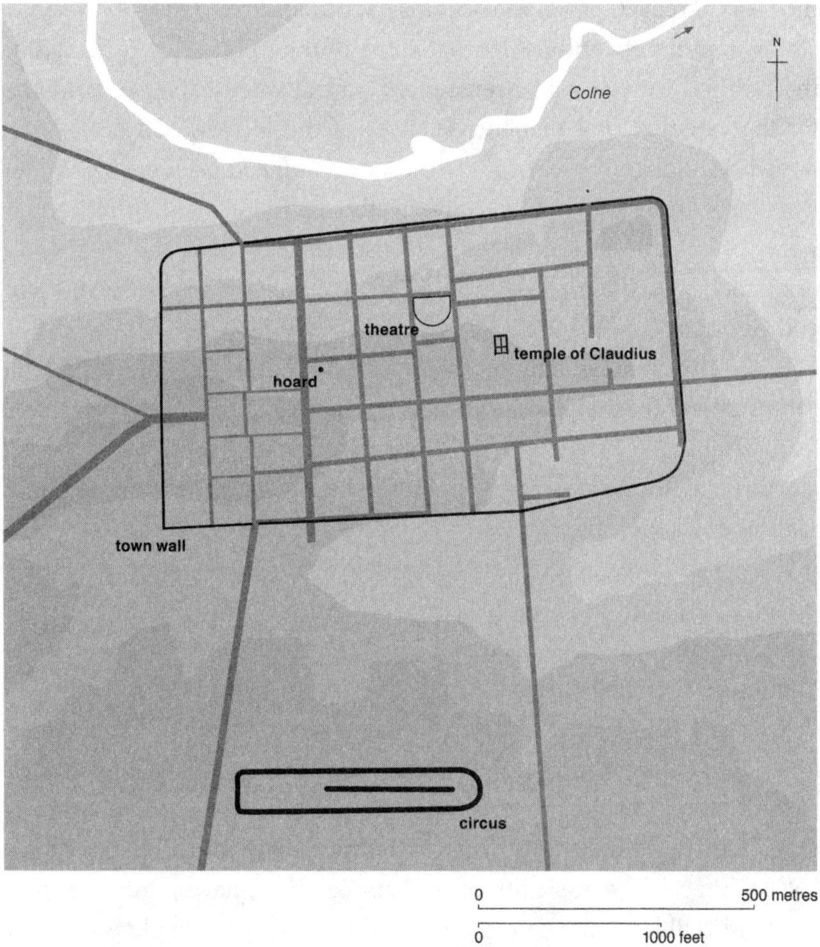

FIG 4.1.
Colonia Victrensis at Camulodunum, in the late first century CE, showing the location of the Fenwick Hoard; Camulodunum was undefended during the Boudican uprising, and the town wall and circus shown on this plan were constructed several decades later (after P. Crummy 2008, fig. 2; N. Crummy 2016, fig. 1, with additions)

the most important administrative and urban centre in Roman Britain, and the temple to the divine Claudius was intended to provide a focus for the loyalty of the pro-Roman elite of the province.[3] Tacitus recorded that by 60 the colony included the temple of Claudius, a statue of Victory, and a theatre, noting also that it was not defended by ramparts and ditches. Most of the buildings of this early colony were constructed of timber with tile roofs. Archaeological excavations have uncovered traces of this flourishing community, indicating that some of the military barracks within the original fortress had been reused and adapted to serve as houses for the veterans, and that the defences of the fortress had been abandoned.[4] Although the fortress at Camulodunum had been the base of the Twentieth Legion, the soldiers who lived there following their retirement were veterans of all four legions garrisoned in Britain and themselves originated from different parts of the empire, including Italy, Spain, Gaul, and Germany.

While this massive temple was constructed of local stone with a tile roof, some of the stone incorporated in the structure was also imported from Tunisia, and fragments of Mediterranean marble found at the site are thought to derive from a monumental inscription commemorating the dedication of the cult to Claudius.[5] The remains of the foundations, which have survived as the basements of the Norman castle built at Colchester, indicate the immense scale of this Roman building, erected to honour the cult of the deceased emperor. At the time of its construction, there were no other masonry buildings in Britain on anything like this scale, and it served as a very impressive statement of the power of Rome and its emperor-gods. At this time, even the most senior leaders of the southern Britons were living in timber-built houses. Since some of these high-ranking Britons would have travelled to visit Rome, the scale and architectural complexity of the temple would have reminded them of grand buildings in the capital of the empire. The temple was also a statement of Nero's determination to continue to build on his stepfather's victories in Britain by conquering additional territories.

The temple was served by a group of priests, senior men of mixed origins recruited from the British peoples whose leaders had submitted to Claudius. It seems likely that the friendly rulers supplied at least some of these priests, since being selected as a priest of the imperial cult would have increased their status, reaffirming the relationship with their former patron, who had now become divine.[6] Senior legionary veterans living in the colony would also have become priests, including some of the highest ranking officers who accompanied Claudius during the march on the *oppidum* at the site of Camulodunum in 43. The rituals associated with the celebration of Claudius' cult was probably funded by the public officials of the colony and by the priests who served the imperial cult. These individuals may also have contributed to the cost of the building of the temple.

The cult of Claudius may have been celebrated at annual gatherings of the priests with other high-ranking Britons. The main festivities, which probably took place on 1 August, the deceased emperor's birthday, would have included a lavish sacrifice to his divine spirit at an altar that stood in front of the temple. At the centres for the worship of Augustus in other provinces, games also formed part of the occasion, spectacular events which may initially have been held in the open air at Camulodunum. A monumental circus for chariot racing was indeed constructed, but not until several decades later.[7] Other regular sacrifices to the divine spirit of the emperor would have taken place at the altar in front of the temple throughout the year.

The lack of defences surrounding the colony indicates that trouble from the Britons was not anticipated, presumably reflecting the enthusiasm with which the friendly rulers of southern Britain had adopted the imperial cult. That such powerful individuals were deeply involved in the cult might have suggested that the colony was secure from any danger. The establishment of the fortress and colony would, however, have been a serious source of grievance among some Britons. The legionaries who retired to live at Camulodunum were given land to cultivate, requiring, for instance, the confiscation of property from the Iron Age communities living there when the Roman legions arrived. The Roman administration pursued a careful policy with members of the British elite, however, and it is clear that not all the powerful families of the Trinovantes had been driven away from Camulodunum at the time of the conquest.

Archaeological excavation at Stanway, 4 kilometres (3 miles) southwest of the colony, has uncovered a cemetery containing the graves of deceased members of the Iron Age elite, and the dead continued to be buried there until about 60 (see fig. 2.3).[8] Although the Britons who had directly opposed the Roman invasion were killed or driven away, some influential families at Camulodunum were clearly allowed to remain and presumably to retain their lands. The area around Stanway and Gosbecks lay within the western part of the territory defined by the dykes of the Iron Age *oppidum*, where a significant cult centre, probably dedicated to King Cunobelin, developed during the second half of the first century CE (discussed later). The information from Gosbecks demonstrates that the administration of the colony tolerated this sanctuary dedicated to a former friendly ruler and that some members of the Trinovantian elite continued to live in and around Camulodunum.

THE EARLY TOWNS OF SOUTHERN BRITAIN

Several other towns were beginning to develop during the 50s, a process which may have been guided by the governor and procurator of the province (fig. 4.2a). The Romans came from a Mediterranean world in which the city-state was the basis of civic life, a political construct they set out to impose upon the peoples they conquered in Britain. As mentioned, the *oppida* of Late Iron Age southern Britain were not urban in the Mediterranean sense but were meeting places. They did not include monumental public buildings, such as marketplaces, temples, and theatres, and were not usually nucleated population centres. This situation began to change when Iron Age peoples were formally incorporated into the territory of the empire.

The Roman policy in Britain was to encourage the elite families of each of the Iron Age peoples to establish their own *civitas* as the basis for local self-government. The leaders of each *civitas* controlled their own people and were encouraged to focus this rule upon a town, a *civitas* capital, where the power of the elite families was now to be centred. Roman governors manipulated local elites when they established this system of *civitates* developed out of the preexisting Iron Age political structures. The governors would have favoured particular British leaders over others and aimed to establish a system disempowering individuals and peoples who had opposed Rome. Many of the *civitates* of Britain covered quite large areas of territory, and in this way Rome would have enabled pro-Roman elites to extend their power over others whom the imperial power did not directly favour.[9]

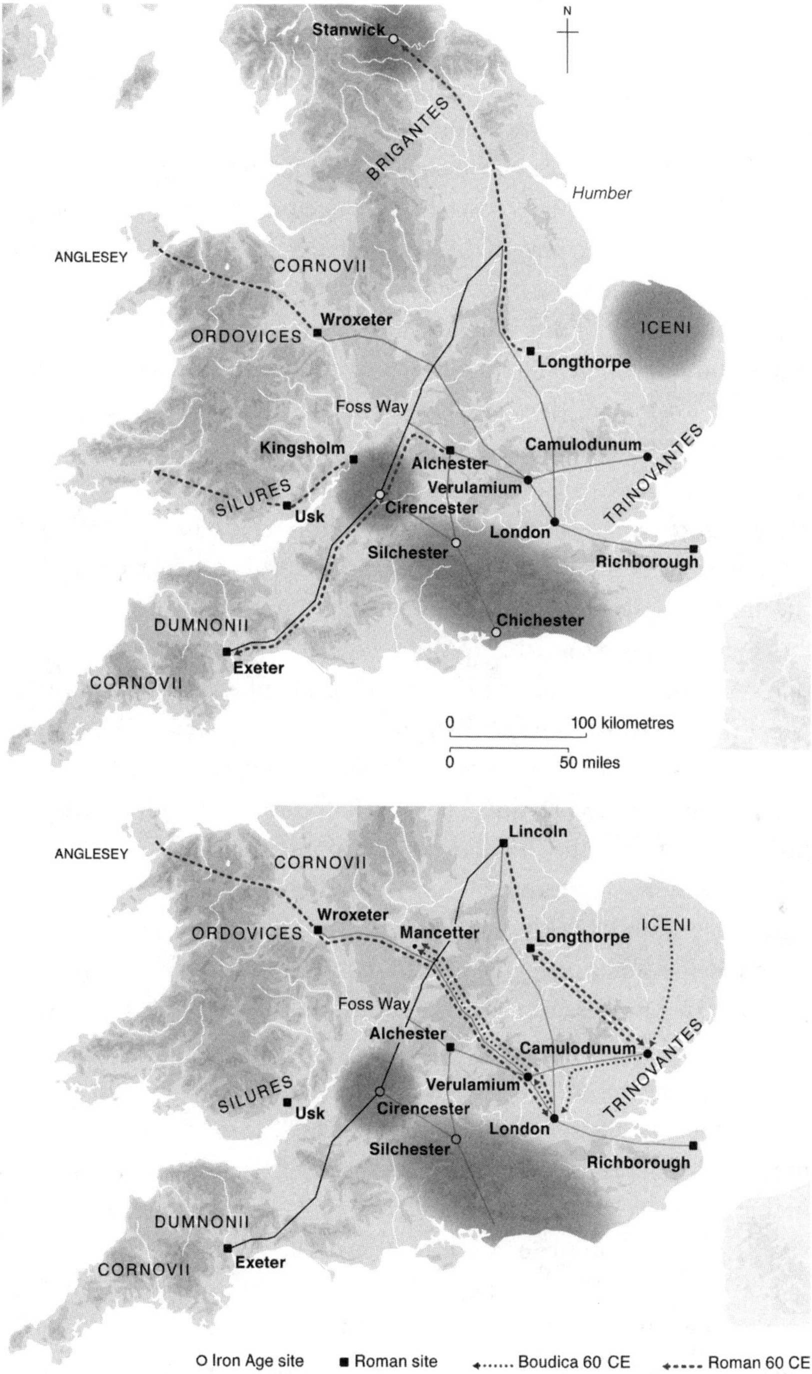

FIG 4.2.

Britain under Nero: (a) (top) the Roman campaigns from 54 to 60, showing forts and towns; (b) (bottom) the events of the Boudican uprising in 60

Little is known about when exactly the individual *civitates* of southern Britain were formally established, except that in the cases of the friendly kingdoms, this would have occurred when their rulers died. At this point, as their territory was formally incorporated into the empire, the elite families of the former kingdom would have been required to supply magistrates and councils to govern their community. Each *civitas* was governed by an annually changing roster of magistrates and a council elected from local landowners.[10] These individuals, recruited from the leading families of the community, depended for their continued influence on the power of Rome. In return, they assisted the imposition of imperial order by ensuring the law-abiding behaviour of their people, while acting as tax collectors for Rome.

As this system was imposed across southern Britain, *civitas* capitals usually developed on the sites of, or in close proximity to, the *oppida* of the Iron Age peoples. These became significant administrative, social, and political centres for their peoples during the later first and early second centuries CE and survived down to the end of Roman rule in Britain, when they were abandoned. Each town eventually included a forum: a monumental building, constructed around a courtyard, where the ruling council administered justice. Tacitus referred to this policy of urbanization when he described the colony at Camulodunum as an example of how the Britons were brought to abide by Roman laws. The government of the colony and its civic buildings, meanwhile, were intended to serve as a model to the British elite of how to urbanize and regulate their own peoples. This process of urbanization did not, nevertheless, occur particularly swiftly, and organized schemes of metalled streets and public buildings were not constructed at the *civitas* capitals of southern Britain until the late first and early second centuries. The main type of building in the early phases of these towns was small, rectangular houses, made of timber. Some well-favoured urban communities were, however, supplied with Roman bathhouses at an early stage of the 50s or 60s.

The first *civitas* in Britain may have been established during the mid-50s, when the king of the Catuvellauni died and was buried at Verulamium. This urban community was no ordinary *civitas*, however, since its urban capital had been awarded the special status of *municipium* by Rome, meaning that the elected magistrates who ruled the town automatically became Roman citizens.[11] Verulamium was the only Roman town in Britain to be accorded the status of *municipium*, reflecting a particular bond of friendship between its ruling elite and the emperor. But despite this close relationship, there was little to mark the early urban centre at Verulamium as particularly Roman.[12] Archaeology has demonstrated that the local population gradually started moving down to the valley floor, to live in timber buildings constructed alongside metalled roads. The transition from Iron Age *oppidum* to Roman town would take several further decades, however, although a Roman bathhouse was probably built before 60. Architects may have been brought in from Gaul or the Mediterranean to construct this bathhouse using technology unknown in Britain before the arrival of the Roman military.[13] Alternatively, it might have been made for the urban community by military engineers. Bathing in the Roman manner was a key element of the Mediterranean lifestyle for the citizen soldiers of Rome, and the pro-Roman elite of southern Britain swiftly adopted the custom. A grand bathing facility would be established at the sanctuary site at Bath (Somerset) during the 70s (discussed later).

At least some other friendly rulers were also establishing urban centres, and Roman bathhouses were constructed at Togidubnus' twin *oppida*. Excavations at Silchester have uncovered the foundations of a bathhouse which must have been one of the earliest Roman urban buildings in Britain, since it appears to have been built during the reign of Claudius (fig. 4.3).[14] An urban centre was also gradually developing within the dykes of Togidubnus' southern *oppidum* at Chichester, featuring a Roman building, perhaps a bathhouse, with an inscription bearing the name Nero and datable to 57–58.[15] The construction of early bathhouses at Silchester, Verulamium, and Chichester is highly significant: bathing was evidently becoming an established part of life for the most wealthy members of the British elite. The friendly kings would also have begun to introduce their British clients to the pleasures of social bathing.

London (*Londinium*) had quite different origins from the other towns of southern Britain. It was not officially constituted like Camulodunum and did not develop from an Iron Age *oppidum*.[16] We hear mention that London in 60 was not a colony but was well known for the large number

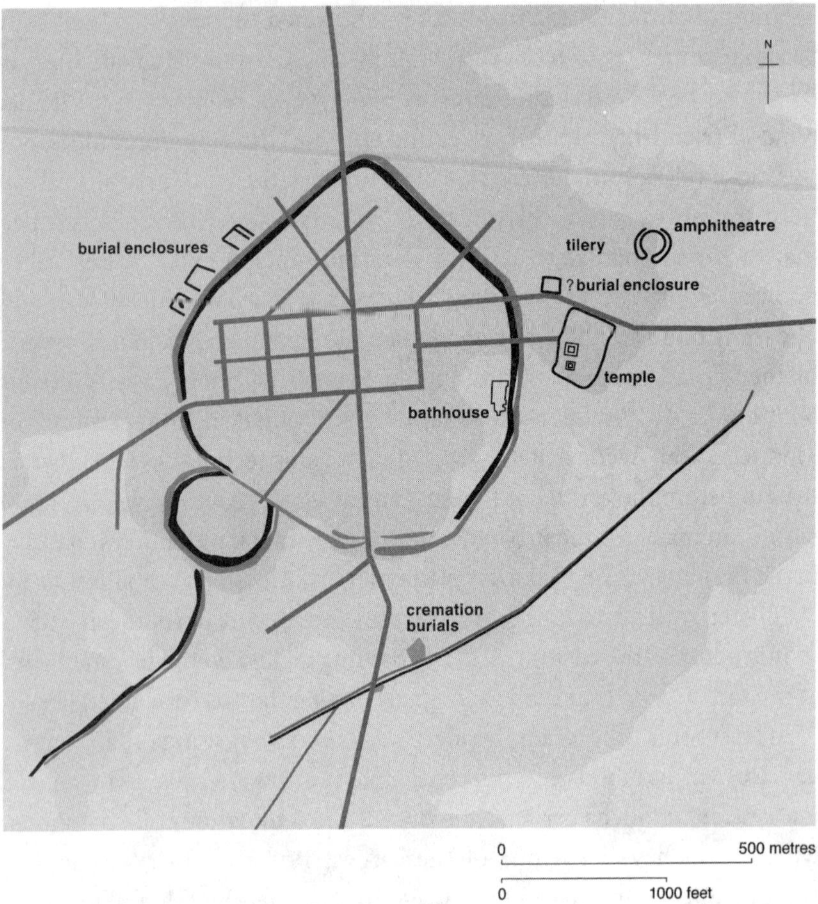

FIG 4.3.
The *oppidum* of Silchester (*Calleva*) at the time of Nero (after Creighton and Fry 2016, fig. 17.1, with additions)

of merchants who traded there and the quantity of their merchandise.[17] The town was established by traders from overseas who settled the riverine landscape on both sides of the Thames during the decade after the invasion. The position of London on the margin of Iron Age society also accorded it a neutral location, well away from the political centres of the British elite. The waterfront on the north bank of the Thames at London had replaced Richborough as the main port of the province by the early 50s, with a substantial settlement of perhaps around 9,000 people developing on both banks of the river. The variety of imports reported in early contexts indicates the substantial scale of the trade passing through this port. The main roads were laid during the 50s, a metalled marketplace was established in the core of the settlement to the north of the Thames, and a bathhouse may have been constructed to the south of the river. Many small timber buildings have been uncovered, including houses, a pottery shop, and granaries, while the presence of roundhouses indicates that Britons also settled in the town.

Of all these towns, the colony at Camulodunum had the highest status since it was home to a large number of Roman citizens. The second most prestigious town in the province was the *municipium* at Verulamium, which served as the *civitas* capital of the Catuvellauni. Togidubnus' kingdom to the south of the Thames remained nominally independent of Rome, and the bathhouses constructed at Silchester and Chichester may have been gifts to this friendly king, who was also a Roman citizen. London had no administrative status at this time, although it had already become the main port and economic centre of Roman Britain, with a resident population that included wealthy merchants from Gaul and other parts of the empire.

THE WESTERN AND NORTHERN FRONTIERS

The strategy of conquest in Britain early in Nero's reign continued to build on that pursued under Claudius. Little is recorded about the activities of Gallus, the new governor, although he must have been kept busy directing the construction of roads and forts across western Britain, thereby establishing Roman control of the lands previously conquered by Plautius and Scapula.[18] The Roman military forces were gradually encroaching into the territories of the Silures and the Ordovices in Wales, constructing a network of forts to help to force these peoples into submission (see fig. 4.2a). The Twentieth Legion advanced from the fortress at Kingsholm into the territory of the Silures, where it built the fortress at Usk (*Burrium*, Monmouthshire); the fortress at Wroxeter (*Viroconium*, Shropshire), constructed by the Fourteenth Legion, was well positioned to act as a base for the campaigns against the Ordovices and into northern Wales.[19] Forts were also being constructed as bases for the auxiliary units campaigning to push the frontier of the territory controlled by Rome further west into Wales.

Meanwhile, the Second Augusta was actively subduing the territory of the Dumnonii in south-western Britain. The Roman fortress at Exeter (*Isca*, Devon) was constructed during the mid-50s as the base of this legion, which had moved there from Alchester.[20] From a strategic location on the Exe estuary, the Exeter fortress controlled shipping routes along the Atlantic seaboard and was evidently intended as a base for campaigning further west. Roman forts were also constructed as bases for auxiliary units in the territory of the Dumnonii, an indication that military campaigning was required to subdue this people. The Iron Age hillforts and enclosed settlements throughout the south-west constituted the local gathering places of decentralized communities, subdued individually by Roman campaigns.[21] Security from external attack was clearly also important, and the two early Roman fortlets on Exmoor were strategically located to observe the north coast of the Bristol Channel.[22] This reflected the instability of the situation across Wales, where the conflict with the Silures was not indeed finally settled until the 70s.

Venutius of the Brigantes

We know of one additional event in central Britain that occurred when Gallus was governor. This involved Venutius of the Brigantes, the most prominent military leader in Britain following the capture of Caratacus.[23] Venutius had long remained loyal to the Romans and was under their protection for as long as he was married to Cartimandua, queen of the Brigantes. Venutius had evidently fallen out with his wife, however, and they had divorced. Cartimandua took his brother and some of his kinsmen prisoner, and in response Venutius sent a band of armed men into her territory. Although he had been married to her and was clearly seen by Tacitus as a leader of a part of the Brigantes, Venutius seemingly had control over another unnamed people, from whose territory he now sent warriors to invade Cartimandua's kingdom. That Venutius was not titled 'king' in the account of these events suggests that much of his power was derived from his marriage to Cartimandua: she inherited her preeminence among her people through the support of Rome, while Venutius led another semiindependent people under her overall control as queen of the Brigantes. By turning against Cartimandua, Venutius had also broken his alliance with Rome.

Venutius' force of armed men was met first by a Roman auxiliary unit and then by a legionary force, presumably a detachment from the Ninth. This indicates the serious resistance that had emerged and suggests that the attack on Cartimandua was defeated only with difficulty. Nevertheless, the Romans succeeded in restoring her to her leadership of the Brigantes, and Stanwick, which was probably her power base, continued to be occupied at this time. The extensive site at Scotch Corner, just south of Stanwick, lay to either side of the Roman road nowadays known as Dere Street, which was constructed during the early 70s to formalize a preexisting route.[24] As the community at Stanwick and Scotch Corner had access to considerable quantities of Samian pottery and imported glassware from the Continent, friendly relations between Cartimandua and the Roman administration evidently provided the opportunity for traders to settle in her territory for a further decade (discussed later).

Quintus Veranius: A Provincial Governor Who Died in Office

Gallus was recalled from Britain in 57 and replaced as governor by Quintus Veranius, an experienced military commander who had previously governed Lycia (part of present-day Turkey); in his term in Britain he conducted 'modest sallies' against the Silures.[25] He died in 58, after only a short time in office; his last words were reported to have been that had he lived another two years, he would have subjected the whole island to Nero. Subsequent events would demonstrate that his assumption of the viability of such rapid conquests was entirely misplaced. By this time, Roman control had been extended across much of the present-day English Midlands. The fortress at Lincoln (*Lindum*) was established during the late 50s as a base for the Ninth Legion, which would have begun campaigning further to the north.[26] Although there is no clear indication that forts were constructed north of Lincoln at this stage, Roman control may have extended as far as the line of the Humber and the River Don.

Suetonius Paulinus: An Ambitious New Governor

Gaius Suetonius Paulinus, the governor appointed in 58 to replace Veranius, already had experience of mountain warfare, having conducted a spectacular campaign in Mauretania (North Africa).[27] Paulinus began his term with two years of successful campaigning in Britain, conquering territory and establishing a permanent garrison in a network of forts throughout the western territory of the Silures, and in central and northern Wales.[28] From this position of strategic strength, he then attacked the island of Anglesey (*Mona*). He manufactured ships with flat hulls to manage the perilous shallows, a sign of the significance he attributed to the conquest. For his enemies were acquiring support from this island which was acting as a sanctuary for fugitives.[29] Apparently, Anglesey also had deeper mystical significance.

In his detailed account of the attack by infantry and cavalry soldiers, Tacitus provides a vivid description of the opposing force of Britons drawn up on the shoreline of Anglesey: 'There stood along the shore a diverse line, dense with arms and men, and with females running in between: in funereal clothing and with tumbling hair, they were flourishing firebrands after the manner of the Furies; and Druids around about, pouring forth ominous prayers with their hands raised to the sky'.[30] Furies were ghastly creatures of Roman mythology who gloried in the violence of military conflict. The presence of Druids, meanwhile, added a mystical touch to the description of the opposition Paulinus faced, suggesting that the island of Anglesey had special significance to the Iron Age peoples as a sacred place. After Paulinus had defeated the assembled forces of the Britons, he ordered the burning of the sacred groves and established a garrison, presumably based in a camp or a fort.[31] Druids were often associated with sacred groves in classical writings, and the emphasis on the otherness of Anglesey as a sacred island lying within Ocean added to its allure as a target for the new governor's thirst for military success.

While he was in north-west Wales, however, Paulinus received news of a serious uprising among the Iceni, far to the east. Despite being a highly effective military commander, he had lost control of a developing crisis there which threatened to put at risk the conquests of the previous seventeen years.

BOUDICA'S UPRISING

In 60, the Roman rule of Britain faced its first major challenge, when Boudica's uprising almost drove the occupying forces out of the province (see fig. 4.2b).[32] This British resistance fighter's fame rests in part on Dio's physical description of her: 'In stature she was very tall, in appearance most terrifying, in the glance of her eye most fierce, and her voice was harsh; a great mass of tawniest hair fell to her hips; around her neck was a large gold necklace; and she wore a tunic of diverse colours over which a thick mantle was fastened with a brooch. This was how she was always dressed. She now grasped a spear to aid her in terrifying all who beheld her.'[33] This is the only detailed description of an ancient Briton recorded anywhere in the classical texts, and the image presented of Boudica as a rough and uncivilized barbarian formed part of Dio's account of the barbarity of the Britons who rebelled against Rome. Tacitus, by contrast, offered a far more positive portrayal of her as a noble woman who had been grievously treated.

The direct cause of Boudica's resistance was the treatment she and her daughters had received at the hands of the Romans: 'The king of the Iceni, Prasutagus, conspicuous for his long-standing wealthiness, had written down Caesar [Nero] as his heir along with his two daughters, deeming that by such compliance both his kingdom and his household would stay clear of injury. The opposite turned out to be the case, so much so that his kingdom was devistated by centurions, his household by slaves—as though both were captured property. At the very start Boudica had beatings inflicted on her and their daughters were violated by rape; all the principals [leading men] of the Iceni, as if they had received the entire district as a gift, were stipped of their ancestral property, and the king's relatives were held like menials'.[34] Prasutagus had apparently aimed to bequeath his kingdom jointly to the emperor and his daughters, whereas the treaty designating Prasutagus as a friendly king would have included the stipulation that the Iceni were to be absorbed into the lands of the Roman province when he died. Prasutagus must have been hoping that if he offered half of his territory directly to the emperor, his daughters would be allowed to take over as joint rulers of the remaining lands.

What drew Roman criticism was not the legality of taking over of the territory of the Iceni but the way the Roman authorities managed the handover.[35] Tacitus' reader in Rome would have been deeply shocked by the idea of Prasutagus' high-ranking family suffering abuse at the hands of slaves. This was a serious reversal of the strict rules of hierarchy and status structuring Roman society and an affront to classical conceptions of moral decency. The king had been a long-standing client of Rome whose wealth is likely to have derived, at least in part, from the gifts he had received from the emperor. Prasutagus, his wife, and his children may well also have been Roman citizens. By this account, Boudica was driven to fight against Rome as a result of the outrageous treatment she, her daughters, and her kin had suffered.

Dio hints at broader concerns among the ruling families of southern Britons, suggesting that an excuse for war was found in the confiscation of the sums of money that had previously lent to the leaders of the Britons during the reign of Claudius, presumably including the leaders of the Iceni and Trinovantes. The provincial procurator, Decianus Catus, the Roman official responsible for the financial management of the province, apparently demanded that these peoples pay these sums back. He may well also have been directly responsible for the abuse Boudica and her daughters suffered. Another reason for the uprising was that Nero's wealthy senior advisor, Annaeus Seneca, had lent some British rulers 40,000,000 sesterces and had also recently recalled these loans. He is known to have loaned money at interest and had clients across the Roman world, presumably employing a number of freedmen to manage his financial affairs.[36] The immense sum of money he allegedly invested in Britain was equivalent to more than thirty tons of silver coins, enough wealth to have fed, supplied, and paid the 40,000 Roman soldiers based in Britain for an entire year. If the sum was recorded accurately, it shows the size of the loans that British leaders had taken.

These loans would have been used by high-ranking Britons, including the friendly rulers, to fund their increasingly lavish lifestyles. Capital may have been used to acquire wine, olive oil, and Roman tableware and to provide the feasts for clients that secured these rulers' patronage. At least some of them probably used the money to finance the priesthood of the cult of Claudius at Camulodunum. We hear that in the view of the Britons involved in the uprising, the 'temple set up to the divine Claudius had the appearance of a citadel of eternal despotism, and its chosen priests were pouring away fortunes in a show of religion'.[37] By recalling loans at the wrong time, Seneca and Catus drove the elite families of the Iceni and Trinovantes to join the uprising. There is little to indicate, however, that the other friendly rulers joined Boudica. As in the earlier campaigns of conquest, the peoples of Britain were by no means united in their resistance to Rome.

Boudica Ascendant

Boudica led an uprising of the Iceni, rousing the Trinovantes and other peoples who had yet to be defeated by Rome in battle. The bitterest hatred, we are told, was reserved for the veterans and the other recent settlers at Camulodunum, who had been driving people from their houses and evicting the Britons from their fields.[38] Worrying portents were recorded. A statue of Victory at Camulodunum fell over without cause, for instance; Ocean acquired a 'gory appearance'; and the 'likenesses of human bodies' were left on the coast by the ebb tide. Camulodunum had been a key location in the victory of 43 and in consequence was the first place to suffer at Boudica's hands. The comments on Ocean refer to earlier Roman concerns about Britain as an otherworldly land inhabited by outlandish creatures, demonstrating that the uprising was as much a numinous as a military threat.

As Paulinus was far away campaigning in Wales, the veterans of Camulodunum sought help from Catus, who sent 200 soldiers to assist the small number of troops based at the colony. He was not a military commander and is likely to have had access to only a small body of soldiers. For further armed assistance, he would have called upon Paulinus to return. In addition, the Ninth Legion, who had been campaigning further north, were soon on their way to help the people at Camulodunum. The colonists had not fortified the colony with a trench and rampart, or moved the old men and women to a place of safety, and we are told that the temple was seen to provide some form of security from the rebels. Although this building may not have been completed by the time of the uprising, it was evidently used as a stronghold by the troops at Camulodunum. The buildings of the colony were pillaged and burnt, except for the temple, into which the soldiers had retreated. The Britons blockaded the temple for two days before it was stormed and its occupants slaughtered.

Archaeological excavations have uncovered a layer of burnt debris across the entire colony, indicating the intensity of this destruction.[39] Human remains and artefacts have only been discovered in small numbers; nonetheless, a bag of Roman coins and jewellery buried in a box under the floor of one of the houses was a standout find. Known as the 'Fenwick Hoard', it provides information about one of the families who died.[40] Silver military awards, including two bracelets and an armlet, indicate that the householder was a legionary veteran of some distinction, and the extremely high-quality and fashionable gold jewellery presumably belonged to his wife (fig. 4.4). The excavation of a neighbouring site has uncovered human remains of several of the hundreds of colonists who died at Camulodunum. It appears that the entire veteran community of the colony were killed, along with their families. The soldiers Catus sent were also slaughtered.

The victorious Britons then attacked the Ninth Legion, which was approaching Camulodunum under the command of Petillius Cerialis, putting the Romans to flight and killing some of the infantry.[41] Cerialis and the cavalry escaped to safety, perhaps retreating to the fortress at Longthorpe. The defeat of the Ninth and the complete destruction of the colony and its population of veterans was a major catastrophe for Rome. We hear of only one occasion when an entire legion was defeated during the conquest of Britain: in Wales in 52. The evidence for the famous event of the 'loss of the Ninth' in northern Britain, during the early part of

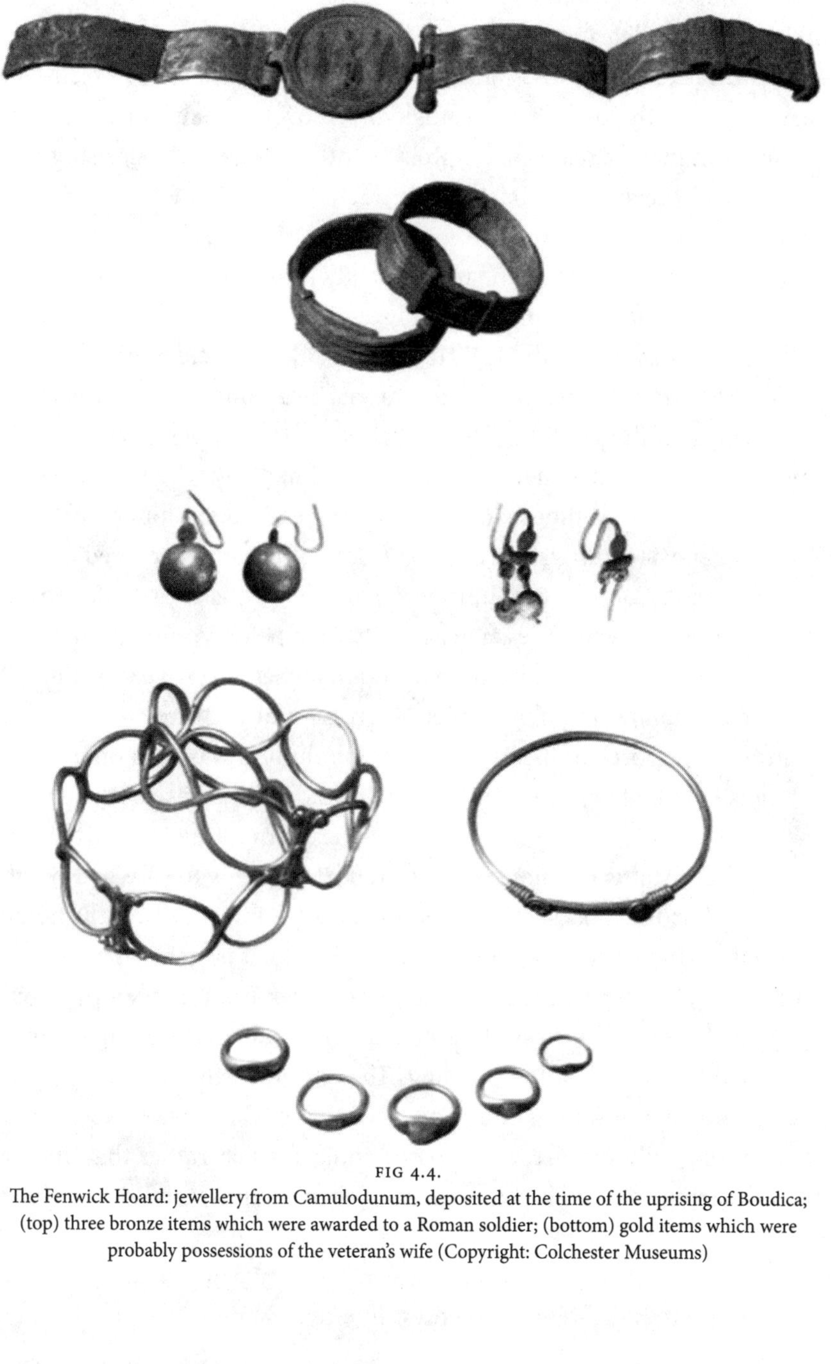

FIG 4.4.
The Fenwick Hoard: jewellery from Camulodunum, deposited at the time of the uprising of Boudica; (top) three bronze items which were awarded to a Roman soldier; (bottom) gold items which were probably possessions of the veteran's wife (Copyright: Colchester Museums)

Hadrian's reign, has recently been reassessed and provides another possible example (discussed later). At any rate, it was very rare for a legion to suffer a serious defeat and be forced to withdraw. We are told: 'Trembling at this disaster and at the hatred of the province which his greed had driven to war, the procurator Catus crossed over to Gaul'.[42] He had evidently been made a scapegoat in Rome for the events of the uprising.

Paulinus, meanwhile, marched through the lands of the enemy to London, travelling at speed from Anglesey.[43] He was accompanied by cavalry and light infantry; the more heavily armed legionary troops followed at a slower pace. Since he had limited forces available and Cerialis had already retreated with his legionaries, Paulinus decided not to take a stand at London. In effect, he chose to sacrifice London as a strategy to save the rest of the province. He allowed the townspeople to join his column; nonetheless, the enemy force overwhelmed any who were delayed by their physical abilities or unwilling to leave their homes behind. A burnt deposit comparable to that at Camulodunum, uncovered during excavations in London, has indicated that the Britons entirely destroyed the developing town.[44] The same calamity then befell Verulamium; some traces of this attack have also been found in archaeological excavations.[45]

Boudica's followers directed their aggression at the three main urban centres to the north of the Thames. Camulodunum was the home of the veterans who had conquered much of Britain and the base of the cult of the divine Claudius. The community at Verulamium had recently been awarded the status of *municipium* to reflect its elite's loyalty to Roman rule. London, the most significant Roman port at this time, was the home of wealthy traders from lands across the sea. Tacitus stated that 70,000 citizens and Roman allies perished at these places, presumably an approximation of the total number of Romans and their allies, including Britons, who died as a result of the uprising. The comment that there was 'neither capturing nor selling or any other feature of the trade of war ... but slaughtering, gibbets, fire, and crosses' indicates that rather than follow the Roman custom of enslaving many of their victims, the Britons killed them instead.[46]

The scale of this crisis can be shown by comparing it to the major Roman defeat in the Teutoberg Forest in 9 CE, when three entire legions, around 15,000 men, and accompanying auxiliaries perished at the hands of the Germanic leader Arminius. The losses across the civil population in Britain in 60 were certainly greater and constituted a direct threat to the Roman possession of the province. The Romans lost far fewer troops, however, in the British uprising, and reinforcements sent to Britain the following year consisted of around 7,000 men (discussed later). Far more damaging to Rome and its reputation was the total destruction of the three towns, including the colony and the temple of Claudius, the main port of the province at London, and the capital of the Rome-allied people at Verulamium. The number of deaths of veteran soldiers and overseas traders would have seriously impacted the province; the uprising must also have caused a concern in Rome that the friendly rulers of southern Britain might turn against the empire.

Other Roman settlements and forts may have been attacked, which would help to explain this high death toll.[47] It has been suggested that the Cornovii of the English West Midlands, were one of the groups who rose in opposition to Rome on the grounds that several forts in their territory were occupied during the 60s. (Rather confusingly, two distinct peoples in southern and central Britain were named 'Cornovii'; the southern one will be discussed shortly.) What is clear is that the uprising was threatening to spread across much of southern Britain to the north of the Thames. The news of the calamity in Britain would also have been swiftly dispatched to Rome, and it was observed that Nero contemplated withdrawing from Britain, probably at this point in the conflict.[48] This did not happen, although Paulinus was undoubtedly in a very difficult strategic situation. Two of his legions were at their bases in Longthorpe and Exeter, and the troops fighting under his command on Anglesey were still marching to join him. Some of the auxiliary units would have been campaigning with the legions, while others were dispersed in forts in potential enemy territory.

A significant factor in helping Paulinus to win his victory, however, was that the peoples of at least two of the friendly kingdoms had not, it seems, joined the uprising. There is no indication that the troubles spread to the peoples south of the Thames, and Togidubnus was later rewarded for his loyalty to Rome. Cartimandua, meanwhile, since she was not driven out of her kingdom at this time, was presumably able to keep control of the Brigantes. There is also little to indicate that the Cantiaci, the Dobunni, or the Corieltavi arose to fight against Rome. The uprising divided the leaders of the Britons, and this lack of a united opposition helped to limit the threat Paulinus faced.

Boudica Defeated

The governor had under his command the Fourteenth Legion, together with detachments of the Twentieth and auxiliaries from the nearest forts, in total amounting to around 10,000 men[49] Tacitus provides a description of the site chosen by Paulinus for the battle: 'he selected a place with narrow jaws [a narrow valley] and enclosed by a wood at the rear, knowing well enough that there were no enemy elements except in front and that the flat ground was open, without the dread of ambush. So the legions stood by in crowded ranks, the light armoured troops [auxiliaries] all around, the cavalry clustered at the edges.'[50] This description was probably derived from a written report compiled at the scene, and a search for the location of the battle has been under way for centuries. In truth, the landscape of the location described bears comparison with hundreds of similar places throughout southern Britain. Paulinus was in the vicinity of London before it was sacked, as we know; he may then have marched north-west along Watling Street to meet the slower-moving legionary troops on their way from Anglesey. A favoured location has been identified as close to Mancetter (*Manduessedum*, Warwickshire), where there is high ground broadly matching this description and an extensive Roman military site.[51]

The Britons are described as 'rioting everywhere' in numbers never seen before. They even brought their wives with them to witness victory from vehicles positioned around the edge of the battlefield. Boudica is described as riding in a chariot with her daughters from one group to the next to ask for their support in her effort to defeat Rome. The leaders of the Iceni evidently still used chariots to enhance the drama of movement and signify their social standing. The recent discovery of an Iron Age chariot burial from Pembrokeshire (Wales) indicates that Iron Age warriors outside the boundaries of the Roman province continued to use chariots at the time of Boudica's uprising.[52] If Boudica was a Roman citizen, she had evidently not entirely abandoned the traditions of her people. The *Annals*, includes a speech that she is purported to have made to rouse her followers for the fight: 'she testified that it was of course customary for the Britons to take to the field under female leadership; yet now she was not, as one sprung from great ancestors, avenging her kingdom and wealth but, as one of the people, her lost freedom, her body battered by beatings, and the abused chastity of her daughters. The desires of the Romans had advanced to the point where they left no bodies, not even old age or virginity, unpolluted.'[53] Despite the idea that women commonly led the Britons in war, Boudica is the only female war leader to be named in the classical texts referring to Britain. The words of her speech were written both to enliven Tacitus' account and, by association, to cast a moral reflection upon Nero's misrule.[54] Unlike the speech of Caratacus in Rome in 52, of course, there were no Roman observers to hear Boudica's words before this decisive battle. Tacitus' comments provide an important insight into how the Roman senatorial elite judged the rule of 'bad' emperors such as Nero.

Boudica's speech is followed by the oration of Paulinus, which is typical of the speeches often attributed to Roman commanders by classical writers.[55] He urged his soldiers to stand fast, and they used their narrow position as a defence. Once they engaged with the Britons, the Romans gradually broke them with a frontal attack, and the Britons were also hampered in their flight by the surrounding vehicles. The Roman soldiers then added to the Britons slain by killing the women and impaling their animals. Tacitus states that by some estimates just under 80,000 Britons fell, while only around 400 Roman soldiers were killed, with a few more than this number wounded. Boudica, he recounted, ended her life with poison, like Cleopatra. Although the number of dead Britons was probably exaggerated for effect, this was certainly a notable victory for the Romans.[56]

The heaped remains of the dead Britons may have been carefully collected by the Roman troops and buried in pits which may eventually be discovered through excavation, thus locating the site of the battle.

Roman victories were sometimes commemorated with monuments, although the place of Boudica's defeat seems not have been marked in this way. Paulinus had won a battle against considerable odds. According to the estimated losses, the Romans faced a force of Britons eight times their number; however, this appears to have included noncombatants. Comparisons with other Roman battles in Britain are restricted by the lack of detail in surviving texts. It was recorded that a third of the 30,000 Caledonian fighters at the battle of *Mons Graupius*, in 84, died. This suggests that the defeat of Boudica may have been one of the largest battles during the Roman campaigns in Britain. The honorary titles awarded to the two legions instrumental in the defeat of Boudica acknowledged their vital role in a very exposed position; the Fourteenth Legion was called 'martial and victorious' (*martia victrix*) while the Twentieth Legion was named 'valiant and victorious' (*valeria victrix*).[57] Others were less fortunate. The legate of the Second Legion, Poenius Postumus, 'having cheated his own legion of... glory' by refusing Paulinus' orders to march into battle, ran himself through with a sword.[58]

For the Britons who opposed Rome's conquests, this defeat was a calamitous event. Boudica's uprising presented a serious threat to Roman rule in Britain and led to her being considered from the sixteenth century as the most famous ancient Briton (discussed in the afterword). Although all knowledge of this uprising was lost in post-Roman times, the classical texts were rediscovered in the Renaissance, and Boudica ('Boadicea') was drawn upon as an ancient and barbaric parallel for Queen Elizabeth I, who defended Britain from the Spanish Armada. In the nineteenth century, Boudica was transformed into a valiant defender of British rights in the face of military problems in their empire. She is celebrated today by a massive Victorian bronze statue on Westminster Bridge in London.

PAULINUS TAKES REVENGE

News of the uprising would have been received in Rome with horror. It was unusual for an entire legion to be defeated in battle; moreover, the colony and two additional towns had been sacked, with the loss of a considerable number of Roman lives. The scale of this calamity would have severely impacted the supply of valuable minerals from the west of the province and the taxes being extracted from its peoples. The extent to which these events were the result of the mismanagement of provincial affairs is unclear, and the critical comments directed toward Catus in Tacitus and Dio suggest that he was made a scapegoat. Although Paulinus must also have had a considerable responsibility for these destructive events, he was not immediately replaced, and in the longer term the opinion of the Senators in Rome attributed much of the blame to Nero.

The uprising would have had a devastating impact on all the Britons involved, whether they had joined the conflict or opted to avoid being drawn in. Furthermore, with winter setting in, Paulinus was determined to mete out harsh punishment to those he suspected of having opposed Rome.[59] Following the defeat of Boudica, the whole of Paulinus' army was assembled and kept 'under canvas'—that is, permanently on campaign—to finish the war in the province. Nero increased the available manpower by sending a substantial force from Germany, including 2,000 legionaries, eight cohorts of auxiliary soldiers, and 1,000 cavalry. The legionaries reinforced the Ninth Legion; the auxiliaries were stationed in new winter quarters across enemy territory. Those peoples still 'wavering' in their loyalty to Rome were 'ravaged with fire and sword'.[60] Such military action as was deemed necessary was directed against peoples to the north of the Thames, and indeed several of the writing tablets recently found at the Bloomberg site in London indicate that London was the main disembarkation point for the auxiliaries arriving in Britain.[61] These writing tablets are a significant discovery. They include the names of almost 100 inhabitants of early Roman London, including a number of men involved in trade. A fort was constructed within the devastated area of London to act as a temporary base for the soldiers who were to be deployed further north.

Few Roman camps and forts have been found in the territories of the Iceni and Trinovantes.[62] Presumably, their warrior elite had been so thoroughly defeated that the Roman soldiers were able to harass the surviving population with impunity. By contrast, several forts in the West Midlands were either first established or continued to be used during the early

60s, probably indicating the suppression of resistance by the Cornovii to Roman rule.[63] This conflict and subsequent Roman acts of revenge were the cause of severe food shortage throughout the entire province during the winter of 60–61.[64] The supplies that were available were allocated preferentially to the Roman forces, and even communities who had taken no part in the uprising would have been negatively affected.

The manoeuvering towards peace was slow, and the new procurator, Julius Classicianus, did not agree with Paulinus' aggressive approach.[65] A member of the aristocracy from northern Gaul, Classicianus was appointed by Nero, or by his advisors, after Catus had fled the uprising. This appointment may have resulted from the emperor's desire to restore order in Britain. After all, there had been sustained contacts between senior leaders from northern Gaul and those of southern Britain since before the time of Julius Caesar. In any case, Classicianus' immediate priority was to reestablish the financial stability of the province and reinstitute the collection of taxes. He died while serving in Britain and was buried under a grand stone monument at London, indicating that this was where he had his operational base as the town was reconstructed.[66] His presence would have helped to reassure both the Gallic traders reestablishing themselves at London and the rulers of the friendly kingdoms that Rome was serious about reestablishing order in Britain, since a procurator from northern Gaul was likely to be trusted.

Classicianus asked Nero to appoint a new governor who would be less angry and conceited, reporting that there would be no end to the war in Britain if Paulinus remained as governor.[67] Boudica's fierce uprising, which had separated Paulinus from the main Channel ports and his family in Rome, may have been leading him to pursue vengeance to an extreme extent. Polyclitus, a freedman of Nero, was sent to inspect the situation in Britain, and although Paulinus remained in command of the province for a while, at some point during the late spring to early summer of 61 he was replaced as governor by Petronius Turpilianus.[68] Paulinus went on to serve as one of the emperor Otho's leading commanders in the struggle against Vitellius for succession after Nero died (in 69), suggesting that Paulinus was not disgraced as a result of his rather tarnished record as governor in Britain.

SETTLING BRITAIN THROUGH DIPLOMACY

The new governor Turpilianus was 'milder' in approach towards the Britons and pacified them without taking any further risks.[69] Turpilianus is thought to have been a nephew or grandnephew of Aulus Plautius, the first governor of Britain, which may have been an important consideration when Nero was looking to appoint a more diplomatic governor. Plautius would have had clients among the senior Britons, and a new governor from the same family may have been particularly welcome to the British elite in the aftermath of the failed uprising. Although little is known of Turpilianus' term of office in Britain, he would have worked closely with Classicianus to restore order across the province.

Turpilianus handed over the governorship of the province to Trebellius Maximus, probably during 63. Trebellius was described as 'idle', in that he never ventured on campaign but governed the province as an 'affable administrator'.[70] This apparently led to the Britons learning to 'condone seductive vices'. Turpilianus and Trebellius were criticized by Tacitus for their lack of military ambition in unfavourable contrast to the actions of those governors, including Paulinus, who had demonstrated the desire to achieve military glory. Imperial conquests were achieved during this period, however, through a combination of both armed violence and diplomacy. The prime task the officials appointed in the aftermath of the uprising pursued was to restore the stable conditions that were required for trade to resume and for the payment of taxes. After stability had been restored, the campaigns of conquest in the west and north would be able to continue.

A find made in 2019 adds a significant detail to the narrative of restoring the province to Roman rule during the early 60s. A metal detector user discovered a lead ingot at Rossett (Wrexham, Clwyd, Wales), stamped with a text recording the names of the emperor Nero and the governor Trebellius Maximus.[71] The inclusion of 'Magul' in this text indicates that this British lead was smelted at a place called Magalonium. It is not known exactly where this place was; it may have been in the Welsh Marches. The early dating of this ingot, together with those from Charterhouse (discussed earlier), shows the speed with which the Roman military exploited the available mineral resources.

Reorganizing the Legions

In the mid-60s, Nero withdrew the Fourteenth Legion from Britain, together with eight cohorts of Batavian soldiers, to join his expedition to the Caucasus.[72] By this time, military order in Britain had been fully restored. As a result of the withdrawal of the Fourteenth, the three remaining legions in Britain required a reorganization. The Second Augusta continued to be based at Exeter, and the Ninth at Lincoln, but the activities of the Twentieth are far from clear.[73] It has been argued that one detachment was stationed at Usk, with another moving to Wroxeter to replace the Fourteenth. A new fortress was constructed, apparently by the Twentieth Legion, at Gloucester (*Glevum*, Gloucestershire), 1 kilometre to the south of the disused fortress at Kingsholm. Legions may often have been split for strategic reasons into several divisions, and the Twentieth seems to have been divided between three fortresses, presumably to provide cover after the departure of the Fourteenth. This may also suggest that Nero intended eventually to return the Fourteenth Legion to Britain.

Despite a reduction in the military forces available, the Romans achieved progress with the conquest of south-western Britain during the second half of the 60s. The south-western people known as the Cornovii occupied the lands of the far west, beyond the territory of the Dumnonii. Several Roman forts in their territory appear to have been constructed at this time, both to control this people and to direct the exploitation of their rich mineral resources, particularly tin.[74]

Reestablishing the Towns

An initial priority after the uprising had been quelled was to reestablish and rebuild the colony at Camulodunum (see fig. 4.1). The street grid and some of the earlier building plots were quickly reestablished. However, because a new generation of legionary veterans was required to replace those slaughtered in the uprising, the reconstruction of the more substantial houses and public buildings would take decades.[75] The building of the town wall appears to have been considered a priority, perhaps to reassure the remaining members of the urban community. The temple of Claudius was eventually rebuilt and enclosed within an enormous and elaborate arcaded wall. The entire enclosure constituted a grand provincial forum, with the temple at its centre and a monumental altar outside the entrance to the temple building.[76] Later in the first century, the complex of enclosures at Gosbecks was also supplemented with a temple and a theatre, indicating the development of meetings connected with the cult of an ancestral king, probably Cunobelin.[77]

The initial rebuilding works at London were focused upon the reconstruction of the harbour front on the north bank of the Thames and the reestablishment of the main roads and the water supply.[78] The writing tablets found at the Bloomberg site indicate that trading recommenced swiftly after the uprising: one bill of sale for the transport of 'twenty loads of provisions' from Verulamium to London was dated to October 62. Although the start of construction of substantial houses and public buildings at London, including a forum and amphitheatre, was still more than a decade away, people were returning to the town, presumably reassured by the presence of the procurator and the Roman troops passing through the port. It is unclear how long it took for the urban centre of Verulamium to be rebuilt, although the bill of sale from the Bloomberg site indicates that market activities at both towns had recommenced.[79]

Rewarding Togidubnus

Tacitus' comment that Togidubnus had remained 'most loyal' until recent times indicates that this friendly king and his senior clients had kept the peoples of the southern kingdom loyal to Rome during the uprising. His loyal behaviour presumably included direct assistance to Rome in 60–61, as the uprising was defeated and order restored to the province. This assistance would have included supplies of vital food and equipment to the Roman military, and he might have been able to spare soldiers to supplement the Roman troops fighting against resistant Britons.[80] Following the violent suppression of the uprising, Togidubnus received rewards in the form of lavish Roman buildings which were constructed at his *oppida* at Chichester and Silchester.[81]

The elaborate and extensive Mediterranean-style palace at Fishbourne (West Sussex) was constructed during the 70s, preceded by an almost equally remarkable, if slightly less extensive, villa built during the second half of the 60s.[82] Although Togidubnus ruled over several peoples, the Fishbourne palace has usually been interpreted as a personal gift to him from Nero. Incorporating Mediterranean marble and Corinthian capitals, this palace included a series of elaborate rooms, a colonnaded courtyard, and a bathhouse, designed for a luxurious lifestyle that would have included meetings with Togidubnus' important clients. Close to the harbour that Roman military forces had used during the early years of the conquest, the palace lay within the area defined by the dykes of the Iron Age *oppidum* at Chichester. It was located 3 kilometres (2 miles) west of the capital town of the Regnenses, which was already developing at Chichester. An inscription from Chichester, mentioning Nero, indicates that one monumental Roman building had already been constructed before the uprising (discussed earlier). A more famous Roman inscription recording the dedication of a temple to Neptune and Minerva dates to the 60s or 70s.[83] At least three monumental Roman buildings were constructed in and around the developing urban centre at Chichester during Togidubnus' reign.

Some archaeological finds from Silchester suggest that the Roman authorities also arranged for the construction of another grand building at Togidubnus' northern *oppidum* (see fig. 4.3).[84] The presence of what may have been a second palace, comparable to Fishbourne, is indicated by fragments of monumental masonry, including Corinthian capitals and tiles stamped with Nero's name, that have been found reused in later buildings. The earlier bathhouse was replaced at this time by a new and more substantial building, and an amphitheatre was constructed. Amphitheatres were built at a number of civil and military sites across Britain, and the one at Silchester may have been used for riding displays, staged fights between gladiators, and meetings of Togidubnus' clients.[85] The developing town at Silchester focused around the network of earth paths of the Late Iron Age *oppidum*, and the new series of streets dates to the 70s; a series of dykes defined the nucleated settlement.

The gifts of these buildings to Togidubnus, representing highly visible rewards to him for his loyal support in 60–61, served to demonstrate to other high-ranking Britons the potential rewards of remaining loyal to Rome. The elites of other British peoples would have been able to draw their own conclusions from the contrasting fates of Togidubnus and Boudica during the uprising of 60 and its aftermath.

NERO AND BRITAIN

Claudius had bolstered his imperial rule through his successes in Britain, and during the early part of Nero's reign the territory Gallus and Paulinus gained in western Britain built on the achievements of earlier commanders. Paulinus may have overstepped the mark in 60 by seeking to conquer Anglesey, however, and poor management of the Iceni following the death of Prasutagus provided a motive for Boudica to lead an uprising that fundamentally threatened Roman possession of the entire province. The senatorial elite and the common people at Rome, meanwhile, would have continued to be aware of the ideology of Claudius' reign, with its emphasis on the significance of the Roman conquest of the lands beyond Ocean. The loss of Britain would have been much to the detriment of Nero's reputation in Rome.

Paulinus defeated Boudica only after serious damage had been inflicted on the infrastructure and population of the province, and the fact that there was no victory parade in Rome to celebrate her defeat suggests that Rome's elite found the events associated with the uprising deeply embarrassing. Nero committed suicide in June 68, causing a significant crisis in Rome. He had remained popular with the ordinary people in Rome as a result of his public largesse, but the senatorial elite had turned against him in the wake of his excesses. These included several high-profile murders, notably that of Nero's mother, Agrippina, in 59 and the great fire of Rome in 64, which destroyed much of the city. Rumours circulated that Nero had deliberately started the conflagration to free up urban land for his new Golden Palace. The disaster in Britain was just one of the high-profile events that undermined his reign, and he became the first Roman emperor whose memory was condemned by the Senate immediately after his death.

Boudica's uprising would provide authors with a powerful means of communicating Nero's failings. In the speech written by Dio, she reflects on Nero's supposed femininity: 'Nero ... has the name of a man but is in fact a woman: the proof is that he sings, plays the lyre and preens himself'.[86] In contrast, Dio portrayed her as far more masculine than the emperor, echoing highly critical contemporary attitudes toward him among members of the Senate. Tacitus was equally critical of Nero, although he provided a more balanced account of the uprising, on which this chapter's narrative has drawn in detail. His version suggests that despite the growth of Nero's extremely negative reputation, order was effectively restored to Britain following the catastrophe of Boudica's uprising.

5

FINDING THE END OF BRITAIN

> Men from the infantry, cavalry, and navy were often stationed together in the same camp [in Caledonia], sharing supplies and high spirits. Each stressed his own exploits and his own dangers: as he boasted, in the way soldiers do. The ravines in the forests and mountains were compared with the dangers of storm and tides, victories on land against the enemy with the conquest of Ocean.
>
> Tacitus, *Agricola*[1]

NERO'S SUICIDE IN JUNE 68 put an end to the Julio-Claudian dynasty of emperors, creating a crisis as several powerful men vied to rule the Roman Empire. The details of these political events, leading to no fewer than four different emperors in the space of eighteen months, do not concern us here. The resulting instability had a deep impact upon the governing of Britannia, as troops were withdrawn on several occasions to support one or other of the imperial aspirants.[2] Trebellius Maximus continued to govern Britain, but in spring 69 the troops rebelled against him. This caused him to flee with some legionaries to join Vitellius, one of the contenders, who subsequently defeated the emperor Otho and seized power in Rome.

Vitellius appointed Vettius Bolanus to replace Trebellius as governor of Britain and, being unsure of its loyalty to his rule, sent the Fourteenth Legion back to serve in the island. The position of the new emperor was now under threat from the influential Flavian family, led by Vespasian. Vitellius sent for troops from Germany, Britain, and Gaul; the governor, Bolanus, was unable to supply the requested reinforcements, as Britannia was not securely under his control. Indeed, the Second and Fourteenth legions in Britain were agitating for Vespasian to become emperor. The Second had served under Vespasian there from 43 to 47 and were joined by the Fourteenth in supporting him. The Fourteenth did not long remain in Britain, in fact: they were once more redeployed to the Rhineland soon after these events.

CARTIMANDUA OVERTHROWN

The quarrels between the legions and rumours of unrest across the empire encouraged an uprising among the Brigantes.[3] The chief instigator was Cartimandua's former husband Venutius, who had already led a rebellion against her rule more than a decade previously. The motivation for the new rebellion, we are told, was a private dispute between Venutius and his former wife. For Cartimandua was of noble birth, and handing over Caratacus to the governor Scapula in 51 had brought her yet more wealth and power. She had divorced Venutius and formed a liaison with his armour-bearer, Vellocatus. That her new lover was Venutius' client only added insult to the injury of the divorce.

Venutius is presumed to have been the leader of another of the peoples of central Britain who had formerly been united under the rule of Cartimandua and therefore allied to Rome (discussed earlier). Cartimandua's family, we are also told, was shaken by this scandal, and Venutius, who had the support of the Brigantes, directly threatened her rule over them.[4] Despite the loyalty she had continued to show to Rome over several decades, Tacitus viewed her actions, including the handing over of Caratacus to Rome in 51 and her marital infidelities, as signs of her moral depravity. Foreign queens such as Cartimandua were often portrayed in Roman texts as subverting an accepted hierarchy of gender roles, and his interpretation of her actions also drew upon moral condemnation of other powerful women in the ancient world, including Cleopatra VII of Egypt.[5]

In this difficult situation Cartimandua requested support from Bolanus, as had also been her tactic more than a decade earlier when Venutius had planned to overthrow her. A mixed force of legionary and cavalry soldiers came to her assistance and fought several battles with what is described as 'varying success'.[6] The Roman forces rescued her, although her kingdom was left to Venutius to rule. The Samian pottery from the excavations at her royal centre of Stanwick has been dated to 65–70, indicating that this *oppidum* was abandoned when her rule ended.[7] The neighbouring site at Scotch Corner, however, continued to be occupied as a trading centre until the later first century. At Aldborough (*Isurium Brigantum*, North Yorkshire), 45 kilometres (30 miles) south of Scotch Corner, a town was becoming established close to the site of an abandoned fort.[8] As the centre of political power shifted from Stanwick, this settlement became the *civitas* capital of the Brigantes during the later first century.

Nothing further is heard of the former queen, and she may have retired to live in Rome. Nor is it known whether Venutius gained control of the entire territory of the Brigantes, but he would certainly have become a direct target of future Roman aggression, to punish him for overthrowing the pro-Roman queen of a friendly kingdom. We are told that Bolanus governed Britain with a gentler hand than was appropriate for an 'untamed province'.[9] It is evident, however, that he faced serious problems arising from the divided loyalties of the legions and a significant reduction in military manpower. When Vespasian's forces defeated Vitellius at Cremona (Italy) in October 69, Vitellius' army included detachments from three of the British legions: the Second, the Ninth, and the Twentieth. The need to keep the territory under Roman control at a time of turmoil across the empire; may have prevented Bolanus from leading a full-scale campaign in support of Cartimandua.

The fact that Julius Agricola was in command of the Twentieth Legion during this period causes us to doubt the accuracy of Tacitus' negative comments about Bolanus. Agricola would become governor of Britain eight years later, and we know a great deal about him from *Agricola,* Tacitus' laudatory biography of him. That we need to read it with care is signalled by Tacitus' statement that he wrote it to honour Agricola soon after he died. In 69–70 Bolanus may have kept the Twentieth under Agricola in reserve rather than sending them to campaign against Venutius.

VESPASIAN AND BOLANUS

Vitellius' position in Rome was always precarious, and after he was murdered in December 69, Vespasian replaced him as emperor. Like Claudius before him, Vespasian now needed military successes to help secure his position as ruler of the Roman world.[10] He was of lower social standing than his predecessors: his family was of equestrian rather than senatorial rank. The *equites*, or equestrians, were the second aristocratic order in Rome, ranking just below the senatorial elite. Senatorial and equestrian families intermarried and alike held senior posts in the empire's administration. The traditional senatorial families, however, continued to be keenly aware of distinctions of status between their leaders, and Vespasian had to overcome such prejudices to prevail.

Unlike Claudius and Nero, however, Vespasian was already a successful military commander. He had established his reputation during the first years of the conquest of Britain, where he had commanded the Second Legion. The year before he became emperor, he had also played a leading role in the suppression of a serious uprising in Judea. Indeed, two further threats to Roman rule demanded quelling during the first year of his reign. In the East, his eldest son, Titus, completed the subduing of Judea by conquering Jerusalem. Petillius Cerialis, meanwhile, who had commanded the Ninth Legion when it was defeated by Boudica's uprising in Britain, led an army to defeat a revolt of the Batavi that was threatening Roman security in the Rhineland. These actions concluded, Vespasian then directed his attention to the conquest of Britain, although the reinforcing of the legions would take a year to accomplish.

Bolanus continued to serve as governor of Britain for the first eighteen months of Vespasian's reign, and although Tacitus gave him little praise, a Roman poet offered a very different account of his achievements.[11] This poet mused upon the actions of Bolanus in 'Caledonian fields', commenting on the watchtowers and forts he built far and wide, and the weapons captured from Britons, including the breastplate of a king. Bolanus may have sent military or diplomatic missions far beyond the northern Roman frontier, seeking alliances with friendly communities in southern Scotland or, since 'Caledonia' referred to the lands north of the Clyde-Forth isthmus, casting even further to the north. Roman campaigning has been interpreted as an entirely offensive process, but it is likely that Bolanus deployed his navy to make contact with potentially friendly Britons in southern Scotland. Roman campaigning often exploited knowledge acquired through naval exploration, and diplomatic activities by sea were then followed up with military campaigns overland.

The extensive lands formerly ruled by Cartimandua may have remained unsettled at this time, but the reference to the capture of weapons from the Britons suggests that Bolanus also commanded military action that resulted in victories. Military units on campaign made camps as they went, and some of the many examples found throughout the territory of the Brigantes and into southern Scotland may indeed have been constructed by forces campaigning under the aegis of Bolanus. The forts the Romans built across these areas would then have been established under the next governor. When Bolanus was recalled to Rome in 71, Vespasian awarded him patrician rank, making him a member of a select and privileged class of Roman citizens. Bolanus had clearly played a significant role in keeping Britain secure at a deeply troubled time.

THE CONQUEST OF WESTERN AND CENTRAL BRITAIN

Vespasian appointed Petillius Cerialis to replace Bolanus in 71. Since he had been commander of the Ninth Legion in 60 when they had suffered a humbling defeat at the hands of Boudica's followers after the sacking of Camulodunum, he might have seemed a strange choice to lead an ambitious offensive campaign. He must, however, have proved his worth in reestablishing order in Britain after the uprising had been suppressed, and he played a leading role in subduing the Batavi in 70. He was a close associate of Vespasian, and his earlier experience of Britain would have made him familiar with the province and its soldiers. He brought the

Second Legion Adiutrix with him to Britain, thereby restoring the legionary garrison to four.[12] The Second Adiutrix had been created in 70 from the troops of the Adriatic fleet based at Ravenna (Italy), who had risen in support of Vespasian's claim to rule in Rome. The name Adiutrix recorded the origin of this legion as an auxiliary unit.

The restoration of the legionary garrison to full strength clearly demonstrated Vespasian's determination to renew the stalled conquest. Nero had removed one legion during the mid-60s, and the garrison had been further reduced by the detachments removed from Britain to support Vitellius in 69. With imperial stability restored, Cerialis had access to around 20,000 legionary troops and larger forces of auxiliaries. The conquest could resume in earnest.

Subduing the Brigantes

Cerialis' first target was the Brigantes, who had challenged Rome by driving out Cartimandua. Bolanus must already have commenced these campaigns, and Cerialis won some significant victories.[13] The main base for this campaigning was the legionary fortress at York (*Eboracum*), which was established for the Ninth Legion (fig. 5.1).[14] York was a significant location in the road network and was also well-positioned to be supplied by sea by way of the Humber estuary. The Second Adiutrix, recently arrived in Britain, meanwhile took over the Ninth's former fortress at Lincoln. Forts began to be constructed to the north of York, as Cerialis focused his attention on the suppression of Brigantian resistance by land and sea.

The extensive territory the Brigantes occupied was divided into east and west by the Pennine uplands. Cerialis is described as fighting many battles, indicating that he had to subdue a number of communities individually. For millennia these upland landscapes had been managed for agriculture, and much of the tree cover had been cleared before the Romans' arrival. These lands were populated by communities living in settlements and hillforts.[15] The power-structure that had held the Brigantes together under Cartimandua's leadership had collapsed, however, and the small discrete areas these communities occupied required the Roman forces to

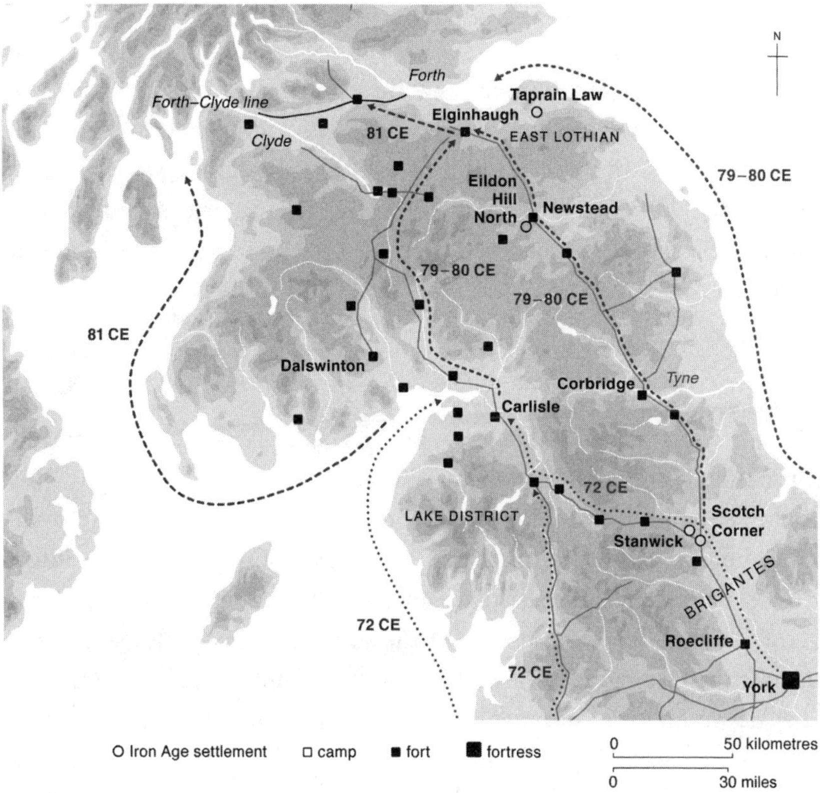

FIG 5.1.
Central and northern Britain under the Flavians, showing lines of advance by land and sea and the Iron Age hillforts at Traprain Law and Eildon Hill North (after Bidwell and Hodgson 2009, fig. 5, and Hanson 2007a, fig. 5, with additions)

undertake localized campaigning, constructing roads with forts at regular intervals.[16] Mobile auxiliary units, meanwhile, became the garrison of occupation.

The early date of the Roman fort at Carlisle (*Luguvalium*, Cumbria) indicates that in 72 Cerialis spearheaded a campaign to target a subruler of the Brigantes with a centre of power in this region; perhaps this was Venutius.[17] There is nevertheless no further mention in the classical texts of Cartimandua's former husband, who would have been a prime target for Rome. The troops marched to Carlisle from York by way of Scotch Corner and across the Pennine uplands.[18] Another military force was simultaneously marching north from the Welsh Marches, following the route of the second major road leading into central Britain. Other forts were swiftly established, and the conquest of the vast territories Cartimandua had ruled may largely have been completed by 77. Certain areas proved more difficult to subdue, it seems, and forts were still being constructed in the Lake District (Cumbria), for instance, several decades later. The building of roads and forts across these extensive territories occupied the Roman forces for several decades.

The Final Defeat of the Silures

Cerialis was replaced as governor around 74 by Sextus Julius Frontinus, a prominent politician and distinguished writer, who directed his attention to completing the conquest of the peoples of Wales. This had stalled after the uprising of Boudica, but Frontinus finally defeated the Silures, overcoming their 'stout resistance and also the difficult terrain' (fig. 5.2).[19] As well as subduing the people of the south, Frontinus also sent troops against the Ordovices of central Wales, and although we hear nothing of this, he would have continued the campaign in central Britain.

At this time, as the legionary garrison moved forward into conquered territories, the Romans established two new fortresses, at Caerleon and Chester.[20] Caerleon (*Isca*, Newport, Wales), was the new base of the Second Augusta, constructed by the side of the River Usk within the territory of the Silures. Chester (*Deva*, Cheshire), strategically located to exploit a harbour on the River Dee, became the base for the Second Adiutrix, redeployed from the fortress at Lincoln. New forts were also constructed to hold down the population. One reason for the Roman interest in Wales was the widespread mineral deposits that would be swiftly exploited.[21] The earliest dating information for lead and silver mining in Flintshire under the Romans comes in the form of the inscriptions on two lead ingots found at Chester which indicate that operations had commenced by 74, although mining had probably started in this area of northern Wales years earlier. The inclusion of the name Deceangli is thought to indicate that enslaved local people provided the industrial workforce, which would have operated under Roman military supervision.

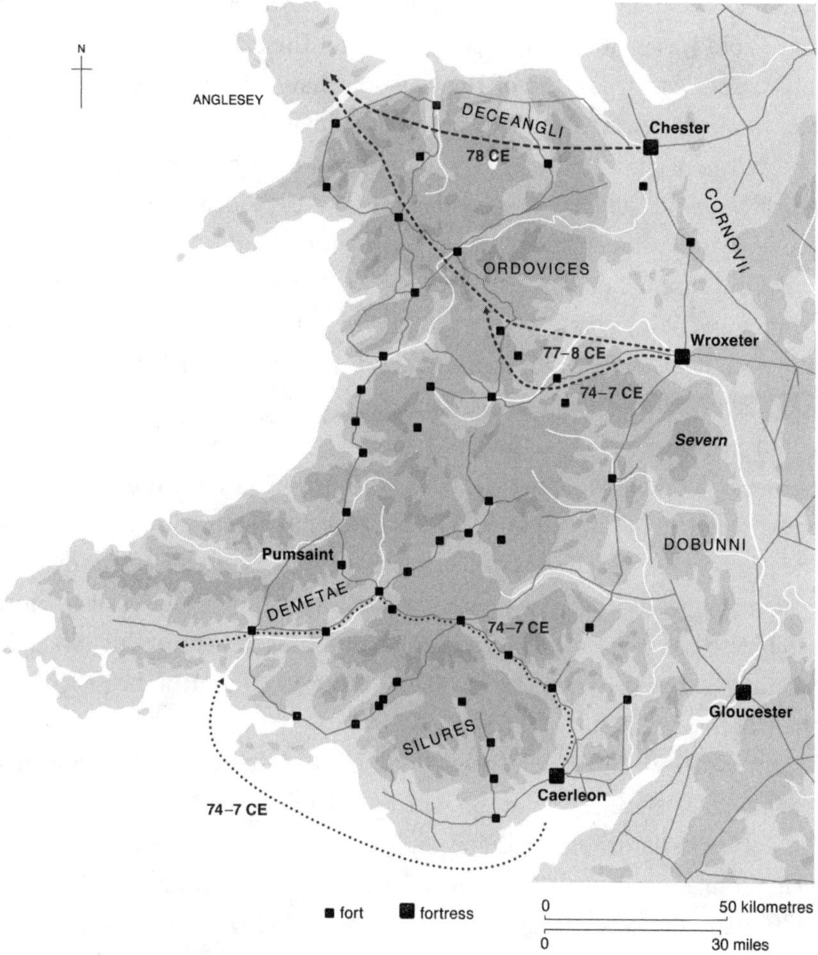

FIG 5.2.
Flavian forts and campaign routes in Wales (after Burnham and Davies 2010, fig. 2.4, with additions)

The gold mines at Dolaucothi (Carmarthenshire) were the main source of this mineral in Britain.[22] This gold had been exploited in prehistoric times, though there is little indication of mining at Dolaucothi during the Iron Age. The mine workings, which are well preserved, included opencast pits, underground galleries, and aqueducts. The Roman fort at Pumsaint, located almost a mile to the north-west, housed the Roman soldiers who supervised the local workforce. Although this fort was constructed during the mid-70s, in fact mining probably started at least two decades earlier, since gold was a vital commodity for Rome. The exploitation of the gold, silver, and lead resources of Wales would have commenced as soon as conditions were safe. The acquisition of gold and silver from Britain was one of the original motives for the invasion of Britain under Claudius, and along with the taxes that local communities paid, also helped to fund the military forces engaged in conquering the island.

By the time Frontinus was recalled to Rome in 78, much of central Britain and Wales had been subdued. The military garrison had gradually been transferred to the frontier lands across the north and west; the four legions were based at Caerleon (Second Augusta), Chester (Second Adiutrix), York (Ninth), and probably Wroxeter (Twentieth). The fortresses at Exeter, Gloucester, and Lincoln had been decommissioned, as they were located in territory which had been subdued and settled. In the previous phases of the conquest, the legions had frequently moved to new fortresses as the frontier was pushed forward. The legions were now established at these four more permanent bases, reflecting the strategic requirement to keep a strong garrison in reserve to control the peoples of the frontier regions.

Much of central Britain, probably including southern Scotland, had now been overrun. An author writing during the mid-70s stated that Roman arms had not expanded their knowledge of Britain beyond the neighbourhood of the Caledonian Forest.[23] This suggests that they had only made diplomatic contacts with peoples living to the south of the Clyde and Forth, to the north of which lay Caledonia.

AGRICOLA'S COMMAND

Gnaeus Julius Agricola is one of the most famous figures of Britain's Roman past.[24] He is thought to have been born in Rome to a family originally from Gallia Narbonensis (southern France). Before his appointment as governor of Britain, he had already served as military tribune in one of Paulinus' legions in the aftermath of Boudica's uprising and then as commander of the Twentieth under Bolanus and Cerialis successively.

By 73 he had returned to Rome, when Vespasian appointed him governor of the province of Aquitania (south-western France). He was appointed to govern Britain in 78. He remained in office there for seven years, an unusually long period of time in provincial service.

Defeating the Ordovices and Conquering Anglesey

Before turning his attention to the north, Agricola determined to defeat the opposition in Wales once and for all (see fig. 5.2). The Ordovices had virtually wiped out a cavalry unit operating in their territory, and although the summer campaigning season was almost over, Agricola dealt with this threat decisively, advancing into the hills with several legionary detachments and a small force of auxiliaries and, Tacitus reported, slaughtering almost the entire population.[25] Although Roman commanders often aimed to kill their adversaries in battle, Tacitus must have exaggerated the violence of Agricola's tactics. The settlements of the peoples in this part of Wales were widely dispersed, and it is unlikely that Agricola's forces planned to destroy systematically all the people living across the lands of the Ordovices. Pursuing a strategy of terrifying the Britons, nevertheless, Agricola then decided to conquer Anglesey, the island off the coast of northern Wales that Paulinus had attacked seventeen years earlier. Although Agricola was campaigning without ships, he used auxiliaries who were experienced swimmers to launch a surprise attack, resulting in the surrender of the island. The speed with which the Romans overcame any resistance by the inhabitants may suggest that the violence of Paulinus' earlier campaign against the people of Anglesey had lived on in memory, allowing the surrender of the island to Agricola in 78 without too much bloodshed. Coins issued in Rome celebrated the conquest of Anglesey by portraying a kneeling captive wearing cloak and trousers, an indication of the fame of Anglesey in Rome.[26]

This is the final mention in classical texts of offensive campaigning in Wales, suggesting that the Ordovices and Silures had finally been defeated. The various other peoples living across Wales would also have surrendered or been defeated by this time. The conquest of the upland areas had required sustained military campaigning, and the network of forts and roads which had been established facilitated the enforced peace. The creation of imperial order naturally required the imposition of taxation, and Roman commanders were expected to negotiate with communities at a local level to achieve stability. The necessity for an established auxiliary garrison to ensure the imposition of peace and to collect the tax in grain and livestock may explain why it took Rome so long to settle Wales. Many of the forts remained occupied for decades, an indication that sustained policing was required.[27]

Taxing the Province

During his first winter in Britain, we are told, Agricola alleviated the burden of taxation by distributing the levy of grain and tribute more widely.[28] Such financial matters were usually the responsibility of the procurator, which suggests that Agricola was working with his financial counterpart to improve the efficiency of the taxation. The implementation of taxation required a province-wide land census, since property holdings formed the basis for the calculation of dues. An initial census would have been conducted during the first decade of the conquest, but substantial territories had since been added to the province. Agricola may have used the winter months of 78–79 to ensure that the census was complete and up to date.

The taxes the conquered peoples paid to Rome helped offset the cost of the large number of soldiers stationed in Britain.[29] Legionary and auxiliary soldiers received their pay in cash and were also supplied with food imported from overseas, including luxury items such as wine and olive oil. Soldiers would also have bought goods from local people, introducing coins into the economy of the *civitates* of southern Britain. During the first century CE, Roman coins spread quite widely across the southern lands. Rome preferred taxes to be paid in cash, and the ruling elites of the *civitates* of Britain must have been required first to collect produce from the peoples they governed and then to obtain the Roman coinage with which to pay their taxes. These wealthy and influential individuals already had direct experience of currency, since communities across southern Britain had produced their own coins during the centuries before Claudius' invasion.

Across the frontier areas of the province—in Wales and south-western, central, and northern Britain—Roman coins are very rarely found away from the Roman military sites. These were also in areas where Iron Age coins had not been produced. Across these regions, the tax was probably paid in kind, in levies of grain and livestock. Since these societies were decentralized and lacked elite groups with sufficient authority to establish or run local government over an extensive territory, the arrangements for taxation would have had to be enforced on local leaders. As a result, few *civitas* capitals would be established across western and central Britain, and Roman auxiliary units probably collected this tax in kind from the local communities (discussed later).

Campaigning in Southern Scotland

During 79, his second season in the province, we are told that Agricola concentrated his forces and then embarked on a tireless military campaign, setting up sites for camps, reconnoitring estuaries and forests, and launching raids for plunder.[30] It is not at all clear where in Britain he was campaigning. However, since the peoples of Wales had been defeated, the new theatre of war was likely to have been southern Scotland, beyond the lands of the Brigantes (see fig. 5.1). Much of this land may have been fought over while Cerialis and Frontinus were governing Britain, in which case Agricola was seeking to establish control over peoples already defeated. The temporary camps that legionary and auxiliary forces created while campaigning in enemy territory are common across much of southern and eastern Scotland.

The only other indication of military activity during this season is the reference to a Caledonian bear which apparently mauled a crucified criminal during the festivities for the opening of the Colosseum in Rome in the summer of 80.[31] The 50,000 people who crowded into this massive new amphitheatre witnessed many violent deaths in the arena, and this exotic wild animal had been brought from beyond the empire's north-western frontier presumably to feed the crowd's fantasies of worldwide conquest. Games in the arena were a popular entertainment at Rome, and past spectacles had featured an assortment of exotic animals from beyond the frontiers, including lions, panthers, leopards, crocodiles, giraffes, and ostriches.[32] The use of the bear in the first event to be held at the Colosseum symbolized Rome's ambitions to complete the conquest of Britain by subduing Caledonia.

Southern Scotland was conquered by way of the two main campaigning routes which followed the roads running north from the forts at Carlisle and Corbridge (Northumberland). Additional roads were constructed to subdue the territories to either side of these two routes. These would often have exploited earlier routes the Iron Age communities used. No details of these campaigns survive in the classical texts; the locations of the roads and forts indicate that a swift advance across southern Scotland was accomplished by bypassing areas that formed no direct threat to the Romans. Much of south-western Scotland, for example, appears to be largely empty of such camps, forts, or roads, presumably because its peoples posed no immediate military challenge to Rome.[33] The fleet was used to explore the coast beyond the lands where the military units were campaigning and to seek diplomatic agreements with communities who could be persuaded to make friendship with Rome.

The coastal plain of East Lothian in south-eastern Scotland is another region that has produced little evidence of Roman fortifications. This area includes a large expanse of fertile land, suitable for the growing of grain, which was intensively occupied by Iron Age farming communities. The hillfort of Traprain Law, first established many centuries earlier on a steep-sided whaleback hill, formed a centre for the people who lived on this prime agricultural land (fig. 5.3).[34] During excavation at Traprain, substantial quantities of Roman imported goods, including Samian pottery, Roman coins, and glass vessels, have been found. Imports such as these are rarely found in any quantity during the excavation of the Iron Age settlements of central, northern, and western Britain, and their presence indicates that the community at this hillfort had a special relationship with Rome. The pottery and glass vessels found at Traprain were used for feasting and drinking, a custom which helped to create the bonds between patrons and clients living at and around this hillfort. It is presumed that this people followed the rule of a single leader who made

FIG 5.3.
The Iron Age hillfort at Traprain Law (East Lothian, Scotland) from the air, showing the ramparts that surround the top of this prominent hill (Crown copyright: Historic Environment Scotland)

a treaty with the Roman governor, securing peace in exchange for loyalty and the payment of tax in kind. The imported goods at Traprain may have been gifts from the governor or traded goods supplied by Roman merchants who visited the hillfort.

Rome had widely adopted the practice of friendly kingship before and during the conquest of southern Britain; there is little to indicate that other peoples in central and northern Britain had comparable treaties. The names of four peoples of southern Scotland were recorded by the Romans: the Votadini, Selgovae, Novantae, and Damononii. Each of these communities, like many of their neighbours to the south, occupied a very extensive territory.[35] There is nothing to indicate that they formed centralized groups comparable to the community which gathered at Traprain Law. Each of these four peoples would have been constituted of a number of different groups which cooperated at certain times, especially when they were collectively threatened by the invasion of hostile forces. There is little to indicate how these broader communities mustered, although the targeting of two hillforts during Roman campaigns in Scotland indicates that some of these traditional centres retained significance as communal meeting places.

The hillfort impressively sited on the Eildon Hill North, broadly comparable in scale to Traprain Law, was one of the largest in southern Scotland.[36] Although this hillfort was not intensively occupied during the late first century, it was clearly a target for Roman strategy. Several camps have been located nearby at Newstead (*Trimontium*), on Dere Street, and the first in a sequence of forts was constructed there during the Flavian advance (fig. 5.4). *Trimontium* means 'Three Hills,' referring to the three Eildon summits, on one of which the hillfort was located. North Eildon evidently constituted one of the traditional meeting places of the Selgovae, the people inhabiting this area of Scotland, which explains why it became an important target for Roman campaigning.[37]

In the second century, the Romans made an even more direct example of the community who maintained their traditional centre at the hillfort at Burnswark Hill (Dumfries and Galloway; discussed later). The Romans besieged this hillfort from two substantial temporary camps built on the slopes below, thought to have been constructed during a Roman campaign of the 140s (see fig. 8.2). The way the Romans treated these two hillforts provides the only direct evidence of the strategy their campaigning forces pursued in Scotland. Nevertheless, many Iron Age communities must have been subdued one by one as Roman military units conquered their lands. Many would have surrendered willingly, although there were doubtless frequent skirmishes as local peoples resisted the Roman forces.

Diplomacy would also have been widely employed to persuade influential local leaders to submit. At some of the settlement sites across southern and central Scotland Roman imports have been found in some quantity, suggesting that Roman officers made efforts to forge alliances with at least some powerful families. The tower-like stone roundhouses known as brochs, which typify the Iron Age Scottish highlands and islands (fig. 5.5), were also built in southern Scotland. Where they have been excavated, Roman artefacts have often been found.[38] These settlements were the homes of influential families in a society with a relatively small degree of social hierarchy, and such leaders may have been given these goods as the result of agreements binding them to maintain peaceful conditions

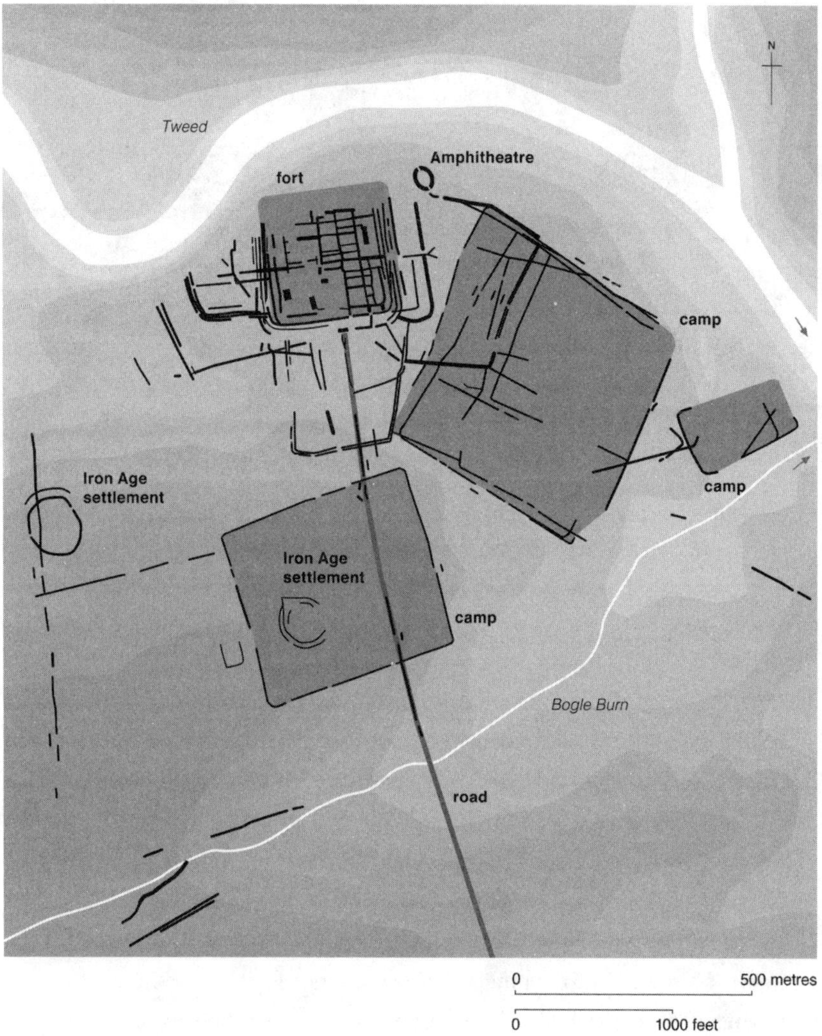

FIG 5.4.
The landscape around Newstead (Borders, Scotland), showing Iron Age settlements, Roman camps, the main fort, and an amphitheatre (redrawn from an image created by the Royal Commission for the Ancient and Historical Monuments of Scotland, with permission)

within their locale. The terms of these treaties may also have provided safe conduct for Roman traders, and some of the imported items on the sites may indeed have been supplied through trade. As taxation in kind, such agreements would also have required local leaders to supply food to the Roman occupying forces.

FIG 5.5.
Clachtoll Broch (Assynt, Highland, Scotland), a substantial stone roundhouse in the far north-west of the Scottish mainland (Photograph by Richard Hingley)

Encouraging Urban Development across the South

During the winter of Agricola's second year in Britain (79–80), we are told that he encouraged the warlike people living in widely dispersed and 'primitive' settlements to become accustomed to peace and ease:

> he gave encouragement to individuals and assistance to communities to build temples, marketplaces [*fora*], and town-houses. He praised those who responded quickly and criticised the dilatory. As a result, the provincials started to compete with each other for honour, rather than having to be persuaded. Furthermore, he educated the sons of leading men in the liberal arts and rated their natural talents above the trained skills of Gauls. The result was that those who had recently rejected the Roman tongue now conceived a desire for eloquence. Thus, even our style of dress came into favour and the toga was to be seen everywhere. Gradually they also became drawn into the allurements of bad ways, public porticoes and warm baths and elegant parties. The Britons had no experience of this and called it 'civilisation', although it was also part of their enslavement.[39]

Temples, marketplaces, and elaborate houses were viewed by Romans as the hallmark of a civilized society, and the ambition of the leading Britons to construct and use such buildings indicated their desire to make themselves Roman. The toga had a comparable significance: it symbolized peace and Roman identity, since it was only worn by Roman citizens. There is another side to the conception of civil order in this quotation, however, since the public porticoes, warm baths, and elegant parties symbolized vice. Such places were notorious in the city of Rome because they provided opportunities for debauched behaviour. By adopting Roman ways, the Britons were considered to be effectively enslaving themselves, an idea Tacitus had already explored in the speeches of Caratacus and Boudica.

The establishment of *civitates* was a vital administrative measure ensuring the stability and order of the province. Agricola was clearly not the first governor to promote this policy of urbanization; Togidubnus' two royal capitals at Silchester and Chichester had been supplied with Roman buildings during the 50s and 60s. Since Togidubnus had been ruling the southern kingdom since 43, however, he may well have been dead by the time Agricola became governor. Togidubnus' kingdom was the last of the Claudian friendly territories to be absorbed into the province when his two royal centres became *civitas* capitals. There is little to indicate that the other *civitas* capitals of southern Britain had monumental stone buildings by the time Agricola was governor. The only exception was Verulamium, where, since the local elites' urban centre was a *municipium*, they evidently enjoyed particular Roman favour. Indeed, magistrates from this community would have become Roman citizens as a reward for their public service. An inscription from the forum at Verulamium, which dates the dedication of this building to 81, names the emperor Vespasian and his sons Titus and Domitian, while also referring to Agricola.[40] Although this urban community would have had the contacts and resources to commission and fund the building of this grand forum, the inclusion of his name on the dedicatory inscription suggests that Agricola may have provided some encouragement and support. Since the forum was the civic focus of the *civitas* of the Catuvellauni, it was a key symbol of the absorption of this self-governing community into the Roman world.

The governors of Britain would actively have encouraged the development of urban life, although the local elite groups who ruled these communities would have taken the initiative in planning and funding the construction of the monumental buildings that came to adorn their capitals. The urbanization of the southern *civitates* was a slow process nonetheless, as the construction of monumental buildings at these towns—with the few exceptions noted—would commence only during the later first and early second centuries. London, since it had special status as the main port and largest market in Britain, was another exception. The forum and amphitheatre there were constructed during the 70s.[41]

Another grand Roman building that had been constructed by this time was the temple at the spa centre at Bath (*Aquae Sulis*, Somerset; fig. 5.6).[42] This substantial classical temple, comparable in significance to the temple of Claudius at Camulodunum, was built to supplement the facilities of the hot spring, already becoming a popular destination for soldiers and other Romans. In this case the dedicatory inscription has not been found during the excavation of the complex, so it is unclear who was responsible for

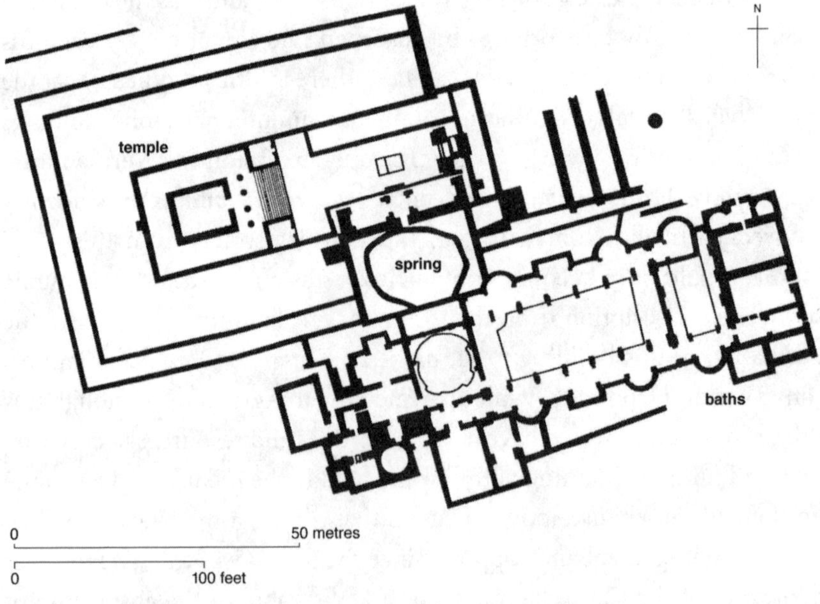

FIG 5.6.
The Roman temple and baths at Bath (after Davenport, Pool, and Jordan 2007, with additions)

commissioning the temple. The patron could equally have been a high-ranking Briton with the connections and resources to sponsor a classical building on this scale or a wealthy settler from some other part of the empire.

A Preliminary Campaign in the Far North

When Vespasian died in 79, his son Titus succeeded him as emperor. Titus had served as a military tribune in Britain in the early 60s and was aware of the potential of Britain to provide him with a military victory.[43] The accession of the new emperor required an assertive expression of Roman power, since Britain was the main focus of Roman campaigning at this time. In 80 Agricola conducted his third season of campaigning, against peoples whose territories extended as far north as the estuary of the River Tay (*Tanaum*), an indication that the Roman forces had reached an advanced location in eastern Scotland (fig. 5.7).[44] The Roman troops apparently so intimidated the enemy that they did not dare challenge them, and they were able to establish 'forts'. This suggests that an advance contingent of Roman soldiers had reached a point far to the north, beyond the lands under Rome's direct control, and presumably expected to overwinter there. This is the first date when we can be confident that Roman campaigning forces had reached the lands of Caledonia. Agricola was clearly already planning further ventures in the far north of Britain with the ambitious aim of conquering the entire island.

The excavation of the fort at Elginhaugh (Midlothian), on the line of the campaigning route of Dere Street, provides a detailed picture of one of the many Roman fortifications built across Scotland (fig. 5.8).[45] Elginhaugh is the only Flavian fort in Scotland to have been extensively examined using modern standards of excavation, and its construction can be dated to around 79–80 with unusual precision, as the result of a hoard of 45 silver *denarii* deposited as a foundation offering when the headquarters building was being constructed. The headquarters was a substantial courtyard building where the most significant military meetings occurred and the standards carried by the military unit were also kept. Roman soldiers sometimes made offerings of this nature to the gods

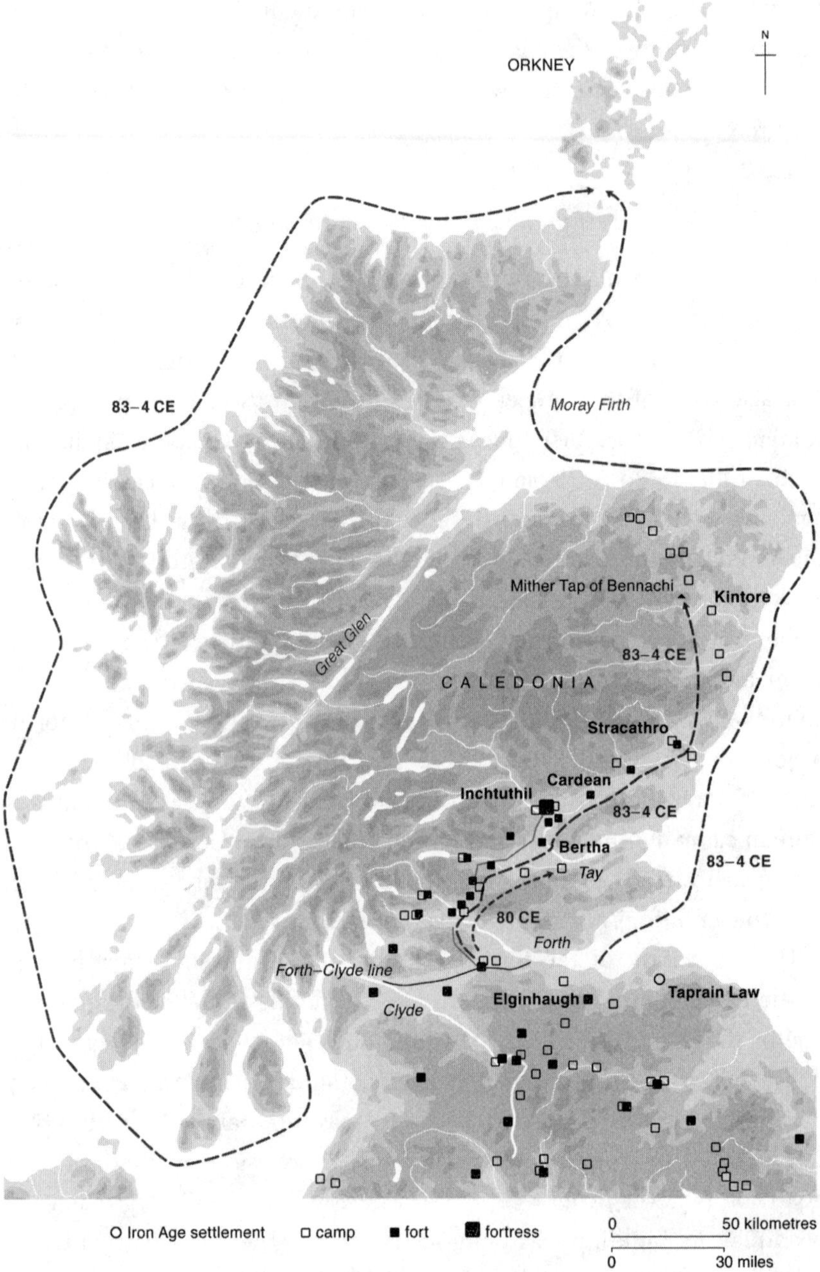

FIG 5.7.
Roman forts and campaign routes in northern Britain under Agricola (after Hanson 2007a, fig. 5, with additions)

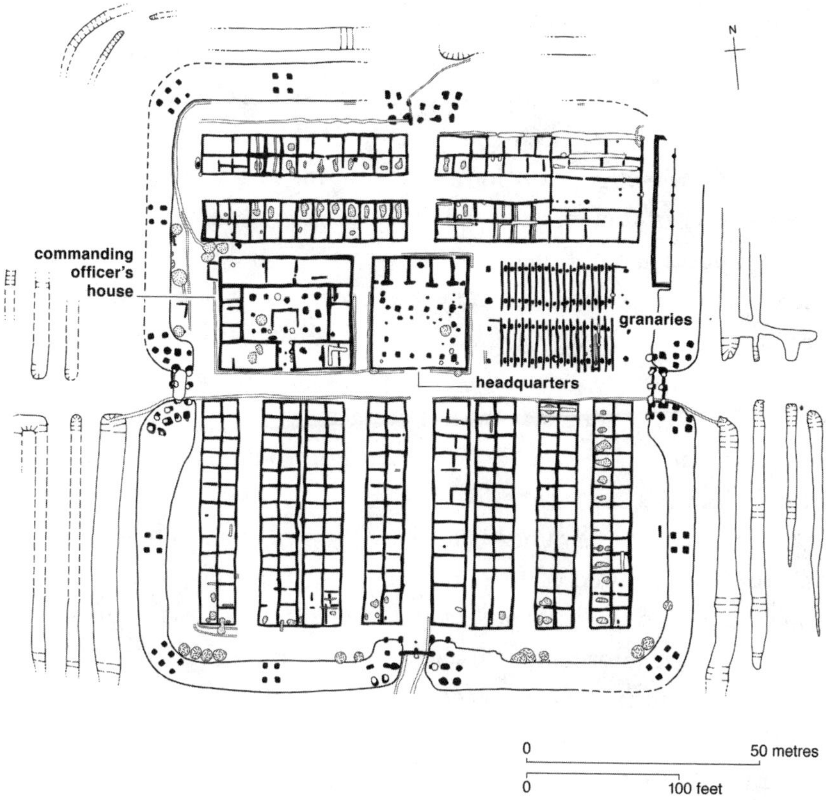

FIG 5.8.
The Roman fort at Elginhaugh, constructed in around 79–80;
the buildings that are not labelled were barrack blocks (after Hanson 2007a, fig. 14)

when new buildings were being constructed, and the close dating of the coins from the hoard ties in with Agricola's third and fourth seasons of campaigning. The hoard would have represented one-sixth of the annual pay of a cavalry trooper, and it may have been deposited during an official ceremony held by the unit when the headquarters building was being constructed. This fort was the base for an auxiliary unit of around 500 troops, and it has been proposed that it may have been a joint infantry and cavalry force. Since there are no burial monuments to soldiers from Elginhaugh, the name of this unit remains unknown.

This fort, of which the headquarters buildings, granaries, and barrack blocks have been uncovered, was built of timber and earth. There was also a fortified enclosure, or annex, attached to the fort, probably home to civilians who had followed the troops into southern Scotland. Campaigning military forces were often accompanied by groups of civilians who helped to supply the soldiers' needs; we have detailed information for the civil community which grew up, for instance, at the fort of Vindolanda (discussed later). Although the soldiers fighting with Agricola were in an exposed position at the edge of Roman territory and may not have been accompanied by a large following, it is known as a result of finds of the production of pots during the excavation that potters from southern Britain accompanied them to Elginhaugh. The soldiers also constructed a stone bathhouse just outside the fort defences. By this stage of the Roman conquest many of the soldiers on campaign would have had access to bathing facilities, regarded as being a key aspect of living in the Roman manner. When military units established more permanent bases, bathing facilities were considered fundamentally important, and the other forts established under Agricola in Scotland would have had such facilities too.

We also have information about the food consumed by the soldiers at Elginhaugh, much of which, was brought from overseas, including wine, olive oil, and figs. The Roman fleet accompanied Agricola into Scotland, and a harbour on the Firth of Forth may have been used to land supplies for all the Roman forces campaigning across southern Scotland, including the soldiers at Elginhaugh. Military units such as these also sourced animals and grain through raiding the property of local communities. Friendly peoples, such as those inhabiting the lands surrounding Traprain Law, probably supplied food to the soldiers as a form of taxation or even traded it directly to them. Despite this, much of the food the Roman military required was transported from further south.

Securing a Temporary Frontier

The progress of the conquest halted for a while in 81 as Agricola established a frontier at the Clyde–Forth line. We hear that 'if the spirit of the army and the glory of the Roman name had permitted it, a frontier would have been found within Britain itself. For the Firths of Clyde [*Clota*] and Forth [*Bodotria*], carried far inland by the tides of the opposing sea, are separated by a narrow neck of land. This was now being securely held by garrisons, and the whole sweep of land on the nearer side was secured; the enemy had been pushed back, as if into a different island'.[46] To secure the conquered lands across southern Scotland, Agricola created a guarded '*terminus*', a frontier, consisting of a patrolled track garrisoned along its length.[47] Tacitus emphasizes the role of the sea and the inflowing of water in the Firths of Clyde and Forth as a natural element of the frontier. He describes the Roman garrisoning of this narrow isthmus as supplementing the divine waters and isolating the Caledonians, in effect, within another Oceanic realm of barbaric islands—including Ireland, Orkney, and Shetland—that remained to be conquered.[48] This strategy would have avoided the necessity of leading campaigns by land and sea to subdue the vast territories of Caledonia, which extend over 300 kilometres (190 miles) further to the north.

Despite the reference to garrisons, however, no camps or forts have yet been confidently identified on the Clyde–Forth line. The Romans continued to establish their network of forts and roads immediately to the south during Agricola's fourth season; this work would have taken several years to complete.

Viewing Ireland across the Sea

Titus reigned over Rome for two years and when he died in September 81 was succeeded by his younger brother Domitian. The establishment of roads and forts continued during 82, Agricola's fifth year of campaigning. He is said to have defeated peoples previously unknown to the Romans, following a sea crossing, and then assembled his forces in a part of Britain that faced Ireland.[49] The sea routes to Ireland and its harbours were apparently well known to the Romans from trading and contact with merchants. Archaeological research has substantiated these statements, since Roman imports, including pottery and coins, have been found in Ireland. Although these were indeed probably the result of trade, it is also possible that the Romans had agreed treaties of friendship with local leaders, who may sometimes have been rewarded with gifts for supporting Rome.[50] Finds of Roman goods have been made at a number of sites, and metal detecting at the Iron Age promontory fort at Drumanagh (Loughshinny, County Dublin) on Ireland's east coast has produced a particularly large assemblage of imported items, including several Roman coins. This was probably one of the main centres for trade.

Tacitus also records that Agricola gave refuge to a 'minor king' from Ireland who had been expelled after a family quarrel. This Irish supplicant, reminiscent of the Iron Age kings who fled to Julius Caesar and Augustus from southern Britain, may have been hoping that Agricola would take the opportunity to invade Ireland and restore him to his dominion in the way Caesar had used Mandubracius, after Cassivellaunus drove him out, as an excuse to invade Britain in 54. The surrender of this Irish princeling may indeed have offered Agricola an opportunity for armed intervention, especially as it was rumoured that Ireland could be conquered and held with a single legion and a small number of auxiliaries. However, since an advance across the Clyde-Forth line was imminent, Caledonia remained Agricola's initial priority.

Crossing into Caledonia

The aggressive campaign to conquer northern Britain resumed as Agricola crossed the Firth of Forth into Caledonia in 83, during his sixth season of campaigning. The name 'Caledonia' means 'hard men', and classical writers wrote of the 'Caledonian Forest', emphasizing the idea of this land as an untamed wilderness.[51] This does not mean that in reality the lands of Caledonia were thickly forested. In fact, archaeological research indicates that the agriculturally fertile lowland, coastal plains, and islands were settled by farming communities and that much of the tree cover had already been cleared during the centuries before the Roman forces arrived.[52] The eastern coastal areas of northern Scotland included extensive areas of low-lying land, with fertile soils, which were intensively settled by Iron Age communities. In Northern Scotland, where the high peaks of the Scottish Highlands make up the highest mountainous terrain in Britain, even the river valleys were sparsely settled.

We have some information about the military forces that accompanied Agricola into Caledonia.[53] At the core of his army were the legionary soldiers, and detachments from all four legions of Britain may have been involved. Agricola would have left substantial garrisons at all four legionary fortresses in the south across central Britain, and he may have been campaigning with detachments from each legion, perhaps around 10,000 troops in total. The light infantry auxiliary soldiers at the battle of *Mons Graupius* numbered 8,000 and the cavalry 3,000, so that he might have had a total of approximately 20,000 soldiers under his command in Scotland. Not all of them were destined for the far north, however, as some were left to guard garrison points and supply routes across southern Scotland.

The majority of Agricola's auxiliary cavalry and light infantry, as in the earlier stages of the conquest, came from other provinces of the empire, especially Gaul and Germany. We also hear of Britons serving with Agricola. These British auxiliaries were recruited from the *civitates* in the south of the province, and it is possible that he had several thousand Britons under his command. Recruiting British auxiliaries would have provided more soldiers for these northern campaigns. Any free man was able to join the Roman auxiliaries, and indeed providing troops was one of the ways the rulers of the *civitates* could demonstrate their loyalty to Rome. The use of auxiliaries from recently conquered lands in military campaigning was not without risks.[54] Although many of these soldiers had received Roman military training and lived under Roman rule while on campaign, their senior officers remained concerned about their loyalty.

The potential risks of using recently recruited auxiliary soldiers in offensives in hostile territory was demonstrated by the actions of a cohort of Usipi, conscripts from Germany, who deserted Agricola's command while campaigning in Caledonia in 83.[55] These auxiliary troops murdered a centurion and other Roman soldiers who had been training them before escaping in three captured warships and sailing around Britain. They were shipwrecked, and reduced to cannibalism, and then managed to return to Germany, where they were enslaved. One of Agricola's priorities, campaigning so far from home, was to ensure the loyalty of his auxiliary troops, and the legions would have played a significant role in keeping order.

The Roman fleet was also a vital element of Agricola's strategy for conquering Caledonia. We hear that the inhabitants were dumbfounded by the sight of this fleet in 83, which may have been the first time the population of northern Britain saw Roman warships. The Roman navy was already familiar with the coast of southern and central Britain, but they needed to explore the coastal waters of northern Britain and find harbours there. The practicalities of navigating the rough waters of the northern sea were not all that concerned Agricola's navy: Romans often thought that storms and the wrecking of vessels at sea were expressions of the gods' disfavour, unavoidable once aroused. In addition, control of the sea was vital to Agricola's success, for although the infantry and cavalry advanced across the territories they conquered on foot or on horseback, the fleet supplied food and equipment and could also be used to ferry small groups of soldiers to selected locations.

After crossing the Forth, the invasion of Caledonia proceeded by way of the low-lying lands along the north-eastern coast. The remains of a large number of Roman camps in this area reveal the route of the march (see fig. 5.7).[56] They mark the movement of Agricola's forces almost as far north as the Moray Firth during these sixth and seventh seasons of campaigning. We hear that as the Romans advanced, Caledonians attacked their camps. Agricola divided his forces into three divisions in order to avoid being encircled by these superior numbers of fighters familiar with the terrain.[57] He himself was in charge of one of these divisions, which continued to campaign separately but in a coordinated fashion.

The Caledonians' force then massed for a night attack on one of the divisions, the Ninth Legion. It was reportedly below strength, and its sentries were cut down as the attackers burst into the camp, before the legionaries drove them back, with the assistance of troops Agricola sent in support. It is unclear exactly where in north-eastern Scotland this conflict occurred. The Roman forces, emboldened by their victory, wanted to 'go deep into Caledonia, and fighting battle after battle, to find the end of Britain at last'.[58] The Britons, after their retreat, reacted by arming their young men, moving their wives and children to places of safety, and cementing alliances between their peoples with meetings and sacrifices.

The Battle of Mons Graupius

Agricola aimed to bring the Caledonians to battle during his seventh season in 84. He dispatched the fleet to put raiding parties ashore while a lightly equipped force moved overland, reinforced by the 'bravest Britons' (who were serving as Roman auxiliaries).[59] The auxiliary cavalry and light-armed infantry were sent into Caledonia in advance of the more heavily armed legionary soldiers. As Agricola's forces were devastating the communities inhabiting the rich farming lands of the eastern part of Caledonia, the scene was set for a major confrontation.

The excavations at one of the camps established on this campaign provide insights into the tactics Agricola used to force the Caledonians to fight a pitched battle. Farming communities had been occupied with the fertile soils of north-eastern Scotland for millennia. A recent excavation at Kintore (Aberdeenshire) in this region uncovered part of a camp large enough to hold all of Agricola's 20,000 soldiers.[60] This is one of four camps of a comparable size that have been found in north-eastern Scotland. The discovery of over 100 cooking ovens shows that the camp was occupied for several weeks at least, perhaps longer, and the traces of an Iron Age settlement suggest that the Romans displaced local people when they arrived. They used Kintore as a temporary military base; however, signs that a substantial military force garrisoned at this location may indicate that they were terrorizing the population of an extensive area. The Romans' offensive strategy may have included the killing of their enemies in large numbers, the assembling of hostages and slaves to be transported south, and the requisitioning of crops and livestock. Once little remained to be destroyed, these troops would have moved on to establish another camp in a new area, in a determined effort to provoke the Caledonians into battle.

The Caledonians already occupied *Mons Graupius* when Agricola arrived. The meaning of *Graupius* is not known; although the Grampian Mountains of Scotland perpetuate the name, it seems that it was first coined during the fifteenth century by scholars quoting *Agricola*. In fact, the text itself does not provide enough information to identify the battle site at all. A better clue is the large number of Roman camps found across north-eastern Scotland, including Kintore; no camps have been found to the north of the Great Glen. These camps' distribution suggests that the battle of *Mons Graupius* was fought in the vicinity of the modern city of Aberdeen, possibly at Mither Tap of Bennachi (Inverurie), a location at the foot of a range of hills with a striking profile.[61]

The Caledonians assembled for the battle with a force of 30,000 gathered from all their peoples and with more still arriving, under the ultimate leadership of the warrior Calgacus. Described by Tacitus as an outstanding leader of valour and nobility, he is otherwise unattested, but his name is thought to have meant 'swordsman'. His power derived both from his military prowess and the ties of patronage which bound clients to his cause. At the same time, his power—like that of the famous Cassivellaunus and Caratacus before him—depended chiefly on his past successes with the sword. That he was taking a significant risk facing Agricola in battle is indicated by the earlier defeats Caratacus and Boudica suffered in pitched battles. But as Agricola's troops were destroying settlements, killing and enslaving large numbers of people, and requisitioning vast quantities of crops and livestock, Calgacus was given no option but to fight. Had he failed to join battle with Agricola in the summer of 84, his numerical advantage over the Romans would have dissipated, and he would have lost authority over his followers. The Caledonians who had elected him leader were desperate for revenge against the violent invaders who were despoiling their lands.

In Tacitus' account Calgacus delivers a long speech before the battle, portraying his followers as resistant barbarians who yet possess the old and acclaimed Roman virtues of nobility and morality.[62] This speech is a narrative device Tacitus uses to criticize the dictatorial behaviour of the emperor Domitian at Rome.[63] It also includes a commentary on the contrasting identities of the Britons and their foes. Calgacus remarks that the Roman force 'has been put together from peoples that are very different from one another. Success has kept it together, but it will fall apart in defeat. Or can you really suppose that Gauls and Germans and—it is shameful to mention them—many Britons too are bound to them by loyalty and goodwill?' Calgacus contrasts this (potential) Roman disunity with the idea of Britain as a united whole, referring to 'Britannia' on four occasions to provide a concept of collective unity. This powerful idea of united 'British' opposition to Rome ignores the fact that most the island was already under Roman rule. Tacitus uses this idea to stress the dangers Agricola faced in the campaigns in the far north and to underline the scale of the victory he was about to achieve at the physical and cultural edge of the world.

Agricola is also given a speech, in which he describes the long marches through forests and across estuaries during seven years of campaigning, noting that the 'furthest point' of Britain is no longer merely a subject of report and rumours but is now being dominated by Roman forts and arms. The battle of *Mons Graupius* then commenced, as the units of the Roman army were drawn up in line, with 8,000 auxiliary infantry in the centre and 3,000 cavalry on the flanks. The legionaries, held in reserve while the auxiliary forces joined battle, were stationed in front of the rampart of the nearby camp, as Agricola was seeking to win a victory with no Roman legionary blood being spilled. He probably had approximately 20,000 soldiers against the 30,000 Britons. The Caledonians were positioned up on the slopes of the mountainous terrain, with their charioteers filling the plain. The Roman auxiliaries, including four cohorts of Batavians, two of Tungrians, and some cavalry, forced the Britons back; the chariots fled the scene. The Batavians and Tungrians were auxiliary soldiers recruited from the Lower Rhine Valley; they would be important in the manning of Britannia's northern frontier in subsequent decades (discussed later).

At the end of the battle, 'a vast and grim spectacle unfolded on the open plains: the cavalry pursued, inflicted wounds, took captives, and, as fresh foes appeared, butchered their prisoners.... Everywhere could be seen weapons, bodies, mangled limbs, and bloodstained earth.'[64] We are told that by nightfall, 10,000 of the enemy had been killed, while a mere 360 Roman soldiers were reported dead; probably, once again, an exaggeration. At dawn the next day there was 'the silence of desolation on all sides, the hills lonely, homesteads smouldering in the distance, not a man to encounter the scouts'. This description evokes the extreme violence Agricola directed against the people of Caledonia who dared to fight against him.

The tombstone of one of Agricola's cavalry soldiers also provides a graphic rendering of the violence of this conflict. It commemorates a trooper of the Treveri, a people of Roman Germany, named Insus, who survived the Caledonian campaign and returned to central Britain, where he died and was buried at the Roman fort at Lancaster (Lancashire). He holds a short sword in his left hand and has just beheaded an enemy. His sword hand holds the detached head by the hair, showing that it has been taken as a trophy from the body of its owner, a naked Briton armed with a large sword.[65] The remains of the Caledonian dead at *Mons Graupius* have yet to be found, but we can presume that many were slaughtered as a warning to the survivors not to stand in the Romans' way. The scale of deaths on the Roman side was probably underestimated.

Burial monuments found at Chester and at Cyrene (Libya) also provide information about some of the soldiers who fought at *Mons Graupius*.[66] The inscription on the monument of Gaius Julius Karus at Cyrene recorded that he was originally from the Roman province of Gallia Narbonensis (southern France). He had commanded the Second Cohort of Asturians from north-west Spain, and was richly decorated with two crowns and an 'untipped spear' (*hasta pura*, or blunt spear) for his actions in a 'British War': probably the campaign in Caledonia. The crowns, described as a 'Wall Crown' and a 'Rampart Crown', were military decorations made from metal. Such decorations were regularly awarded to legionaries for valour, but rarely to auxilairies such as Karus. The blunt spear was another traditional reward for bravery. A long way from Cyrene, six tombstones at the Roman fortress of Chester name legionaries of the Second Legion Adiutrix who died during their period of service, including Voltimesis Pudens, who had served for thirteen years. These men may have been wounded at *Mons Graupius* and returned to their home base. Alternatively, they may have died on the battlefield, where their bodies may have been cremated and their ashes carried back to the fortress for burial.

The Aftermath of Conflict

The day after the battle, Roman scouts reported that enemy fugitives were not massing at any point, and as the summer campaigning season was already over, Agricola led his entire forces further into the northern territories, taking hostages with him.[67] He instructed the Roman fleet to sail around Britain and then, in order to intimidate the inhabitants, proceeded in a sedate manner through territory the Romans had not previously reached, stationing his infantry and cavalry in winter quarters across Caledonia. Since we know that temporary camps were replaced by forts, a sizable garrison was clearly being established in the conquered lands. The distribution of forts across the eastern parts of Caledonia indicates the areas that were garrisoned in the winter following the great victory at *Mons Graupius*.

For the first time, the fleet sailed around the coast of the 'remotest sea' and managed to confirm travellers' previous claims that Britain was in fact an island. Although this was the first occasion on which we can be sure a Roman fleet sailed around the northern coast of Britain, other Mediterranean travellers had been further north on previous occasions. We hear that Agricola's fleet discovered and subdued the islands of the Orkneys (*Orcades*) and observed Shetland (*Thule*) in the distance.[68] The islands lying off the western and northern coasts of Scotland at this time were inhabited by communities living in impressive stone-built houses called brochs.[69] The architectural complexity of some of the broch settlements of Orkney illustrates that these were the homes of people of influence. The Romans may already have had some contacts with the inhabitants of Orkney, as already mentioned, and Agricola's navy seems to have dictated terms of surrender to some of the leaders of the peoples living on these islands.

Thule, a semimythical, far distant land, had first been mentioned by Pytheas centuries before, but the Romans had continued to doubt its existence. By '*Thule*' Pytheas may have meant Iceland; Tacitus used '*Thule*' to refer to Shetland. Agricola's fleet was only able to sight this fabled island and do no more, because of the lateness of the season, but Tacitus' reference to *Thule* added a significant element to Agricola's victory in

Caledonia and raised the possibility of further conquests beyond the northern limits of the British mainland.

The Conquest of Ocean

Agricola must have claimed in his dispatches to Domitian that his victory at *Mons Graupius* had completed the conquest of Britain. Certainly, there are indications that it was trumpeted in Rome as the final conquest of Ocean embarked upon by Claudius forty years before. During the campaigns in Caledonia, we hear, the soldiers and sailors in Agricola's forces compared the ravines in the forests and mountains with the dangers of storm and tides at sea, while victories on land against the enemy were thought to represent the conquest of Ocean. Elsewhere, Tacitus wrote of Caledonia: 'nowhere is the dominance of the sea more extensive. There are many tidal currents flowing in different directions. They do not merely rise as far as the shoreline and recede. They flow far inland, wind about, pushing themselves into the highland and mountains as if in their own realm'.[70] The rivers that flowing far inland across Scotland would have presented a challenge to the campaigning forces. Educated Romans conceived of the conquest of Britannia as the subjection of Ocean and his children.

The Romans had adopted from the Greeks the worship of Oceanus, an ancestral god of the sea, as mentioned earlier. Alexander the Great had once sacrificed to Oceanus and his divine wife, Tethys, during a campaign at the eastern end of the known world, in India.[71] As the Romans had conquered and subdued the southern parts of Britannia and explored their coasts, Caledonia had thus become Ocean's domain. At the time Agricola was invading Caledonia, a Roman poet writing to a friend who was soon to travel to Britain observed: 'you are going to visit the Caledonian Britons and green Tethys and Father Ocean'.[72] Tethys, in Greek mythology the wife of Oceanus and the mother of the river gods, would also have been a highly appropriate deity to celebrate when visiting the northern lands where the waters of the sea flowed far inland. Demetrius of Tarsus, a professional teacher of Greek, explored the coast of Britain during Agricola's campaigns and is likely to have been the same Demetrius who dedicated two silvered bronze tablets to Oceanus and Tethys while visiting a shrine at the legionary fortress of York.[73] A short account survives of his voyages around northern Britain, recalling that some of the islands were named after divinities and heroes and many were isolated, inhabited only by holy men revered by the Britons.[74] We cannot know which islands Demetrius visited; his comments reflect the classical conception of the numinous quality of Ocean off the coast of Caledonia.

Victory Celebrations

The Roman forces overwintered in Caledonia and started to construct a network of forts, although Agricola himself would have travelled back to his base in the south for the cold season, leaving a trusted legionary commander in charge of the troops. Agricola was recalled to Rome in 85, where on the orders of Domitian he received 'triumphal ornaments' and a statue.[75] Domitian evidently welcomed Agricola's victory, since it credited him with completing the fabulous quest to conquer Britain begun by Julius Caesar almost 140 years earlier. Successful Roman generals were sometimes awarded a magisterial toga, as were Plautius and Scapula, which is probably what 'triumphal ornaments' meant. Agricola was the only successful general honoured in this way during Domitian's long reign. The statue of Agricola would have been located in the Forum of Augustus, where famous Roman generals were commemorated.

The claim that the conquest of Britain had been completed was also commemorated by the construction of a vast four-sided triumphal arch at the port of Richborough in Kent.[76] The surviving foundations of this remarkable structure were excavated during the early twentieth century. Although the dedicatory inscription and the sculpture decorating this arch have survived only in fragments, we know of no other event in Britain around this time that would have warranted the installation of so grand a monument. Faced with sculpted and inscribed panels of white Carrara marble imported from Italy, the Richborough arch was designed as a symbolic gateway to Britain through which travellers from the Continent would pass. It was located on a small island joined to mainland Britain by a causeway and as such marked a point of transition from Ocean to the mainland, close to the place where the invading forces of Julius Caesar and Claudius had come ashore.

What better place to celebrate the claim that the conquest of Ocean had been completed than a sacred island lying off the mainland at the point of entry to Britain, a location identified with the famous expeditions across Ocean of Julius Caesar and Claudius?

TOTAL CONQUEST?

Between 70 and 85, the governors of Britain led a remarkable series of campaigns across a vast area that was equivalent to half of mainland Britain. These campaigns came close to achieving Vespasian's objective of completing the conquest of the island. The three governors before Agricola had conquered much of Wales and central Britain, leading campaigns into southern Scotland and constructing the network of roads and forts that effectively secured Roman control. Agricola built on these achievements by completing the conquest of Wales and central Britain and pushing his forces far into Caledonia. His defeat of the massed forces of the Caledonians at *Mons Graupius* was used by Agricola and Tacitus to claim that the conquest was completed, bar some limited campaigning.

This victory was celebrated in Rome and in Britain, though the events of the following two years demonstrated that the people of Caledonia were far from conquered entirely. Indeed, the conquest of the mountainous Scottish Highlands would never be achieved, and the Roman forces withdrew to south of the Clyde-Forth line in approximately 86–87. Agricola's relationship with Domitian deteriorated after his return to Rome.[77] This may, in part, reflect the strategic need to withdraw from Caledonia despite the complete conquest of this Oceanic territory having being proclaimed at Rome two years before. Tacitus, however, wrote a very different account of these events, suggesting that Domitian held Agricola back from further appointments since he was jealous of

Agricola's achievements in Britain. By emphasizing Agricola's deteriorating relationship with Domitian, Tacitus effectively distanced his father-in-law's achievements from the dictatorial actions of a hated emperor. Domitian had died and been damned in memory in 96, two years before Tacitus finished writing *Agricola*.[78]

6

THE NORTHERN FRONTIER

The empire was cordoned by the sea of Ocean or distant streams.

Tacitus, *Annals*[1]

DURING THE FIRST FOUR decades of the Roman conquest of Britain, campaigning encompassed almost the entirety of the mainland, and when the emperor Domitian recalled Agricola to Rome in 85, his successor as governor would have been instructed to complete the subjugation of Caledonia. That Rome's ruling classes considered the conquest of mainland Britain to be virtually complete is indicated by the honours Domitian bestowed on Agricola upon his return to Rome and explains the construction of the massive triumphal arch at Richborough on the Kent coast. Although Agricola's report to Domitian in the aftermath of the battle of *Mons Graupius* presumably stated that further campaigning was required to secure the lands of northern Britain, this may have been overlooked in the immediate wake of so great a victory beyond the north-western edge of the Roman world.

LUCULLUS IN CALEDONIA

We are informed that Agricola handed over the province of Britannia 'peaceful and secure' to his successor.[2] After his recall, it appears that a senior member of the Roman aristocracy named Sallustius Lucullus was appointed to govern Britain.[3] Very little is known of his background; nonetheless, the appointment was undoubtedly made as a result of his military and diplomatic experience. The task of commanding the four legions stationed in the province, an unusually large force even for a frontier province of Rome, made the governorship of Britain a significant role. Under the generalship of Lucullus, however, these four legions were about to be reduced to three.

Campaigning in the Far North

The battle at *Mons Graupius* marked the end of any large-scale resistance to Rome's annexation of territory in northern Britain, and this victory was followed by the military forces' construction of a network of forts and roads across the lands of north-eastern Scotland (see fig. 5.7). The limited territorial reach of these forts and roads also is an indication that the campaigns to conquer and settle Caledonia were restricted to an area to the east.

The most significant element of the garrison was the legionary fortress established at Inchtuthil (Perth and Kinross; fig. 6.1). The presence of this substantial fortification, large enough to hold at least 5,000 troops, indicates that Lucullus was indeed intent on completing the conquest of the far north of Britain.[4] Since burial monuments have yet to be found at Inchtuthil, it is not clear which legion (or legions) was based there, although it is possible that the Twentieth Legion moved north to there from Wroxeter. The construction of the fortress may have commenced during the winter of 84–85, immediately after the battle of *Mons Graupius*, and continued for at least two years under Agricola's successor. Built on an area of raised ground, the defences of the fortress and the buildings that lay within, which were standard for such a military establishment, have all been mapped. Although many of these buildings had been completed by 86, it is instructive that the commanding officer's house and the bathhouse remained under construction. The scale of such a fortress required that it would take more than two years to construct it.

The rampart and the buildings inside the fortress were built of timber and earth, adopting the techniques the Roman military had used

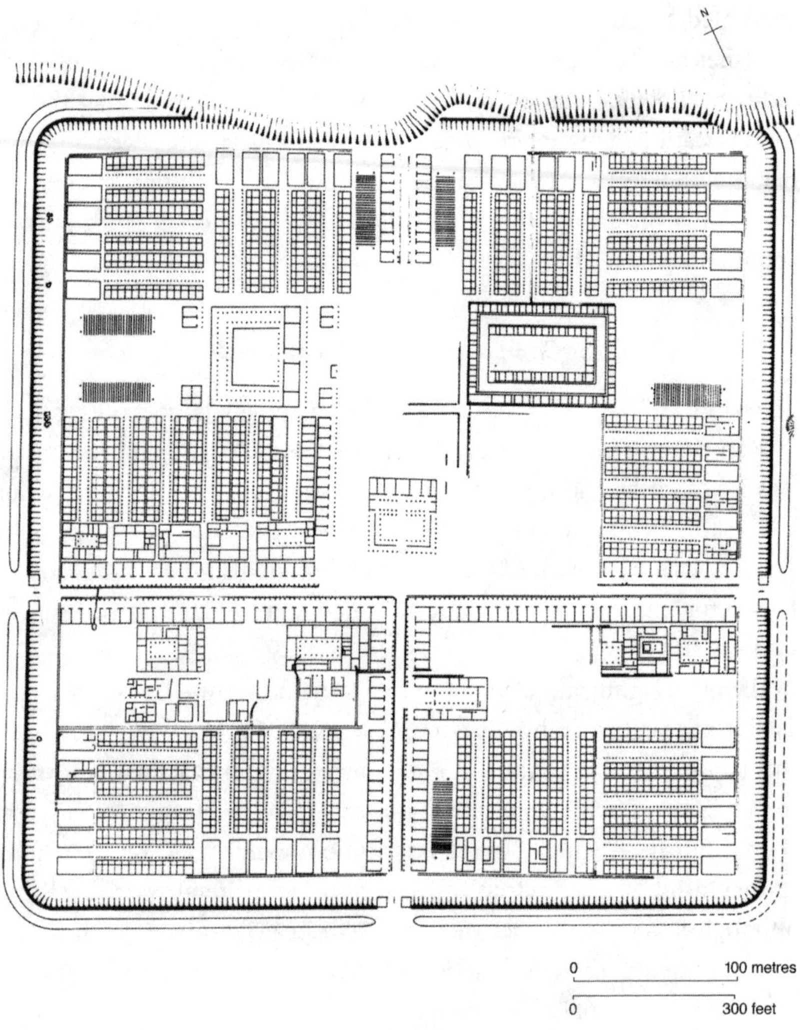

FIG 6.1.
The Roman fortress at Inchtuthil, constructed around 84–86 (from Pitts and St Joseph 1985)

to construct their fortifications across Britain during the previous four decades. Timber forts required regular rebuilding, as the ramparts and buildings deteriorated in the wet climate of northern Britain. After the early second century, therefore, Roman fortresses and forts came to be constructed in more durable stone, with the result that they did not have to be repaired and rebuilt quite so frequently. One highly important discovery at Inchtuthil is that the timber-and-earth rampart that surrounded the fort was subsequently rebuilt with a stone wall to provide facing.[5] This reconstruction of the defences in stone indicates that the fortress was intended to provide a long-term home for legionary soldiers during the conquest of the extensive territories to the north and west.

Forts and fortresses often included workshops for the production of weapons, pottery, and tile, and Inchtuthil was no exception.[6] Local industries were established for the production of pottery, tiles, and iron, and indeed much of the material required to build the fortress was acquired and processed locally. Fortresses were constructed in territories that had already been conquered, to serve as secure winter bases and bases for further campaigns against resistant peoples living in lands not yet subdued. The construction of Inchtuthil, the only legionary fortress north of York, was thus a remarkably ambitious statement of Roman intent to conquer Caledonia.

Inchtuthil was the focal point in a line of forts, the 'glen-blocking forts', located at the places where the principal rivers emerge from the Scottish Highlands.[7] These forts, to the north-east and south-west of Inchtuthil, guarded the exit points from the Highlands for enemy forces moving down the major glens to the north-west. The presence of Inchtuthil indicates that the glen-blocking forts were also intended as a base for offensive campaigning into the mountainous uplands by way of the glens. However, since no Roman camps and forts have been found in these mountainous uplands, which would have proved extremely difficult terrain for campaigning, it appears that the advance into the Scottish Highlands was never mounted.

A second line of Roman forts, fortlets, and watchtowers, known as the 'Gask System', was built just to the rear of the glen-blocking forts, along part of the road that carried military supplies through eastern Scotland. This heavily defended and closely supervised line of forts was constructed to support the campaigns of Agricola and Lucullus. The recently conquered lands across south-eastern Caledonia and also in southern Scotland, to the south of the Clyde-Forth line, were held in check by auxiliary units based in forts located at regular intervals. The strategy was to take control of these lands by dominating their people with treaties and taxation, a policy that had already been used to considerable effect across Wales and much of northern Britain. Very few metalled roads were constructed across the south-east of Caledonia, indicating that supplies were transported along dirt tracks to the campaigning forces and garrison. Transport along such tracks must have been hampered by the extremely wet weather northern Britain experiences during the winter seasons.

Although much of Caledonia remained to be conquered, a line of temporary Roman camps extended most of the way up the east coast of Caledonia toward the Moray Firth. Some of these camps may have marked the northward march of Agricola's forces immediately before the battle of *Mons Graupius* in 84, although the sites cannot themselves be dated to this degree of accuracy and could equally well relate to the campaigns Lucullus commanded in 85–86. At this time, the strategic objective may have been to subdue the agricultural communities in the extensive and relatively low-lying lands across eastern Caledonia. The military forces who suppressed the local population, by killing those who resisted and looting livestock and grain, may have used these camps as bases. Potentially friendly communities would also have been recruited as allies. Forts which were used for overwintering have not been found to the north of Stracathro (Angus), indicating that the conquest had not progressed to the stage at which the troops were settled. During the cold season, the campaigning forces would have withdrawn to forts in the south-east of Caledonia.

The distribution of the camps and forts indicates that from 83 to 86 the Roman military forces were preoccupied with the challenge of taking control of a relatively small region of eastern Caledonia, and that Lucullus was not able to extend the campaign as far as the Moray Firth or into the Scottish Highlands.[8] Much of the land that remained to be conquered was very mountainous and sparsely populated. Traces of farming settlements have been found in the lower lying valleys and coastal lands, and the western and northern isles are known to have been well settled by communities living within brochs (see fig. 5.5). The conquest and subjugation of the peoples living across these difficult terrains, as already mentioned, might have taken Rome decades of sustained campaigning to achieve. Agricola's ambition to conquer Caledonia had resulted in an untenable military situation, and Lucullus would swiftly have become aware of the scale of sustained campaigning required to complete this project. He must have communicated this news to Domitian at a time when the Empire was coming under considerable threat from Decebalus, the king of Dacia.

WITHDRAWING FROM THE FAR NORTH

Dacia, beyond the River Danube, had been united under a single king over a century before, having become a threat to Rome at the time of Augustus. Decebulus, a shrewd and resourceful leader, had revived this threat and led his forces across the Danube to the south from Dacia to invade the Roman province of Moesia in 85–86, resulting in the death of the Roman provincial governor and many of his troops.[9] Domitian decided to respond by leading Roman forces against Decebalus, becoming the first reigning emperor to campaign in person since Claudius' invasion of Britain. Domitian's campaigns against Dacia were only partly successful, and several years would pass before a Roman victory led to a treaty with Decebalus. If, by this stage, Domitian retained any desire to complete the objective of his father, Vespasian, to fully conquer Britain, events on the Danube would have dissuaded him from committing the manpower required to subdue Caledonia. Although Britannia had been the stage for impressive Roman victories for over forty years, ultimately it was only a small and remote province. The crisis on the Danube, by contrast, threatened the security of the entire empire. And so Domitian apparently decided that some of the forces maintaining Rome's control of Britain would have to be withdrawn and reassigned to more pressing needs. Coming two years after the celebration of Agricola's conquests, the news of the withdrawal from Caledonia would not have been welcomed by the Senators in Rome.

The Second Legion Adiutrix was moved from Britain to Budapest (*Aquincum*, Hungary) on the River Danube by the early 90s.[10] We do not know exactly when this move occurred, and although it may have resulted from the strategic need in 85–86 to reassign troops to face an escalating crisis on the Danube, there is another possibility. The Second Adiutrix had been moved to Britain in 71 to support the campaigns to complete the conquest of Britain. Instead of remaining as part of the permanent garrison, this legion could have been removed from Britain shortly after the Roman victory at *Mons Graupius*, when it was supposed that the conquest had effectively been completed. The three legions remaining in Britain were settled in fortresses at some distance from the frontier, as the ambition to conquer the far north receded and Inchtuthil was abandoned. The Twentieth Legion replaced the Second Adiutrix at Chester, the Second Augusta was based at Caerleon, and the Ninth at York. The fortress at Wroxeter, meanwhile, the former base of the Twentieth Legion, was abandoned.

This reduction in the legionary garrison by a quarter was followed by further transfers of troops to the Danube. Relatively little is known of these withdrawals. One clue may be found on an epitaph from the temple of Jupiter at Heliopolis (Baalbek, Lebanon) commemorating the achievements of the Roman commander Gaius Velius Rufus.[11] This inscription is thought to indicate that Rufus commanded a campaign on the Danube in 89 with detachments from at least eight legions. These detachments included troops from the Second Adiutrix and from two of the legions remaining in Britain, the Second Augusta and the Ninth. This indicates that the legionary forces in Britain were considerably reduced as a result of the continuing conflict with Dacia. Auxiliary units would also have accompanied the legionaries to the Danube. We know little of these troops, although the burial monument of a cavalryman from the legionary fortress of *Carnuntum* (Petronell, Austria) on the Danube provides the name of an auxiliary who had previously served in Britain.[12] Auxiliaries who had been recruited in Britain during the late 70s and 80s are also known to have served in conflicts on the Danube during the late first and early second centuries.[13] The conflict Decebalus initiated was destined not to be settled swiftly.

The Assassination of Lucullus

The Roman military's withdrawal from Caledonia led Tacitus to make the histrionic remark that Britain, having been conquered, was 'immediately given up'.[14] In reality, only the far north was abandoned.

The evidence for this abandonment is derived from the date range of the Roman coins found at forts excavated in northern Britain.[15] The salaries of Roman soldiers were paid in cash, which required large numbers of Roman coins to be transported to the frontier regions of the empire. Locations where troops were stationed on the frontier in Britain usually received new batches of coins from the mints on the Continent soon after they were issued. The soldiers dropped and lost some of these coins—and sometimes hoarded them—at the forts where they were serving, so the approximate dates of occupations of fort sites can be established from the coins found there. Coins of a distinctive issue produced in 87 have been found on archaeological sites throughout southern and central Britain but are notably absent from the forts of northern Scotland. This suggests that the Romans abandoned the northern territories before this issue of coins reached Britain. The forts in Caledonia, together with several of the forts located immediately to the south of the Clyde-Forth line, were evacuated as part of an orderly withdrawal, which involved the levelling and burning of sites as they were abandoned.[16] At Inchtuthil, the buildings were demolished and the flagstone floors of the bathhouse lifted. At Elginhaugh, the internal buildings of the fort were demolished, although excavation has indicated that the ramparts may have been left standing, to be used by military units patrolling the area. Several other forts in this area were also decommissioned at this time. An immense quantity of iron nails was deposited in a pit inside a workshop at Inchtuthil, possibly with the intention of preventing the local population from reusing the iron to produce weapons.

The governor Lucullus was put to death by Domitian, apparently because he allowed a new spear to be named after himself.[17] This is an unlikely story, however, as Lucullus was probably executed on the emperor's orders in the autumn of 86 at a time when Domitian's authority had been destabilized by the military crisis on the Danube. It is possible that Lucullus was among those conspiring against him. He may also have fallen foul of Domitian because of the Roman withdrawal from Caledonia.

THE STANEGATE AND THE EARLY HISTORY OF VINDOLANDA

Nothing is known about the identity of the two men who governed Britain in the aftermath of the retreat from northern Scotland. Northern Britain had not been entirely abandoned in the late 80s, and a handful of forts in southern Scotland continued to be garrisoned during the later first century (fig. 6.2).[18] Rome followed a strategy of creating a wide military area

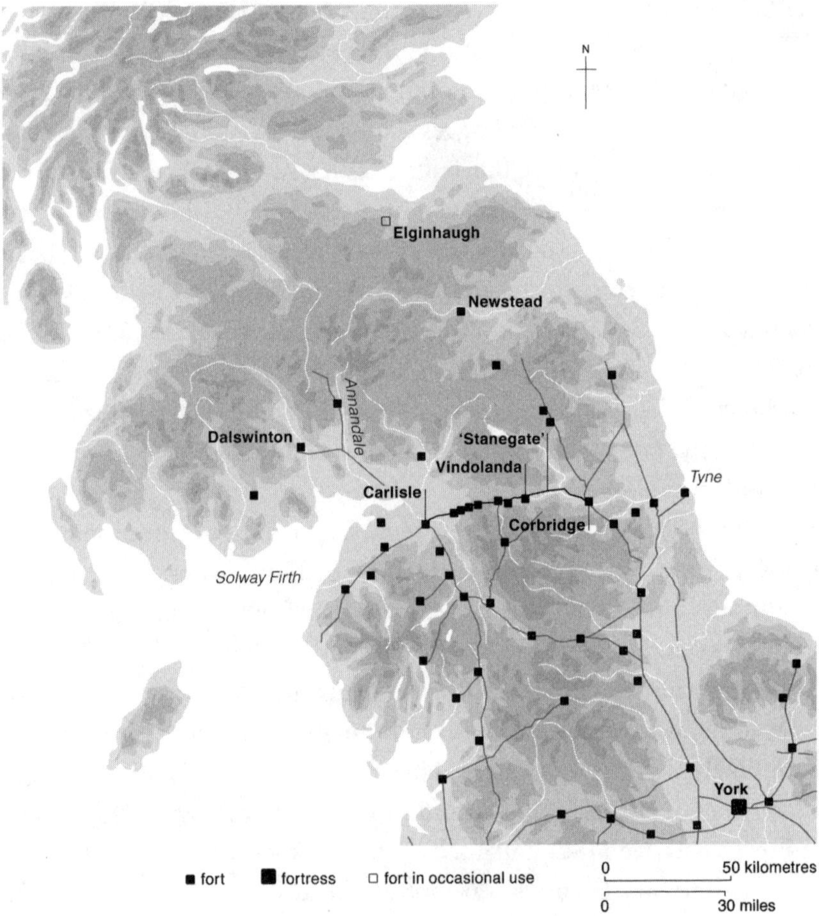

FIG 6.2.
Roman forts in northern and central Britain after the withdrawal from Caledonia (after Hanson 2007a, fig. 12, and Bidwell and Hodgson 2009, fig. 5)

of supervision across this northern frontier. The forts continuing in use across southern Scotland formed fortified outposts along the roads running north into the lands beyond the province. They included the forts of Newstead and Dalswinton (Nithsdale, Dumfries, and Galloway), which underwent major refurbishments. Newstead was a large, heavily defended fort, accommodating a garrison of cavalry and infantry soldiers. The new fort at Dalswinton was established as a base from which to control the western Scottish lowlands.

Although Roman claims to the territory to the north of Newstead had been abandoned, they may have continued to enforce treaties negotiated with local leaders in previous decades, requiring communities to continue to pay taxes in grain and animals and to supply military recruits. The decommissioned fort at Elginhaugh continued to be visited for some time after the Romans withdrew to the south, as indicated by the construction of paved surfaces and wells within the defended area and signs that the ramparts may have continued to be maintained.[19] The continued use of this fort suggests that Roman patrols travelled to Elginhaugh, perhaps on an annual basis, to collect tax in livestock and grain from the local people. A coin of Trajan has been found at Elginhaugh, suggesting that these patrols continued until the end of the first century at least. Many of the other decommissioned forts in the lands to the north of Newstead may similarly have been used as bases for the collection of taxes in produce from local communities. The Roman military would also have monitored potential threats brewing across this territory and would have met any hint of resistance with a violent response.

One important route, known now by the medieval name Stanegate, ran at right angles to the two campaigning routes across a neck of relatively low-lying land that separated the Solway Firth from the valley of the River Tyne.[20] This garrisoned track was developed, from the mid-80s, as a northern frontier line to the province.

The Stanegate followed an ancient east-west route which crossed the relatively low ground between two ranges of high hills, the Pennines to the south and the Cheviots to the north, and exploited the courses of several rivers immediately to its south. This important route was initially a dirt track; units of the Roman army constructed an engineered metalled road during the early second century, at which point more forts were added to its line of fortifications (see fig. 6.3). Before this time, travel along the muddy and waterlogged course of the Stanegate would have been extremely difficult, particularly during the winter months. At least three Roman forts, and possibly as many as five, were constructed along this track during the mid to late 80s.[21] The fort at Carlisle was extensively reconstructed during the winter of 83–84—closely dated by tree rings preserved in the wood. The building of the first fort at Vindolanda has been accurately dated to the mid-80s. The fort at Corbridge (*Coria*?) was probably also built around this time, perhaps replacing an earlier fort.

Since forts were still in use in southern Scotland, the Stanegate was not the northern limit of Roman control, which may have been located at the Clyde-Forth isthmus. The troops garrisoned on the Stanegate controlled movement across the frontier lands. Auxiliary units also continued to man forts within the province, to the south of the Stanegate. The construction of forts along the road from Manchester to Carlisle and across the Lake District, for example, indicates that the settling of these lands continued for decades after a garrison was first established along the Stanegate.[22]

The First Cohort of Tungrians at Vindolanda

The groundbreaking discoveries at the fort of Vindolanda provide vital information about the establishment of the northern frontier. The name *Vindolanda* may have signified 'white season' in Celtic and was probably a reference to the winter frost that settled across the plateau where a sequence of Roman forts was constructed during the centuries of Roman rule (fig. 6.4).[23] Among all the Roman fort sites excavated in Britain, Vindolanda is exceptional in the very high quality of information that five decades of fieldwork and research have derived from it. The early forts were built of timber and are deeply buried below the foundations of the later stone-built forts. Each fort was constructed on top of the demolished remains of its predecessor, preserving many artefacts in sealed deposits and creating anaerobic conditions that preserved very large quantities of organic remains, including the famous 'letters' (fig. 6.5). The lifespan of

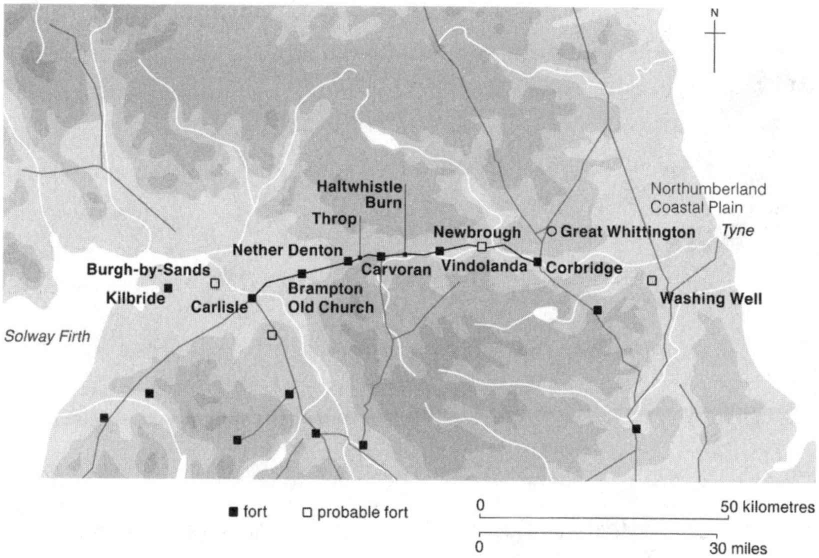

FIG 6.3.
The Stanegate in around 105 (after Symonds 2018a, fig. 29, with additions)

FIG 6.4.
The Roman fort and civil settlement at Vindolanda from the air, showing the later Roman forts and *vicus* (civil settlement); the early timber forts are buried below these visible remains (Copyright: Vindolanda Trust)

FIG 6.5.
One of the most famous of the Vindolanda letters: a birthday invitation to the commanding officer's wife (Copyright: Vindolanda Trust)

these four early forts has been established by tree-ring dating, pottery dating, and the discovery of letters with calendar dates in their texts.

The texts on these writing tablets, most of which date approximately to 90–120, include personal letters to colleagues and friends and documents recording lists of people and materials that were stored at the forts. When the first letter was discovered in 1973 it was a considerable surprise, as archaeologists had not been aware of the existence of this type of text. 'Stylus'-type writing tablets had regularly been found in Roman contexts across the empire prior to this, but the vast majority of the Vindolanda letters are of a very different type. They were made from thin leaves of wood, about the size of a modern postcard, with writing on the smooth surface in ink. Several hundred have been uncovered, and new examples continue to be found on a regular basis during the annual excavations. The recovery of a large quantity of leather shoes from within the fort itself has also provided a significant insight into the military communities at Vindolanda, as many were worn by women and children (fig. 6.6).

The earliest fort was manned by the First Cohort of Tungrians. The Tungri were a people of the middle Meuse Valley (Belgium), where the unit must originally have been raised.[24] This same auxiliary cohort was still, moreover, the garrison at Vindolanda around 90, when the second fort was constructed. The wider significance of the discovery of letters related to this unit is that it has led to a reassessment of the military

FIG 6.6.
Two shoes belonging to children from Vindolanda (Copyright: Vindolanda Trust)

strategy the Romans adopted for holding these frontier lands. It used to be assumed that each fort in Britain, often occupied by an auxiliary garrison (cohort) of around 500 men, was located on a road one day's march from the next and that each garrison was charged with maintaining order and taxing the people in its designated locale. This may indeed have been the basic tactic used during the conquest of Wales and central Britain, but documents from Vindolanda indicate that by the 90s, the Roman forces had adopted a far more flexible approach which spread the available manpower more widely across the frontier regions of the province.

The letter which is most informative on military strategy is a strength report of the garrison when the First Cohort of Tungrians was commanded by Julius Verecundus, the senior officer in periods 1 and 2 of the fort.[25] The cohort's full strength was 752, including six centurions, although only 296 of these soldiers were present at Vindolanda itself; others were stationed elsewhere, including *Coria* (probably Corbridge), London, and five other locations. The names of these places unfortunately cannot be recovered because the document is too damaged. It reports that thirty-one of the men at Vindolanda are unfit for duty, fifteen are unwell, six are wounded, and ten others were suffering from an inflammation of the eyes. This letter and several others from Vindolanda indicate that soldiers were regularly sent out from their home base to support units on patrol and to obtain supplies. These letters also imply that Roman military control of the conquered lands could evidently be maintained with fewer soldiers than the physical distribution of forts might have suggested, since rather than a garrison of 500 men, only around 300 were stationed at Vindolanda at this time.[26]

These letters convey the impression of the Roman frontier as a landscape of forts and roads that provided the basis for a flexible strategy of policing, organization, and control across a very extensive territory.[27] This strategy involved the widespread exchange of information by letters across the frontier zone itself, involving the military units based both on the Stanegate and at the forts to the north and south. Many of the forts across late first-century Britain may not have been fully manned, with scattered detachments assembling on occasions when a show of strength was required. Western, central, and northern Britain had been subdued so very swiftly between 71–84 that it seems likely that this flexible strategy was developed in the decades before the Tungrians arrived at Vindolanda. The Roman military forces evidently worked in a highly strategic manner, making the best use of the manpower available, and the distribution of the garrison reflected this policy. The garrison of each unit's home base may also have strengthened during the winter months, when campaigning conditions were compromised by the inclement weather.

This letter contains yet another indication of the character of the northern frontier zone: if only six men were recorded as injured, conditions at and around Vindolanda may have been relatively settled and peaceful. Although some Roman weapons have been found during the excavations, including lances, spears, bolt-heads, swords, and slingshots, the letters give little indication of armed conflict. Since the garrison remained in place across southern Scotland, the fort was at some distance from the front line of Roman territory as it was established in the late 80s and 90s.

The auxiliary units based at forts further to the north might have seen more regular military action. Nonetheless, the relatively peaceful conditions across this frontier during the late first and early second centuries was probably the result of the devastation the Flavian campaigns had wrought on the communities of northern Britain. The image of peace across this extensive frontier landscape which this chapter emphasizes derives from the information the Vindolanda letters provide. Much of our knowledge of the first forty years of the conquest of Britain derives from the writings of Julius Caesar, Tacitus, and Dio. If the frontier was at peace during the late first to the early second centuries, that could actually explain the absence of surviving classical texts referring to campaigning and conquest.

Several of the letters refer to the acquisition, by purchase or import, of a wide variety of commodities, providing some indication of how the presence of the garrison at Vindolanda affected the lives of the local Iron Age peoples of the frontier. Some of the entrepreneurs and merchants who prospered by supplying Vindolanda may have been Britons, although this is not clear from the names in the letters. We read of some wagons belonging to Britons bringing grain to the garrison of the second fort.[28] This might have been food requisitioned as tax, perhaps from farms in the frontier zone or further south. The military occupation of the frontier zone may also, however, have provided opportunities for wealthy Britons living in the southern parts of the province to sell their surplus agricultural produce, which may have been transported by cart to Vindolanda and other forts in the frontier region to be sold to the soldiers living there.

TWO NEW COLONIES IN THE PROVINCE

A military diploma found at Flémalle (Belgium) is inscribed with the name Publius Metilius Nepos, the man whom Domitian probably appointed to govern Britain in 94.[29] The same diploma also tells us that Titus Avidius Quietus replaced Nepos as governor in 97. This diploma is one of several providing important information about military affairs in

Britain. On discharge from the military after a certain term of service, each auxiliary soldier was presented with such a diploma: a bronze folding tablet that granted him particular rights, usually including Roman citizenship, permission to marry, and citizenship for his wife and children.[30] Auxiliary troops were not officially allowed to marry until after they had retired, although many had unofficial families, and these diplomas granted citizenship to the soldier's whole family. Military diplomas are not uncommon finds, and they provide both vital information about the distribution of military units across the empire and insight into the lives of individual soldiers, their families, and their commanders.

All that is known about events in Britain under these two governors is that the decision was made to award colonial status to the two urban communities at Lincoln and Gloucester.[31] Before this time, the only colony in Britain was at Camulodunum, which had been established in 49 and refounded after the Boudican uprising in 60–61. Rome granted colonial status to urban communities across the empire to enhance the political position of their ruling elites. All three of the first-century colonies established in Britain were, however, designed to provide homes for military veterans from the legions. They were the highest-ranking towns in the province and had constitutions modelled on Rome itself. The formal titles of the two new colonies indicate the date when they received colonial status. Lincoln was known as *Colonia Domitiana Lindensium*, indicating that it was refounded as a colony late in the reign of Domitian, before 96. Gloucester was named *Colonia Nerviana*, indicating the granting of colonial status under Nerva, who succeeded Domitian and ruled as emperor in 96–98.

When Lincoln and Gloucester were awarded colonial status, they were already developing as urban centres on the sites of decommissioned legionary fortresses, and their populations included veterans who had decided to settle permanently at the sites of their former bases. The decommissioned fortresses at Exeter and Wroxeter were not awarded colonial status, although towns were also developing at these sites. These urban communities were awarded the lesser status of *civitas* capitals; Exeter was the capital of the Dumnonii and Wroxeter of the Cornovii. It is not entirely clear why only two new colonies were founded during the 90s. Perhaps the three colonies in Britain reflected the presence of three legions in the province after the Second Adiutrix had been moved to the Danube.

THE NINTH COHORT OF BATAVIANS AT VINDOLANDA

The third fort was constructed around 98, when the Ninth Cohort of Batavians replaced the Tungrians. Neighbours of the Tungri, the Batavians came originally from a territory in the Lower Rhine Valley. The interior of the second fort had been entirely flattened, and its successor was centred slightly further to the southwest.[32] The discoveries from the remains of this fort have provided the most exciting and remarkable insights of all the excavations at Vindolanda. Some of the most informative letters come from the fort of this third period, when the Batavians were under the command of two prefects in succession, whose names appear in the tablets.

The first, Flavius Genialis, had been appointed by around 100 and remained at Vindolanda for two or three years. Relatively little is known about activities along the Stanegate while he was in command, although one of the letters from this period, together with a commemorative inscription from Fulginiae (Umbria, Italy), provide important insights into the activities of the Roman military in the frontier lands of Britain.[33] The letter and inscription record an officer named Titus Haterius Nepos who, among his other duties, had been asked to conduct a census of a people named the Anavionenses. This people probably lived in Annandale (Dumfries and Galloway; see fig. 6.2), 45 kilometres (30 miles) northwest of Carlisle; Nepos was probably based at the fort at Corbridge while he undertook the task.

Another of the Vindolanda letters comments: 'the Britons are unprotected by armour. There are very many cavalry. The cavalry do not use swords nor do the wretched Britons [*Brittunculi*] mount in order to throw javelins'. This text may have referred to the poor quality, in Roman terms, of the auxiliaries recruited from among the Britons of the frontier regions, including the Anavionenses.[34] The reference to the lack of armour and swords is reminiscent of Tacitus' comment that the Silures and Ordovices, who fought for Caratacus against Rome in 51, had no breastplates or helmets. Iron Age weapons have been found in western and northern Britain, and members of the local elite would have had access to swords and spears. Evidently, however, this report was commenting on the absence of armour and weapons amongst the Iron Age peoples of the frontier region generally. The auxiliary recruits would then be trained up to serve in the Roman forces in other parts of the empire, following a career path already pursued by several generations of Britons.

Flavius Genialis was replaced as commander at Vindolanda by Flavius Cerialis, who is very well attested in the letters. 'Flavius' was the family name of the previous ruling dynasty in Rome and may suggest that Cerialis' father was granted Roman citizenship after 70, when the emperor Vespasian was establishing his rule.[35] The cognomen 'Cerialis' might even suggest a personal connection with Petillius Cerialis, the former governor of Britain who also led the defeat of the Batavian uprising of 69–70. That Flavius Cerialis was a Batavian may signify that his father had remained loyal to Rome during the uprising and then been rewarded with citizenship, which his son inherited. Flavius Cerialis owed his position and status at Vindolanda to his Roman citizenship and his command of the Ninth Cohort of Batavians.

Auxiliary units had traditionally been recruited to serve Rome under their own leaders, a practice that seems to have continued at Vindolanda among the Ninth Cohort of Batavians.[36] Allowing auxiliary units to be recruited from a single people could, however, result in trouble, as the desertion of the Usipi during Agricola's campaigns in Caledonia had demonstrated. By the late first century, auxiliary units were instead increasingly being formed by combining soldiers from different geographical backgrounds into a single fighting force, as the evidence for the 'mixing' of the Tungrian regiment when returned to Vindolanda indicates (discussed later). This suggests that the Batavian cohort stationed at this fort may have had a special status, enabling them to serve as a single unit under the command of a member of their own aristocracy.[37] In one letter, a certain Masclus (Masculus) asks Flavius Cerialis to send more beer for his comrades, referring to Cerialis as 'his king'. This highly unusual terminology in a Roman context suggests the survival of the traditional form of address to a member of the Batavian aristocracy and may also indicate that Masclus was being cheeky and not entirely respectful toward an authority figure.[38]

The letters also provide fascinating insights into the lifestyle of Flavius Cerialis' family, including his wife, Sulpicia Lepidina, and his children, freedmen, and slaves (see fig. 6.5). The famous birthday invitation to Lepidina from Claudia Severa, the wife of the commanding officer of another fort, shows that wives of such officers on the northern frontier created strong social bonds and were free to attend parties and family gatherings at some distance from their homes.[39] This suggests that such women were able to travel in the frontier region, although they would surely have required a military guard. Fragments of several other tablets contain well-known quotations from Virgil's *Aeneid* and *Georgics* and were probably exercises to teach the commander's children to write in Latin.[40]

The commanding officer's house within the fort has been partly excavated, revealing, among other things, that Cerialis and his family had access to luxuries at Vindolanda, including wine, olives, and spices as well as chickens and geese.[41] Built of timber and floored with bracken, this house was constructed around a courtyard in the manner of a Mediterranean villa. The excavations at the fort have also produced a vast quantity of leather shoes in styles and sizes that indicate the gender, age, and status of their wearers. Those from the commanding officer's house have been described as 'very high-end' and included fashionable and well-made shoes for women and children. One sandal in particular, clearly an expensive and fashionable item, probably belonged to Lepidina herself. Cerialis' house was typical of commanding officer's houses at Roman forts across Britain, indicating the senior status of these important individuals. Legionary commanders and provincial governors had even greater status, reflected in their households' access to more slaves and greater quantities of luxuries.

The letters also provide information about the role of the soldiers stationed at Vindolanda in building projects, in manufacturing, and in acquiring food.[42] It was always assumed that auxiliary forts across Britain were built by legionary construction teams, with the auxiliary units moving into the completed forts. Scenes depicted on Trajan's Column in

Rome, which commemorates the conquest of Dacia during the early second century, show legionary soldiers constructing military fortifications during the campaign, although it should not be assumed that this carving was intended to represent the actions of campaigning in accurate detail. A letter from the third fort certainly has cast some doubt on the idea that all building work at this fort was entirely undertaken by legionaries.[43] It lists a work party, including twelve men, who were to build the bathhouse, suggesting that auxiliaries helped to construct or maintain some of the buildings. The remains of the bathhouse at Vindolanda, just to the south of the south-east corner of the fort, have also been excavated (fig. 6.7). Unlike the other buildings of the fort, the bathhouse required large quantities of brick, tile, and stone. As the remains of buildings like these indicate, by the 90s the Mediterranean style of bathing had spread among both auxiliary and legionary units throughout Britain. Moreover, bathing was not available to the officers only, and some of the Vindolanda letters show that soldiers in the ranks spent money on soap and towels. Other

FIG 6.7.
The late first-century bathhouse at Vindolanda from the air (Copyright: Vindolanda Trust)

leisure activities for the officers, such as hunting with dogs, were a key feature of Roman elite entertainment. Two leather boxing gloves found during recent excavations indicate another pastime of the soldiers stationed at the fort.

A record of a brewer called Atrectus appears among other entries on an accounts list. He may even have been based at Vindolanda, for beer appears to have been widely available there.[44] The discovery of such a range of written documents, providing information about ordinary, everyday life, emphasizes the extent of literacy among the military community.[45] The variability of handwriting styles may suggest that many, if not all, of the soldiers were literate. Although it is no surprise that commanding officers such as Flavius Cerialis and their families were able to speak and to write in Latin, the tablets show the extent to which literacy was fundamental to the entire community of the fort, for managing military activities, and for social and economic life. The letters concerning commercial activity indicate that traders also needed to be able to communicate in a common language, attesting the supply of a wide range of goods that soldiers at the fort were able to purchase.

The information from these excavations has also challenged the image of Roman forts as predominantly masculine environments.[46] During the first and second century common soldiers were not officially allowed to marry. Comments in classical texts have suggested that the presence of women was considered contrary to proper military discipline, and it used to be assumed that women and children did not accompany military units on campaign. Recent discoveries indicate, however, that women and children were an integral part of the military communities that developed everywhere on the frontiers of the Roman empire. At Vindolanda, although soldiers would have made up the greater proportion of the personnel, women and children were also present in considerable numbers (see fig. 6.6). The recovery of shoes of many sizes and types from the excavated deposits clearly demonstrates their presence, including many items of footwear notably less 'high-end' than those from the commanding officer's house. Military men were often accompanied by slaves, and this may be how many women and children came to live at Vindolanda.[47]

One of the letters was sent from a slave named Severus to another slave, Candidus, referring to payment for an item connected with the Saturnalia, the December festival at which slaves were allowed to change places with their masters.[48] This is one of the few letters providing any information about the religious beliefs and practices of the inhabitants of the garrison. We also read of the celebration of the *Matronalia*, a festival held in honour of the goddess Juno Lucina, who was associated with childbirth.[49] The idea of slaves exchanging places with their masters would have been attractive, as most slaves would have led miserable lives with little influence over their destinies. These documents indicate that some of the women living on the Roman frontier, however, led lives of privilege and leisure. Flavius Cerialis was an important military commander with high status in this frontier community, and his wife, Lepidina, and his children were the wealthiest family at Vindolanda. Although their domestic slaves may have been treated with some respect, they will have had little real freedom.

Even though information about the lives of slaves in Roman Britain is limited, one piece of evidence to survive is a writing tablet from London that records the sale of the Gallic slave Fortunata, listing her value as 600 denarii and stating that she is in good health and unlikely to run away.[50] Although Fortunata was certainly too valuable to be destined for a brothel, female and male prostitution was common in Roman society, and may provide another explanation for some of the shoes of women and children at Vindolanda.[51] Life was nasty, brutish, and short for many slaves, female and male alike, and Roman military life, like Roman politics, was dominated by powerful men.

REINFORCING THE STANEGATE UNDER TRAJAN

Trajan succeeded Nerva as emperor in 98, already an accomplished commander with military experience in Spain and Germany. Trajan craved further military glory and led two wars against the kingdom of Dacia in 101–2 and 105–6 which resulted in the acquisition of a new province for the empire.[52] The strategy in Britain during Trajan's reign, by contrast, was of retrenchment, and clearly indicates that the conquest of the north was no longer a priority. A military diploma from Malpas (Cheshire) records that Lucius Neratius Marcellus, one of a pair of distinguished brothers from Saepinum in Italy, was appointed by Trajan to govern Britain in 103 and may have continued in the post until 105–6.[53] Marcellus was nevertheless a man of very limited military experience, suggesting a shortage of suitable candidates as the result of the deployment of many more experienced commanders in the Dacian Wars as well as lack of interest on the part of the new Emperor in further campaigning in Britain.

Details in several letters from the third fort at Vindolanda suggest that Marcellus thoroughly reorganized and strengthened the garrison of the Stanegate (see fig. 6.3). This was necessary, in part, because the military forces available to him continued to be reduced by the removal of troops to fight in Dacia. Information for military withdrawals is scarce, but we know that the Ninth Cohort of Batavians left Vindolanda for Dacia in around 105.[54] To maintain a stable frontier, therefore, Marcellus moved units from other parts of Britain to the Stanegate. The remaining forts in southern Scotland were probably abandoned at this time, and as Wales gradually became settled, the auxiliaries stationed there were also reduced.[55] During the first decades of the second century, some forts in Wales were maintained. This was evidently part of a flexible strategy of military occupation, aimed both at keeping control over newly conquered peoples still requiring to be settled and, in all likelihood, at guarding against any possible incursions from across the Irish Sea. Auxiliary manpower, however, was increasingly concentrated along the northern frontier.

The Stanegate was reinforced as the frontier was redesigned to form a 'closed' system of control.[56] This included the rebuilding of the forts at Corbridge, Vindolanda, and Carlisle and the addition of further troops stationed along the line of the Stanegate. The network was designed to support and protect military traffic travelling along this important east–west corridor of communication while also fulfilling the vital role of patrolling the fords across the rivers just to the south of the Stanegate.[57] The soldiers in the forts and fortlets along this communication route superintended movement across the line, first and foremost to prevent unauthorised incursions into Roman lands.

Before this time, Roman frontiers in Britain had operated as 'open' zones of control, bases from which military forces could move forward to conquer additional territory. The garrisoning of Agricola's forces along the *terminus* on his advance at the Clyde-Forth line, for example, had formed only a temporary halt, and was crossed the year after it was established in 81 during the campaign into Caledonia. The 'closing' of the Stanegate frontier during the early second century was part of a broader strategy that was also implemented along the Rhine and Danube during Trajan's reign.[58] Although these rivers in Germany had played a significant role in Roman military strategy for over a century, the change in policy focused on exercising closer control over people who wished to enter Roman territory from the northern lands in Britain and Germany.

Despite the increase in its garrison, however, the Stanegate did not extend right across the neck of low-lying land separating the Solway Firth from the mouth of the River Tyne. No Roman forts have been located to the east of Corbridge, leaving a length of the north bank of the Tyne apparently ungarrisoned for 45 kilometres (30 miles).[59] Despite searches for forts along this bank for over a century, none have been found, which tends to indicate that fortification did not continue east from Corbridge to the coast. To the east of Corbridge, there were several fords across the Tyne which would have made it possible for people living north of the frontier to cross into Roman lands by bypassing the Stanegate at its eastern end. The open character of the Tyne section of the frontier probably indicates that a treaty of friendship had been agreed with the people living to the north-east of Corbridge.[60]

There is evidence of a parallel strategy in operation on the Danube frontier, where a Germanic people known as the Hermunduri were allowed to cross the river into Roman territory without hindrance to trade while the other Germanic peoples 'see only our arms and our forts'.[61] The Hermunduri must have been able to control the fords and river crossings spanning the Danube, regulating the movements of people travelling from their lands into the empire. Their provision of this security meant that Roman fortifications were not required. The absence of military infrastructure along the Tyne to the east of Corbridge suggests that a comparable treaty existed here, ensuring that an open frontier could be maintained. Any movement of people across the line of the Stanegate to the west, meanwhile, was closely supervised by the soldiers stationed at the forts.

This strategic arrangement on the frontier was dictated by the topography of the lands through which the Stanegate ran, as well as by the character of the Iron Age peoples who occupied them. There were many Iron Age enclosed settlements in the area of the northern frontier.[62] Across the upland ground, including the vicinity of Vindolanda, these enclosed settlements were usually small in scale and dispersed, indicating a preference for pastoral farming. Relatively little is known about the settlements in the Cumbrian plain to the west of the Stanegate, although excavations on the low-lying Northumberland coastal plain, to the north-east of the Stanegate, have indicated a densely settled farming landscape. The substantial scale of these settlements suggests that these communities were capable of producing a considerable agricultural surplus, from which the Roman garrison was supplied. For example, one Iron Age settlement that has been extensively excavated was almost as large as a Roman auxiliary fort (fig. 6.8). The amount of labour involved in constructing the enclosures surrounding these settlements clearly illustrates that these Iron Age peoples were not the primitive barbarians depicted on Roman tombstones. Their long-established agricultural regimes required that peace and order be maintained.

Where these settlements have been excavated, finds of Roman goods are comparatively rare, although fragments of wheel-made pottery, amphorae, and a few Roman coins have occasionally been discovered.[63] Other finds from these Iron Age sites include quern-stones, handmade pottery, and glass bangles. This scarcity of Roman finds forms a dramatic contrast with the vast quantities found when forts have been excavated; the Roman troops were very well supplied with wine, foodstuffs, and pottery, and were paid in cash. The lack of Roman coins on the excavated Iron Age settlements of the frontier zone suggests that surplus agricultural supplies, including grain and livestock, were requisitioned from these communities as tax. It seems unlikely that local farmers traded their surpluses to the fort garrisons, since they did not take any quantity of coins or pottery home in return.

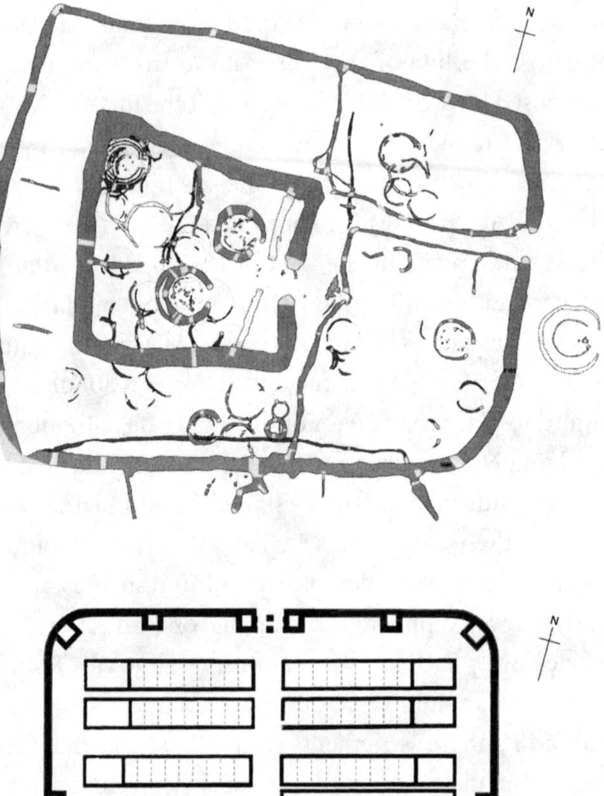

FIG 6.8.

Comparative plans of an excavated Iron Age settlement from the coastal plain north of Newcastle (top) and the Roman fort at Wallsend (bottom), drawn to the same scale (redrawn from an image by Nick Hodgson, with permission)

That some trading was occurring is indicated by the archaeological finds from a significant site at Great Whittington (Northumberland). This lies 7 kilometres (5 miles) to the north of Corbridge by the side of a Roman road known as the Devil's Causeway.[64] Iron Age items, Roman coins, and brooches have been located by metal detecting at this site, which, as it was situated just beyond the eastern limits of the Stanegate, probably served as a local market. The number of Roman coins at Great Whittington peaked during the late first and early second centuries, before the building of Hadrian's Wall, although later coins indicate that the market continued to be frequented in later years. The treaty with the local people living in the area to the north-east and east of Corbridge would have secured safe access for traders to this market, which served the peoples living to the north of the frontier. Little more is known about this Iron Age people, although they were evidently capable of maintaining peace along an extensive length of the frontier for several decades, enabling them to keep the terms of their treaty with Rome.

THE TUNGRIANS RETURN TO VINDOLANDA

The name of Marcellus' successor as governor of Britain is unknown, although Marcus Atilius Metilius Bradua may have been serving as governor around 111.[65] The Stanegate required continuous management, and a garrison was maintained in the forts and fortlets. When the Ninth Cohort of Batavians was redeployed to Dacia, the First Cohort of Tungrians, after an absence of ten years, returned to garrison the fourth fort at Vindolanda. A completely new fort was built on top of the remains of the earlier forts. It was the largest of the four early forts at Vindolanda and may have garrisoned 700 men at full capacity. Military strategy on the Stanegate remained highly flexible.[66] One letter from this fourth fort mentions the supply of grain to soldiers, including legionaries. Another contains a record of sums received and debts outstanding, referring to the Vardullian cavalrymen, a unit originally raised in northern Spain. The barracks for the Vardullian cavalry was recently located and excavated.[67] The Tungrians clearly continued to constitute the main garrison, although the makeup of this cohort may have become more varied as a result of reinforcement by soldiers from other frontier areas of the empire, such as Spain.

The Military Community

The distribution of footwear from the excavations at Vindolanda suggests that women and children continued to live within the fort during the early second century.[68] In addition to the nonmilitary personnel living within the ramparts, an extramural settlement was also developing in an area to the north of the period 3 and 4 forts. Settlements (*vici*), lying outside the gates of forts, were a regular feature of the northern frontier landscape of Hadrian's Wall during the late second and early third centuries (discussed later). The recent excavations at Vindolanda and Carlisle, however, have indicated that extramural settlements were also an element of military life on the northern frontier earlier than this: from the late first century. In addition to the wives and children of the troops living in the fort, these military communities would have included people attracted to trade with the garrison.

The Vindolanda letters include references to a shrine, cottage, brewery, and guesthouse, indicating that an extramural settlement was developing during the late first and early second centuries. Part of this settlement, which lay to the north of the early forts, has been excavated.[69] A particularly important recent discovery is that the wattle-and-daub structures of the houses in the extramural settlement that developed alongside the period 4 fort included several round and rectangular buildings. A large assemblage of finds was uncovered, including stylus pens, writing tablets, shoes, and Roman coins. The roundhouses were an Iron Age building tradition and were probably the homes of Britons who had settled in the *vicus*. Vindolanda may not have been the only fort where Britons were settling; excavations at Carlisle, another of the Stanegate forts, have uncovered a roundhouse, as well as rectangular buildings, just outside the fort gates.[70]

Some of the people who were drawn to live outside the forts at Vindolanda and Carlisle may have moved from Iron Age settlements in the frontier region nearby so as to exploit the economic opportunities the military community offered. This is uncertain, however, since roundhouses were a common building type throughout Britain during the early second century, and these settlers may equally have travelled to live on the Stanegate from further south in the province. They might even have been families who had moved south from beyond the Stanegate frontier. Nevertheless, the development of these extramural settlements is an additional indication, along with the open character of the eastern part of the frontier along the River Tyne, that the personnel of the military garrison of the Stanegate were cooperating with the Britons who were drawn to trade with them.

This situation indicates that the Roman commanders overseeing the fort garrisons were seeking to create stable conditions along the northern frontier. Across the south of the province, many of the fortresses and forts constructed during the initial phases of the conquest had attracted extramural settlements. The continued Roman presence provided opportunities for local people to offer various services to the soldiers. That the soldiers were paid in coin enabled them to buy goods and services from traders living close to their forts. When territories became settled and the military forces moved forward, towns developed on the sites of their decommissioned garrisons. This is how the *civitas* capitals at Exeter and Wroxeter originated during the first century. The extramural settlements at the Stanegate forts indicate that a comparable process was under way, suggesting that conditions on the frontier were relatively peaceful.

Sacred Waters

Excavation at forts along the Stanegate has produced information about the religious beliefs of the soldiers stationed there, providing a reminder that Roman conquest was as much a religious as a military activity. One remarkable discovery, made at Vindolanda in 2012, was a fragmentary inscription lending insight into the worship of the water goddess Ahvardua, who was not previously attested in the Roman Empire.[71] We know the names of several different goddesses who were worshiped at sacred springs across the province of Britain, including Sulis Minerva, whose cult was at the focus of the classical temple and baths at Bath.[72] Coventina, another water goddess, was worshipped at a temple outside one of the forts on Hadrian's Wall later in the second century (discussed later).

The inscription from Vindolanda records a dedication to the goddess Ahvardua by the First Cohort of Tungrians. In the course of earlier excavations, a stone temple was found on high ground close to a spring the Tungrians attributed to her. During the earlier decades of fort construction, this spring had been channelled into a number of stone basins; it may have been a sacred location even before the Romans arrived on the Stanegate. Iron Age peoples viewed rivers, pools, and springs as sacred sites, as witnessed by the many offerings found in such contexts.[73] The spring at the temple of Sulis Minerva at Bath is also thought to have been sacred in the Iron Age before it was converted into an important Roman cult site. Although Ahvardua's temple was built several decades after the first Tungrian garrison arrived at Vindolanda, they may have adopted the worship of a goddess from the local people.

The exact meaning of the Celtic name Ahvardua is uncertain, although it probably signified 'high water' or even 'high tide water'. Although Vindolanda is far from the sea, in the central section of the frontier, the reference to the tide in the name of this spring goddess might perhaps have referred to her identity as a child of Oceanus. All sources of water in the Roman world were considered to be the offspring of this ancient divinity. The water flowed from Ahvardua's spring into a brook that fed the River South Tyne, which then flowed east into the sea. The numinous presence of watery deities was attributed to the rivers and springs of the frontier landscape. Maintaining a friendly relationship with such deities during the construction of the forts along the Stanegate would have formed an element in the diplomacy of creating control and order along the frontier.

BRITAIN AT THE TIME OF TRAJAN'S DEATH

Trajan died in 117 after a highly successful reign. He had led the Roman Empire to impressive military victories leading to the incorporation of new territories, including Dacia, into the empire. It was even more significant for his legacy that, unlike many of his predecessors, he had remained popular with the Senate in Rome. He had become known by the title 'Best' (*Optimus*), which survived his death. The policy of the governors he appointed to manage Britain had been to hold the frontier with reduced manpower, as lowland Scotland was abandoned. Roman control over the northern peoples was maintained by diplomacy and by threats of violence if communities did not remain at peace and willingly pay their taxes. The territories to the south of the Stanegate had been conquered and largely subdued by this time, although some forts across Wales and central Britain remained garrisoned.

The distribution of forts over an extensive area of central Britain demonstrates that the frontier was a wide military zone where the presence of soldiers was required to maintain order and to collect taxes from the local population. The relative peace characterizing the state of the northern frontier was, at least in part, the result of the effort of the Roman military command to establish friendly relations with local people across the frontier region. It stands in stark contrast to the lengthy conflicts with Dacia on Rome's frontier on the Danube. Five decades of conflict across mainland Britain appear to have temporarily exhausted the will of the northern Britons to resist. This situation was about to change, however, as serious trouble erupted on the frontier at about the time Hadrian succeeded Trajan as emperor.

7

EMPEROR OF THE OCEAN

Lord of the waves, Father of the sea, Arbiter of the globe,
Oh Ocean, who embraces all things in your placid loop,
You who regulate the land within your confining limits
You who form every sea, spring and lake . . .

—Hymn to Oceanus[1]

WHEN THE ELDERLY EMPEROR Trajan died in August 117, his adopted heir and successor, Hadrian, faced uprisings on several frontiers of the empire. One of the few texts to mention Britain during Hadrian's reign explains that he resumed the policy of some of his predecessors in devoting his attention to making peace. This was because 'the nations conquered by Trajan were in revolt; the Moors were on the rampage; Britons could not be kept under Roman control; Egypt was ravaged by uprisings; finally, Libya and Palestine displayed a spirit of rebellion'.[2] Trajan had made extensive territorial conquests in his search for military glory, including in Dacia and Parthia. Indeed, the Roman Empire reached its greatest extent under his rule. In view of the problems created by his predecessor's policy of expansion, Hadrian quickly abandoned three of the new provinces (Armenia, Mesopotamia, and Assyria) and turned his attention to securing the imperial frontiers. During his lengthy reign, he travelled throughout these frontier provinces, inspecting the troops and making reforms. Britain was one of the first provinces to receive an imperial visit, as it was one of several requiring urgent attention.

QUELLING AN UPRISING

As we are told that the Britons could not be kept under control, this may suggest that there was a serious uprising in the province at about the time Hadrian assumed power. Another brief account of the troubles of his reign, written forty years after it ended, records 'what great numbers of soldiers were killed by the Jews, what great numbers by the Britons!'[3] The Jewish revolt of 132–35 resulted in a massive loss of life in the Roman military, and the coupling of the Britons with the Jews as enemies of Rome implies that an equally disastrous uprising may have occurred in Britain. In the spring of 118, Hadrian swiftly appointed Pompeius Falco governor of Britain.[4] He had significant previous military experience, including the command of a legion during Trajan's First Dacian War and the governing of the unsettled province of Judaea. The successive decisions by Domitian and Trajan to withdraw portions of the military forces stationed in Britain and send them to fight on the Danube also suggests that Falco may have had to make the best of a depleted garrison in his efforts to settle the uprising.

The surviving fragments of a dedicatory inscription from a victory monument discovered at the mouth of the River Tyne (discussed later) are thought to say that a frontier (Hadrian's Wall) was established between the two shores of the Ocean after the 'scattering of the barbarians'. Another inscription, from Vindolanda on the Stanegate, commemorates an officer named Titus Annius of the First Cohort of Tungrians who was 'killed in the war'.[5] The exact date of Annius' death is uncertain, as is his exact rank, although one possibility is that he was the commanding officer of the garrison at Vindolanda, in which case he would have been a very serious loss. The inscription is thought to have come from a mausoleum, and the wording suggests that his comrades were unable to recover his remains from the battlefield. Since they had not been able to lay them to rest, his friends were concerned that he would return to haunt them as a ghost, and to avoid this the mausoleum was raised as a cenotaph to his memory.

It was once thought that during this uprising, the Ninth Legion was wiped out at an unidentified location to the north of the Stanegate. The idea remains current, as it formed the central premise of the enduringly popular novel *The Eagle of the Ninth*, which was several times adapted for BBC Radio and Television in the twentieth century and more recently inspired the film *The Eagle* (2011).[6] The latest indication of the presence of the Ninth in Britain is an inscription dated to 108 from the fortress at York, although the legion is believed to have remained in the province for some years after this date.[7] It is now known that a detachment of troops from the Ninth was stationed at Nijmegen (*Noviomagus*, Netherlands) on the Rhine during the early second century.[8] It has often been suggested that the Ninth cannot have been wiped out in Britain. The considerable disruption during the early years of Hadrian's reign and the substantial scale of the wall he ordered constructed during the early 120s has led to a reassessment of the information. It is now again thought that the Ninth may have suffered a serious defeat on the northern frontier in Britain and been disbanded.[9] This would have been the third occasion on which a legion suffered defeat in Britain.

The Restoration of Order

One clear indication of Rome's determination to restore order to Britain is provided by an issue of coins, produced between 119 and 121, that feature an image of Britannia in divine form (fig. 7.1a).[10] Other coins issued during Hadrian's reign depict many of the provinces of the empire as divinities, illustrating its extent and the variety of peoples it had subsumed. Each province is shown with a distinctive symbol. Hispania, for example, grasps an olive branch, to indicate the large-scale production of olive oil. Britannia is portrayed as a hooded divinity sitting upright on a rock and armed with a spear and a shield with a spiked boss. The hooded cloak (*birrus Britannicus*), a characteristic British garment, serves to indicate the cold climate, while the rocks on which Britannia sits represent the wildness of these outlying frontier lands of the empire. On coins of Hadrian Dacia is also shown armed and sitting on rocks.

FIG 7.1.
Two coins of Hadrian: (a) Britannia (reverse) (Copyright: Roma Numismatics Ltd, lot no. 598, E-sale 22; https://www.acsearch.info/search.html?id=2775844, reproduced with permission); (b) Oceanus reclining on a dolphin, holding an anchor, and distinguished by the crab's claws on his head (Copyright: National Museum of Wales, NMGW no. 2008. 19H/421, DAL 40441, DAL 40442)

An earlier representation of Britannia in human form, from the imperial sanctuary at Aphrodisias, portrayed the divine Claudius overwhelming the province (see fig 3.4). Seventy years had passed since the commissioning of this sculpture, and the image of Britannia on the coins of Hadrian illustrates a change in perceptions at Rome. This image reflected eighty years of campaigning in Britain, during which civic life had been introduced across the southern lands and a large number of auxiliary troops recruited from the province to serve Rome.[11] The coins also portray Hadrian's determination to hold on to Britannia as an imperial possession.

HADRIAN COMMANDS THE CONSTRUCTION OF THE WALL

A classical text explains that 'having reformed the soldiers in royal fashion [in Germany], he [Hadrian] set out for Britain, where he corrected many things and, as the first to do so, built a wall for eighty miles, which was to separate the barbarians from the Romans'.[12] This statement suggests that the order to build the wall was given when Hadrian visited Britain in 122. In reality it is likely that his initial directive was issued the previous year, when he was making his plans to visit the provinces of Germany, Britain, and Gaul.[13] He is thought to have issued the order before his arrival, so he could inspect the building work along the frontier during his expedition to Britain. The work to construct the Roman frontier (*limes*) along the Rhine and Danube in Germany also commenced during 121.[14]

Hadrian was famous for his appreciation of Greek culture, and he may have drawn on his knowledge of the long walls of classical Greece in creating his plan for the frontier in Britain. Many of these walls were constructed across narrow necks of land.[15] During previous military campaigns, Roman commanders had rarely built linear fortifications, and the frontier works constructed in Germany and Britain under Hadrian were an innovation. The Stanegate under Trajan, for instance, was a patrolled road with troops stationed along its line, not a line of fortifications. The regularity of Hadrian's Wall as initially planned, including the stone curtain and the milecastles (fortlets) and turrets along its length, suggests that it was designed according to a blueprint Hadrian supplied. This regularity of the design was remarkably at odds with the highly flexible strategy of frontier defence practiced along the Stanegate road during previous decades.[16]

The wall was to be constructed just to the north of the Stanegate road and the rivers its forts controlled (fig. 7.2). Hadrian ordered the construction of linear defensive works in many of the frontier areas of the empire.

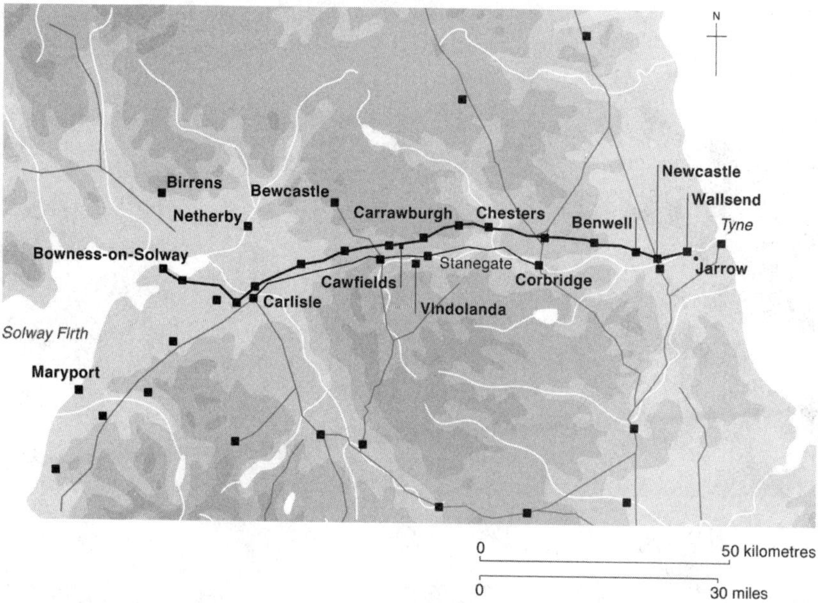

FIG 7.2.
Hadrian's Wall and the northern frontier (after Bidwell and Hodgson 2009, fig. 6, with additions)

The wall in Britain was a particularly substantial example, reflecting the unsettled conditions in Britain at the start of Hadrian's rule, which evidently required a substantial and monumental frontier. It is significant that the wall was mostly constructed of stone: a direct contrast with the building of earlier forts and fortresses from timber and earth (fig. 7.3). The excavations of the four successive early forts at Vindolanda indicate problems with constructing fortifications and buildings in turf and timber, since they required regular rebuilding. The earliest example in Britain of the Roman practice of using stone to build such fortifications was at the fortress at Inchtuthil in the mid-80s. Here the timber and earth ramparts were supplemented with a stone facing wall. The ramparts surrounding the other fortresses and colonies of Britain were refaced with stone during the early second century, and Hadrian's new wall was mainly to be constructed from the same material.

Building in stone provided a clear indication that the military installation was intended to be permanent, and Hadrian may also have regarded

FIG 7.3.
The curtain wall of Hadrian's Wall at Cuddy's Crags (Photograph by Richard Hingley)

stone as a more prestigious building material than earth and timber. A monumental inscription at Lambaesis (Tazzoult, Algeria) records a speech he delivered to troops on his visit to North Africa in which he commended a cavalry unit, the Second Cohort of Spaniards, for its proficiency in building a highly regular rampart from 'huge, heavy, and uneven blocks of stone', contrasting this with the works of other units who had constructed temporary turf walls it was possible to build 'without trouble', from materials that were 'smooth and malleable'.[17] His words imply that the building of military fortifications in stone was a more difficult task but created a more regular and satisfying result. Such a wall, in addition, made the statement that the Roman military forces had found a place to remain, and that decades of attempting to push the frontier forward were at an end.

The use of such immense quantities of stone to build forts may also reflect the fact that timber of the required size and quality was in short supply across the frontier region in Britain.[18] Pollen analysis indicates that much of the tree-cover had been cleared from these lands before the Romans arrived. The Iron Age communities would have managed local timber resources to provide building materials for their own settlements, but the construction of the Stanegate forts during the previous decades would have depleted the available timber. The Roman military used local materials to construct their fortifications and may not have had access to sufficient quantities of wood in this case. The scale and essential uniformity of Hadrian's Wall, however, also reflected his directive to create a highly regular, impressive, and permanent frontier; to this end, stone may always have been the material of choice.

The curtain wall was to be about 3.5–4.5 metres high; it probably originally supported an elevated sentry walk and parapet. The highly regular original plan for the wall included gateways at each of the milecastles to provide access across the line of the frontier.[19] To maintain surveillance along the entire frontier line, two turrets were constructed between each pair of milecastles. The wall was initially intended to run from the Solway Firth in the west to Newcastle upon Tyne in the east, and the line was surveyed and marked out as construction began. The eastern two-thirds was built in stone, and the western third, initially, of turf. Broadly comparable in form to the stone curtain, the turf wall was later rebuilt in stone.

Once the line the wall was to follow had been surveyed, the foundations of the curtain wall were laid along much of its course. According to surviving evidence for the sequence of building, a few of the milecastles and turrets were also constructed before the curtain wall was raised. These advance phases of construction were probably dictated by the emperor's wish to inspect some of the works in an already completed condition during his visit to Britain.[20] Along the north side of the wall, a large V-shaped ditch was separated from it by a berm. The ditch was continuous, except where the precipitous crags in the central part of the wall made it unnecessary. Between the ditch and the curtain wall, at certain points along the frontier, forked branches were inserted into the berm as an obstacle to attackers approaching from the north.[21] It is not clear whether these were an original feature of the wall or were added later.

Several of the forts along the Stanegate were retained as bases for the soldiers who manned the milecastles. These included those located at Carlisle, Vindolanda, and Corbridge. Hadrian's Wall was also designed to harness the potential of rivers to serve as natural barriers along the course of the frontier. In this way, a far more structured frontier system was created which blocked and controlled movement along the traditional routes crossing the frontier. The seventy-nine milecastles could accommodate a garrison of approximately 2,500 auxiliary soldiers, divided into small units, to enforce Roman authority across the frontier. A charge was probably also levied on any civilians who were permitted to cross the wall.

The construction of selected milecastles and turrets along the line as a first stage of the building campaign may also have been a deliberate strategy. It would have enabled the troops involved in the building works to observe activity in the surrounding landscape while operations were under way. The construction of the wall had an immense impact upon the landscape and would have created considerable unrest among the communities inhabiting the frontier lands.

Renewed Troubles

Indeed, the scale of the works required to construct the wall appears to have escalated unsettled conditions along the frontier. Although Roman auxiliaries had garrisoned these lands for over four decades, diplomacy had helped to maintain friendly relations with some of the local people. The scale of the building works involved the arrival of many thousands of legionary and additional auxiliary soldiers, which must have placed a considerable strain on the treaties. The construction project also necessitated the requisitioning of immense quantities of stone, timber, and turf from along the entire course of the wall.[22] Building works on the wall would have increased the traffic on the Stanegate, and during the early 120s, substantial resources were allocated to providing a metalled surface for this road. The construction of the temporary camps, the curtain wall, the ditch, and the milecastles drove local people from their lands, and it is clear from excavations that the various components of the fortification were built across previously cultivated and occupied territory.[23] The frontier works also severely limited the ability of local people to travel around the lands their ancestors had occupied and farmed for generations. The wall was designed to close, or at the very least tightly control, access along ancient tracks and routes, severely restricting the movements of farmers, traders, and people visiting their kin.

One indication of the scale of this disruption is that the treaty of friendship maintaining peace on the frontier to the east of the Stanegate collapsed at about the time the wall was under construction. As mentioned earlier, the northern bank of the River Tyne to the east of Corbridge had been left unfortified when the Stanegate was established, allowing local people to ford the river and gain access to the Roman province. The building of the wall, which extended from sea to sea, entirely closed this open section of the frontier. As a result of this disruption, long-established farming communities across the Northumbrian coastal plain abandoned their settlements.[24] While this may have been the direct result of Roman aggression, it is also possible these people, when faced with the prospect of a closed frontier line, chose to move to join friends and kin living in the lands to the south of the wall. As a result, a wide area of agricultural land beyond the eastern section of the frontier was abandoned. Roman aggression may also have pushed the Iron Age communities living just outside the central and western sections of the wall much further to the north, leaving an area of unoccupied territory immediately beyond the frontier along the entire course of the wall.

HADRIAN IN BRITAIN

Hadrian travelled to Germany, Britain, and Gaul at the start of a sustained programme of touring the frontier provinces. His visits, during which he introduced reforms, were primarily tours of inspection of military organization. A description of his actions in 121–22 describes how, 'travelling through one province after another, visiting the various regions and cities and inspecting all the garrisons and forts... he [Hadrian] personally examined and investigated absolutely everything, not merely the usual accessories of the camps, including weapons, trenches, ramparts, and palisades, but also the private affairs of everyone'.[25] Coins issued later in Hadrian's reign depict him inspecting soldiers in frontier provinces around the empire, including Britain.[26]

When Hadrian travelled to Britain from Germany, he probably sailed from the mouth of the River Rhine to the Tyne estuary, at the eastern end of the course chosen for his new wall. He would have crossed the Channel at some point between April and September 122, the favoured time for crossing Ocean. A substantial entourage accompanied him, including his wife, the empress Sabina, and a detachment of the praetorian guard.[27] Two accounts tell of him dismissing several officials during his visit and spying on others. He may have remained in Britain for only a few weeks. We know nothing about his activities, even where in Britain he travelled, other than that he brought military reinforcements with him. The legionary and auxiliary forces accompanying him indicate the importance he attributed to securing control over the British frontier.

By mid-July 122, Hadrian appointed Platorius Nepos as governor of Britain.[28] Nepos, who had previously governed the province of Lower Germany, was accompanied on his journey to Britain by the Sixth Victrix, one of the legions already under his command. The Sixth had been based at Xanten (*Vetera*, Germany) and now moved to the fortress at York, where it replaced the Ninth, which by this date had already left Britain or been disbanded. An inscription from Viterbo (*Ferentium*, Italy), honouring Titus Pontius Sabinus, indicates that Hadrian's expedition also brought to Britain three legionary detachments, a total of 3,000 troops.[29] Sabinus commanded detachments from the Seventh Gemina, Eighth Augusta, and Twenty-Second Primigenia, which probably provided some of the skilled masons and engineers required for the immense task of constructing the wall. The name Junius Dubitatus, a soldier of the Eighth, is known, since he accidentally dropped a shield inscribed with his name over the side of a boat while his unit was either landing at or disembarking from a port at the mouth of the Tyne.

Although much of the building work on the wall was undertaken by legionaries, the forts, when constructed, were manned by auxiliary units, reflecting the common Roman policy of placing noncitizen soldiers on the front line. One of the auxiliary units brought to Britain to construct the wall was the First Cohort of Spaniards, commanded by Marcus Maenius Agrippa.[30] An inscription from Camerino (*Camerinum*, Italy) records information about Agrippa's career, mentioning that he was 'singled out by ... Hadrian and sent on the British expedition' with this unit. Agrippa was a friend of Hadrian and was also later appointed to command the

British fleet. Information about Agrippa and the cohort under his command is provided by four altars found at the fort at Maryport (*Alauna*) on the coast of Cumbria, newly constructed at this time. Dedicated by Agrippa and the First Cohort of Spaniards to the most popular of the gods, Jupiter the Best and Greatest (Jupiter Optimus Maximus), these altars were built as offerings by the key Roman garrison on the Cumbrian coast during the years following their arrival.

A military diploma from Szõny (*Brigetio*) in Hungary provides considerable information about the military personnel stationed in Britain at this point, listing fifty auxiliary units, including thirty-seven infantry cohorts and thirteen cavalry *alae*, discharging soldiers on 17 July 122.[31] The unusually large number of veterans recorded on the diploma suggests that at least one ceremony was organized to coincide with Hadrian's visit, enabling him to address the soldiers assembled on the British frontier. Military order had evidently been reestablished there: otherwise, so many soldiers could not have retired at this time. The diploma records many of the auxiliary units stationed in Britain; it has been estimated that around fourteen additional units had no veterans retiring during Hadrian's visit.

The Szõny diploma was presented to a cavalryman, Gemellus, a Pannonian by birth (from Hungary) who had been third-in-command of thirty men. He returned home when he retired; as already mentioned, many other veterans remained close to the bases in Britain where they had last served. The sixty-four light infantry and cavalry units stationed in the province suggests an auxiliary strength of around 38,000 troops, although these units may not all have been operating at full strength.[32] The three legions would have amounted to 15,000 men, and since a further 3,000 legionaries were brought to Britain as part of Hadrian's expedition, the total provincial garrison may be estimated at 55,000 men.[33] The initial invasion force under Claudius had numbered between 30,000 and 40,000 troops. Although the size of the provincial garrison had fluctuated according to the ambitions of successive emperors, Hadrian considerably increased it. A tenth of the total of the military forces available to Rome across the entire empire where then based in Britain, guarding a province that constituted only around 4 percent of the total land area held by Rome.

The population of the province of Britannia is estimated to have been about 2,000,000.[34] These people were based predominantly in rural settlements, since the towns were not heavily populated at this time. London, the largest of the towns, is thought to have been home to about 26,000 people. This suggests that the Roman garrison may have constituted 3 percent of the total population of Britain when Hadrian visited. Most of these military personnel were stationed along the frontier. The legionaries were occupied with constructing the wall and the auxiliaries with assisting with building work and garrisoning both the Stanegate forts and, as they were completed, the milecastles of the new frontier line. The ceremony at which the retiring troops received their diplomas may have been held at the eastern end of the wall at Newcastle.

Bridging the Tyne and the Harnessing of Ocean

The bridge over the river at Newcastle bore the emperor's name, and he probably visited the site during the summer of 122.[35] He may have delivered his speech to the assembled troops, including those who were about to retire, near there. The Roman name for Newcastle was Hadrian's Bridge (*Pons Aelius*); it was quite unusual for a bridge outside Rome to be named after an emperor. Perhaps he visited this place to lead the ceremonies accompanying the start, or the completion, of the building of the bridge, which would provide access to a strip of ground beyond the River Tyne where the linear barrier of the wall was under construction.

Little survives to indicate the character of Hadrian's Bridge at Newcastle. Much more is known about a second bridge, also bearing his name, which spanned the River Tiber in the city of Rome. This bridge, which has survived the ensuing centuries, is known today as the Ponte S. Angelo.[36] Images of it on bronze medallions indicate that the parapets supported tall columns surmounted by statues, four on each side of the carriageway. The parapets of other bridges across the empire are known often to have supported columns, and in the case of one particularly well-preserved example over the River Cendere Çay (*Chabinas*, Turkey), the columns were accompanied by altars. The only significant surviving traces of the Newcastle Bridge, which were found in the Tyne during the nineteenth century, are two large altars (fig. 7.4). These were probably placed at the sides of columns supported by the parapet, which may also have been surmounted by statues. Dedicated to Oceanus and Neptune, these altars bore short inscriptions naming the Sixth Legion. They make no reference to Hadrian, however; the bridge would presumably have supported a dedicatory inscription in stone honouring him.

Classical writers addressing the Roman conquest of Britain regularly mentioned Oceanus, and an issue of coins from about the time Hadrian visited Britain depicts this divinity reclining on a dolphin and holding an anchor in his right hand (fig. 7.1b).[37] On a few of these coins, he grasps a trident rather than an anchor.[38] The same three symbols—the dolphin, anchor, and trident—were inscribed on the two altars from Hadrian's Bridge. Neptune was a Roman god of water in all its forms, including the sea and all rivers. Perhaps the didication to Neptune in this case called upon his role as a river god. The sacrifice at Hadrian's Bridge, therefore, included offerings to the divinities of both Ocean and Tyne.

FIG 7.4.
The altars dedicated to Oceanus and Neptune from the site of the Roman bridge at Newcastle upon Tyne (from Bruce 1933, p. 42)

Roman commanders who bridged major rivers on the imperial frontiers often sought the support of the divinities of watercourses.[39] A notable example is depicted on Trajan's Column in Rome, which was constructed to celebrate the conquest of Dacia (in 105–6). One of the most remarkable features of this column, which would have been highly visible at its base, is the massive, bearded figure of the Danube, shown guiding the Roman troops across an elaborate bridge. Trajan had ordered the construction of this bridge, over half a mile long, to carry his troops over the river to victory. The Danube is portrayed as an immense, beneficent deity, tamed and harnessed in support of Trajan's military ambitions. The deity of the River Tyne, while far less imposing than the Danube, would still have needed to be assuaged through sacrifice as part of the ceremonies that accompanied Hadrian's visit to the eastern end of the wall.

A stone sculpture from the fort on the wall at Chesters (*Cilurnum*, Northumberland) portrays the divinities of both the Tyne and Ocean (fig. 7.5).[40] The statue must have been commissioned, after the wall was constructed, by one of the succession of officers who commanded the unit stationed at the fort. It was found during the excavation of the bathhouse which formed part of the commanding officer's house. The Tyne is

FIG 7.5.
The river god from the Roman fort at Chesters (from Bruce 1851, 178)

portrayed as a bearded divinity clad in a long flowing cloak and reclining against the head of a larger god with a thick beard and flowing locks. That this larger god is shown as the source of the Tyne's waters suggests that this is Oceanus himself, the father of all waters. This statue links the worship of Tyne with Ocean and mirrors the joint sacrifice to these aquatic gods at Hadrian's Bridge. Roman troops living along the wall regularly reflected on the divinity of the springs and rivers along its line (discussed later).

Hadrian's act of sacrifice also recalled the exemplar of Alexander the Great's sacrifice to Oceanus and Tethys in India which would have been familiar to those present. Hadrian sought to emulate Alexander's achievements, just as Alexander had aimed to emulate the widespread travels of the mythical Heracles,.[41] Several issues of coins produced during Hadrian's reign include the figure of Hercules, and in some of these issues the divine hero is shown in the guise of the emperor, standing over and subduing the reclining figure of Oceanus.[42] Hercules had required the gods' permission to venture beyond the pillars that bore his name; the coins portray Hadrian engaging in his Herculean campaign of travelling across the empire and his mastery of Ocean.

The image of frontier and sea is also reflected in the fragmentary remains of the inscription from a victory monument that once stood at the eastern end of the wall.[43] Although the original plan had been to terminate the wall at Newcastle; a change to this design, which Hadrian may have ordered, extended the curtain 7.5 kilometres (5 miles) further east to Wallsend (*Segedunum*, Tyne and Wear). Here an arched masonry mole, projecting into the Tyne, provides the most likely location for this monument. Two fragments of the inscription survive, and the text has been reconstructed: 'son of all the deified emperors, the emperor Caesar Hadrian Trajan Augustus, after the necessity of keeping the empire within its limits had been laid upon him by divine injunction ... after the scattering of the barbarians and the security of the province of Britain was restored, added a frontier line between the two shores of the Ocean for 80 miles'. This statement is reminiscent of Tacitus' claim about the actions of Agricola in 80 when he established a string of forts along the Clyde-Forth isthmus. Hadrian's Wall, like Agricola's fortified line, was harnessing Ocean and the rivers to push the scattered barbarians back 'as if into a different island.'

Onward to Gaul

After a few weeks on the frontier, Hadrian may have travelled south by road via the colony at York. If so, he probably used the port at London as his point of disembarkation to sail to Boulogne on his way to inspect the provinces of Gaul. The discovery of the head of a statue of Hadrian in the River Thames at London may indicate that he visited this town, the largest urban settlement in the province.[44] This statue may originally, indeed, have been one of a collection depicting the emperors of Rome decorating the new and very substantial forum in London, completed, after several decades of construction, at about the time of Hadrian's British expedition. This building replaced a far smaller forum, and its substantial scale reflected the growing importance of an urban community which may have become the provincial capital by this time.

Other public buildings had been constructed across London. One unusual structure in an urban context is the auxiliary fort that lay on the north-western edge of the town. None of the other towns in the south of the province had a garrison of Roman auxiliaries, and the presence of this fort may reflect London's status as one of the two bases of the fleet controlling the Channel. A second fort was built for the fleet at Dover (*Dubris*, Kent), its other major port.[45] Although the British fleet was based in the south-east, it would have sailed regularly around the coasts of Britain, visiting the ports of the province and providing logistical support for the military during the building of the wall. The fleet would also have been given the responsibility of transporting Hadrian to Gaul.

REVISING THE PLANS SO AS TO CONSTRUCT A STRONGER WALL

A decision was made around the time of Hadrian's British expedition to strengthen the design of the new frontier line radically by adding twelve forts to supplement the small garrison of the milecastles.[46] This change of plan may have been a command direct from Hadrian, following his observation of the frontier under construction. A second significant change subsequently involved the construction of an immense second linear earthwork, known as the Vallum, to the south of the curtain wall. The need to strengthen the wall suggests that the Roman troops faced resistance from local communities during building operations. These two changes of plan strengthened the frontier (discussed later).

Who Built the Wall?

A large number of building inscriptions were placed in the south face of the curtain wall and built into the ramparts and internal structures of the forts and milecastles along its line. These inscriptions serve to identify the units responsible for constructing each element of the frontier (fig. 7.6).[47] They indicate that the three legions based permanently in Britain, the Second Augusta, the Sixth Victrix, and the Twentieth Valeria Victrix, were all fully involved in the construction work. The legionary soldiers were quartered in temporary camps for the summer months. During the winter, they returned to their fortresses in the south, leaving an auxiliary garrison stationed at the forts and milecastles to maintain order along the frontier. Much of the construction of fortifications was undertaken by the legions, although the inscription from Lambaesis (discussed earlier) indicates that auxiliary units could build stone ramparts, and some of the inscriptions from the wall indicate that the governor called upon labour from across the province to support this massive building project. Three inscriptions record building works undertaken by the British fleet, while an inscription from the Vallum indicates that a Dacian auxiliary unit undertook work on the frontier to the west of Newcastle.

Britons may also have been involved in the building works, and seven '*civitas* stones' suggest that peoples from the south provided assistance.[48] These inscriptions are known by this term because they record the efforts of work gangs from *civitates* of the south of the province, naming the Durotriges, the Dumnonii, and the Catuvellauni; one damaged stone may also name the Brigantes. Although they cannot be closely dated, it has usually been assumed that the *civitas* stones derive from a later time, when the wall was reconstructed. Since by this time southern Britain had been part of the empire for almost 80 years, however, and because all the other centurial stones are considered to date to the 120s, it is more

FIG 7.6.

Three Roman stones that commemorate the construction of Hadrian's Wall (Photograph by Richard Hingley) (Reproduced by permission of English Heritage and the Trustees of the Clayton Museum) probable that military veterans from the British *civitates* travelled to the frontier to assist with the construction work.

The Fort Decision

The strengthening of the frontier resulted in the addition of twelve forts to the line of the wall, at regular intervals approximately 10 kilometres (7 miles) apart. In addition to these, several of the forts along the Stanegate were retained. More forts were later added to the wall, bringing the total number of forts along and immediately behind the wall to nineteen by the 130s. Beyond the western end of the wall, another group of forts, fortlets, and towers continued this line of surveillance for a distance of 45 kilometres (30 miles) southwards along the Cumbrian coast, including the fort at Maryport with its auxiliary garrison of Spaniards (mentioned earlier).[49]

Each of the forts was large enough to be able to accommodate about 500 troops, in addition to those based at the seventy-seven milecastles. The contingent stationed immediately along the wall was in this way increased to an estimated total of around 9,000 men.[50] The auxiliary units took up residence in the forts as soon as the legionary work parties withdrew, and the twelve extra forts were fully operational by the mid-120s. The width of the curtain wall at its base was changed at this time from a 'broad wall' to a 'narrow wall', indicating the need to conserve stone building material and to accelerate the construction of the frontier.[51] At about the same time that the decision was taken to narrow the wall, the plan was probably also amended to build an extra 7.5 kilometres (5 miles) of curtain wall from Newcastle to the easternmost fort at Wallsend, terminating in the victory monument (discussed earlier).

The positioning of several of the forts straddling the curtain wall indicates how these installations were intended to operate. At Chester, for example, a third of the fort and three of the gateways lay to the north of the curtain wall. This would have enabled the swift deployment of soldiers into the lands beyond (fig. 7.7). The wall was evidently designed, in part, to play a protective role, although the large number of soldiers stationed along its line would also have provided the manpower for offensive action. At least three outpost forts, at Birrens, Netherby, and Bewcastle,

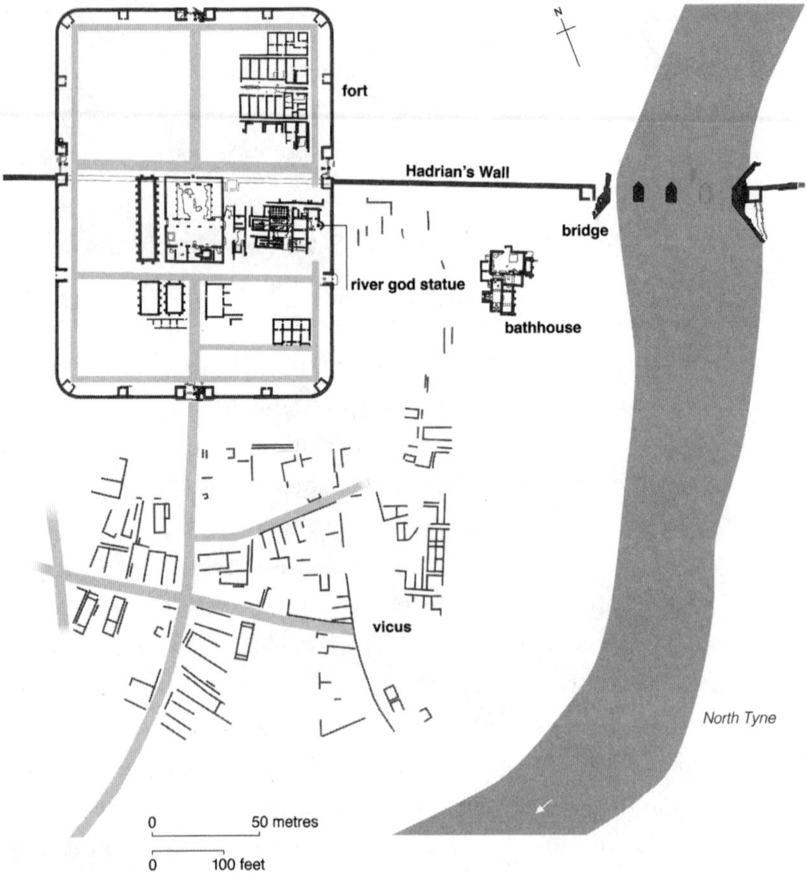

FIG 7.7.
The Roman fort at Chesters, showing the location of the *vicus* (civil settlement), bathhouse, Hadrian's Wall, and the Roman bridge over the River North Tyne (Redrawn from an illustration in the English Heritage guidebook to Chesters [Hodgson 2011], with additions)

were located on the roads running to the north beyond the wall, indicating that Roman territory did not end at the line of the wall (see fig. 7.2). During the late first century, outpost forts had existed beyond the line of the frontier along the Stanegate, and the planning of Hadrian's Wall indicates a comparable policy of defence in depth.

Each fort was the base for a single auxiliary unit of infantry or cavalry, and the names of several of these units, for example the First Cohort of

Spaniards at Maryport under their commander Agrippa, survive on stone inscriptions. Other units are recorded in a late Roman document called the *Notitia Dignitatum*. Despite the regularity of the wall—with its systematic placement of milecastles and turrets—auxiliary troops probably continued to move around the frontier region in a flexible fashion, following the strategy practised on the Stanegate in previous decades. Many of these auxiliary soldiers originated from the north-western provinces of the empire, although units came from other parts of the empire too.

The complete plan of the Hadrianic fort at Wallsend has been uncovered, but most of the evidence for buildings within the forts has been derived from the later phases of their use.[52] Each of the forts was supplied with a bathhouse outside the walls, indicating that Roman-style bathing had become a habit for the auxiliary soldiers. Auxiliary units were presumably accompanied by their families, and women and children may have lived with the soldiers within the forts or in extramural settlements beyond the Vallum. Very little is known, however, about these extramural settlements along the wall before the later second century (discussed later). It is possible that the unsettled conditions on the frontier during the 120s prevented such communities from becoming established outside the gates of the forts, a development perhaps awaiting a more peaceful time.

The 9,000 troops on the wall constituted over quarter of the entire auxiliary manpower in Britain, and many more troops were stationed at forts in the hinterland and at the outpost forts. This focusing of troops on the frontier required the reorganization of the military personnel throughout the province, reducing the strength of auxiliary units based in Wales and across parts of central Britain.[53] Nevertheless, many forts also continued to be occupied in lands well to the south of the wall, indicating that extensive military supervision was still thought to be required within the frontier of the province.

The Vallum Decision

Around the time of this fort decision came a second change of plan, involving the construction of the Vallum to the south of the line of the curtain wall (fig. 7.8).[54] The sequence of construction of the various works making up the wall during the years after 122 indicate that construction of the Vallum started a short time after forts began to be added to the curtain wall. Much of the course of the curtain wall had been laid out by this time, although its construction was not yet completed. The Vallum was a substantial steep-sided ditch, often with a flat base, with earth mounds along its northern and southern edges. An excavation of one of the Vallum crossings at Benwell (*Condercum*, Newcastle) indicates that the sides of the Vallum were very steep and that it would have been very difficult for anyone who fell in to get themselves out again without a ladder.[55] This monumental earthwork extended from Bowness-on-Solway in the west to the mouth of the Tyne at Newcastle in the east.

The patrolled causeways at each of the twelve wall forts, that at Benwell being one example, constituted the majority of the crossings of the Vallum. This indicates the significant change of plan that the decision to build the Vallum represented, as follows. The milecastles punctuating the curtain wall acted as guarded gateways providing access across the frontier. Each of these forts provided a route of access through the frontier at the gates in their south and north walls. This indicates that, theoretically, the wall as originally planned could be crossed at many regularly spaced locations along its line. After the plans for the wall were amended

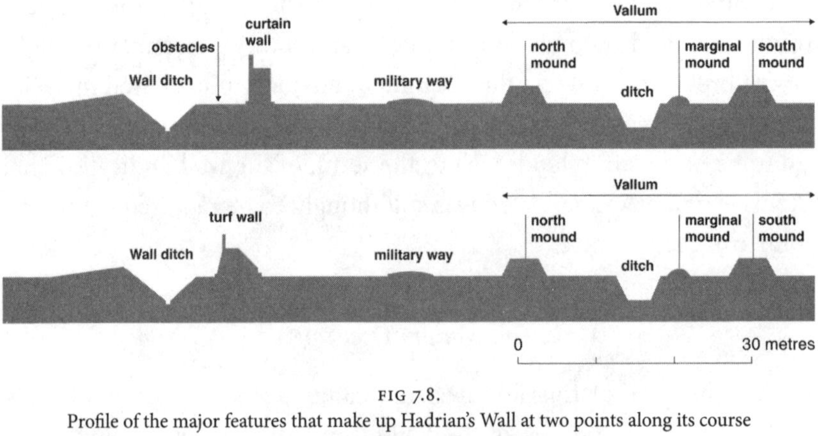

FIG 7.8.
Profile of the major features that make up Hadrian's Wall at two points along its course (after a drawing by Maxfield 1982, fig. 2).

with the addition of the Vallum, however, the movement of nonmilitary personnel across the frontier became extremely tightly controlled. At Benwell the fort lay just to the north of the Vallum causeway. This causeway supported a monumental gateway with two portals through which all travellers crossing the Vallum had to pass. The gateway was opened from the north, indicating that the garrison at the fort controlled, with the curtain wall and the Vallum, the access to and from the territory that lay between. Comparable gateways may have existed at some of the other Vallum crossings, each guarded by the auxiliary unit stationed at the nearby fort. In this way, the Vallum effectively defined the southern limits of a patrolled area of military territory along the frontier, including the forts and milecastles.

The construction of the Vallum enabled the garrison at each of the twelve wall forts to control the movement of travellers from the south into the military territory along the frontier, as well as to keep a watch on whom the garrisons at the milecastles were letting through the gateways they patrolled. Moving across a Vallum causeway would have required permission from the garrison at the local fort and would have brought the traveller into a heavily garrisoned strip of land immediately to the south of the curtain. Access through the northern gate of the fort into the lands beyond the frontier would only presumably have been granted to troops or imperial officials. Civilian travellers and traders wishing to move across the frontier on the other hand would have had to pass through the two closely guarded access points at a milecastle and a Vallum crossing. This would have required an awkward journey through an area under heavy military control, skirting one of the forts.

After the wall's design was amended in 122, it must have become very difficult for the local people to cross the frontier, which suggests that the intention was to cut off the populations on either side from one another. The forts on the Cumbrian coast to the west of the wall and the Roman fleet in the Solway and Tyne would also have ensured that travellers could not bypass the infrastructure of the frontier by sea.

After the completion of the wall, a number of additional crossings were created across the Vallum by filling the ditch and moving the earth mounds to the south and north. In addition, some sections of the Vallum were filled in not long after it was first dug. This may indicate that the provision of only twelve crossing-points proved too strict a control over military movements across the frontier. When the design of the wall was amended in 122, however, the intention appears to have been to close access across the frontier for local people while maintaining a system of access to multiple routes north for the troops serving along the frontier.

THE 'MAGIC AND MILITARY WALL'

The exploration of Benwell crossing provided another important insight into the Vallum: that it channelled running water.[56] Excavated into boulder clay, the straight sides of the causeway were revetted in masonry. About halfway up the profile of the ditch, a drain was found in the edge of the causeway, indicating that the western, uphill side of the causeway formed a pool of water over a metre deep. Through the drain, the surplus water flowed from this pool under the gateway on the crossing and into the eastern section of the Vallum ditch. The position of the drain indicates that the pooling of water in the ditch to the west of the gateway must have been intentional. The wet weather on the frontier would regularly have caused water to run through the drain, emptying into the Vallum to the east of the gateway before joining a stream and eventually reaching the Tyne.

Only the foundations of the Benwell gateway survive, although these were clearly substantial and may have supported a monumental edifice modelled on the triumphal arches constructed throughout the empire. These grand imperial victory monuments were often constructed in close proximity to waterways, or near the sea, and in the case of the Benwell gateway the Vallum took the place of a watercourse. Recall that the Arch of Claudius in Rome carried an aqueduct over one of the main roads running into the city, and the monumental Richborough Arch was built on an island lying just off the south-east coast of Britain, at one of the major points of entry to the province.[57] The gateway at Benwell, together with Hadrian's Bridge at Newcastle and the victory monument at Wallsend, celebrated the harnessing of the waters eventually flowing east into the Tyne.

The impervious soils through which much of the course of the Vallum was dug would have retained water, channelling and redirecting the flow of springs and streams toward the rivers flowing east into the Tyne and west into the Irish Sea.[58] Few excavations have explored the Vallum. One of the most informative discoveries was made during the nineteenth century, close to the fort at Carrawburgh (*Brocilita*, Northumberland).[59] The military unit responsible for constructing this section of the Vallum came across a spring. Intent on draining the area as part of their building campaign, they built a stone cistern to contain the water and channel it away. In the 130s, after a fort was constructed to the east of the spring, this cistern (named by the Victorians as 'Coventina's Well') became the focus of the cult of a goddess or nymph named Coventina. The excavation of the Well uncovered a great number of offerings donated to the sanctuary during the second and third centuries and later placed in the Well. These included many altars and an image of this goddess reclining on the flowing waters of a stream or spring (fig. 7.9), a pose typical of the representations of water nymphs found across the empire.

There has been a lengthy debate about whether Coventina was a goddess the local people worshipped before the Roman auxiliaries arrived in the area or the troops brought her cult with them. Very little is known about the religious beliefs of the local peoples across the frontier region; Iron Age communities elsewhere are known to have worshipped the spirits of many natural places, including hills, wetlands, and springs. The stone inscriptions from Coventina's Well are all dedicated by troops who were recruited in the northern frontier provinces. A dedication to Coventina has also been found in southern Gaul, showing that she was worshipped at places other than Carrawburgh. Water goddesses were commonly worshipped at springs across the empire, and several other sanctuaries are known in Britain, including the shrines of Ahvardua at Vindolanda, Sulis Minerva at Bath (Somerset), and Senuna at Ashwell (Hertfordshire).[60] Sulis and Senuna were local goddesses whose worship the Romans adopted, and Coventina and Ahvardua may well have been comparable. That none of the dedications to Coventina were inscribed by Britons merely reflects the fact that local people did not

FIG 7.9.
One of the commemorative stones from Coventina's Well at Chesters, now at Chesters Museum, showing the goddess in the guise of a classical nymph (Photograph by Richard Hingley) (Reproduced by permission of English Heritage and the Trustees of the Clayton Museum)

inscribe stones with Latin text. Some of the thousands of Roman coins offered to the goddess at Coventina's Well, however, could equally have been offerings from local people who visited the Well, just to the west of the Roman fort.

Troops stationed along Hadrian's Wall made numerous votive offerings to the spirits of special places during the second and third centuries.

These inscriptions, and the statue of the Tyne from Chesters (discussed earlier), indicate that it was the custom of military men to placate and seek the support of the deities of springs and rivers.[61] Worship of nymphs, almost invariably by soldiers, was particularly common, although the dedication on an altar from Carvoran (*Magnis*, Northumberland) is by a woman named Vettia Mansueta and her daughter Claudia Turianilla. Another altar, from the outpost fort at Risingham (*Habitancum*, Northumberland), reads: 'forewarned by a dream the soldiers bade her who is married to Fabius to set up an altar to the nymphs who are to be worshipped'. Nothing more is known about the identity of the persons these inscriptions mention, but they demonstrate that military settlers and their families often sought to placate the local spirits inhabiting the springs and rivers of the frontier landscape. Neptune also received dedications from soldiers at four of the forts along the wall.

Many other local deities connected with other features of the landscape also received dedications, including several war gods.[62] One of the most popular was Cocidius, who was worshipped along the western section of the frontier. He is shown armed with a spear and shield on several of the dedications he received, and one made by the First Cohort of Batavians, found at a milecastle, includes the words 'Genio Vali'. This is thought to be a reference to the 'genius', or guardian spirit, of the wall. The wall soldiers also regularly worshipped the official gods of the Roman pantheon—Jupiter, Minerva, Mars, and Juno—and made dedications seeking their protection of the reigning emperor's welfare. Occasionally, local gods were linked with classical gods; a dedication has been found to Mars Cocidius, for example. The linking of local deities with classical gods was common in Britain, as in the case of Sulis Minerva, who was worshipped by both soldiers and civilians at the Roman spring sanctuary of Bath (Somerset).

Many of the gods whose worship is recorded on the wall are not directly connected with Ocean and rivers, but the regular offerings to Neptune and the nymphs, recalling the altars dedicated at Hadrian's Bridge, indicate the numinous character of the springs, streams, rivers, and ports along the frontier.

COMPLETING THE WALL AND THE STABILIZATION OF THE PROVINCE

The inscriptions found along the wall provide a detailed chronology of its construction, indicating that by about 130 the main elements were completed.[63] Platorius Nepos, governor in Britain from 122 to perhaps 127, is named on seven building inscriptions, indicating that much of the work on the curtain wall and the forts was completed before he was recalled. Lucius Trebius Germanus succeeded him as governor, and the fact that his name does not appear on any such building inscriptions suggests that the main phase of construction was completed by the time of his arrival. Nevertheless, several additional forts, including Carrawburgh, were added to the line of the wall during the 130s, and it may have taken several decades to replace the turf wall along the western part of the frontier with the stone curtain.[64]

By the early 120s, the Roman military had been occupying the northern frontier lands for over four decades. Although the frontiers had needed substantial reinforcement after the uprising early in Hadrian's reign, the province had been part of the empire for long enough that British auxiliaries had been serving on Rome's other frontiers for decades. The southern lands of the province, meanwhile, were well settled, with *civitates* whose ruling elites kept order over their own people and collected tax for the Roman authorities (fig. 7.10). Throughout these settled lands where the military forces had moved on, as across much of the rest of the empire, the leading families of the local communities had taken over the governing of their peoples and fostered and created a settled provincial life. The establishment of local self-government for these peoples was a vital element of the Roman strategy of conquest. It enabled the Roman governors who were pushing the frontier forward to campaign with the knowledge that their supply lines were secure. The taxes paid by the communities of the south also helped to support the cost of maintaining the military forces. These communities also produced surpluses of agricultural produce which were requisitioned to supply the troops. During the second century, forts were few and far between in the south-east, although the forts at Dover and London provided bases for the British fleet.

FIG 7.10.
The *civitates* and legionary fortresses of Britain

Although the *civitas* centres of these southern peoples had been established during the second half of the first century, the street systems and public buildings in most of these towns, including the fora and bathhouses, were constructed during the early second century.[65] Some of these buildings were commissioned and completed under Hadrian, as is indicated, for instance, by the monumental inscription adorning the entrance to the forum at Wroxeter. This refers to Hadrian by name and records the completion of this building by the *civitas* of the Cornovii in 130. As noted earlier, some of the southern *civitates* may even have provided work gangs to help with the massive project of constructing the wall.

It proved impossible, however, to implement this highly effective strategy for encouraging local self-government across much of western and central Britain, where few *civitas* capitals ever developed. The Iron Age peoples of these regions met together for regular festivities and would join forces to repel incomers. Their leaders were warriors who reacted to the Roman invasion either by uniting their peoples to fight or by submitting. After these communities capitulated, or after their eventual defeat in battle, the treaties imposed required them to accept Roman rule, keep the peace, and pay taxes. The *civitas* capitals at Exeter and Wroxeter were located at the margin of the area of Britain where local self-government was established and were founded with significant input from veterans from the recently decommissioned legionary fortresses at both places. Because it was impossible to establish local self-government across most of western and central Britain, Rome found it necessary to retain a military presence based at the forts, to keep watch, enforce order, and collect the tax from the local population.

OCEAN HARNESSED

The troops along the frontier would also have continued to supervise the local peoples and, on occasion, to conduct armed campaigns against peoples living beyond the imperial limits when Rome feared an uprising. This range of activities cannot, however, entirely explain why the wall was designed to be so physically imposing. The Roman frontier works between the Rhine and the Danube fulfilled a broadly comparable purpose and were also manned by very substantial military garrisons.[66] Although the palisades and ramparts delimiting this Hadrianic frontier system were less monumental in scale than Hadrian's Wall, they extended much further and represented an equally daunting building campaign for the provincial garrison. They had the vitally important role of keeping order on a frontier protecting the lands to the south, which formed the core territory of Rome's empire.

The monumental proportions of Hadrian's Wall have sometimes been taken to indicate that the peoples living to the north were too fierce to be conquered and that the military situation along the British frontier required a particularly strong defensive fortification and a substantial garrison to match.[67] The territory directly beyond the barriers constructed between the Rhine and Danube in Germany appears from current research to have been sparsely populated; some sections are several days' travel from the nearest known Iron Age settlement. Hadrian's Wall divided settled landscapes that had been occupied for centuries and so the building of this frontier would seem to have provoked more sustained resistance.[68]

The size of the Roman garrison certainly shows that the province was an important imperial possession. The exploitation of Britain's natural resources cannot provide the entire explanation for this lavish expenditure of military manpower. The most important resources were derived from farming and mineral extraction and included access to Britons living beyond the wall as well. Slaves were obtained from beyond the imperial frontiers to meet the demands of the Mediterranean market. By leaving the lands to the north and west of the province free of their control, the Romans effectively maintained a reserve of slaves to be acquired through trade and occasional campaigning. Despite this, the resources of Britain would not have generated enough profit to offset the cost of the entire garrison.

It seems probable that the number of Roman troops stationed in Britain and the scale of the wall were due to the significance of the province in the imagination of the Mediterranean elite as a semibarbaric territory set within Ocean. Although civil life had been established throughout the settled lowlands, Britain retained in the Roman mind much of its earlier status as a barbaric place.[69] Classical texts had long called their readers' attention to Ocean's status as the boundary of the earth's orb, and the campaigns in Britain had added the most profitable part of this large island to the empire. This imperial possession now lay within the tightened security provided by Hadrian's magical and military wall. The control of this otherworldly and semibarbaric land outweighed any consideration of the economic lure of raw materials, crops, auxiliary recruits, and slaves. Britain had long played a significant role in Roman conceptions of Ocean and universal empire, connecting the actions of emperors and military commanders from Julius Caesar to Caligula, Claudius, Agricola, Hadrian, and beyond. The wall was the latest manifestation of the conceptual and physical conquest of the island that lay beyond the shores of Ocean.

8

THE LATER HISTORY OF THE ROMAN NORTHERN FRONTIER

They live in tents, naked and without shoes, possess their women in common, and rear all offspring in common.

—Dio (on the Caledonians and Maeatae)[1]

When he ordered the construction of his wall, Hadrian aimed to establish a permanent boundary to the lands under Roman control; to separate the peoples of the north from the imperial lands of the province. The roads running beyond Hadrian's Wall were garrisoned by auxiliary units based at several outpost forts. Their role was to monitor these frontier lands, to prevent opponents from assembling, and to enforce the payment of tax in agricultural products, auxiliary recruits, and slaves. A decade after the completion of the wall Hadrian died, and his successor embarked on a new campaign of conquest in Britain.

ANTONINUS PIUS AND THE ADVANCE INTO SOUTHERN SCOTLAND

In 138, when Antoninus Pius succeeded Hadrian as emperor, he required a military victory and selected northern Britain as the venue.[2] Having no military experience himself, however, he decided to stay in Rome and appointed Lollius Urbicus, a seasoned military commander, to lead the campaign as governor of Britain. Urbicus, whose family came originally from Numidia (North Africa), commanded the invasion of southern Scotland from 139 to 142.[3] The legions and auxiliary units already in Britain were supplemented by reinforcements from other provincial garrisons. An inscription from the Roman fort of Birrens (*Blatobulgium*, Dumfries and Galloway), for example, records the presence in southwestern Scotland of two legionary detachments from the Rhine frontier, the Twenty-Second Primigenia (based at Mainz) and the Eighth Augusta (from Strasbourg).[4]

The Roman troops campaigning across southern Scotland were based in camps and constructed a network of roads and forts to hold the territory once its peoples were subdued (fig. 8.1). Otherwise, little is known of

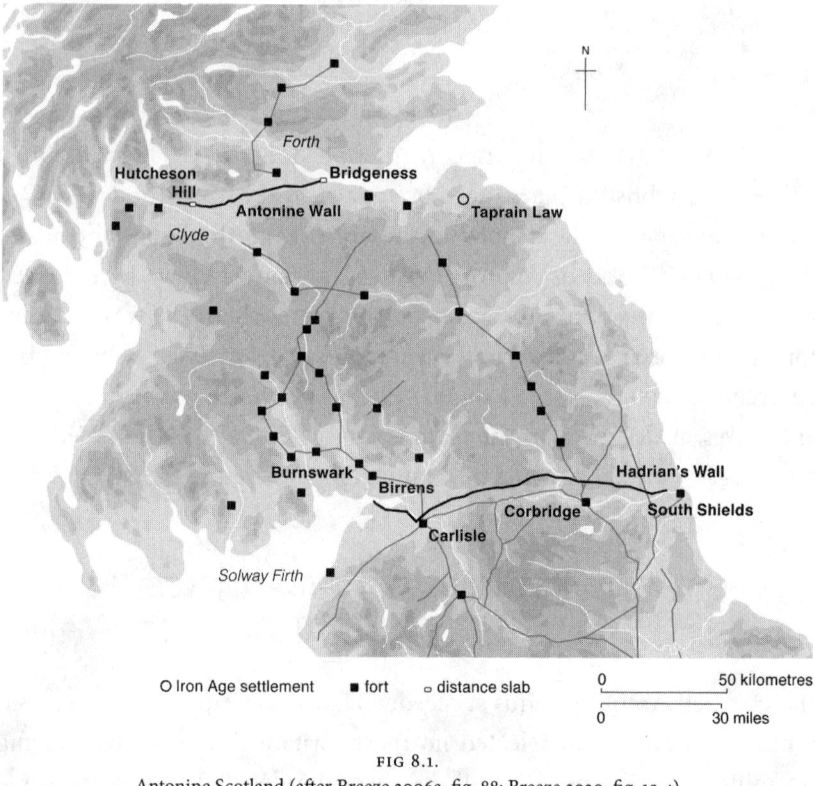

FIG 8.1.
Antonine Scotland (after Breeze 2006a, fig. 88; Breeze 2020, fig. 19.4)

these campaigns, although there is evidence that one of the largest hillforts of southern Scotland, Burnswark Hill (Dumfries and Galloway) may have been besieged by Roman forces at this time (fig. 8.2).[5] The ramparts of this hillfort crowned the summit of a hill that was visible across an

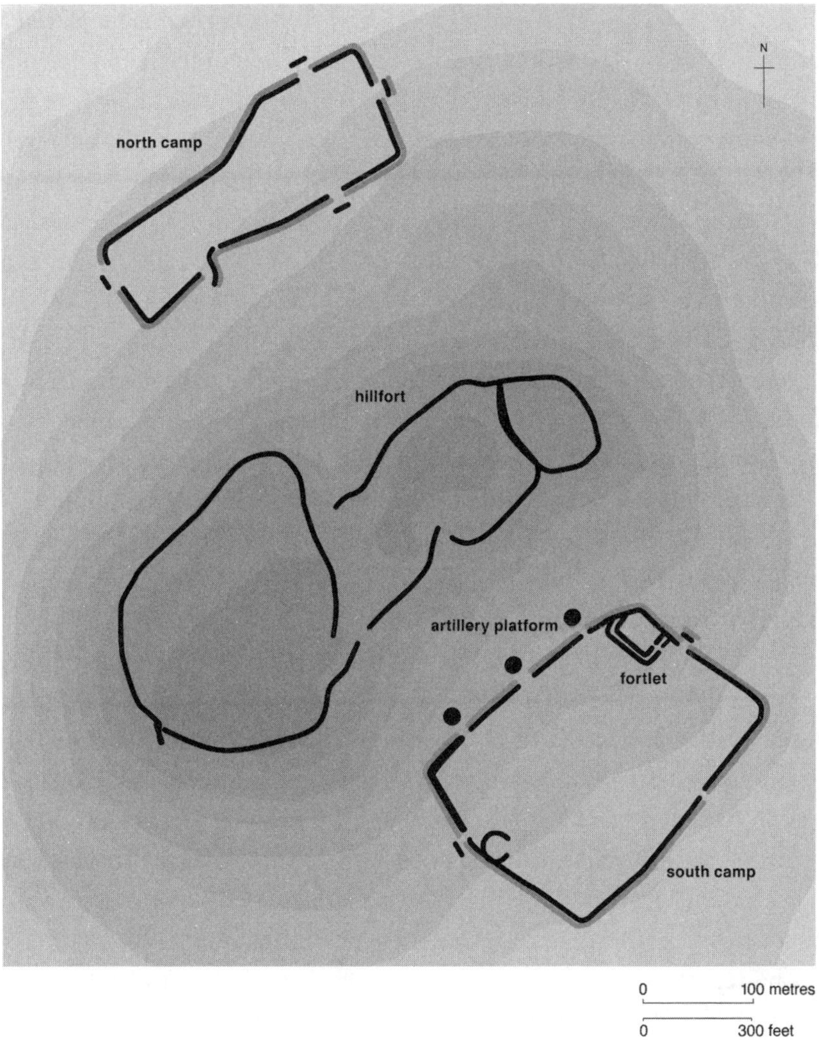

FIG 8.2.
Burnswark Hill (Dumfries and Galloway, Scotland), showing the Iron Age hillfort and the two Roman camps on the lower slopes (redrawn with permission from a survey by the Roman Commission on the Ancient and Historical Monuments of Scotland)

extensive area of south-western Scotland. Two substantial Roman camps were constructed on the slopes below the hillfort, and those defending it were subjected to a sustained attack with lead ballista bolts and sling-shots. Although this protracted siege is not closely dated, it is thought likely to have occurred during the campaigns of Urbicus. The fort of Birrens is located 4.5 kilometres (3 miles) to the south-east of Burnswark Hill, and the legionary detachments stationed there presumably played a prominent role in besieging the hillfort. Quite what offence the defenders of Burnswark Hill had committed to warrant an attack of this severity is unclear. The scale of the siege works here is comparable, however, with those at the sites of two famous attacks on high-profile centres of resistance: Numantia (Soria, Castile and Leon) in northern Spain in 133 BCE and Alesia in Gaul under Julius Caesar in 52 BCE.[6] It is not known whether Urbicus besieged any of the other hillforts of southern Scotland during his campaign.

As in earlier invasions, conquest was not merely a matter of defeating those who resisted. Urbicus would have continued to divide the opposition by reinforcing preexisting alliances with friendly peoples across southern Scotland. One such was the community focused around the hillfort of Traprain Law (discussed earlier). During the Flavian advance, sixty years earlier, many treaties may have been negotiated with communities prepared to cooperate and maintained in the subsequent decades. The Roman imports found during the excavation of Iron Age settlements, including pottery, glass, bronze ornaments, and the occasional Roman coin, were the result of such alliances.[7] And it was not just across southern Scotland that Rome sought friendship with powerful local communities. Small quantities of Roman imports have also been found at Iron Age settlements across central, northern, and western Scotland. These alliances and contacts with more distant peoples would have been maintained by sea, and the sites producing Roman imports are located in close proximity to the coast.

The recent excavations at Birnie (Moray) have cast considerable light on an Iron Age community living around 300 kilometres' march (190 miles) north of Hadrian's Wall, which was nevertheless in close contact with Rome during the second century.[8] This settlement included a group of substantial roundhouses, and the site has yielded a quantity of Roman imports, the most remarkable of which are the two late second-century coin hoards (discussed later). Imports of pottery and bronze ornaments which date earlier than these indicate that diplomatic contacts with the community spanned the second century and may have commenced under the Flavians. Roman imports found on other sites suggest that the people at Birnie were not unique in this respect but belonged to one of a number of influential communities across northern and eastern Scotland maintaining friendly relations with Rome during this time. Indeed, it was not just to the north of Hadrian's Wall that the Romans sustained diplomatic efforts with Iron Age communities. Archaeological finds show that Roman diplomacy and trade continued with the peoples of Ireland during the second century and after.[9] Relations were not always peaceable across the western seaboard, and several forts were retained in Wales and on the west coast to the south of Hadrian's Wall, in part as a defence of Roman lands against the threat of invasion from the west.[10]

The Antonine Wall

Antoninus may originally have planned to conquer the entirety of northern Britain, completing the campaign spearheaded by Agricola. By 142, however, when the emperor celebrated a victory in Rome, it had already been decided to construct a new frontier at the southern boundary of Caledonia on the Clyde-Forth isthmus (see fig. 8.1).[11] This was to become known as the Antonine Wall. Urbicus was recalled to Rome around this time, and the Antonine Wall, almost 120 kilometres (75 miles) to the north of Hadrian's Wall, took the three legions about three years to construct. The distance between the mouths of the Clyde and the Forth enabled this boundary—as it was now constituted, at 60 kilometres (38 miles) in length—to be half as long as Hadrian's Wall (117 kilometres; 73 miles). The seventeen forts constructed along the Antonine Wall indicate that the garrison was intended to be approximately the same size as that of the earlier wall had been. Several outpost forts also lay on the roads running to the north of the Antonine Wall, demonstrating the implementation of the same strategy of defence as had operated on the earlier Stanegate and Hadrian's Wall frontiers.

Despite Antoninus' desire to impress, his wall, in contrast to the stone edifice of Hadrian's Wall, was built mainly from timber and turf. If the original intention had been to build this new wall entirely in stone, a change in materials was evidently authorized at an early stage of construction. The turf wall itself was built on a stone foundation to provide stability, while the forts along the line were also turf-built. This method of construction may have been thought necessary in order to speed up the construction work in response to local resistance to it. The scale of the disruption of the local communities along the line of the Antonine Wall undoubtedly caused conflict, as did the construction of Hadrian's Wall twenty years earlier.

The Antonine Wall was nevertheless a highly impressive and monumental mural barrier, one of its most remarkable features being the twenty 'distance slabs' found along its line.[12] These stones are broadly comparable to the commemorative inscriptions found along Hadrian's Wall but are far more elaborate. Their Latin inscriptions emphasize that the building of this wall was part of a great military campaign led by the imperial legions and under the instruction of Antoninus himself. The slabs are also carved with depictions of Roman deities and scenes of conquest, which, like the sculptures on all Roman triumphal monuments across the empire, would have been picked out in colour. They were originally set up immediately to the south of the Antonine Wall, probably by the side of the military way running behind the frontier works.

One of the most impressive of the slabs is from Bridgeness (Bo'ness, Falkirk) on the Firth of Forth, at the east end of this wall (fig. 8.3). This elaborate carving records the emperor's name and the role of the Second Legion Augusta in the construction work. To the right of the panel is a vignette of the ritual purification of the legion through the celebration of the *suovetaurilia*, involving the sacrifice of a pig, a sheep, and a bull at an altar. This was a ceremony marking the culmination of Antoninus' conquest of southern Scotland at the time that the building of the new wall commenced. In 122 Hadrian had presided over a sacrifice at the east end of his wall; the Bridgeness slab suggests a comparable ceremony at the east end of the Antonine Wall, where it met the waters of the Firth of Forth; this sacrifice was probably led by Aulus Claudius Charax, the

FIG 8.3.
The Bridgeness distance stone from the Antonine Wall (Image © National Museums Scotland)

commander of the Second Legion, a famous Greek writer and philanthropist. On the left side of the inscription, a second vignette depicts the fighting that preceded the building of the Antonine Wall. A cavalry soldier is shown riding down a disorganized rabble of barbarians, including one victim who has been beheaded.

Further west along this wall, at Hutcheson Hill (Bearsden, East Dunbartonshire), a second distance slab recorded the Twentieth Legion Valeria Victrix as the builders of this section. The panels to the sides of the slab feature captives who watch, bound and submissive, as the empress Faustina, wife of Antoninus, welcomes home the victorious troops after their campaign in Scotland. Vanquished barbarians were regularly featured on Roman sculptures and on coins, and the Hutcheson Hill slab is a reminder that an important objective of all the offensive wars Rome fought was to obtain slaves for the Mediterranean markets. Defeated enemies were almost always killed, as depicted at Bridgeness, or enslaved, as shown at Hutcheson Hill.

These images of defeated and enslaved barbarians communicate the scale of Rome's violence against the resistant local peoples of southern Scotland. Along with the siege works at Burnswark Hill, these slabs remind us of the acts of slaughter and enslavement these peoples experienced during Rome's military occupation of their lands. It is unlikely that local people were the intended audience of these images or of the earlier depictions of defeated Britons on the tombstones of Roman cavalry soldiers. Unless they were trusted friends of Rome, such people would have been kept well away from the wall.

Abandoning the Antonine Wall

Antoninus must have planned this new frontier both to replace Hadrian's Wall and to protect the lands his campaign had added to the empire. The decommissioning of Hadrian's Wall so as to provide the troops needed to man the forts along the new frontier must have been part of the scheme. Inscriptions indicate, however, that several units remained in place on Hadrian's Wall and that during the late 150s the decision was made to decommission the Antonine Wall and to pull the garrison back south to the earlier wall.[13] The forts along the Antonine Wall were carefully demolished and the distance slabs removed and buried as part of a ritual act marking the closure of the frontier. Several outpost forts to the north of Hadrian's Wall were retained, and the treaties previously agreed with friendly communities across Scotland remained in place.

Why, after less than twenty years, was the Antonine Wall abandoned? Antoninus' need for a military victory to secure his rule had motivated his military campaign in northern Britain. By the time of the withdrawal to the south, he had ruled for more than a decade and was well established as emperor. Britain was a long way from Rome, moreover, and he evidently felt able to allow the abandonment of these lands. This was the second time in just over seventy years that the Romans withdrew from southern Scotland. This withdrawal was presumably in response to the strategic difficulties the military units faced in attempting to keep the newly conquered lands and their peoples under Rome's control. To understand why this might be the case, consider that the Antonine conquest of southern Scotland extended the frontier of the province across a vast area almost 300 kilometres (190 miles) in depth, from Chester in the south to the Clyde-Forth isthmus in the north. Although the conquest of the peoples of Wales and central Britain had been achieved many decades before, much of this territory remained to be garrisoned.[14] In this context, the construction of the forts across southern Scotland must have stretched the available military manpower almost to breaking point.

Once the Antonine forts were constructed, the legions withdrew to their fortresses far to the south: the closest fortresses lay almost 300 kilometres away at Chester and York. Although legionary detachments may have remained on the ground in southern Scotland, any threat of a serious uprising in northern Britain would have required the summoning of the legions from their distant bases. The conquest of southern Scotland may also have overextended the lines of military communication and supply, for much of the food consumed on the Antonine Wall was produced in the fertile lowland areas of southern Britain. Food for the winter had to be stored in each fort, and the Roman fleet also helped to supply the garrison of central, western, and northern Britain. The harsh winter conditions made sailing difficult, however, and extra food may have had to be brought several hundred kilometres by road.

The problems the governors of Britain faced in maintaining order across such a deep frontier region probably explains the decision to withdraw to Hadrian's Wall. After the late 150s, we know of only one more serious attempt to subdue the lands to the north—under Septimius Severus in the early third century. On this occasion, a series of campaigns were undertaken against peoples who were threatening the security of Rome's northern frontier in Britain; these actions appear to have been intended to quell potential resistance and do not seem to have resulted in the conquest of territory. From the 160s until the collapse of Roman rule in Britain during the late fourth and early fifth centuries, the northern frontier of the province remained on the line of Hadrian's Wall.

THE PEOPLE OF HADRIAN'S WALL

There are hints of trouble on the British frontier during the early 180s, when Rome was ruled by the emperor Commodus. One account speaks of peoples from the north crossing Hadrian's Wall, causing a great deal of damage and cutting down a general and his soldiers.[15] To reestablish the stability of the frontier, extra troops were sent to the province under an experienced commander. A diplomatic strategy was also developed to maintain order and peace across the lands that lay between the two walls, creating a buffer zone where Iron Age communities were bribed with coinage and other Roman goods to remain friendly.[16] Despite this reference to troubles under Commodus, the development of towns and extramural settlements provides evidence of settled conditions on Hadrian's Wall.

During the second century, the town at Carlisle developed outside the gates of the fort and became, possibly later the same century, the *civitas* capital of the Carvetii.[17] Carlisle was well to the north of the other *civitas* capitals of Britain and was a late development. In southern Britain, many of the *civitas* capitals evolved under the leadership of the elite families among the peoples for whom they had served as a centre, although the towns at Exeter and Wroxeter developed on the sites of former legionary fortresses, and their elites included military veterans (discussed earlier). It is unlikely that the Carvetii, the Iron Age people settled around Carlisle, had enough elite families to run the administration of this *civitas*, for the local administrators were drawn mainly, if not entirely, from veterans, as in the towns at Exeter and Wroxeter. All three of these towns would also have attracted local peoples to trade and settle. A second town on Hadrian's Wall, at Corbridge, grew up on the site of an abandoned Roman fort. This urban community may also have become a *civitas* capital during the late second or early third century.[18] These towns at Carlisle and Corbridge were located on the two main roads running across the wall and became thriving communities. Their location on these roads suggests that trading across the frontier was one reason for their success.

The settled condition of life on Hadrian's Wall is also indicated by the extramural settlements (*vici*) which developed outside the gates of the forts along its line (see fig. 7.7).[19] Earlier in the history of the conquest of Britain, many forts were accompanied by extramural settlements, as at Vindolanda, on the Stanegate (discussed earlier). Many more of these settlements, however, were established during the later second century and became extensive and important urban centres in the following century. The most fully excavated example is the early third-century extramural settlement at Vindolanda (see fig. 6.4). After the early second century, this site continued to be used for a succession of forts, built one on top of each other. The extramural settlement of the early third century was located outside the western gate of the fort and was populated by settlers attracted to the place by the possibility of producing goods there and trading with the soldiers. The extramural settlements at the forts along

Hadrian's Wall were characterized by small rectangular buildings, serving as houses and shops, located along metalled roads. From the late second century onwards, these *vici* became successful economic centres as a result of the purchasing power of the soldiers, who were paid in cash. Inscriptions from Hadrian's Wall can be a valuable source of information about the variety of people living in the forts and extramural settlements. Two evocative and particularly interesting burial monuments from the fort and *vicus* at South Shields (*Arbeia*, Tyne and Wear) provide a vivid insight into the diversity of these communities.[20] South Shields, a port and supply base situated on the south bank of the River Tyne in the eastern hinterland of the wall, was evidently home to people originally from very different parts of the empire.

One of the tombstones commemorates Victor, a Moor from North Africa, who died aged twenty. He was a freedman of Numerianus, a trooper of the First Cavalry Regiment of Asturians, who according to the inscription had 'most devotedly conducted Victor to his tomb'. This inscription informs us that Numerianius, an auxiliary soldier from Spain, had previously freed his slave and then demonstrated his devotion after his untimely death by commissioning an impressive monument from an accomplished sculptor. On the carved stone relief, Victor is richly dressed, reclining upon a couch in front of a tree representing paradise. A slave offers him a cup of wine as part of a funeral banquet, representing the idea of a joyful afterlife. Slaves commonly accompanied their masters to military postings, as attested in the Vindolanda letters. It was not only the commanding officers of auxiliary units in Britain who owned slaves, however, for here there is nothing to indicate that Numerianus was anything other than a common soldier. He evidently had some resources, however, as he was able to commission a lavish memorial to his friend.

Many of the soldiers who served along Hadrian's Wall were recruited from Spain and the Rhine frontier, although troops are also known to have come from other frontier regions of the empire, including North Africa and the Near East. During the second century auxiliary units continued often to be moved around the empire, and many of the troops may not have served on the wall for more than a few years before their unit was transferred elsewhere. Some soldiers became settled in the region of the wall, however, and continued to live on the northern frontier after they retired from military service.[21] Some of the soldiers had unofficial families; until the early third century, serving auxiliaries were not allowed by law to marry. As a result, the extramural settlements along the wall would have included some local women and the children from these relationships, although we do not know their names or anything about their lives.

Traders also came to Hadrian's Wall from overseas to exploit the market created by the presence of the soldiers. The second—and more famous—tombstone from South Shields brings us face to face with the Catuvellaunian wife of a Syrian, named Regina (see fig. I.8). Originally a slave owned by Barates, whom he later freed and married, she died at the age of thirty. Victor and Regina were both honoured with rich burial monuments by their former masters, as part of the lavish ceremonies that accompanied their funerals. This may, however, provide an unduly positive impression of the lives of many Roman slaves along the wall.

Regina's tombstone provides additional information about her and her husband, Barates. She is named on the inscription as being of the Catuvellauni, the people targeted during the invasion of Claudius in 43, when he marched on the *oppidum* of Camulodunum. She is not described as a Briton on her tombstone because the peoples of Roman Britain identified themselves by reference to their *civitas* rather than thinking of themselves as British. When the work parties which had been recruited from the province to help to build Hadrian's Wall left a record of their contribution, they also identified themselves by their *civitates* (discussed earlier). British legionaries who served and died in other areas of the empire, by contrast, are described as Britons on their memorials, suggesting that it was only when these individuals moved overseas that they ceased to be identified primarily by the name of their *civitas*.[22] The concept of Britannia was a Roman creation.

Regina is shown clothed in a sleeved tunic with a floor-length skirt, a type of dress familiar from representations of women from Rome's northern frontier regions of Gaul and Germany. Portrayed sitting on a chair while spinning and wool-working, she is engaged in the activities traditionally carried out by women in the Roman domestic sphere. Around her neck is a twisted neck ring, or torc, which indicates her wealth and references her barbarian ancestry as well. Recall that although torcs ceased to be commonly worn in Britain at about the time of Caesar's invasion, Tacitus described Boudica as wearing a torc during the uprising she led. It may appear surprising that an ex-slave, whose name in translation meant 'Queen', was portrayed wearing a torc, as these artefacts denoted high status. The two bracelets Regina wears provide a further clue to the significance of the torc: her jewellery helped to indicate the status she acquired when she married Barates.

The symbolism of Regina's memorial emphasizes the wealth of her husband, and the elaborate tombstone suggests that although he was not a Roman citizen he may have played a significant role in the frontier community. The name 'Barathes' is recorded in the inscription on a far less elaborate tombstone, from the Roman town at Corbridge, commemorating a sixty-eight-year-old 'flag-bearer', and, although the name is spelt slightly differently, he may have been the same Barates who married Regina. There is some debate about the meaning of the term 'flag-bearer'—whether Barates was a retired soldier who had carried the standard of an auxiliary unit into battle or a trader selling banners to the soldiers along the wall. Every Roman auxiliary and legionary unit had its own standard, kept for security in the headquarters building of their fort. Whatever his profession, Barates had made enough money to own at least one slave and to commission a lavish tombstone for his freed wife at her death. One of the most fascinating aspects of this monument is that the inscription describing her relationship to him is inscribed in both Latin and Aramaic. Barates was evidently part of a community of Syrians at South Shields; otherwise, why would the information included on the memorial have been given in both languages? This offers an insight into the diverse nature of the communities living along the wall during the late second century.

The literary texts describing the invasion and settlement of Roman Britain mainly emphasize the actions of high-ranking male members of the Roman elite, while these two inscriptions, together with some of the letters from Vindolanda, provide alternative perspectives. They provide some clues about the lives of rather less high-ranking men, and a few women as well. The people whose lives can be reconstructed from these sources are used today to communicate a positive image of life on the Roman wall to the many visitors who travel to explore the remains. It is important to keep in mind that the province of Britannia was conquered and maintained as a result of considerable and sustained aggression by Rome, which led to the killing, displacement, and enslavement of many anonymous victims.

SEPTIMIUS SEVERUS AND BRITAIN

Around the time the emperor Septimius Severus took power in Rome, in 193, the governor of Britain, Virius Lupus, had to pay a people called the Maeatae to keep the peace, since, we are told, they and the Caledonians had broken the treaties previously agreed with them.[23] Nothing is known about where the Maeatae lived, although they were described as being close to the 'cross wall', a possible reference to the Antonine Wall, which had been abandoned. The author who recorded these actions provided a highly fanciful description of the way of life of the people who lived in the lands beyond Hadrian's Wall: 'there are two principal peoples of the Britons, the Caledonians and the Maeatae.... Both inhabit wild and waterless mountains and desolate and marshy plains, and they possess neither walls, nor cities, nor tilled fields. They live on their flocks, and by hunting and on certain fruits.... They live in tents, naked and without shoes, possess their women in common, and rear all offspring in common.'[24] The potential threat these peoples posed to Roman control of the frontier lands is emphasized with a description of their savagery. In more recent times, the excavation of Iron Age sites across Scotland indicating that the peoples there were agriculturalists who lived in well-established settlements places these highly exaggerated statements in their true context.

During the late second century a threat to the security of the Roman frontier seems to have developed. The Iron Age peoples of Scotland were decentralized and had no well-established political hierarchies, so it seems unlikely that the Caledonians and the Maeatae were planning coordinated resistance to Rome. In these conflicts, the leaders of some communities chose to take their followers to war, while others sought friendship with Rome. The reference to Lupus resorting to bribery reflects a time-honoured strategy, employed since Julius Caesar and Augustus, of offering gifts to the leaders of prominent British peoples to secure their friendship. As a result, indeed, of the decentralized character of these Iron Age communities, rival leaders were evidently threatening the security of the frontier zone. The alternative strategies Roman governors pursued to counter such threats were to resort to bribery or to mount an armed invasion to defeat the threat.

The discovery of silver coins of Severus across southern and central Scotland bears testimony to the gifts used to secure friendship, and to keep order, in the lands beyond the wall (fig. 8.4). The other Roman imports, such as pottery, glass, and bronze ornaments, found at some Iron Age settlements are likely to have arrived there as diplomatic gifts. No fewer than six hoards of Severan coins have been found on sites in eastern Scotland to the north of the Clyde-Forth isthmus, including two hoards of over 600 denarii on the site of the Iron Age settlement at Birnie.[25] The exact dating of these coins suggests that they arrived at Birnie in batches during the late 190s. Roman emissaries presumably sailed up the east coast of Scotland on several occasions to negotiate with this community, and the earlier finds from the site (discussed previously) indicate that these diplomatic activities aimed to maintain a friendly relationship spanning generations. The other hoards of Severan coins have all been found at locations in the coastal regions of eastern Scotland, suggesting that in this way Rome bribed several communities there to remain friendly. Coins of the same date have also been found scattered singly in other locations across Scotland; it is not clear how many communities were being bribed as part of this strategy of buying peace.

It is unclear whether this strategy was successful, and the emperor Severus, who had already commanded military campaigns in Syria and Parthia, decided to make an example of the peoples of northern Britain. In 208, despite being sixty-three years old and suffering badly from gout, he became the first emperor to visit the province since Hadrian. Some of the coins issued during his reign also drew upon Hadrianic precedent in depicting Oceanus as a reverse motif to record his expedition to

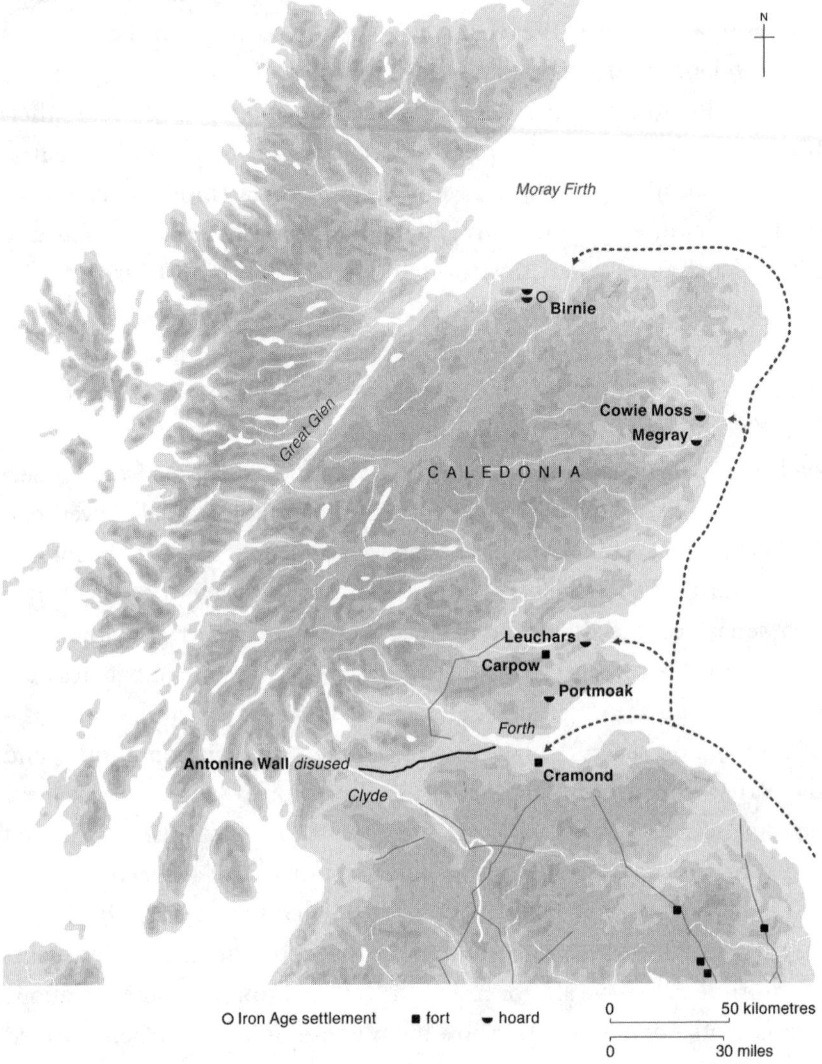

FIG 8.4.
Scotland under Septimius Severus, showing the sites of some forts known to have been occupied at this time, the location of the Iron Age settlement at Birnie, and the location of additional Severan hoards (after Breeze 2006a, fig. 91)

Britain.[26] Severus brought his entire family with him, including his wife, Julia Domna, and his sons, Caracalla and Geta, and took up residence at the legionary fortress at York, the base of the Sixth Legion. An extensive extramural settlement had developed to the south of the River Ouse alongside this fortress and had grown into a substantial town by the time Severus adopted York as his imperial capital. At some point during the early third century, this urban community was awarded the status of colony and became the fourth of such urban settlements in Britain.[27]

The three campaigning seasons Severus spent in Britain indicate the high importance he placed on subduing the province. He was probably familiar with Tacitus' account of Agricola's exploits in Britain and clearly aimed to conquer the entire island and provide his sons with experience of campaigning in the process. In 209 and 210 he and his older son, Caracalla, directed two major campaigns to the north of Hadrian's Wall. Little is known about these events, except that supply bases were established at South Shields and Corbridge and some of the marching camps discovered across southern and eastern Scotland presumably date to his campaigns. Several forts are also known to have been constructed under his reign. One classical account, which undoubtedly exaggerates his achievements, records that he pursued the retreating Britons to the end of the island and that 50,000 of them perished.[28] Perhaps he was consciously following in Agricola's footsteps by campaigning into Caledonia up the east coast of Scotland. Tacitus' account of his father-in-law's adventures was well known during Severus' lifetime.

Severus died at York in February 211. He was cremated, and his ashes were returned to Rome in a jar of purple stone, perhaps Egyptian porphyry. He was succeeded jointly by his sons, Caracalla and Geta. They had a fractious relationship, however, and Caracalla soon arranged to have his brother murdered and took up sole control of the empire. Caracalla straightaway cancelled his father's plan to conquer northern Britain and made peace with the northern peoples in 211.[29] To ensure the security of the northern frontier, Hadrian's Wall was then recommissioned. Most of the classical writers in fact attributed the building of this wall to Severus, reflecting the claims in his propaganda that he had restored the security of Britain. Since it appears to have been his intention to conquer the lands to the north of the wall, however, the restoration of the wall more likely was ordered by Caracalla. The wall was now almost a century old, and the curtain wall would have required substantial rebuilding. A new fort was constructed at Newcastle, and several other forts along the line of the wall were also rebuilt. A policy of in-depth defence was reestablished. and some of the outpost forts to the north of the wall were rebuilt after a period of abandonment.

Caracalla also divided the province of Britain into two, with York becoming the capital of *Britannia Inferior* (Lower Britain), again demonstrating the importance of the fortress and town. The prosperous town of London was probably the capital of the other province, *Britannia Superior* (Upper Britain). Famously, Caracalla also extended Roman citizenship to almost the entire free population of the Roman Empire, meaning that auxiliary soldiers and free residents of the province of Britannia alike were now citizens of Rome. Most of the original benefits of Roman citizenship had, however, already been eroded by this time, and the most important privileges had become restricted to the hereditary Roman elite.

THE WALL DURING THE LATE THIRD AND EARLY FOURTH CENTURIES

Little is known about the frontier during the third century. In 286 Carausius, a senior Roman army officer, rebelled against the rule of the joint emperors Diocletian and Maximian, and Britain was caught up in these events.[30] The emperors had appointed Carausius to suppress the 'barbarian' raiders in the Channel and restore Roman supremacy at sea. Instead, he seized personal control of Britain and part of Gaul, establishing and building up a fleet to defend his territory. Following the precedent of Hadrian and Severus, Carausius' desire to control the sea was symbolized on some of his coinage by Oceanus, the ancestral god of the sea who had long been associated in the Roman mind with Britain.[31]

This threat to Rome's control of the sea led to the construction of substantial forts which defended the ports on either side of the Channel. The fleet was also reinforced to combat the piracy threatening Roman control of the sea. These coastal forts required a large garrison, which must have resulted in a reallocation of troops from elsewhere and a consequent reduction in manpower along the northern frontier. Although some of the forts across Wales and south of Hadrian's Wall remained in use until well into the third century, the provincial garrison as a whole was gradually being thinned out to support the new coastal defences.[32]

Carausius was quickly overthrown by Allectus, his second in command. The Roman emperors were clearly determined to take Gaul and Britain back from the usurpers, however, and in 296 Constantius Chlorus (Constantius I) crossed Ocean to Britain, defeated Allectus, and restored Britain to the empire.[33] Constantius returned to Britain in 305, accompanied by his son, Constantine, to campaign against a people known as the Picts, or the 'painted people'.[34] This name was often used in classical texts addressing the troubles on Britain's northern frontier during the fourth century. The Picts represented a loose confederation of peoples, uniting from time to time, as Roman power weakened, to threaten the province with raiding and looting. Little is known about Constantius' campaigns, although he clearly led an invasion of the lands beyond the wall. He claimed a victory in Rome, and although his campaign probably did not result in the permanent conquest of any territory, the garrison of the wall was evidently restored.

The following year, Constantius died while visiting York, the second Roman emperor to pass away there in just under 100 years. Constantine was declared emperor at York by the troops under his command, giving him control over the western empire. An account of the final weeks of Constantius' life by a panegyrist, though fanciful, provides an insight into the continuing status of Britannia, in the minds of at least some senior Romans, as a mythical place: 'at the moment when he [Constantius] was to go to the gods, he gazed upon Ocean, the father of the gods, who restores the fiery stars of heaven, so that, when about to enjoy eternal light, he might already see the almost unending daylight there'.[35] Gazing across the North Sea into the twilight, Constantius glimpses the leap from history to eternity that awaits him in York. By crossing Ocean, he has joined the fellowship of divine commanders who travelled to campaign in Britain, including Julius Caesar, Claudius, Vespasian, Hadrian, and Septimius Severus.

The presence of the emperors Severus and Constantius and their entourages at York clearly demonstrates the importance of this fortress and colony to the Roman government of Britain. The fortress remained the base of the Sixth Legion, which may have continued there for some time into the fourth century.[36] The fortresses at Chester and Caerleon were also maintained into the fourth century, although the total number of soldiers located at these legionary bases were reduced.[37]

THE LAST CENTURY OF ROMAN RULE

The events of the late third century impacted the security of the northern frontier, since they led to the reduction of its garrison. Although the infrastructure of the wall continued to be maintained, and most of the forts would still have been manned, life for the communities settled along the frontier frontier deteriorated.[38] Some forts were decommissioned, and the extramural settlements which had developed outside the gates of the forts along the wall were abandoned. During the fourth century the soldiers were paid in kind, with food and clothing, rather than in coin. This reduced the opportunities for trade at the forts and helps to explain why people began to leave the extramural settlements.[39] In many of the forts the families of the soldiers may have been rehoused within the ramparts, as the excavations indicate at Vindolanda, where artefacts associated with women and children are common within the walls of the fourth-century fort. In contrast to the disused extramural settlements at the forts along the wall, the towns at Carlisle and Corbridge continued to prosper well into the fourth century.

Despite deteriorating conditions, Rome's strategy for keeping the frontiers stable appears to have succeeded throughout the fourth century, with only occasional breakdowns of order. Peace was maintained through the two-pronged strategy of continuing to garrison the wall and bribing the peoples who lived beyond it. The wealthy elites of southern Britain clearly prospered; local self-rule at the *civitas* capitals continued, and a number of elaborate and substantial villas were constructed across southern lands.[40] Southern Britain at this time provided corn not only for the Roman garrison on the British frontier but also for the garrison on the River Rhine. The mosaics in some of these villas portray religious scenes that are comparable to houses of the elite in the Roman Mediterranean.

There are also some indications that Christianity, which Constantine introduced as the official religion of the empire, started to replace older forms of worship across the province. For instance, three bishops and a priest from Britain attended the Council of Arles in 314, although direct evidence for Christian worship in Britain is scarce.[41] The new religion also spread to the northern frontier, although it did not completely sweep away older religious practices.

Classical accounts described the condition of the frontier during the fourth century as unsettled, provoking further interventions by Rome. The emperor Constans visited in 343, possibly to campaign against an uprising.[42] He also issued coins featuring Oceanus, drawing upon imagery on the coinage of earlier emperors who had crossed the sea to Britain. The organization of the frontier garrison had changed by this time, as sons tended to follow their fathers into military service, establishing settled communities at the forts. This may also have helped to maintain stability. In 367, the commander Theodosius visited the province to campaign against a 'barbarian conspiracy', and in the early 380s, Magnus Maximus won a victory against the Picts and Scots.[43] The Scots were a people from Ireland who came to settle in northern Britain during the late fourth and fifth centuries, eventually leading to the naming of northern Britain as Scotland. Very little is known about these campaigns.

During the late fourth century some military personnel may have been removed from the province to serve in the serious conflicts resulting from invasions of Germanic peoples on the Continent, but many of the forts across the frontier region of Britain continued to be occupied. In the second half of the fourth century, as the security provided by the frontiers gradually deteriorated, the towns and villas of the civil zone declined in wealth, although many remained occupied. The classical texts begin to mention Saxon invaders from Germany, in addition to the Picts and Scots. After about three and a half centuries of Roman rule, the campaigns by emperors and military commanders to conquer and hold Britain finally ceased. The first decade of the fifth century is usually taken to mark the end of Roman rule in Britain. Archaeological excavations, however, have revealed that although some military units may have been withdrawn, many of the forts along the wall and the northern frontier region continued to be occupied.[44] The role of Hadrian's Wall as a manned Roman frontier, however, ended when the imperial administration abandoned Britain during the first decade of the fifth century. The communities at the forts on the northern frontier gradually transformed themselves into local bands of warriors who strove to keep order in the areas immediately surrounding their defended settlements.

Occupation also continued at many of the towns and rural settlements across the south of the province, although the supply of imperial coinage and the manufacture of industrial goods gradually declined as the Roman provincial government collapsed.[45] Many of the walled towns of the south probably served as the focus for regional kingdoms under single rulers, and by the 440s, groups of settlers from northern continental Europe settled over much of southern and eastern Britain.[46] By this time Roman rule in Britain was, well and truly, over.

AFTERWORD: 'WHAT HAVE THE ROMANS EVER DONE FOR US?'

Roll on, thou deep and dark blue ocean—roll! . . .
Time writes no wrinkle on thine azure brow—
Such as creation's dawn beheld, thou rollest now.

—Byron, *Childe Harold's Pilgrimage*

After the ending of the Roman rule of the province of Britannia during the late fourth and early fifth centuries, knowledge of its Roman past was almost entirely lost. The ruins of masonry buildings, including the walls surrounding the towns and forts, and the frontier works of Hadrian's Wall survived into medieval times, however, providing evidence for the Roman investment in the conquest of Britain. Many of the classical texts narrating events in the Roman past were also lost, and it was the rediscovery of these ancient writings during the sixteenth century which brought tales of Britain's distant past to the attention of knowledgeable scholars.[1] In conjunction with the discovery of many Latin stone inscriptions throughout central and western Britain, this stimulated an interest in antiquarian pursuits during the ensuing centuries. Scholars and artists mused upon the Roman past and the origins of the contemporary population of the British Isles. During the eighteenth century, knowledge of the settlements and possessions of the people who had inhabited Roman Britain also advanced, as inscriptions were collected and excavations were occasionally made at villas and military sites.

THE RECOVERY OF ROMAN BRITAIN

Two interconnected themes in particular were explored in the classical texts addressing Britain: the actions of the invading Roman forces and the resistance of named ancient Britons. Boudica is a particularly enlightening example of this.[2] While the complexity of her character, as narrated in the writings of Tacitus and Dio, has sometimes been used to construct a positive view of rightful British resistance to foreign domination, at other times she has been viewed in an entirely negative manner as a savage barbarian. During the late sixteenth and early seventeenth centuries Queen Elizabeth I (r. 1558–1603) was compared with Boudica to encourage the English people to resist the threat of invasions from the Continent (see fig. I.6). Later in the seventeenth century, plays and poems portrayed Boudica in far more negative terms. During the nineteenth century her image was reinvented as a primitive parallel with Queen Victoria (r. 1837–1901). At a time when Britain was developing an empire of its own, Boudica's valiant resistance to Rome provided Victorian scholars and poets with a powerful message of national unity in pursuit of imperial might.

The classical texts supplied details about other individuals that British authors also used to illustrate the significance of the Roman past. Caratacus and Calgacus were sources for musings upon the ancestry and identity of the peoples of Britain.[3] During the late sixteenth century, meanwhile, the name of the British king Cunobelin was identified on pre-Roman coins. William Shakespeare's play *Cymbeline* (1611) drew very creatively upon the limited information in the classical texts about this powerful pre-Roman king. Narrating events that had taken place in the century between Julius Caesar's invasion and the arrival of Claudius, Shakespeare portrayed the growing civility of the Britons under Roman tutelage and emphasized Cymbeline's status as a civilized ruler as a favourable reflection on the contemporary politics of the court of James I (r. 1603–23).

Hadrian's Wall was generally known at this time as 'Picts' wall' and was thought to have been constructed during the late fourth and early fifth centuries, when the Roman forces were withdrawing from Britain. James I tried to unify the formerly independent kingdoms of Scotland and England into 'Great Britain', and poets used the ruination of Picts' wall to symbolize this policy.[4] On the map of Northumberland included in Michael Drayton's poetic vision of Britain, *Poly-olbion* (1622), 'aged Pictswall' was personified as a water god, dressed in contemporary clothing, with the Roman wall sprouting from his head (fig. A.1). In this image, the illustrator, William Hole, was drawing upon a classical conception that the River Tyne supplemented the physical wall in the formation of the frontier. In Drayton's poem, Pictswall describes how he maintained control over the unsettled frontier in Roman and medieval times.

As the lead characters in plays and poems, pro-Roman figures generally proved less popular than the freedom fighter of ancient Britain. Until the

FIG A.1.
The detail of William Hole's image of 'Aged Picstwall' taken from the map of Northumberland in Michael Drayton's *Poly-Olbion* (1622) (from a print in the possession of Richard Hingley)

famous inscription was uncovered during building work in Chichester in 1723, the friendly king Togidubnus, for example, was known only from a single reference in Tacitus' *Agricola*.[5] The inscription fascinated antiquarians. It provided the important information that Togidubnus was a Roman citizen and gave rise to speculation (incorrect) that he was a Christian. Romans were also sometimes adopted as honorary Englishmen during the eighteenth century. In Edward Barnard's *New, impartial and complete history of England* (1790), Agricola was portrayed as a senior Roman official who made a formative contribution to English social and cultural history (fig. A.2).[6]

The civilizing contribution of classical Rome to Britain could be a difficult concept to accept, since, as Tacitus outlined, Agricola had also enslaved the Britons. Such images of civilization and barbarism have derived much of their potency from the nuances in the classical texts.[7] The powerful idea of Roman civilization developed partly from a notion that the arrival of the Romans introduced 'civilization' to southern Britain, or what was now England, as the title of Barnard's book indicated, rather than to the whole of Great Britain. Southern Britain appeared to have been particularly privileged by the Romans, as this was where the most impressive Roman towns and rural villas were to be found. By contrast, although a military presence had been maintained throughout the Roman period in Wales and northern England, Roman culture appeared not to have flourished to the same extent. Scotland and Ireland lay beyond the limits of Roman 'civilization' entirely, and from the medieval period Hadrian's Wall was considered to be the dividing line between 'civilized' England and 'barbarian' Scotland.[8]

Archaeological research increased substantially in scale during the nineteenth century, inspired in part by the idea that the Romans had played a formative part in the development of early society across Britain. Excavation focused mainly on the villas and towns of the south; towards the end of the century, military sites, including Hadrian's Wall and the Antonine Wall, also began to be investigated on a large scale.[9] The early excavations were undertaken by clearing the soil from the buried remains of stone buildings. Little recording of archaeological structures was undertaken, but detailed records of particular projects were

FIG A.2.
'Julius Agricola ... introducing the Roman Arts and Sciences into England' (from a print in the possession of Richard Hingley)

increasingly produced. The second half of the nineteenth century was also vitally important for the emergence of knowledge of the artefacts and settlements of the pre-Roman populations.[10] The scale of archaeological research during the past century has transformed the quantity and quality of information available both for the Iron Age and for the Roman invasion of Britain,[11] as this book clearly demonstrates.

THE MODERN WORLD

As Britain's own empire grew, the public's sense of the relevance of the Roman past was transformed. In their parody of history teaching in schools, *1066 and All That* (1930), W. C. Sellar and R. J. Yeatman jokingly remarked that 'the Roman conquest was … a *Good Thing*, since the Britons were only natives at that time.'[12] The settled ways of life of many generations of people across the British Isles prior to the Roman invasion were linked, through the use of the term 'native', to the ways of life of the colonized nonwestern peoples of Britain's own empire.[13] Sellar and Yeatman were referring to a commonly held belief that the Roman conquest of Britain had assisted the peoples of lowland Britain to develop over time until, in the Victorian era, they in turn had conquered and incorporated 'natives' within their expanding empire across the globe.[14]

The Monty Python comedy *Life of Brian* (1979) follows a broadly comparable logic. Although the action is set in Judaea during the Roman period, this film also provides a commentary on the teaching of the Roman past in elite ('public') schools in Britain. John Cleese as Reg, a representative of the People's Front of Judaea, famously demands: 'What have the Romans ever done for us?'[15] He is responding to the observations of his fractious followers, who, in answer to his initial statement that the Romans had 'bled us white' and 'taken everything that we had', list a variety of innovations—including the aqueduct, sanitation, roads, irrigation, medicine, education, wine, public baths, and order. As Reg's anti-Roman stance is seen to be more than a little unbalanced, we can infer from this scene that Britain's elite schools taught that the Roman Empire was a formative influence in social development in the Mediterranean, Europe, and Britain. This reflects the sentiment that overall the Roman invasion was a 'good thing' for the English, despite Tacitus' observation that it had led to the enslavement of the Britons.

In today's media, the perceived contribution of the Romans to contemporary society is often given a less ironic and more direct emphasis.[16] The 'televisual' character of Roman sites and finds, together with the prominence of the classical texts dealing with Britain, account in part for the public prominence of Rome today. In Scotland and Wales ideas about resistance to Rome have long been far more popular. The length of time it took Rome to conquer Wales is suggestive of a highly resistant Iron Age population, and it was also there that Caratacus, having transferred his centre of resistance from south-east Britain, made his final stand before being captured and taken to Rome. Scotland had apparently resisted with even greater success and, like Ireland, remained free of direct Roman control. Despite his ultimate defeat, Calgacus is seen as a valiant model of resistance to southern invaders, whether Roman or English.[17]

Current views of the Roman period remain highly variable. Roman Britain's role as a military province continues to be emphasized by the media and in education. Many of the Roman monuments that are accessible to the public are military in character, and Roman legionary reenactment is very popular.[18] Prominent among Roman monuments open to the public are numerous sites along Hadrian's Wall (notably Vindolanda, Housesteads, and Chesters) and the legionary fortresses at Chester and Caerleon (see app. 2). The 'loss of the Ninth Legion' has inspired two films, both released in 2011 (*The Eagle* and *Centurion*), while novels about the Roman military invasion and settlement of Britain are particularly popular, as exemplified by the writings of Simon Scarrow and Adrian Goldsworthy. Goldsworthy, an acknowledged expert on the Roman army, has written a four- novel series inspired by the excavations at Vindolanda.[19] Civil life in the south of Britain is somewhat less well served by the media, although the public can visit Roman remains of towns and rural villas. These include museum displays of Roman towns at Verulamium, Camulodunum, London, and York and the impressive Roman villas at Chedworth and Fishbourne.

The Iron Age is also less well represented in the media, although Boudica has inspired a series of novels, of which Manda Scott's trilogy is an excellent example.[20] More recently, first Theresa May and then Boris Johnson have been portrayed as Boudica/Boadicea with ironic humour in cartoons in newspapers as they have attempted to extricate Britain from the European Union.[21] Although the impressive ramparts of the most substantial Iron Age monuments—the hillforts of England, Scotland, and Wales—may project the idea of Iron Age peoples as having been in a constant state of conflict and warfare, since the 1970s a very different view has been communicated at open-air museums in all three countries. The displays emphasize the idea of peaceful, settled, and egalitarian communities (fig. I.5).[22]

The leading Roman actors in these scenes of imperial conquest outline above are male, reflecting the ways the classical texts expressed an elite masculine desire for status and wealth through the exercise of military power. The province, however, is portrayed in female guise on a sculpture from Aphrodisias and coins from Hadrian's reign. Prominent women of the Roman conquest and settlement of Britain included a queen and a powerful female warrior. The wife of the commanding officer at Vindolanda had the freedom to visit friends on the frontier, and female slaves and prostitutes lived among the military communities of the lands of campaign and conquest. The tale of conquest remains, however, primarily one of men who campaigned to enhance their masculinity, status, and wealth through military aggression. This tale of conquering Ocean narrated in this book are aimed to communicates the futility of such imperialistic acts and the death and enslavement they occasion.

APPENDIX 1

TIMELINE OF MAIN EVENTS

FIRST CONTACT AND DIPLOMACY

BCE

320s: The Greek sailor **Pytheas** sails along the western coast of Europe to Britain and beyond

55: The first invasion of **Julius Caesar**

54: The second invasion of **Julius Caesar**

51: The Gallic ruler **Commius** is sent across Ocean to rule in Britain, establishing the southern kingdom

30s and 20s: **Augustus** considers invading Britain on three occasions; diplomacy is used to keep the British kings at peace

14: **Tiberius** succeeds as emperor on Augustus' death and maintains the same diplomatic policy with regard to Britain

CE

16: The fleet of **Germanicus** is destroyed on the north sea; some shipwrecked soldiers are returned to Rome from Britain

30s: **Cunobelin**, a friend of Rome, rules over a large kingdom in southern Britain

39–40: The emperor **Caligula** considers invading Germany and Britain but fails to follow through on the plan

INVASION

43: The emperor **Claudius**, who has replaced Caligula, personally commands the successful invasion of south-eastern Britain, receiving the surrender of a number of kings

43–47: The first Roman governor of Britain, **Aulus Plautius**, conquers much of southern Britain

49–51: The second provincial governor, **Ostorius Scapula**, attacks the peoples of Wales, defeating **Caratacus**

52: **Caratacus** is paraded in Rome

54–60: Further campaigns are waged in Wales and central Britain during the reign of the emperor **Nero**

60–61: **Boudica** of the Iceni leads a significant uprising, which almost drives the Romans out of Britain

61–62: Roman order is restored in the province

68–69: The emperor **Nero** commits suicide, plunging the empire into crisis

69–70: **Cartimandua,** queen of the Brigantes, is overthrown and rescued by Rome; the new emperor, **Vespasian,** starts to restore order to the empire

70–71: The governor **Vettius Bolanus** undertakes some campaigns in central Britain

71: Vespasian appoints **Petillius Cerialis** to replace Bolanus as governor, commanding him to conquer the rest of mainland Britain

71–74: Conquest of the **Brigantes**

74–77: The succeeding governor, **Sextus Julius Frontinus,** campaigns in central Britain and Wales

78: **Julius Agricola** takes over as governor; he completes the conquest of Wales

79–80: Roman campaigns of conquest continue in southern Scotland under Agricola; the emperor **Titus** replaces Vespasian

81–82: A temporary halt is called to the invasion at the southern boundary of Caledonia**;** **Domitian** replaces Titus

83: Agricola leads his military forces and navy to invade **Caledonia** in pursuit of the conquest of northern Britain

84: Campaigning in north-eastern Scotland, Agricola defeats the massed forces of the Caledonians and their leader, **Calgacus,** at the battle of ***Mons Graupius***.

ESTABLISHING THE NORTHERN FRONTIER

85: Agricola is recalled to Rome and replaced by **Sallustius Lucullus** as governor of Britain

85–86: Campaigns in the far north continue, but a decision is soon made to **withdraw from Caledonia** as the result of the imperial crisis caused by conflict with Dacia

85–90: Initial establishment of the Stanegate, a guarded road along the northern frontier, including the first fort at **Vindolanda**

98: **Trajan** replaces Nerva as emperor; Britain, apparently, remains fairly quiet

103–11: The **Stanegate** is reinforced with additional garrisons as a relatively stable frontier is developed

117: **Hadrian** becomes emperor at the death of Trajan; a significant **uprising** breaks out in Britain

118–20: The uprising is suppressed

121: **Hadrian** embarks on a tour of the provinces and plans to visit Britain, ordering the construction of **Hadrian's Wall**

122: Hadrian visits Britain and inspects the wall under construction; two decisions are made, to strengthen the wall by adding forts to the line and by constructing the Vallum

122–30: The building of Hadrian's Wall

THE LATER HISTORY OF THE FRONTIER

138: Hadrian dies; **Antoninus Pius**, who succeeds him, commands the invasion of Scotland

142–45: The **Antonine Wall** is constructed

Late 150s: The Antonine Wall is abandoned and the Roman garrison withdrawn back to Hadrian's Wall

180s–190s: Further unrest on the British frontier

208–11: The emperor **Septimius Severus** visits Britain with his sons to campaign in Scotland

286–96: **Carausius and Allectus** break away from the rule of the Roman emperors, withdrawing soldiers from the northern frontier

296: Emperor **Constantius I** reconquers Britain

305: Constantius travel to Britain to campaign against the Picts and dies in York; he is succeeded as emperor by his son **Constantine**

343: Emperor **Constans** visits Britain, probably to lead a campaign in the north

367: The commander **Theodosius** campaigns in Britain

383: **Magnus Maximus** leads another campaign in Britain

400–430: The province of **Britain** ceases to be part of the Roman Empire

APPENDIX 2

NAMES OF THE PLACES AND THE PEOPLES OF LATE IRON AGE AND ROMAN BRITAIN

THESE PLACE NAMES AND names of the Iron Age peoples and Roman *civitates* are mainly derived from Rivet and Smith (1979), updated here with the results of additional research. The final column gives an indication of the remains that can be visited at these sites (for more information see Hingley 2020c).

Place Names

Modern name	Ancient name	Meaning of ancient name	Role of site	Visible remains*
Benwell	*Condercum*	Place for looking around	Fort	T, V
Colchester	Camulodunum	Fortress of Camulos (a war god)	*Oppidum*, then Roman fortress	M
Colchester	*Colonia Victricensis*	Colony of the victorious	Colony/town	F, M, TW, T
Caerleon	*Isca*	Name of local river	Fortress	BH, FW, M, T
Carlisle	*Luguvalium*	Town of Luguualos (war god)	Fort and town	M
Carrawburgh	*Brocilita*	Covered with heather	Fort	T
Chester	*Deva*	Name of a goddess	Fortress	A, FW, M
Chesters	*Cilurnum*	Cauldron pool	Fort	BH, FW, M
Chichester	*Noviomagus Regnorum*	New market of the Regni	*Oppidum* then town	BH, M, TW
Cirencester	*Corinium Dobunnorum*	[uncertain] of the Dobunni	Town	A, M
Corbridge	*Coria?*	Meeting place?	Fort then town	BH, H, M, T,
Dorchester	*Durnovaria*	Low lying	Town	A, H, M
Exeter	*Isca*	Name of local river	Fortress then town	M, TW

Gloucester	*Glevum*	Bright, noble place	Fortress then colony	M
Leicester	*Ratae Corietavorum*	Fort of the Corieltavi	Possible *oppidum* then town	BH, M
Lincoln	*Lindum*	Pond or lake	Fortress then colony	M, TW
London	*Londinium*	River which requires swimming	Town	A, T, M
Mancetter	*Manduessedum*	Horse chariot	Fort	
	Mons Graupius	Mountain of?	Battle site	
Newcastle	*Pons Aelius*	Hadrian's bridge	Bridge and fort	M
Richborough	*Rutupiae*	Muddy estuary	Camp then port	FW
Silchester	*Calleva Atrebatum*	Town in the woods, of the Atrebates	*Oppidum* then town	A, TW
St Albans	Verulamium	[Uncertain]	*Oppidum* then town	A, H, TW, M
Usk	*Burrium*	Stout, big	Fortress	
Vindolanda	*Vindolanda*	White season	Fort	BH, FW, H, T, M
Wallsend	*Segedunum*	Strong fort	Fort	BH, FW, M
Winchester	*Venta Belgarum*	Market of the Belgae	*Oppidum* then town	M
Wroxeter	*Viroconium Cornoviorum*	Town of Uirico, of the Cornovii	Fortress then town	F, H, M
York	*Eboracum*	Estate of Eburos	Fortress, town and then colony	FW, M

*A = theatre/amphitheatre; BH = bathhouse; F = forum; FW = fort/fortress wall; H = private house; M = museum; T = temple; TW = town walls; V = Vallum crossing

Names of Peoples

Name	Location	Possible meaning
Atrebates	Southern Britain	Settlers, inhabitants
Belgae	Southern Britain	Proud ones
Brigantes	Central Britain	Mighty ones
Caledonia	Northern Britain	Tough men
Cantiaci	Southern Britain	[Unknown]
Carvetii	Central Britain	Deer-men
Catuvellauni	Southern Britain	Men good in battle
Corieltauvi	Southern Britain	[Unknown]
Cornovii	Western Britain	Worshippers of Cerunnos [a horned god]
Cornovii	South-western Britain	Worshippers of Cerunnos [a horned god]
Deceangli	Western Britain	[Unknown]
Demetae	Western Britain	[Unknown]
Dobunni	South-western Britain	[Unknown]
Dumnonii	South-western Britain	Worshippers of Dumnu
Iceni	Eastern Britain	[Unknown]
Ordovices	Western Britain	Hammer-fighters
Regni	Southern Britain	People of the kingdom?
Silures	Western Britain	[Unknown]
Trinovantes	Eastern Britain	Most vigorous

NOTES

PREFACE

1. Salway (1981) and Todd (1981) are examples (see Cunliffe 1984).

2. Millett, Revell, and Moore (2016).

3. E.g. Braund (1996a), Clarke (2001), A. R. Birley (2005), Gambash (2016).

4. The discussion of Britain and the image of Ocean also evidently draws deeply upon the work of Braund (1996a).

5. In the notes, along with the abbreviation *RIB*, the number of the inscription is also given.

6. See Roymans and Fernández-Götz (2019).

7. The intellectual focus on the undermining of dualities, developed here, and the focus on the uses of the Roman past to interpret current identities has been deeply informed by this project (see Hingley, Bonacchi, and Sharpe 2018).

INTRODUCTION

1. Romm (1992), Braund (1996a), Barry (2011).

2. Diodorus Siculus, 17.104.

3. Romm (1992, 18), Cartledge (2004, 216–7).

4. Carreras and Morais (2012, 420–1), McPhail (2014), Rippon and Holbrook (2021, 30–1).

5. For an explanation of italicization of names in this book, see the note at the end of this introduction.

6. As recorded in Suetonius, *Julius Caesar* 7; see Barry (2011, 36 n. 138).

7. As the term 'tribe' has imperial connotations that link the actions of classical Rome to those of modern empires, it has not been used in this book (Moore 2011).

8. Mattingly (2006, 31–2), Woodman (2014, 103).

9. A. R. Birley (2005); see Malloch (2010, 121).

10. Madsen (2020).

11. These reconstructions are, however, limited. For decades, archaeologists have located Roman forts and excavated them as an aid to mapping the chronology of Roman military campaigns. Archaeological discoveries have often been simply ordered into a chronological sequence of events derived from the fragmentary classical texts. Advanced archaeological techniques of excavation and scientific analysis now allow us to challenge some of these earlier assumptions about the timing and extent of the Roman conquest.

12. See appendix 1 for a timeline of the main events of the conquest.

13. Rivet and Smith (1979, 114–6), Mattingly (2006, 31), Moore (2011, 337–9). Wales was made up of several distinct kingdoms that were rarely under the rule of a single king.

CHAPTER 1

1. Plutarch, *Caesar* 23. Translations from this work in this chapter are by Pelling (2011).
2. Caesar, *Gallic War* 4.20–36; 5.4–23; see Raaflaub (2017a), Raaflaub (2017b). Translations from this work in this chapter are by Hammond (1996).
3. Plutarch, *Caesar* 23.
4. Caesar, *Gallic War* 3.7–19.
5. Evidence for this trade is provided by the imported artefacts, including coins and amphorae, that have been found in in southern Britain (Webley 2015).
6. Romm (1992, 19–26).
7. Arnold (1999), Creighton (2000, 13), Riggsby (2006, 71), Moore (2011).
8. See Brunaux (2018).
9. Plutarch, *Caesar* 15.
10. Caesar, *Gallic War* 1.43.
11. Creighton (2000, 12–3).
12. Caesar, *Gallic War* 2.4.
13. See Hornung (2018, 201). Roman military units were regularly reduced in size as the result of casualties.
14. Bishop and Coulston (2006, 48–72).
15. For the dates of Caesar's activities in Britain in 55 and 54, see Raaflaub and Ramsay (2017).
16. Caesar records this as 7 miles; a Roman mile was about 92 percent of a modern mile.
17. Fitzpatrick (2019, 146).
18. The Romans knew of other peoples who used war chariots, such as the Achaemenids, and chariot racing was one of the most popular spectacles staged in Rome (Dunkle 2014, 441–2).
19. Hunter (2005, 50–6), Inall (2014, 44).
20. Giles (2012, 203).
21. Hingley (2020a).
22. Florus, *Roman History* 1.45.16. Translations from this work in this chapter are by Seymour Forster (1984); interpolations in square brackets are by the author.
23. Cicero, *Letters to Atticus* 4.16.7. Translation by Shackleton Bailey (1999, 341).
24. In 2010 archaeologists uncovered a deep ditch with pottery dating from the first century BCE. Further excavation and survey work during 2015–17 revealed an unusually shaped ditched enclosure with at least one entrance (Fitzpatrick 2018 and Fitzpatrick 2019, 149–54; see Reddé 2018, 290, and Roymans and Fernández-Götz 2019, 416). Human remains were also found, and one of the iron artefacts uncovered has been identified as a Roman *pilum* or spear.
25. Thompson (1983), Holman (2005, 24), Champion (2007, 119), Wallace and Mullen (2019, 78).
26. Harding (2012), Moore (2017a).
27. D. Allen (1944, 12–5). However, this is far from established (see chapter 2).
28. Riggsby (2006, 26, 57–8).
29. Haselgrove (2009).
30. Garrow and Gosden (2012).
31. P. Stewart (1995, 2), E. Scott (2018).
32. Garrow and Gosden (2012).
33. Caesar, *Gallic War* 6.13.
34. Ralston (2017).

35. It has usually been supposed that Cassivellaunus' *oppidum* was located north of London, although the site has yet to be located (Niblett 2001, 48–9).

36. Roymans (2018).

37. Braund (1984), Marshak (2015, 7–8).

38. Caesar, *Gallic War* 7.76–80; see Riggsby (2016, 195).

39. Caesar, *Gallic War* 8.23; 8.48.

40. Frontinus, *The Stratagems* 2.13.

41. Creighton (2000, 26–8, 59–64, 73–4), Leins and Farley (2015, 110), Fanello (2016, 16), see Hoffmann (2013, 31–3).

42. Strabo, *Geography* 4.5.2, mentioned the export of British gold and silver, although there is little to indicate that these minerals were exploited in Britain during the Iron Age (discussed later).

43. However, it is also important to note that the coins with the name Commius that have been found in Gaul are of an entirely different type.

44. Taylor, Weale, and Ford (2014, 59–64), Taylor et al. (2020).

45. Suetonius, *Julius Caesar* 37.1.

46. Strabo, *Geography* 4.5.2.

47. Pliny, *Natural History* 9.116; see Hind (2003, 272), Rutledge (2012, 228), Woodman (2014, 156).

48. Florus, *Roman History* 1.45.19.

CHAPTER 2

1. Pedo's poem is lost but this excerpt was preserved in Seneca, *Suasoria* 1. 16–23. The sections of this work quoted in this chapter are from the translation of Senaca's *Declamations* by Winterbottom (1974, 505–6); see also Gambash (2016, 30).

2. Dio 39.38; 53.22; 53.25.

3. B. Campbell (2001, 16), Marshak (2015, 21–2).

4. Diodorus Siculus 5.21.6.

5. Strabo, *Geography* 4.5.2–3. Translations from this work in this chapter are by Roller (2020, 207–8).

6. Braund (1996a, 85), Beard, North, and Price (1998, 157), Gambash (2016, 25).

7. Strabo, *Geography* 4.5.2–3.

8. Creighton (2000, 24); see May (2001), Williams (2005, 73).

9. Caesar's comment on the four kings ruling in Kent in 54 BCE indicates the potential complexity of the peoples subject to the rule of these two kingdoms.

10. The narrative in this chapter is simplified, and there are considerable gaps in our knowledge of the political history of Late Iron Age Britain (see Creighton 2000, 74–5).

11. Creighton (2000, fig. 3.8), Fanello (2016, 236). On these coins, *F* is taken to indicate the Latin word *filius* ('son of').

12. Creighton (2000, 24).

13. As indicated by scientific analysis of gold and silver artefacts from Britain (Creighton 2000, 68–70, La Niece et al. 2018, 421–5). Strabo, however, does refer to the export of gold and silver from Britain to the Continent (discussed later).

14. Hill et al. (2004).

15. Rose (1990), Creighton (2006, 42), see Sande (2015, 8).

16. Augustus, *Res Gestae* 31–2; see Cooley (2009). The *Res Gestae* refers to 'Tinco', which is thought to relate to Tincomarus.

17. Creighton (2000, 74–9). At the time of Caesar's invasion, two of the rulers from this area are known to us as Cassivellaunus and Mandubracius, although their names do not occur on coins.

Other rulers, named Addedomarus and Dubnovellaunus, are also named on coins to the north of the Thames and could have been ruling before or at the same time as Tasciovanus.

18. D. Allen (1944, 12–5), Rivet and Smith (1979, 304–5).
19. Hill (2007, 31–2), Williams (2007, 1), Moore (2017b, 289).
20. After the Roman conquest, Camulodunum was within the territory of the Trinovantes, while the Catuvellauni had their capital at Verulamium.
21. Niblett (2001, 37–42), Creighton (2000, 124–5).
22. Niblett (2004, 33), Gascoyne and Radford (2013, 42–53).
23. Niblett (2004, 31–3), Fitzpatrick (2007, 129–31); see Haselgrove (2016, 389–90).
24. Potter (2002, 20), Williams (2005, 73–4).
25. Fanello (2016, 235), Haselgrove (2018, 81, 83).
26. Creighton (2006, 58–61), Haselgrove (2018, 91), Fulford (2018, 374–8, 381–4), Fulford (2021, 42).
27. Fulford (2015, 64).
28. Haselgrove (2004, 15), Haselgrove (2016).
29. Fell (2020, 669–70, 677–8).
30. Alston (2015, 327–31).
31. Meyer (2018).
32. Tacitus, *Annals* 2.24. Translated by Woodman (2004, 51).
33. Romm (1992, 142–4), Braund (1996a, 202), Gambash (2016, 30).
34. Strabo, *Geography* 4.5.3.
35. Clarke (1999, 327–8).
36. Webley (2015, 129–30).
37. Farley (2012, 13–23).
38. See Pitts (1989, 46–7).
39. Willis (2007, 117).
40. Caesar, *Gallic War* 3.13.
41. Suetonius, *Caligula* 44. Translated by Edwards (2000, 159).
42. Dio 60.21.
43. Creighton (2006, 132–5), P. Crummy et al. (2007, 447–56).
44. Haselgrove (2004, 14), Haselgrove and Score (2014, 311).
45. See Moore (2012, 394–5), Moore (2020).
46. Creighton (2000, 77, 191–5).
47. Creighton (2000, 111–2).
48. Barrett (2001, 125), Braund (1996a, 92–6), Osgood (2011, 87), Gambash (2016, 31–2).
49. Gambash (2016, 31–2), Roncaglia (2019, 67–8).
50. Suetonius, *Caligula* 44–7.

CHAPTER 3

1. Tacitus, *Agricola* 12. Transaltions from this work in this chapter are from A. R. Birley (1999).
2. Osgood (2011, 86).
3. Dio provides the only detailed account of the first months of the conquest to survive (Dio 60.19–23). This was written a century and a half after the event, although clearly relying on at least one earlier text, lost in antiquity (see Lange and Madsen 2016). Translations from this work in this chapter are by Cary (1924).
4. It is possible that Dio's use of the word 'son' also related to a more distant family relationship.
5. Suetonius, *Claudius* 17.
6. A. R. Birley (2005, 19–25).

7. It has usually been claimed that four legions came to Britain in 43 (Todd 2004, 45; A. R. Birley 2005, 227; Tomlin 2018, 2–3, 30), although this is not stated by Dio or any other classical author (see Hoffmann 2013, 56–7).

8. Tacitus, *Histories* 3.44; see A. R. Birley (2005, 22).

9. Fitzpatrick (2019, 154), Andrew Fitzpatrick (personal communication 2020).

10. Millett and Wilmott (2003, 185).

11. See Hind (2007, 107–13), Mason (2009, 78–83).

12. Chris Rudd (personal communication 2020).

13. Dio 60.20. Dio's text is unclear at this point.

14. Dio 60.20.

15. Sauer (2000, 39), see Hind (2007).

16. Dio 60.20.

17. Hingley (2018, 23).

18. Hind (2007, 99–100), Mattingly (2011, 90–1).

19. Suetonius, *Claudius* 17. Translations from this work in this chapter are by Edwards (2000), except where noted. Dio evidently drew on a contemporary account that had exaggerated the role the emperor played in the military events of the conquest.

20. Tomlin (2018, 2–11).

21. Dio 60.21.

22. Tomlin (2018, 17–8).

23. Hoffmann (2013, 203–4).

24. Pomponius Mela, writing during Claudius' reign, mentioned the thirty islands of Orkney, information that must have derived from a knowledgeable source (Romer 1998, 2–3, 115–7).

25. Unfortunately, the section of Tacitus' *Annals* that addressed the first five years of the Roman conquest was lost in antiquity, and as a result we are dependent on fragmentary classical accounts and archaeological discoveries.

26. Tacitus, *Agricola* 14; see Barrett (1979, 234), Braund (1996a, 134–5), Creighton (2006, 31), Tomlin (2018, 34), *RIB* 91.

27. Tacitus, *Annals* 31.

28. See Williams (2000, 278–9).

29. Davies (2009, 120–6).

30. Tacitus, *Histories* 3.45; see Braund (1996a, 124–5), Haselgrove (2016, 472–6).

31. Niblett (2004, 32), Creighton (2006, 125).

32. Wacher (1995, 219). Dio (60.20) inferred that Caratacus and Togodumnus, sons of Cunobelin, were leaders of the Catuvellauni. The *oppidum* of Verulamium would develop into the urban centre of the Catuvellauni.

33. See Creighton (2006, 14), Holbrook (2008, 311), Creighton and Fry (2016, 365–8), Tomlin (2018, 24–5), Moore (2020, 580).

34. Roman military equipment has also been found in the early Roman phases of the towns at Silchester and Chichester, indicating that troops may have been stationed at the capitals of several of the friendly kingdoms (see Creighton and Fry 2016, 365–8; Fulford et al. 2020, 560–70).

35. Score (2011), Haselgrove and Score (2014).

36. See Schörner (2009, 121–1) and Haynes (2013, 96–7) for a comparable helmet from Bizye in Turkey, a gift to a friendly ruler of Thrace called King Rhoemetalkes.

37. See Creighton and Fry (2016, 366–8).

38. Roncaglia (2019, 61–3).

39. Suetonius, *Claudius* 17.

40. Dio 60.23; see Tomlin (2018, 3–11), Rothe (2020, 72–4).

41. Suetonius, *Claudius* 21; see Coleman (1990, 71–2).

42. See A. R. Birley (2005, 15–135).

43. R. Jones (2012).

44. Gascoyne and Radford (2013). 'Fortresses' are usually distinguished from 'vexillation fortresses' in accounts of the early conquests in Roman Britain (e.g. Bidwell 2007). The former were considered to have been constructed for an entire legion and the latter for a 'vexillation' or part of a legion. All of these covered larger areas than forts, which usually accommodated around 500 soldiers. The fortresses of the first twenty years of the conquest, however, varied considerably in size, and it is now thought that legions usually campaigned in flexible units of fewer than 5,000 men (Sauer 2005, 116; see D. Stewart, Cheetham, and Russell 2000, 314). The distinction between fortresses and vexillation fortresses is therefore not very useful.

45. Tomlin (2018, 19–20), *RIB* 200, *RIB* 201.

46. Haynes (2013, 373).

47. Sauer (2005), Bidwell (2007, 17), Tomlin (2018, 21–2). The particularly accurate date for the construction of Alchester was derived from the dendrochronological dating of timber from the excavation of a gateway.

48. Sauer (2000, 39); see Hoffmann (2013, 56).

49. Frere, St Joseph, and Charlesworth (1974, 36–9); see Keppie (2000, 85).

50. Suetonius, *Vespasian* 4. Translated by A. R. Birley (2005, 17).

51. D. Stewart, Cheetham, and Russell (2020).

52. Sharples (2010, 289, 305), Sharples (2014).

53. Roymans and Fernández-Götz (2019, 417).

54. Goldsworthy (1996, 219–20); see Redfern (2011), Harding (2012, 179–82).

55. Richmond (1968); see Sparey-Green (2015, 122).

56. S. Jones and Randal (2010), Harding (2012, 181–2).

57. P. Crummy (1984, 94–7).

58. Suetonius, *Claudius* 24; see Beard (2007, 69–70), Woodman (2014, 289), Rothe (2020, 72–4).

59. Bishop (2014, 1–17).

60. M. Jones (2002, 34), Todd (2004, 52), White (2018, 23–5).

61. Tacitus, *Annals* 12.31–40. This text provides much of the information available for the next phase of the conquest. The chronology of these events has been discussed by A. R. Birley (2005, 25–31).

62. Todd (2007), M. Allen et al. (2017, 193–4).

63. Tacitus, *Agricola* 12.

64. Tacitus, *Annals* 12.31; see Rivet and Smith (1979, 450–1, 478), A. R. Birley (2005, 29–30).

65. Philpott and Potter (1996, 43–4).

66. Tacitus, *Annals* 12.32, see Holbrook (2015, 95–6), Henig and Tomlin (2008).

67. Tacitus, *Annals* 12.33. Translations from this work in this chapter are by Woodman (2004).

68. Pottery finds from the excavations of the fortress may support this early date (Paul Bidwell, personal communication 2019; see Manning 2004, 66; Tomlin 2018, 29–31).

69. R. Jones (2012, 120–1).

70. Gwilt (2007, 304–7), Guest (2008, 38–43), Britnell and Silvester (2018), Evans (2018), G. Smith (2018).

71. Bellino (2011, 18).

72. Symonds (2018a, 92).

73. Burnham and Davies (2010, 37–48).

74. Tacitus, *Annals* 12.33.
75. Meyer (2018).
76. Tacitus, *Annals* 12.36; see Braund (1996a, 115).
77. Tacitus, *Annals* 12.37.
78. This image is reproduced in Barrett (1991, plate 1b).
79. Barrett (1991, 17).
80. Roncaglia (2019, 69), see Barry (2011, 7).
81. Tacitus, *Annals* 12.38–9.
82. Tacitus, *Annals* 12.40; A. R. Birley (2005, 32–4).
83. P. Stewart (1995, 7–9), Tomlin (2018, 16), Roncaglia (2019, 68–9).
84. Tacitus, *Annals* 12.23; see Braund (1996a, 107–8), Beard, North, and Price (1998, 178), Roncaglia (2019, 68–9).
85. Osgood (2011, 102–3).
86. Beard (2007).
87. R. Smith (2013).

CHAPTER 4

1. Suetonius, *Nero* 18. Translated by Edwards (2000, 203).
2. See Rivet and Smith (1979, 312).
3. Comparable centres for the worship of the divine Augustus had already been established at Lyon (*Lugdunum*, France) and Tarragona (*Tarraco*, Spain) and served as models for the cult of Claudius at Camulodunum.
4. Gascoyne and Radford (2013, 77–8, 82, 88).
5. Fishwick (1995), Fishwick (1997), Drinkwater (2019, 15).
6. See Fishwick (1995, 20–5), drawing on information about the organization of the cult of Augustus at Lyon.
7. P. Crummy (2008, 28), Gascoyne and Radford (2013, 117–9).
8. P. Crummy et al. (2007), Gascoyne and Radford (2013, 78, 95–6).
9. Moore (2011).
10. Wacher (1995, 20), Mattingly (2006, 260–6), Rogers (2016, 743–5), Tomlin (2018, 243); see Moore (2011, 348).
11. Tacitus, *Annals* 14.33; see A. R. Birley (2005, 30). Other towns may have been awarded the status of *municipium* in Britain; epigraphic information for the status of these urban centres is very limited.
12. Niblett (2005, 52–3, 85, plans 1 and 2).
13. Revell (2009, 172–9), Laurence, Esmonde Cleary, and Sears (2011, 214–23). The fortress at Exeter, which was constructed around the middle of the 50s, was supplied with a monumental bath-house which provided bathing facilities for the soldiers of the Second Legion (discussed later).
14. Fulford (2019); see Fulford et al. (2020, 8), Fulford (2021, 60–1).
15. Wacher (1995, 259), Fulford (2015, 64–6, 69).
16. Hingley (2018, 25–56).
17. Tacitus, *Annals* 14.33.
18. See Tacitus, *Agricola* 14, and Tacitus, *Annals* 14.29, 14.31–2.
19. White and Barker (1998, 38–42), Manning (2000, 75), Todd (2004, 55), Burnham and Davies (2010, 62, 193).
20. Bidwell (1979, 1, 13–5), Bidwell (2007, 33), Holbrook (2015, 96), Bidwell (2021).
21. Nowakowski (2011, 243–45), A. Smith et al. (2016, 335–7).

22. Symonds (2018b, 48–54).

23. Tacitus, *Annals* 12.40. There is a dispute about whether Veuntius rebelled against Cartimandua on two separate occasions, in 52–57 and 69, or whether Tacitus made an error with the chronology and described the same event twice at two different times; A. R. Birley (2005, 36), Haselgrove (2016, 470–6).

24. Haselgrove (2016, 459–60), Fell (2020, 678).

25. Tacitus, *Annals* 14.29. Translations from this work in this chapter are by Woodman (2004).

26. M. Jones (2002, 32–3), Bidwell and Hodgson (2009, 8), Wilson (2009, 11–2), Tomlin (2018, 22, 30–1).

27. A. R. Birley (2005, 43–50); see Tacitus, *Agricola* 15; Tacitus, *Annals* 14.29–30.

28. Manning (2004, 68), Burnham and Davies (2010, 42).

29. Tacitus, *Annals* 14.30.

30. Tacitus, *Annals* 14.30.

31. This site has yet to be located (Hopewell 2018, 313).

32. The information about this event is included in the writings of Tacitus and Cassius Dio; archaeological research has offered further insights (Tacitus, *Agricola* 14–16; Tacitus, *Annals* 14.29–39; Dio 62.1–12; see Hingley and Unwin 2005).

33. Dio 62. 2. Translation adapted from Cary (1925, 85).

34. Tacitus, *Annals* 14.31.

35. Braund (1996a, 133–5).

36. See Romm (2014, 4.1, 5.1), Tomlin (2018, 36), Drinkwater (2019, 138–9).

37. Tacitus, *Annals* 14.31.

38. Tacitus, *Annals* 14.31–2.

39. Gascoyne and Radford (2013, 96–7).

40. N. Crummy (2016), Lyons (2018, 374–5).

41. Tacitus, *Annals* 14.32.

42. Tacitus, *Annals* 14.32.

43. Tacitus, *Annals* 14.33.

44. Hingley (2018, 52–4).

45. Niblett (2005, 52–3).

46. Tacitus, *Annals* 14.33.

47. Hoffmann (2013, 102).

48. Suetonius, *Nero* 18.

49. Tacitus, *Annals* 14.34.

50. Tacitus, *Annals* 14.34.

51. See Booth (2018, 36).

52. Krakowka (2019).

53. Tacitus, *Annals* 14.35.

54. Braund (1996a, 132–46), Shumate (2006, 88), Adler (2011, 117–62), Gillespie (2018, 37–8).

55. Goldsworthy (1996, 146–7).

56. Dio's description of this battle suggests that it was a far more protracted event; Dio 62.8–12; see Levene (2010, 229–31).

57. A. R. Birley (2005, 227).

58. Tacitus, *Annals* 14.37.

59. Tacitus, *Annals* 14.38.

60. Tacitus, *Annals* 14.38.

61. Tomlin (2016, 56).

62. Brown (1986), Potter and Robinson (2000), Davies (2009, 147–52).

63. Blake, Dean, and Wardle (2018, 140), Booth (2018, 36), White (2018, 23–4).

64. Tacitus, *Annals* 14.38.

65. Tacitus, *Annals* 14.38; see A. R. Birley (2005, 304), Tomlin (2018, 37–8).

66. Hingley (2018, 57, 59).

67. Tacitus, *Annals* 14.38.

68. Tacitus, *Annals* 14.39; see A. R. Birley (2005, 49–50).

69. Tacitus, *Agricola*, 16; see A. R. Birley (2005, 51–6). Translations from this work in this chapter are by A. R. Birley (1999, 13).

70. Tacitus, *Agricola* 16.

71. Tomlin (2020).

72. Tacitus, *Histories* 2.11.

73. Burnham and Davies (2010, 42, 188), Holbrook (2015, 95–6); see Rogers (2016, 743).

74. Todd (2004, 54–5), Nowakowski (2011, 256), M. Allen et al. (2017, 197), Bidwell (2021, 152–5).

75. Gascoyne and Radford (2013, 99, 104).

76. Fishwick (1997, 32–4), P. Crummy (2016, 7).

77. Creighton (2006, 130–5), Gascoyne and Radford (2013, 104, 116, 145–6).

78. Hingley (2018, 57–68), Tomlin (2016, 55–6).

79. Niblett (2005, 53, 150).

80. Creighton and Fry (2016, 365–8).

81. Fulford (2008, 6).

82. Cunliffe (1991, 161), Fulford (2015, 64–6, 69), see Tomlin (2018, 34–5).

83. Tomlin (2018, 33–5), *RIB* 92.

84. Fulford (2008, 5–7), Fulford (2019), Fulford et al. (2020, 7–8), see Creighton and Fry (2016, 435–7).

85. See Creighton and Fry (2016, 424), Hingley (2018, 79–80).

86. Dio 62.6; Translated by Braund (1996a, 142–3), Schulz (2019, 202).

CHAPTER 5

1. Tacitus, *Agricola* 25. Translations from this work in this chapter are by A. R. Birley (1999).

2. The details of this confusing period in the history of Roman Britain are included in books 1–3 of Tacitus' *Histories* (see Morgan 2005).

3. Tacitus, *Histories*, 3.45.

4. Tacitus, *Histories*, 3.45.

5. Braund (1996a, 125–9).

6. Tacitus, *Histories*, 3.45. Translated by Levene (1999, 143).

7. Steve Willis (personal communication 2019); Fell (2020, 967). Samian pottery, finely made with a glossy red surface, was produced in Gaul and is very common at Roman-period sites in Britain, including *oppida*, forts, and towns.

8. Ferraby and Millett (2020, 94–100).

9. Tacitus, *Agricola* 7–8; see A. R. Birley (2005, 61–2).

10. Braund (1996a, 147–8), A. R. Birley (2005, 67, 227), Goodman (2012, 67).

11. Statius *Silvae* 5.2.142–9; see A. R. Birley (2005, 58–62), Gibson (2006, 248), Shotter (2009, 15).

12. Tomlin (2018, 46).

13. See Tacitus, *Agricola* 17.

14. M. Jones (2002, 37), A. R. Birley (2005, 67), Wilson (2009, 9–10), Ottaway (2011, 23–4), Ferraby and Millett (2020, 94).

15. Ottaway (2013, 53–76), Haselgrove (2016, 358–75), A. Smith et al. (2016, 315–20).

16. Bishop (2005), Bidwell and Hodgson (2009, 8–15), Symonds (2015, 89–90), Symonds (2018a, 59). The archaeological information that has been used to date most of the Flavian forts in central Britain and Scotland usually provides only a general indication of when they were constructed, so it is impossible to be certain about the progress of the Flavian campaigns.

17. See Bidwell and Hodgson (2009, 10–1, fig. 3). Dendrochronological analysis of felled timbers from the building of the fort at Carlisle has revealed that construction work was under way during the winter of 72–73 CE (Zant 2009, 413, 447–50; McCarthy 2018, 294).

18. The excavation at Scotch Corner has indicated that the earliest course of Dere Street turned north-west, directly towards Carlisle (Fell 2020, 702–3).

19. Tacitus, *Agricola* 17; see A. R. Birley (2005, 68).

20. The dating of preserved timbers has indicated that the construction works at Caerleon was under way in 71–74 (Burnham and Davies 2010, 43; see Bidwell 2021, 154–5); the date 74 was stamped on two lead ingots which were brought to Chester during construction (Mason 2012, 34, 49).

21. Hirt (2010, 334), M. Allen et al. (2017, 194–6).

22. Burnham and Burnham (2004, 107, 111), Burnham and Davis (2010, 276–80), Darvill and Wainwright (2016, 195), La Niece et al. (2018, 412).

23. Pliny, *Natural History* 4.102; see Hanson (2009, 51–4), Hoffmann (2009), Woolliscroft (2009), Hunter and Caruthers (2012a, 11), Symonds (2018a, 67–8).

24. See A. R. Birley (2005, 71–6), A. R. Birley (2010). Our knowledge is mainly derived from Tacitus' laudatory account of his father-in-law, which provides a great deal of information on the conquest of northern Britain. I have taken the chronology of events from I. Smith (2015), which is derived directly from *Agricola* and thus may be far from reliable as a chronological account (see Woodman 2014, 25–30). We have no alternative and more reliable text on which to draw for the chronology or the actions of Agricola in Britain.

25. Tacitus, *Agricola* 18.

26. I. Smith (2015, 183).

27. Burnham and Davies (2010, 43–53).

28. Tacitus, *Agricola* 19; see Woodman (2014, 194–6).

29. Mattingly (2006, 494–6), Walton and Moorhead (2016, 838–40).

30. Tacitus, *Agricola* 20; see Dobson (2009, 30), A. R. Birley (2005, 67), Breeze (2006a, 34–5), Woodman (2014, 199).

31. Martial, *On the Spectacles* 7.3; see Woodman (2014, 207).

32. See Beacham (1999, 13).

33. Flavian fortifications may be discovered in south-western Scotland in the future, since a previously unknown camp which appears to have no enclosing rampart has recently been located; see Arabaolaza (2019).

34. Macinnes (1984, 243), Hunter (2001, 294), Hunter (2009); see Haselgrove (2009, 236).

35. Breeze (2006a, 44–7), Hunter and Caruthers (2012b, 84); Hunter (2016, 181).

36. Rivet and Smith (1979, 475), Owen (1992, 70), Hanson (2012, 69), Keppie (2012).

37. See Roymans and Fernández-Götz (2019).

38. Macinnes (1984), Armit (1997, 103–6), Hunter (2016, 190–1).

39. Tacitus, *Agricola* 21; see Millett (1990, 69), Woodman (2014, 200–7).

40. Tomlin (2018, 24–9), *RIB* 3123; see I. Smith (2015, 189).

41. Hingley (2018, 74–9).

42. Cousins (2020).

43. Tacitus, *Agricola* 22; see I. Smith (2015, 186–7).

44. See Woodman (2014, 35–6, 207–8).

45. Hanson (2007a), Hanson (2007b); see Hodgson (2009a, 368).

46. Tacitus, *Agricola* 23.

47. Hanson and Maxwell (1983, 39), Brickstock (2020, 62–3).

48. See Braund (1996b), Clarke (2001, 101), B. Campbell (2012, 374–6), Woodman (2014, 220).

49. Tacitus, *Agricola* 24. It is not known whether Agricola was campaigning in south-western Scotland or in Kintyre.

50. Cahill Wilson (2014, 23–9); see Freeman (2001, 60–1).

51. See Pliny, *Natural History* 4.102.

52. Hunter and Caruthers (2012b, 15, 89–91).

53. See Mann (1985, 23), R. Jones (2012, 55), Tomlin (2018, 59–60).

54. Clarke (2001, 109–110), Master (2016, 2–3).

55. Tacitus, *Agricola* 28.

56. However, very few have been excavated, and they cannot be precisely dated since later Roman campaigns may also have reached Caledonia; R. Jones (2012, 19–20, 109).

57. Tacitus, *Agricola* 25–6.

58. Tacitus, *Agricola* 27.

59. Tacitus, *Agricola* 29.

60. See Cook and Dunbar (2008), R. Jones (2012, 55, 116).

61. Murison (1999, 186), D. Campbell (2010, 59), R. Jones (2012, 15), Hunter and Caruthers (2012a, 30); see A. R. Birley (2005, 89).

62. Tacitus, *Agricola* 29–32; see Woodman (2014, 236–56).

63. This dictatorial behaviour had put Domitian at odds with the Senate and caused his memory to be subject to official *damnatio* after his death in 96. Tacitus wrote *Agricola* in the aftermath of this event.

64. Tacitus, *Agricola* 37.

65. *RIB* 3185.

66. A. R. Birley (2005, 93–4), Tomlin (2018, 55–6, 59–60).

67. Tacitus, *Agricola* 38; see A. R. Birley (2005, 90), Woodman (2014, 13, 283).

68. Tacitus, *Agricola* 10; see Woodman (2014, 138), A. R. Birley (2019, 301).

69. See Armit (1997).

70. Tacitus, *Agricola* 10.

71. Diodorus Siculus 17.104; see Caplan and Newman (1976, 173), A. R. Birley (1997, 131).

72. Martial, *Epigrams* 10.44. Translation by Shackleton Bailey (1993, 357).

73. Tomlin (2018, 317–8).

74. Plutarch, *Moralia* 410 A; 419 E; see A. R. Birley (2005, 92).

75. Tacitus, *Agricola* 40; see Woodman (2014, 289), I. Smith (2015).

76. Strong (1968, 42–9, 73), Wilmott (2012, 35).

77. As described in the final chapters of Tacitus, *Agricola* 39–42.

78. Braund (1996a, 171–2), Sailor (2008, 61–2, 92–6); see I. Smith (2015, 177–8).

CHAPTER 6

1. Tacitus, *Annals* 1.9. Translated by Woodman (2004, 7).

2. Tacitus, *Agricola* 40. Translated by A. R. Birley (1999, 29). The chapters of Tacitus' *Histories* describing events during the period covered in this chapter have not survived, and in the absence of other classical texts to pick up the narrative, this chapter is highly dependent on archaeological finds.

3. A. R. Birley (2005, 95–9).

4. Inchtuthil was excavated in 1952–65; geophysical survey and aerial photography have since helped to put these excavations into context (Pitts and St Joseph 1985; Hunter and Caruthers 2012a, 14–5). The regularity of the plan of this fortress, shown in fig. 6.1, relates to the very small percentage of the site that was excavated using narrow trenches (Lynn Pitts, personal communication 2021), and a much more detailed understanding exists of the fully excavated fort at Elginhaugh.

5. Pitts and St Joseph (1985, 31), Bidwell (2007, 47).

6. Bidwell (2007, 107–17).

7. Pitts and St Joseph (1985, 44), Breeze (2006a, 57–8), Hanson (2007a, 28); see Symonds (2018a, 67–72). The term 'glen blocking' has been used to refer to the role of these forts (e.g. Breeze 2006a, 57–8).

8. See Mann and Breeze (1987, 87), Hunter and Caruthers (2012a, 89–91, fig. 2).

9. Hanson (2007a, 36–7), Oltean (2007, 51–2).

10. Tomlin (2018, 66).

11. Kennedy (1983, 189–91, 196), Strobel (1986, 266), Tomlin (2018, 66).

12. Tomlin (2018, 67–8).

13. Haynes (2013, 126), Tomlin (2018, 72–6).

14. Tacitus, *Histories* 1.2. Translated by Levene (1999, 3).

15. Hobley (1989, 69), Hanson (2007a, 34–5), Hanson (2007b, 253, 649), Bateson and Holmes (2013, 253–4); see Brickstock (2020, 63–4).

16. Pitts and St Joseph (1985, 109–113, 279–80), Breeze (2006a, 102), Hanson (2007a, 35).

17. Suetonius, *Domitian* 10.2–3; see A. R. Birley (2005, 95–9).

18. Breeze (2006a, 103–4), Hanson (2012, 70), Hodgson (2017, fig. 14), Hanson, Jones, and Jones (2019); see Brickstock (2020, 63–4). These forts were all excavated decades ago; new excavations would be required to provide new insights.

19. Hanson (2007a, 143–52), Hunter and Caruthers (2012a, 35).

20. Collins and Symonds (2019, 27–9).

21. Bishop and Dore (1989, 126–9, 140), Breeze (2006b, 452–3), R. Birley (2009, 45), Symonds and Mason (2009, 85, 147), Zant (2009, 413).

22. Bidwell and Hodgson (2009, 11–7).

23. A. R. Birley (2002), R. Birley (2009).

24. A. R. Birley (2002, 42), A. R. Birley et al. (2013, 291–6), Haynes (2013, 127), Roymans (2014), Bowman, Thomas, and Tomlin (2019, 227).

25. Bowman (2003, 16–7), A. R. Birley (2017, 7), Bowman, Thomas, and Tomlin (2019, 228) for VT (Vindolanda Tablet) 154.

26. Hanson (2007b, 655), Haynes (2013, 14).

27. Bowman (2003, 18).

28. A. R. Birley (2002, 50) for VT 1108.

29. A. R. Birley (2005, 101–4).

30. Haynes (2013, 56–7, 342–3).

31. Rogers (2016, 743); see Rivet and Smith (1979, 368–9), Hassall (1999, 183–5), Hurst (1999, 114), M. Jones (2002, 51–2), Tomlin (2018, 253–4).

32. A. R. Birley (2002, 122–3), A. R. Birley (2005, 322).

33. A. R. Birley (2005, 321–2), Bowman (2006, 78–9) for VT 611 and the inscription. Another of the letters (VT 594) mentions the Anavionenses.

34. A. R. Birley (2002, 50) on VT 164. Alternatively, this may have related to enemy activity.

35. Bowman (2003, 20–1).

36. Cuff (2011, 146) for VT 628; see Bowman (2006, 86–7), Haynes (2013, 13–4, 286).

37. A. R. Birley (2000, 245, 258). Indeed, the Tungrian cohort at Vindolanda appear to have been recruited differently. A recently discovered letter indicates that troops from Raetia were serving with the Tungrians in the first fort, while two letters from the fourth fort indicate that soldiers from other units were stationed alongside the Tungrians after they returned to Vindolanda during the early second century (Bowman, Thomas, and Tomlin 2019, 239–43).

38. Andrew Birley (personal communication 2021).

39. Greene (2013a, 376) on VT 291.

40. Bowman (2006, 89).

41. Van Driel-Murray (1994), R. Birley (2009, 71–80, fig. 24), Bowman (2006, 87), Greene (2014).

42. Bowman (2003, 36), A. R. Birley (2002, 94).

43. R. Birley (2009, 59–61) on VT 155.

44. Bowman (2003, 39) on VT 182.

45. Bowman (2003, 60–72), Haynes (2013, 318–36).

46. Van Driel-Murray (1994), Greene (2013a), Greene (2013b, 17), Green (2015).

47. Goldsworthy (1996, 72–3), James (2006, 32).

48. A. R. Birley (2002, 155), Bowman (2003, 52) on VT 301.

49. Bowman (2006, 87–8), Greene (2013a, 378–9) on VT 581.

50. Tomlin (2003).

51. Van Driel-Murray (1994, 353–5), Mattingly (2006, 175), Foubert (2013, 393).

52. Bennett (1997, 94–110), A. R. Birley (2005, 109), Oltean (2007, 54–5).

53. Bowman (2003, 45–6), A. R. Birley (2005, 104–12).

54. A. R. Birley (2002, 51, 69).

55. Hodgson (2000), A. R. Birley (2005, 108–9), Breeze (2006a, 105), Burnham and Davies (2010, 47–53), Hunter and Caruthers (2012a, 13).

56. Hodgson (2000, 18–9), Hodgson (2009b, 11–4), Zant (2009, 413, 419), Hanson (2012, 4–5), Hodgson (2017, 34–7).

57. Symonds (2020a).

58. Hodgson (2000, 13–7), B. Campbell (2012, 186–97), Hanson (2014, 5).

59. Collins and Biggins (2013, 247), Symonds (2018a, 103), Collins and Symonds (2019, 27–9), Symonds (2020a, 104). There may have been a single fort at Gateshead (Tyne and Wear) to the east of Corbridge.

60. Symonds (2020a, 104); see Hodgson (2012, 212).

61. Tacitus, *Germania* 41. Translated by Birley (1999, 58).

62. Hodgson (2012), A. Smith et al. (2016, 315–22), Hodgson (2017, 28–30), Collins and Symonds (2019, 19–20).

63. A. Smith et al. (2016, 324), M. Allen et al. (2017, 272–7).

64. Collins and Biggins (2013), Collins and Symonds (2019, 145–6).

65. A. R. Birley (2005, 111–4).

66. A. R. Birley (2000, 242–3), Bowman (2003, 20), Bowman, Thomas, and Tomlin (2010, 190) on VT 180 and VT 181.

67. This excavation was in 2017. Collins (2018, 242–3), Andrew Birley (personal communication 2021).

68. Greene (2013a, 24–7), Greene (2014, 33–4).

69. A. Birley (2013, 86), A. Birley, Meyer, and E. Greene (2016, 247–8).

70. McCarthy (2018, 298–9).

71. Tomlin (2013, 384–5), A. R. Birley, A. Birley, and de Bernardo Stempel (2013), A. Birley, Meyer, and Greene (2016, 246–7).

72. Irby-Massie (1999, 270–1), Jackson and Burleigh (2018, 140).

73. Garrow and Gosden (2012).

CHAPTER 7

1. Translated by Barry (2011, 27).

2. Historia Augusta, *Hadrian* 5.2–3, Translated by A. R. Birley (1997, 80).

3. Fronto, *The Parthian War* 2. Translated by A. R. Birley (1998, 303).

4. A. R. Birley (1997, 3–4, 84), A. R. Birley (2005, 117–8); see Breeze, Dobson, and Maxfield (2012, 19–20), Hodgson (2017, 39–41), Hodgson (2021).

5. A. R. Birley (1998, 303), A. R. Birley (2017, 8–9), Tomlin (2018, 83–4), *RIB* 3364.

6. Sutcliff (1954).

7. Keppie (2000, 92–4), D. Campbell (2018), Tomlin (2018, 78).

8. It has been suggested that the Ninth was probably moved overseas early in Hadrian's reign, before being defeated and disbanded during either the Jewish uprising of 132–35 or the Parthian War of 161 (see Hodgson 2021).

9. Hodgson (2021).

10. Abdy (2019, 11, 42–7, 184).

11. Haynes (2013, 126–8), Ivleva (2016, 251–2).

12. Historia Augusta, *Hadrian* 11.2. Trasnslated by A. R. Birley (2005, 121).

13. Graafstal (2018); see Hodgson (2017, 63–6), Collins and Symonds (2019, 32), Hodgson (2021).

14. Breeze (2011).

15. A. R. Birley (1997, 132–4), Crow (2004, 129), Hodgson (2017, 170–1).

16. Breeze (2009, 91–2), Symonds (2018a, 115).

17. A. R. Birley (1997, 210), Thomas (2007, 27–8).

18. Breeze (2009), Hodgson (2017, 47).

19. Symonds and Mason (2009, 45–7), Symonds (2018a, 112–4), Symonds (2020a).

20. Hodgson (2017, 49–50), Graafstal (2018, 95–7).

21. Hodgson (2017, 163), Symonds (2018a, 125).

22. A. R. Birley (2017, 11), Hodgson (2017, 41), Graafstal (2018, 84, 98–100).

23. Collins and Symonds (2019, 22), Symonds (2020b, 752–3).

24. As indicated by the large number of radiocarbon dates from several of the settlements (Hodgson 2012, 213–9; Hodgson 2017, 98).

25. Dio 69.9. Translated by Cary (1925, 441).

26. Abdy (2019, 203–7).

27. Historia Augusta, *Hadrian* 11.3–6; 12.1; see A. R. Birley (1997, 114, 125), Abdy (2019, 51).

28. A. R. Birley (1997, 124), A. R. Birley (2005, 121), Ottaway (2011, 57–8), Tomlin (2018, 92–4).

29. A. R. Birley (1997, 123), Breeze, Dobson, and Maxfield (2012, 20–5), Tomlin (2018, 94–6), Graafstal (2018, 81).

30. A. R. Birley (2005, 307–9), Tomlin (2018, 97–100).

31. A. R. Birley (1997, 127), Tomlin (2018, 87–9).

32. This estimate suggests that some of the units were double strength, explaining the total figure.

33. See Breeze (2006a, 43), Mattingly (2006, 166).

34. Mattingly (2006, 293).

35. Caplan and Newman (1976), Rivet and Smith (1979, 441), A. R. Birley (1997, 131), Bidwell and Holbrook (1989, 43, 99–103, fig. 28), Collins and Symonds (2019, 128), *RIB* 1316, *RIB* 1320.

36. Bidwell and Holbrook (1989, 43–4, 99–103), Abdy (2019, 216). Medallions were in the form of coins but were larger and heavier; they were presented as gifts to senior military officers and friends of the emperor.

37. The epigraph to this chapter is quoted in Barry (2011, 16–8).

38. Arnaldi (2001–2, 235), Abdy (2019, 14, 16, 42, 51, 111). This god can be identified by this attribute on sculptures, mosaics, and paintings from around the empire.

39. B. Campbell (2012, 377–8), Braund (1996a, 19), Braund (1996b, 45–6), Serban (2009).

40. Bidwell and Holbrook (1989, 7–14, 47), Barry (2011, 23, 36 n. 150).

41. Cartledge (2004, 216–7).

42. Barry (2011, 22–3, figs. 34–36), Stafford (2012, 154); see Abdi (2019, 15, 114, 311).

43. The surviving fragments of the inscription were removed from the original location of the monument and reused in the fabric of a Saxon church at Jarrow (Tyne and Wear) (*RIB* 1051; Bidwell 2015; see Richmond and Wright 1943; E. Birley 1961, 157–9; A. R. Birley 1997, 132–3; Graafstal 2018, 92–5).

44. Hingley (2018, 126).

45. See Hingley (2018, 131).

46. Graafstal (2018, 86–8, 95–7).

47. Hodgson (2017, 51–4, 57–8), Tomlin (2018, 102–11).

48. *RIB* 1843, 1844, 1672, 1673, 1962, 2022, 3376; see Fulford (2006, 68–9), Breeze (2012, 71–2), Symonds (2018b, 20).

49. Hodgson (2017, 51), Symonds (2018a, 121–2).

50. Breeze (2006b, 36–8), Breeze (2009, 95–6), Symonds and Mason (2009, 153), Symonds (2018a, 116, 122–3).

51. Hodgson (2017, 53–4).

52. Hodgson (2017, 80–3, 86–7).

53. Bidwell and Hodgson (2009, 15–7), Breeze (2009, 94–5), Burnham and Davies (2010, 50–1), Symonds (2018a, 117, 118).

54. Breeze (2006b, 85–6), Symonds and Mason (2009, 53), Breeze (2015), Hodgson (2017, 173–5), Graafstal (2018, 83–4), Symonds (2018a, 116).

55. E. Birley (1934, 178–9), Hodgson (2017, 70); see Breeze (2006b, 85–6).

56. This concept is derived from Barry (2011, 23) who has written about the magical function of the Hadrianic frontiers.

57. Several triumphal arches across the empire also included iconography associated with rivers, the sea, and naval conquest, including the arches of Tiberius at Orange (France), of Titus in Rome, of Trajan at Benevento (Italy), and of Septimius Severus in Rome (Midford 2014).

58. The Vallum is known from excavations at Benwell, Black Carts, and Denton to have held water. At Limestone Corner, where it was dug through freely draining soils, it remained dry (Wilmott 2008, 122; Heywood 2009, 419).

59. Allason-Jones and McKay (1985, 5–6), Irby-Massie (1999, 155–7, 286).

60. See Irby-Massie (1999, 155), Jackson and Burleigh (2018, 140), Cousins (2020, 114).

61. Symonds and Mason (2009, 148, 157), Hodgson (2017, 92–3), Ferris (2021, 179–82).

62. Hodgson (2017, 91–3); see Ferris (2021).

63. A. R. Birley (2005, 120, 123–7), Hodgson (2017, 54, 61, 64), Tomlin (2018, 103–6), Collins and Symonds (2019, 37–8).

64. Breeze (2006b, 60), Breeze (2015, 20).

65. As at Alborough (Ferraby and Millett 2020, 106–8), Canterbury (Millett 2007, 156–9), Caerwent (Webster 2003, 214), Caistor by Norwich (Bowden 2013, 165), Cirencester (Holbrook 2008,

313), Leicester (Cooper and Buckley 2003, 33–4), and Wroxeter (White and Barker 1998, 78–9, 184–91; Tomlin 2018, 244–50).

66. Breeze (2011), Graafstal (2018, 90).

67. See O'Gorman (1993) and Johnson (2019).

68. Matthew Symonds (personal communication 2020).

69. Hingley (2017, 103).

CHAPTER 8

1. Dio, 76[77].12). Translated by A. R. Birley (2005, 195).

2. A. R. Birley (2020).

3. Tomlin (2018, 119–31), Hanson and Breeze (2020).

4. Tomlin (2018, 119–20), *RIB* 3486.

5. Reid and Nicholson (2019). It has been suggested that these siege works were practice works constructed by the Roman military forces, but recent research at Burnswark indicates convincingly that the hillfort was besieged. The date of the siege has also not been clearly established, but it is thought to have been undertaken under Urbicus rather than Agricola.

6. See Fernández-Götz and Roymans (eds) (2018).

7. Macinnes (2020, 52–3).

8. Hunter (2007, 31–2), Fraser Hunter (personal communication 2021).

9. Cahill Wilson (2016, 53).

10. Bidwell and Hodgson (2009, 22–5), Burnham and Davies (2010, 54–7).

11. Tomlin (2018, 131), Hanson and Breeze (2020, 28), Hodgson (2020).

12. Thomas (2007, 43–6), Breeze and Ferris (2016), Tomlin (2018, 125–7), L. Campbell (2020), Ferris (2020).

13. Hodgson (2017, 77–9), Tomlin (2018, 145), Hanson and Breeze (2020, 30–1).

14. Burnham and Davis (2010, 50–3), Bidwell and Hodgson (2009, 15–7).

15. A. R. Birley (2005, 162–70), Hodgson (2017, 106–7).

16. Holmes (2014, 150–1).

17. Tomlin (2018, 245–6), McCarthy (2018).

18. Hodgson (2017, 130).

19. R. Birley (2009, 162–8), Hodgson (2017, 125–8).

20. Carroll (2012), Hingley (2012, 321–4), Tomlin (2018, 223–5); see Ferris (2021, 133–42).

21. A Roman military diploma dating to 145 was found in the gatehouse of the east gate to Chesters, which gave rights of citizenship to retiring auxiliary soldiers from the fort.

22. This is illustrated by the inscriptions from burial monuments to British legionary soldiers who served in other parts of the empire (Tacoma, Ivleva, and Breeze 2016, 38).

23. Dio 75(76).5; see A. R. Birley (2005, 184).

24. Dio 76(77).12; Translated by A. R. Birley (2005, 195).

25. Hunter (2007, 31–2), Holmes (2014).

26. Arnaldi (2001–2, 229), A. R. Birley (2005, 195–203), Holmes (2014, 144), Tomlin (2018, 182–93).

27. A. R. Birley (2005, 333), Ottaway (2011, 83).

28. Dio 76(77).13; see A. R. Birley (2005, 196).

29. A. R. Birley (2005, 198–202), Hodgson (2017, 109–11).

30. A. R. Birley (2005, 371–84), Hodgson (2017, 136–8).

31. Williams (1999), Arnaldi (2001–2, 227–39), Davenport (2019).

32. Burnham and Davies (2010, 54–7), Bidwell and Hodgson (2009, 22–5).

33. A. R. Birley (2005, 388–93).

34. A. R. Birley (2005, 406–10), Hunter (2007, 6).
35. Translated by A. R. Birley (2005, 407), see Barry (2011, 23).
36. Ottaway (2011, 134).
37. Burnham and Davies (2010, 167, 177).
38. Tomlin (2018, 417–20).
39. Hodgson (2017, 146).
40. Esmonde Cleary (2016, 141–3).
41. Mattingly (2006, 348), Hodgson (2017, 149–50).
42. A. R. Birley (2005, 414–6), Breeze (2006a, 115–7), Collins and Symonds (2019, 68–70).
43. A. R. Birley (2005, 430–40, 443–50), Hodgson (2017, 176–7).
44. Collins and Symonds (2019, 71–4).
45. Mattingly (2006, 529–32).
46. Mattingly (2006, 535–6), see Esmonde Cleary (2016, 144–6).

AFTERWORD: 'WHAT HAVE THE ROMANS EVER DONE FOR US?'

1. Hingley (2008).
2. Hingley and Unwin (2005, 111–221).
3. Hingley (2008, 109, 29–30, 54, 128–9).
4. Hingley (2012, 66, 76–8).
5. Hingley (2008, 184–91).
6. M. Bradley (2010, 131).
7. Hingley, Bonacchi, and Sharpe (2018, 285).
8. Hingley (2020b).
9. Hingley (2016, 9–13).
10. Hingley (2011).
11. See Millett, Revell and Moore (2016).
12. Sellar and Yeatman (1930, 10–11).
13. This is why I have used the term 'people' rather than 'tribe' to address the Iron Age populations of Britain.
14. Hingley (2008, 60).
15. Monty Python (n.d.).
16. Hingley, Bonacchi, and Sharpe (2018).
17. Hingley (2008, 128–9).
18. Appleby (2005), Hingley 2020(c).
19. Goldsworthy (2017).
20. See M. Scott (2003).
21. See Bonacchi, Altaweel, and Krzyanska (2018, 184).
22. Hingley (2020a).

BIBLIOGRAPHY

ANCIENT WORKS

Caesar, *The Gallic War*. Translated by C. Hammond (1996). Oxford, Oxford University Press.

Cicero, M. T., *Letters to Atticus, Volume 1*. Translated by D. R, Shackleton Bailey (1999). Harvard, Loeb Classical Library.

Dio Cassius, *Roman History, Books 56–60*. Translated by E. Cary (1924). Harvard, Loeb Classical Library.

Dio Cassius, *Roman History, Books 61–70*. Translated by E. Cary (1925). Harvard, Loeb Classical Library.

Florus, *Epitome of Roman History*. Translated by Seymour Forster, edited by J. Henderson (1984). Harvard, Loeb Classical Library.

Martial. *Epigrams, Volume II*. Translated by D. R. Shackleton Bailey (1993). Harvard, Loeb Classical Library.

Plutarch. *Caesar*. Translated with an Introduction and Commentary by C. Pelling. (2011). Oxford, Oxford University Press.

Seneca the Elder, *Declamations, Volume 1, Controversiae, Books 1–6*. Translated by M. Winterbottom (1974). Harvard, Loeb Classical Library.

Strabo, *The Geography of Strabo*. Translated by D. W. Roller (2020). Cambridge, Cambridge University Press.

Suetonius, *Lives of the Caesars*. Translated by C. Edwards (2000). Oxford, Oxford University Press.

Tacitus, *Agricola and Germany*. Translated by A. R. Birley (1999). Oxford, Oxford University Press.

Tacitus, *Annals*. Translated by A. J. Woodman (2004). Indianapolis, Hackett.

Tacitus, *The Histories*. Translated by W. H. Fyfe, revised and edited by D. S. Levene (1999). Oxford, Oxford University Press.

MODERN WORKS

Abdy, R. A. (2019). *The Roman imperial coinage*. Vol. 2. Pt. 3. *From AD 117–38, Hadrian*. London, Spink.

Adler, E. (2011). *Valourizing the barbarians*. Austin, University of Texas Press.

Allason-Jones, L., and B. McKay (1985). *Coventina's Well*. Gloucester, Alan Sutton.

Allen, D. (1944). 'The Belgic dynasties of Britain and their Coins'. *Archaeologia* 90, 1–46.

Allen, M., L. Lodwick, T. Brindle, M. Fulford, and A. Smith (2017). *New visions of the countryside of Roman Britain.* Vol. 2. *The rural economy of Roman Britain.* Britannia Monograph Series 30. London, Society for the Promotion of Roman Studies.

Alston, R. (2015). *Rome's revolution.* New York, Oxford University Press.

Appleby, G. A. (2005). 'Crossing the Rubicon: Fact or fiction in Roman re-enactment'. *Public Archaeology* 4, 257–65.

Arabaolaza, I. (2019). 'A Roman marching camp in Ayr'. *Britannia* 50, 330–49.

Armit, I. (1997). *Celtic Scotland.* London, Batsford/Historic Scotland.

Arnaldi, A. (2001–2). 'Oceanus su monete ed epigrafi'. *Scienze dell'Antichità: Storia, archeologia, antropologia* 11, 227–39.

Arnold, B. (1999). 'Drinking the feast'. *Cambridge Archaeological Journal* 9(1), 71–93.

Barnard, E. (1790). *The new, comprehensive, impartial and complete History of England.* London, Alex Hogg.

Barrett, A. A. (1979). 'The career of Tiberius Claudius Cogidubnus'. *Britannia* 10, 227–42.

Barrett, A. A. (1991). 'Claudius' victory arch in Rome'. *Britannia* 22, 1–19.

Barrett, A. A. (2001). *Caligula: The corruption of power.* Rev. ed. New York, Routledge.

Barry, F. (2011). 'The mouth of truth and the Forum Boarium'. *Art Bulletin* 93(1), 7–37.

Bateson, J. D., and N. M. McQ Holmes (2013). 'Roman and medieval coins found in Scotland, 2006–10'. *Proceedings of the Society of Antiquaries of Scotland* 143, 227–63.

Beacham, R. C. (1999). *Spectacle entertainments of early imperial Rome.* New Haven, CT, Yale University Press.

Beard, M. (2007). *The Roman triumph.* Cambridge, MA, Harvard University Press.

Beard, M., J. North, and S. Price (1998). *Religions of Rome.* Vol. 1. *A history.* Cambridge, Cambridge University Press.

Bellino, V. (2011). 'Romans, Silures and Ordovices'. *Archaeologia Cambrensis* 160, 13–38.

Bennett, J. (1997). *Trajan Optimus Princeps.* London, Routledge.

Bidwell, P. (1979). *The legionary bath-house and basilica and forum at Exeter.* Exeter, Exeter City Council/University of Exeter.

Bidwell, P. (2007). *Roman forts in Britain.* Reprint: Stroud, History Press.

Bidwell, P. (2015). 'The Branch Wall at Wallsend'. *Arbeia Journal* 10, 1–34.

Bidwell, P. (2021). 'The legionary fortress and its landscape context'. In S. Rippon and N. Holbrook (eds.), *Roman and medieval Exeter and their hinterlands: From Isca to Excester.* Oxford, Oxbow, 127–60.

Bidwell, P., and N. Hodgson (2009). *The Roman army in northern England.* Kendal, Titus Wilson.

Bidwell, P., and N. Holbrook (1989). *Hadrian's Wall bridges.* London, English Heritage.

Birley, A. (2013). 'The fort wall: A great divide?' In R. Collins and M. Symonds (eds.), *Breaking down boundaries: Hadrian's Wall in the 21st century.* Portsmouth, RI, *Journal of Roman Archaeology*, 85–104.

Birley, A., A. Meyer, and E. M. Greene (2016). 'Recent discoveries in the fort and extramural settlement at Vindolanda'. *Britannia* 47, 243–85.

Birley, A. R. (1997). *Hadrian: The restless emperor.* London, Routledge.

Birley, A. R. (1998). 'A new tombstone from Vindolanda'. *Britannia* 29, 299–306.

Birley, A. R. (2000). 'The names of the Batavians and the Tungrians in the *Tabulae Vindolandenses*'. In T. Grünewald (ed.), *Germania inferior.* Berlin, de Gruyter, 241–60.

Birley, A. R. (2002). *Garrison life at Vindolanda.* Reprinted 2010. Stroud, History Press.

Birley, A. R. (2005). *The Roman government of Britain.* Oxford, Oxford University Press.

Birley, A. R. (2010). 'The Agricola'. In A. J. Woodman (ed.), *The Cambridge companion to Tacitus*. Cambridge, Cambridge University Press, 47–58.

Birley, A. R. (2017). 'Roman roadworks near Vindolanda and the *Cohors I Tungrorum*'. *Britannia* 48, 1–17.

Birley, A. R. (2019). 'A new dispute about Thule and Agricola's last campaign'. *Lexis* 37, 299–309.

Birley, A. R. (2020). 'Antoninus Pius' guard prefect Marcus Gavius Maximus'. In D. J. Breeze and W. S. Hanson (eds.), 313–32.

Birley, A. R., A. Birley, and P. de Bernardo Stempel (2013). 'A dedication by the "Cohors I Tungrorum" at Vindolanda to a hither unknown goddess'. *Zeitschrift für Papyrologie und Epigraphik* 186, 287–300.

Birley, E. (1934). 'Report for 1933 of the North of England Archaeological Committee'. *Archaeologia Aeliana* 4(11), 176–84.

Birley, E. (1961). *Research on Hadrian's Wall*. Kendal, Titus Wilson.

Birley, R. (2009). *Vindolanda*. Stroud, Amberley.

Birley, R., and A. R. Birley (1994). 'Four new writing-tablets from Vindolanda'. *Zeitschrift für Papyrologie und Epigraphik* 100, 431–46.

Bishop, M. C. (2005). 'A new Flavian military site at Roecliffe, North Yorkshire'. *Britannia* 36, 135–223.

Bishop, M. C. (2014). *The secret history of the Roman roads of Britain*. Barnsley, Pen and Sword.

Bishop, M. C., and J. C. N. Coulston (2006). *Roman military equipment*. 2nd ed. Oxford, Oxbow.

Bishop, M. C., and J. N. Dore (1989). *Corbridge: Excavations of the Roman fort and town*. London, Historic Buildings and Monuments Commission for England.

Blake, S., S. Dean, and C. Wardle (2018). 'Staffordshire in the Roman period'. In R. White and M. Hodder (eds.), 136–57.

Bonnachi, C., M. Altaweel, and M. Krzyanska (2018). 'The heritage of Brexit'. *Journal of Social Archaeology* 18(2), 174–92.

Booth, P. (2018). 'Roman Warwickshire'. In R. White and M. Hodder (eds.), 33–45.

Bowden, W. (2013). 'The urban plan of "Venta Icenorum" '. *Britannia* 44, 145–69.

Bowman, A. K. (2003). *Life and letters on the Roman frontier*. Rev. ed. London, British Museum.

Bowman, A. K. (2006). 'Outposts of empire'. *Journal of Roman Archaeology* 19, 75–93.

Bowman, A. K., J. D. Thomas, and R. S. O. Tomlin (2010). 'The Vindolanda writing tablets (*Tabulae Vindolandenses* IV, Part 1)'. *Britannia* 41, 187–224.

Bowman, A. K., J. D. Thomas, and R. S. O. Tomlin (2019). 'The Vindolanda writing tablets (*Tabulae Vindolandenses* IV, Part 3): New letters of Iulius Verecundus'. *Britannia* 50, 225–51.

Bradley, M. (2010). Tacitus' *Agricola* and the conquest of Britain'. In M. Bradley (ed.), *Classics and imperialism in the British Empire*. Oxford, Oxford University Press, 123–57.

Braund, D. (1984). *Rome and the friendly king*. London, Croom Helm.

Braund, D. (1996a). *Ruling Roman Britain*. London, Routledge.

Braund, D. (1996b). 'River frontiers in the environmental psychology of the Roman world'. In D. L. Kennedy (ed.), *The Roman army in the east*. Portsmouth, RI, *Journal of Roman Archaeology*, 43–7.

Breeze, D. J. (2006a). *Roman Scotland*. Rev. ed. London, Batsford/Historic Scotland.

Breeze, D. J. (2006b). *J. Collingwood Bruce's handbook to the Roman Wall*. 14th ed. Newcastle upon Tyne, Society of Antiquaries of Newcastle upon Tyne.

Breeze, D. J. (2009). 'Did Hadrian design Hadrian's Wall?'. *Archaeologia Aeliana* 5(38), 87–103.

Breeze, D. J. (2011). *The frontiers of imperial Rome*. Barnsley, Pen and Sword.

Breeze, D. J. (2012). 'The civitas stones and the building of Hadrian's Wall'. *Transactions of the Cumberland and Westmorland Antiquarian and Archaeological Society* 3(12), 60–80.

Breeze, D. J. (2015). 'The Vallum of Hadrian's Wall'. *Archaeologia Aeliana* 5(44), 1–29.

Breeze, D. J. (2020). 'The army of the Antonine Wall'. In D. J. Breeze and W. S. Hanson (eds.), 286–99.

Breeze, D. J., B. Dobson, and V. Maxfield (2012). 'Maenius Agrippa, a chronological conundrum'. *Acta Classica* 55, 17–30.

Breeze, D. J., and I. Ferris (2016). 'They think it's all over: The face of victory on the British frontier'. *Journal of Conflict Archaeology* 11(1), 19–39.

Breeze, D. J., and W. S. Hanson (eds.) (2020). *The Antonine Wall*. Oxford, Archaeopress.

Breeze, D. J., L. M. Thoms, and D. W. Hall (eds.) (2009). *First contact: Roman and northern Britain*. Monograph 7. Perth, Tayside and Fife Archaeological Committee.

Brewer, R. J. (ed.) (2000). *Roman fortresses and their legions*. London, Society of Antiquaries of London/National Museum of Wales.

Brickstock, R. J. (2020). 'Pre-Antonine coins from the Antonine Wall'. In D. J. Breeze and W. S. Hanson (eds.), 61–6.

Britnell, W. J., and R. J. Silvester (2018). 'Hillforts and defended enclosures of the Welsh borderlands'. *Internet Archaeology* 48. doi.org/10.11141/ia.48.7.

Brown, R. A. (1986). 'The Iron Age and Romano-British settlement at Woodcock Hall, Saham Toney, Norfolk'. *Britannia* 17, 1–58.

Bruce, J. C. (1851). *The Roman Wall*. London, John Russell Smith.

Bruce, J. C. (1907). *The hand-book to the Roman Wall*. 5th ed. London, Longmans.

Bruce, J. C. (1933). *The handbook to the Roman Wall*. 9th ed. Edited by R. G. Collingwood. London, Longmans.

Brunaux, J.-L. (2018). A battle between Gauls in Picardy'. In M. Fernández-Götz and N. Roymans (eds.), 79–88.

Burnham, B., and H. Burnham (2004). *Dolaucothi-Pumsaint*. Oxford, Oxbow.

Burnham, B., and J. L. Davies (eds.) (2010). *Roman frontiers in Wales and the Marches*. Cardiff, Royal Commission on the Ancient and Historical Monuments of Wales.

Byron, G. G. (1841). *Child Harold's pilgrimage*. London, C. Daly.

Cahill Wilson, J. (2014). 'Romans and Roman material in Ireland'. In J. Cahill Wilson (ed.), *Late Iron Age and 'Roman' Ireland*, Report 8, Dublin, Worldwell/Discovery Programme, 11–58.

Cahill Wilson, J. (2016). '*Et tu, Hibernia*? Frontier zones and cultural contact'. In S. Gonzáles Sánchez and A. Guglielmi (eds.), *Romans and barbarians beyond the frontiers*. Oxford, Oxbow, 48–70.

Campbell, B. (2001). 'Diplomacy in the Roman world'. *Diplomacy and Statecraft* 12(1), 1–22.

Campbell, B. (2012). *Rivers and the power of ancient Rome*. Chapel Hill, University of North Carolina Press.

Campbell, D. B. (2010). *Mons Graupius AD 83*. Oxford, Osprey.

Campbell, D. B. (2018). *The fate of the Ninth*. Glasgow, Bocca della Vetità.

Campbell, L. (2020). 'Monuments on the margin of empire: The Antonine Wall sculptures'. In D. J. Breeze and W. S. Hanson (eds.), 96–109.

Caplan, C., and T. G. Newman (1976). 'Museum notes'. *Archaeologia Aeliana* 5(4), 171–6.

Carreras, C., and R. Morais (2012). 'The Atlantic Roman trade during the Principate'. *Oxford Journal of Archaeology* 31(4), 419–41.

Carroll, M. (2012). 'The insignia of women'. *Archaeological Journal* 169, 281–311.

Cartledge, P. (2004). *Alexander the Great*. London, Macmillan.

Champion, T. (2007). 'Prehistoric Kent'. In J. H. Williams (ed.), 67–134.

Clarke, K. (1999). *Between geography and history*. Oxford, Oxford University Press.

Clarke, K. (2001). 'An island nation: Re-reading Tacitus' "*Agricola*"'. *JRS* 91, 94–112.

Coleman, K. M. (1990). 'Fatal charades'. *JRS* 80, 44–73.

Collins, R. (2018). 'Hadrian's Wall: Roman Britain in 2017'. *Britannia* 49, 342–7.

Collins, R., and J. A. Biggins (2013). 'Metal-detecting and geophysical survey at Great Whittington, Northumberland'. *Archaeologia Aeliana* 5(42), 235–67.

Collins, R., and F. McIntosh (eds.) (2014). *Life in the Limes*. Oxford, Oxbow.

Collins, R., and M. Symonds (eds.) (2013). *Breaking down boundaries: Hadrian's Wall in the 21st century*. Portsmouth, RI, *Journal of Roman Archaeology*.

Collins, R., and M. Symonds (eds.) (2019). *Hadrian's Wall 2009–2019*. Kendal, Titus Wilson.

Cook, M., and L. Dunbar (2008). *Rituals, roundhouses and Romans: Excavations at Kintore, Aberdeenshire 2000–2006*. Vol. 1. *Forest Road*. Edinburgh, Scottish Trust for Archaeological Research.

Cooley, A. (2009). 'Text, translation and commentary', included within the translation of Augustus, *Res gestae divi Augusti*. Cambridge, Cambridge University Press.

Cooper, N. J., and R. Buckley (2003). 'New light on Roman Leicester (*Ratae Corieltauvorum*)'. In P. Wilson (ed.), 31–43.

Cousins, E. H. (2020). *The sanctuary at Bath in the Roman Empire*. Cambridge, Cambridge University Press.

Creighton, J. (2000). *Coins and power in Late Iron Age Britain*. Cambridge, Cambridge University Press.

Creighton, J. (2006). *Britannia: The creation of a Roman province*. London, Routledge.

Creighton, J., and R. Fry (2016). *Silchester: Changing visions of a Roman town*. Britannia monograph series 28. London, Society for the Promotion of Roman Studies.

Crow, J. (2004). 'The northern frontier of Britain from Trajan to Antoninus Pius'. In M. Todd (ed.), 114–35.

Crummy, N. (2016). 'A Hoard of military awards, jewellery and coins from Colchester'. *Britannia* 47, 1–28.

Crummy, P. (1984). *Colchester archaeological reports 3: Excavations at Lions Walk, Balkern Lane, and Middleborough, Colchester, Essex*. Colchester, Colchester Archaeological Trust.

Crummy, P. (2008). 'The Roman circus at Colchester'. *Britannia* 39, 15–32.

Crummy, P. (2016). 'It started with a fire, never thought it would come to this'. *Colchester Archaeologist* 28, 2–7.

Crummy, P., S. Benfield, N. Crummy, V. Rigby, and D. Shimmin (2007). *Stanway: An élite burial site at Camulodunum*. Britannia monograph series 24. London, Society for the Promotion of Roman Studies.

Cuff, D. B. (2011). 'The king of the Batavians'. *Britannia* 42, 145–56.

Cunliffe, B. W. (1984). 'Images of Britannia'. *Antiquity* 58, 175–8.

Cunliffe, B. (1991). 'Fishbourne revisited'. *Journal of Roman Archaeology* 4, 160–9.

Darvill, T., and G. Wainwright (2016). 'Neolithic and Bronze Age Pembrokeshire'. In H. James, M. J. Kenneth Murphy, and G. Wainwright (eds.), *Pembrokeshire county history*, Vol. 1, *Prehistoric, Roman and early medieval Pembrokeshire*. Haverfordwest, Pembrokeshire County History Trust, 55–222.

Davenport, C. (2019). 'Carausius and his brothers'. *Antichthon* 53, 108–33.

Davenport, P., C. Poole, and D. Jordan (2007). *Archaeology in Bath*. Oxford, Oxford University Press.

Davies, J. (2009). *The land of Boudica: Prehistoric and Roman Norfolk*. Oxford, Oxbow.

Dobson, B. (2009). 'The rôle of forts'. In W. S. Hanson (ed.), 25–32.

Drayton, M. (1622). *The Second Part, or a continuance of Poly-Olbion from the eighteenth song*. London, John Marriott and John Grismand.

Drinkwater, J. F. (2019). *Nero: Emperor and court*. Cambridge, Cambridge University Press.

Dunkle, R. (2014). 'Overview of Roman spectacle'. In P. Christesen and D. G. Kyle (eds.), *A companion to sport and spectacles in Greek and Roman antiquity*. London, Wiley–Blackwell, 441–55.

Esmonde Cleary, S. (2016). 'Britain at the end of empire'. In M. Millett, L. Revell, and A. Moore (eds.), 134–49.

Evans, E. M. (2018). 'Romano-British settlements in south-east Wales'. *Internet Archaeology* 48. doi.org/10.11141/ia.48.8.

Fanello, M. (2016). 'Later Iron Age coinage in Britain'. Ph.D. diss., University of Leicester.

Farley, J. (2012). 'At the edge of empire: Iron Age and Roman metalwork in the East Midlands'. Ph.D. diss., University of Leicester.

Fell, D. (2020). *Contact, concord and conquest: Britons and Romans at Scotch Corner*. Monograph 5. Barnard Castle, Northern Archaeological Associates.

Fernández-Götz, M., and N. Roymans (eds.) (2018). *Conflict archaeology*. London, Routledge.

Ferraby, R., and M. Millett (2020). *Isurium Brigantum*. London, Society of Antiquaries of London.

Ferris, I. (2020). 'Building an image: Soldier's labour and the Antonine Wall distance slabs'. In D. J. Breeze and W. S. Hanson (eds.), 110–20.

Ferris, I. (2021). *Visions of the Roman North*. Oxford, Archaeopress.

Fishwick, D. (1995). 'The temple of Divus Claudius at "Camulodunum"'. *Britannia* 26, 11–27.

Fishwick, D. (1997). 'The provincial centre at Camulodunum'. *Britannia* 28, 31–50.

Fitzpatrick, A. P. (2007). 'The fire, the feast and the funeral'. *Revue du Nord* 11, 123–42.

Fitzpatrick, A. P. (2018). 'L'enceinte d'Ebbsfleet sur l'île de Thanet (Kent): Un camp césarien en Angleterre'. In M. Reddé (ed.), 273–85.

Fitzpatrick, A. P. (2019). 'Caesar's landing sites in Britain and Gaul in 55 and 54 BC'. In A. P. Fitzpatrick and C. Haselgrove (eds.), *Julius Caesar's battle for Gaul*. Oxford, Oxbow, 135–58.

Foubert, L. (2013). Female travellers in Roman Britain'. In E. Hemelrijk and G. Woolf (eds.), 391–403.

Freeman, P. (2001). *Ireland and the classical world*. Austin, University of Texas Press.

Frere, S. S. (1967). *Britannia*. London, Routledge and Kegan Paul.

Frere, S. S., J. K. St Joseph, and D. Charlesworth (1974). 'The Roman fortress at Longthorpe'. *Britannia* 5, 1–129.

Fulford, M. (2006). 'Corvées and the *civitates*'. In R. J. A. Wilson (ed.), *Romanitas: Essays on Roman archaeology in honour of Sheppard Frere*. Oxford, Oxbow, 65–71.

Fulford, M. (2008). 'Nero and Britain'. *Britannia* 39, 1–14.

Fulford, M. (2015). 'The towns of south-east England'. In M. Fulford and N. Holbrook (eds.), 59–89.

Fulford, M. (2018). 'Concluding discussion'. In M. Fulford et al. (eds.) , 373–85.

Fulford, M. (2019). 'Silchester's Roman baths'. *Current Archaeology, CA Live*, 5 December. www.archaeology.co.uk/articles/silchesters-roman-baths.htm.

Fulford, M. (2021). *Silchester revealed*. Oxford, Windgather.

Fulford, M., A. Clarke, E. Durham, and N. Pankhurst (2018). *Late Iron Age Calleva*. Britannia monograph series 32. London, Society for the Promotion of Roman Studies.

Fulford, M., A. Clarke, E. Durham, and N. Pankhurst (2020). *Silchester insular IX*. Britannia monograph series 33. London, Society for the Promotion of Roman Studies.

Fulford, M., and N. Holbrook (eds.) (2015). *The towns of Roman Britain*. London, Britannia monograph series 27.

Gale, R. (1723). 'An account of a Roman inscription, found at Chichester'. *Philosophical Transactions* 32, 391–400.

Gambash, G. (2016). 'Estranging the familiar'. In D. Slootjes and M. Peachin (eds.), *Rome and the worlds beyond its frontiers*. Leiden, Brill, 20–32.

Garrow, D., and C. Gosden (2012). *Technologies of enchantment: Exploring Celtic art*. Oxford, Oxford Unversity Press.

Gascoyne, A., and D. Radford (2013). *Fortress of the war god: An archaeological assessment*. Oxford, Oxbow.

Gibson, B. (2006). 'Introduction, translation and commentary'. In P. P. Statius, *Silvae 5*. Oxford, Oxford University Press, .

Giles, M. (2012). *A forged glamour: Landscape, identity and material culture in the Iron Age*. Oxford, Oxbow.

Gillespie, C. C. (2018). *Boudica*. New York, Oxford University Press.

Goldsworthy, A. K. (1996). *The Roman army at war*. Oxford, Clarendon Press.

Goldsworthy, A. K. (2017). *Vindolanda*. London, Head of Zeus.

Goodman, M. (2012). *The Roman World: 44 BC–AD 180*. 2nd ed. New York, Routledge.

Graafstal, E. (2018). 'What happened in the summer of A.D. 122?' *Britannia* 49, 79–111.

Greene, E. M. (2013a). 'Female networks in military communities in the Roman West'. In E. Hemelrijk and G. Woolf (eds.), 369–90.

Greene, E. M. (2013b). 'Before Hadrian's Wall: Early communities at Vindolanda and on the northern frontier'. In R. Collins and M. Symonds (eds.), 17–32.

Greene, E. M. (2014). 'If the shoe fits: Style and status in the assemblage of children's shoes from Vindolanda'. In R. Collins and F. McIntosh (eds.), 29–36.

Greene, E. M. (2015). '*Conubium cum uxoribus*: Wives and children in Roman military diplomas'. *Journal of Roman Archaeology* 28, 125–59.

Guest, P. (2008). "The early monetary history of Roman Wales'. *Britannia* 39, 33–58.

Gwilt, A. (2007). 'Silent Silures?' In C. Haselgrove and T. Moore (eds.), 297–328.

Hanson, W. (ed.) (2009). *The army and frontiers of Rome*. Portsmouth, RI, *Journal of Roman Archaeology*.

Hanson, W. S. (2007a). *A Roman frontier fort in Scotland: Elginhaugh*. Stroud, Tempus.

Hanson, W. S. (2007b). *Elginhaugh: A Flavian fort and its annex*. Britannia monograph series 23. London, Society for the Promotion of Roman Studies.

Hanson, W. S. (2009). 'The fort at Elginhaugh and its implications for Agricola's role in the conquest of Scotland'. In D. J. Breeze, L. M. Thoms, and D. W. Hall (eds.), 49–58.

Hanson, W. S. (2012). 'Newstead and Roman Scotland'. In F. Hunter and L. Keppie (eds.), 63–76.

Hanson, W. S. (2014). 'The nature and function of Roman frontiers revisited'. In R. Collins and F. McIntosh (eds.), 4–17.

Hanson, W. S., and D. J. Breeze (2020). 'The Antonine Wall: The current state of knowledge'. In D. J. Breeze and W. S. Hanson (eds.), 9–36.

Hanson, W. S., R. E. Jones, and R. H. Jones (2019). 'The Roman military presence at Dalswinton, Dumfriesshire'. *Britannia* 50, 285–320.

Hanson, W. S., and G. Maxwell (1983). *The Antonine Wall*. Edinburgh, Edinburgh University Press.

Harding, D. (2012). *Iron Age hillforts in Britain and beyond*. Oxford, Oxford University Press.

Haselgrove, C. (2004). 'Society and polity in Late Iron Age Britain'. In M. Todd (ed.), 12–29.

Haselgrove, C. (2009). 'The Iron Age'. In J. Hunter and I. Ralston (eds.), *The archaeology of Britain*. New York, Routledge, 149–74.

Haselgrove, C. (2016). *Cartimandua's capital? The late Iron Age royal site at Stanwick, North Yorkshire*. York, Council for British Archaeology.

Haselgrove, C. (2018). 'The Iron Age coins'. In M. Fulford et al. (eds.), 77–91.

Haselgrove, C., and T. Moore (eds.) (2007). *The Later Iron Age in Britain and beyond*. Oxford, Oxbow.

Haselgrove, C., and V. Score (2014). 'The Iron Age open-air ritual site at Hallaton, Leicestershire'. In C. Gosden, S. Crawford, and K. Ulmschneider (eds.), *Celtic art in Europe*. Oxford, Oxbow 304–14.

Hassall, M. (1999). 'Soldier and civilian'. In H. Hurst (ed.), 181–5.

Haynes, I. (2013). *Blood of the provinces*. Oxford, Oxford University Press.

Hemelrijk, E., and G. Woolf (eds.) (2013). *Women and the Roman city in the Latin West*. Leiden, Brill.

Henig, M., and R. S. O. Tomlin (2008). 'The sculptural stone'. In A. Simmonds, N. Márquez-Grant, and L. Loe (eds.), *Life and death in a Roman city*. Oxford, Oxford Archaeology, 116–8.

Heywood, B. (2009). 'The vallum at Limestone Corner'. In T. Wilmott (ed.), *Hadrian's Wall, archaeological research by English Heritage 1976–2000*. Swindon, English Heritage, 419.

Hill, J. D. (2007). 'The dynamics of social change in Later Iron Age eastern and south-eastern England c. 300 BC–AD 43'. In C. Haselgrove and T. Moore (eds.), 16–40.

Hill, J. D., A. Spence, S. La Niece, and S. Worrell (2004). 'The Winchester Hoard'. *Antiquaries Journal* 84, 1–22.

Hind, J. G. F. (2003). 'Caligula and the spoils of Ocean'. *Britannia* 34, 172–4.

Hind, J. G. F. (2007). 'A. Plautius' campaign in Britain'. *Britannia* 38, 93–106.

Hingley, R. (2008). *The recovery of Roman Britain*. Oxford, Oxford University Press.

Hingley, R. (2011). 'Iron Age knowledge: Pre-Roman peoples and myths of origin'. In T. Moore and X.-L. Armada (eds.), *Atlantic Europe in the first millennium BC*. Oxford, Oxford University Press, 617–37.

Hingley, R. (2012). *Hadrian's Wall: A life*. Oxford, Oxford University Press.

Hingley, R. (2016). 'Early studies in Roman Britain'. In M. Millett et al. (eds.), 3–21.

Hingley, R. (2017). 'The Romans in Britain'. In C. Beaule (ed.), *Frontiers of colonialism*. Gainesville, University Press of Florida, 89–109.

Hingley, R. (2018). *Londinium: A biography*. London, Bloomsbury.

Hingley, R. (2020a). 'Egalitarianism and the southern British Iron Age'. In B. X. Currás and I. Sastre (eds.), *Alternative Iron Ages*. London, Routledge, 109–26.

Hingley, R. (2020b). 'Hadrian's Wall: An allegory for British disunity'. In F. Kaminski-Jones and R. Kaminski-Jones (eds.), *Celts, Romans and Britons: Classical and Celtic Influences in the construction of British identities*. Oxford, Oxford University Press, 201–22.

Hingley, R. (2020c). 'Iron Age and Roman ancient monuments that are available to visit in England, Scotland and Wales'. Ancient Identities Output. https://figshare.com/articles/online_resource/Iron_Age_and_Roman_ancient_monuments_and_open-air_museums_that_are_available_to_visit_in_England_Scotland_and_Wales_Ancient_Identities_Output_2019_/12807236/1.

Hingley, R., C. Bonacchi, and K. Sharpe (2018). 'Are you local?' *Britannia* 49, 283–302.

Hingley, R., and C. Unwin (2005). *Boudica: Iron Age warrior queen*. London, Bloomsbury.

Hirt, A. M. (2010). *Imperial mines and quarries in the Roman world*. Oxford, Oxford University Press.

Hobley, A. S. (1989). 'The numismatic evidence for the post-Agricolan abandonment of the Roman frontier in northern Scotland'. *Britannia* 20, 69–74.

Hodgson, N. (2000). 'The Stanegate'. *Britannia* 31, 11–22.

Hodgson, N. (2009a). 'Review: Elginhaugh'. *Britannia* 40, 365–8.

Hodgson, N. (2009b). 'A review of research on Hadrian's Wall'. In N. Hodgson (ed.), *Hadrian's Wall 1999–2009*. Kendal, Titus and Wilson, 5–52.

Hodgson, N. (2012). *The Iron Age on the Northumberland coastal plain*. Newcastle upon Tyne, Tyne and Wear Archaeology and the Arbeia Society.

Hodgson, N. (2016). *Chesters Roman Fort and the Clayton Museum*. Rev. ed. London, English Heritage.

Hodgson, N. (2017). *Hadrian's Wall: Archaeology and history at the limit of Rome's empire*. Marlborough, Robert Hale.

Hodgson, N. (2020). 'Why was the Antonine Wall made of turf rather than stone?'. In D. J. Breeze and W. S. Hanson (eds.), 300–12.

Hodgson, N. (2021). 'The end of the Ninth Legion, war in Britain and the building of Hadrian's Wall'. Britannia, First View Articles. doi:10.1017/S0068113X21000015.

Hoffmann, B. (2009). 'Cardean: The changing face of Flavian forts in Scotland'. In D. J. Breeze, L. M. Thoms, and D. W. Hall (eds.), 29–32.

Hoffmann, B. (2013). *The Roman invasion of Britain*. Barnsley, Pen and Sword.

Holbrook, N. (2008). 'Cirencester and the Cotswolds'. *Journal of Roman Archaeology* 21, 304–23.

Holbrook, N. (2015). 'The towns of south-west England'. In M. Fulford and N. Holbrook (eds.), 90–116.

Holman, D. (2005). 'Iron Age coinage and settlement in east Kent'. *Britannia* 36, 1–54.

Holmes, N. M. McQ (2014). 'The Synton and Kippilaw denarius hoards'. *Proceedings of the Society of Antiquaries of Scotland* 144, 133–67.

Hopewell, D. (2018). 'Roman Anglesey'. *Britannia* 49, 313–22.

Hornung, S. (2018). 'Tracing Julius Caesar'. In M. Fernández-Götz and N. Roymans (eds.), 193–203.

Hunter, F. (2001). 'Roman and native in Scotland'. *Journal of Roman Archaeology* 14, 289–309.

Hunter, F. (2005). 'The image of the warrior in the British Iron Age'. In C. Haselgrove and D. Wigg-Wolf (eds.), *Iron Age coinage and ritual practices*. Mainz am Rhein, Von Zabern, 25–68.

Hunter, F. (2007). *Beyond the edge of the empire*. Inverness, Groam House Museum.

Hunter, F. (2009). 'Traprain Law and the Roman world'. In W. S. Hanson (ed.), 225–40.

Hunter, F. (2016). 'Beyond Hadrian's Wall'. In M. Millett, L. Revell, and A. Moore (eds.), 179–202.

Hunter, F., and M. Carruthers (eds.) (2012a). Scotland: The Roman presence: ScARF summary Roman panel document. https://scarf.scot/national/roman-scotland-panel-report/.

Hunter, F., and M. Carruthers (eds.) (2012b). Iron Age Scotland: ScARF panel report. https://scarf.scot/wp-content/uploads/sites/15/2015/12/ScARF%20Iron%20Age%20Sept%202012.pdf.

Hunter, F., and L. Keppie (eds.) (2012). *A Roman frontier post and its people: Newstead 1911–2011*. Edinburgh, National Museum of Scotland.

Hurst, H. (1999). 'Topography and identity in *Glevum colonia*'. In H. Hurst (ed.), 113–35.

Hurst, H. (ed.) (1999). *The coloniae of Roman Britain*. Supplementary series 36. Portsmouth, RI, *Journal of Roman Archaeology*.

Inall, Y. L. (2014). 'Burials of martial character in the British Iron Age'. In G. J. R. Erskine, P. Jacobsson, P. Miller, and S. Stetkiewicz (eds.), *Proceedings of the 17th Iron Age Research Student Symposium, Edinburgh*. Oxford, Archaeopress, 44–61.

Irby-Massie, G. (1999). *Military religion in Roman Britain*. Leiden, Brill.

Ivleva, T. (2016). 'Britons on the move'. In M. Millett, L. Revell, and A. Moore (eds.), 245–61.

Jackson, R., and G. Burleigh (2018). *Dea Senua*. London, British Museum.

James, S. (2006). 'Engendering change in our understanding of the structure of Roman military communities'. *Archaeological Dialogues* 13(1), 31–6.

Johnston, A. C. (2019). 'Rewriting Caesar: Cassius Dio and an alternative ethnography of the north'. *Histos* 13, 53–77.

Jones, M. J. (2002). *Roman Lincoln*. Stroud, Tempus.

Jones, R. H. (2012). *Roman camps in Britain*. Stroud, Amberley.

Jones, S., and C. Randall (2010). 'Death, destruction and the end of an era'. In M. Sterry, A. Tullett, and N. Ray (eds.), *In search of the Iron Age*. Oxford, Oxbow, 165–84.

Kennedy, D. (1983). 'C. Velius Rufus'. *Britannia* 14, 183–96.

Keppie, L. (2000). 'Legio VIII in Britain'. In R. Brewer (ed.), 83–100.

Keppie, L. (2012). 'The search for Trimontium'. In F. Hunter and L. Keppie (eds.), 11–22.

Krakowka, K. (2019). 'New finds from the Pembrokeshire chariot burial'. *Current Archaeology*. 3 September. www.archaeology.co.uk/articles/new-finds-from-the-pembrokeshire-chariot-burial.htm.

Lange, C. H., and J. M. Madsen (2016). 'Between history and politics'. In C. H. Lange and J. M. Madsen (eds.), *Cassius Dio: Greek intellectual and Roman politician*. Boston, Brill, 1–10.

La Niece, S., J. Farley, N. Meeks, and J. Joy (2018). 'Gold in Iron Age Britain'. In R. Schwab, P.-Y. Milcent, B. Armbruster, and E. Pernicka (eds.), *Early Iron Age gold in Celtic Europe*. Forschungen Zur Archäometrie Und Altertumswissenschaft. Verlag Marie Leidorf GmbH, Rahden, Westfalia, 407–30.

Laurence, R. S., S. Esmonde Cleary, and G. Sears (2011). *The city in the Roman West*. Cambridge, Cambridge University Press.

Leins, I., and J. Farley (2015). 'A changing world, c. 150 BC–AD 50'. In J. Farley and F. Hunter (eds.), *Celts: Art and identity*. London, British Museum Press, 108–27.

Levene, D. S. (2010). 'Warfare in the *Annals*'. In A. J. Woodman (ed.), 225–38.

Lyons, A. (2018). 'Sites explored, 6. East Anglia'. *Britannia* 49, 372–9.

Macinnes, L. (1984). 'Brochs and the Roman occupation of lowland Scotland'. *Proceedings of the Society of Antiquaries of Scotland* 114, 235–49.

Macinnes, L. (2020). 'The impact of the Antonine Wall on Iron Age society'. In D. J. Breeze and W. S. Hanson (eds.), 47–60.

Madsen, J. M. (2020). *Cassius Dio*. New York, Bloomsbury.

Malloch, S. J. V. (2010). '*Hamlet* without the prince? The Claudian *Annals*'. In A. J. Woodman (ed.), 116–26.

Mann, J. C. (1985). 'Two "topoi" in the *Agricola*'. *Britannia* 16, 21–4.

Mann, J. C., and D. J. Breeze (1987). 'Ptolemy, Tacitus and the tribes of north Britain'. *Proceedings of the Society of Antiquaries of Scotland* 117, 85–91.

Manning, W. H. (2000). 'The fortresses of the *legio* XX'. In R. Brewer (ed.), 69–82.

Manning, W. H. (2004). 'The conquest of Wales'. In M. Todd (ed.), 60–74.

Marshak, A. K. (2015). *The many faces of Herod the Great*. Grand Rapids, MI, Eerdmans.

Mason, D. (2009). *Roman Britain and the Roman navy*. Reprint: Stroud, History Press.

Mason, D. (2012). *Roman Chester*. Reprint: Stroud, History Press.

Master, J. (2016). *Provincial soldiers and imperial instability in the 'Histories' of Tacitus*. Ann Arbor, University of Michigan Press.

Mattingly, D. J. (2006). *An imperial possession: Britain in the Roman empire*. London, Allen Lane.

Mattingly, D. J. (2011). *Imperialism, power, and identity*. Princeton, NJ, Princeton University Press.

Maxfield, V. A. (1982). 'Mural controversies'. In B. Orme (ed.), *Problems and case studies in archaeological dating*. Exeter, Exeter University, 57–82.

May, J. (2001). '*Coins and power in Late Iron Age Britain*, by J. Creighton' (review). *British Numismatic Journal* 71, 199–200.

McCarthy, M. (2018). 'Carlisle: Function and change between the first and seventh centuries AD'. *Archaeological Journal* 175, 292–314.

McPhial, C. (2014). 'Pytheas of Massalia's route of travel'. *Phoenix* 68(3/4), 247–57.

Meyer, M. (2018). 'The Germanic-Roman battlefields of Kalkriese and Harzhorn'. In M. Fernández-Götz and N. Roymans (eds.), 205–17.

Midford, S. (2014). 'Roman imperial triumphal arches'. *Iris* 27, 11–26.

Millett, M. (1990). *The Romanization of Britain*. Cambridge, Cambridge University Press.

Millett, M. (2007). 'Roman Kent'. In J. H. Williams (ed.), 135–86.

Millett, M. (2011). 'Roman Britain since Haverfield'. In M. Millett et al. (eds.), 22–42.

Millett, M., L. Revell, and A. Moore (eds.) (2016). *The Oxford handbook of Roman Britain*. Oxford, Oxford University Press.

Millett, M., and T. Wilmott (2003). 'Rethinking Richborough'. In P. Wilson (ed.), 184–94.

Monty Python (n.d.). 'Scene 10: Before the Romans things were smelly'. Another Bleeding Monty Python Website, Life of Brian. http://montypython.50webs.com/scripts/Life_of_Brian/10.htm.

Moore, T. (2011). 'Detribalising the later prehistoric past'. *Journal of Social Archaeology* 11(3): 334–60.

Moore, T. (2012). 'Beyond the oppida: Polyfocal complexes and Late Iron Age societies in southern Britain'. *Oxford Journal of Archaeology* 31(4), 391–417.

Moore, T. (2017a). 'Caesar on Britain'. In K. A. Raaflaub (ed.), 44–7.

Moore, T. (2017b). 'Alternatives to Urbanism? Reconsidering oppida and the urban question'. *Journal of World Prehistory* 30, 281–300.

Moore, T. (2020). *A biography of power: Research and excavations at the Iron Age 'oppidum' of Bagendon, Gloucestershire*. Oxford, Archaeopress.

Morgan, G. (2005). *69 AD: The year of four emperors*. Oxford, Oxford University Press.

Murison, C. L. (1999). *Rebellion and reconstruction, Galba to Domitian*. Atlanta, GA, Scholars Press.

Niblett, R. (2001). *Verulamium*. Stroud, Tempus.

Niblett, R. (2004). 'The native elite and their funerary practices from the first century BC to Nero'. In M. Todd (ed.), 30–41.

Niblett, R. (2005). 'Roman Verulamium'. In R. Niblett and I. Thompson (eds.), Alban's buried towns. Oxford, Oxbow, 41–165.

Nowakowski, J. A. (2011). 'Appraising the bigger picture—Cornish Iron Age and Romano-British lives and settlements 25 years on'. *Cornish Archaeology* 50, 241–61.

O'Gorman, E. (1993). 'No place like Rome: Identity and difference in the Germania of Tacitus'. *Ramus* 22(2), 135–54.

Oltean, I. A. (2007). *Dacia: Landscape, colonisation and romanisation*. Abingdon, London.

Osgood, J. (2011). *Claudius Caesar*. Cambridge, Cambridge University Press.

Ottaway, P. (2011). *Roman York*. Reprint: Stroud, History Press.

Ottaway, P. (2013). *Roman Yorkshire*. Pickering, Blackthorn Press.

Owen, O. (1992). 'Eildon Hill North'. In J. S. Rideout, O. A. Owen, and E. Halpin (eds.), *Hillforts of southern Scotland*. Edinburgh, AOC (Scotland), 21–72.

Philpot, S., and T. W. Potter (1996). 'Excavations at Stonea Camp'. In R. P. J. Jackson and T. W. Potter (eds.), *Excavations at Stonea, Cambridgeshire*. London, British Museum, 27–44.

Pitts, L. F. (1989). 'Relations between Rome and the German 'kings' on the middle Danube'. *JRS* 79, 45–58.

Pitts, L. F., and J. K. St. Joseph (1985). *Inchtuthil: The Roman legionary fortress*. London, Society for the Promotion of Roman Studies.

Potter, T. W. (2002). 'The transformation of Britain: From 55 BC to AD 61'. In P. Salway (ed.), *The Roman era*. Oxford, Oxford University Press, 11–38.

Potter, T. W., and B. Robinson (2000). 'New Roman and prehistoric aerial discoveries at Grandford, Cambridgeshire'. *Antiquity* 74, 31–2.

Raaflaub, K. A. (2017a). 'Gallic War'. In K. A. Raaflaub (ed.), *The Landmark Julius Caesar*. New York, Anchor Books, 1–268.

Raaflaub, K. A. (ed.) (2017b). *The Landmark Julius Caesar: Web essays*. New York, Pantheon.

Raaflaub, K. A., and J. T. Ramsey (2017). 'Reconstructing the chronology of Caesar's Gallic Wars'. *Histos* 11, 1–74.

Ralston, I. (2017). 'Oppida: Towns in Caesar's world'. In K. A. Raaflaub (ed.), 52–7.

Reddé, M. (2018). 'L'armée romaines en Gaule à l'époque républicaine'. In M. Reddé (ed.), 287–300.

Reddé, M. (ed.) (2018). *L'armée romaines en Gaule à l'époque républicaine*. Collection Bibracte 28. Glux-en-Glenne, Bibracte-Centre archéologique européen.
Redfern, R. C. (2011). 'A re-appraisal of the evidence for violence in the Late Iron Age human remains from Maiden Castle Hillfort, Dorset'. *Proceedings of the Prehistoric Society* 77, 111–38.
Reid, J. H., and A. Nicholson (2019). 'Burnswark Hill'. *Journal of Roman Archaeology* 32, 459–77.
Revell, L. (2009). *Roman imperialism and local reactions*. Cambridge, Cambridge University Press.
Richmond, I. A. (1968). *Hod Hill*. Vol. 2. *Excavations carried out between 1951 and 1958*. London, British Museum.
Richmond, I. A., and R. P. Wright (1943). 'Stones from a Hadrianic war memorial on Tyneside'. *Archaeologia Aeliana* 4(21), 93–120.
Riggsby, A. M. (2006). *Caesar in Gaul and Rome*. Austin, University of Texas Press.
Rippon, S., and N. Holbrook (2021). 'Exeter's local and regional hinterland'. In S. Rippon and N. Holbrook (eds.), *Roman and medieval Exeter and their hinterlands: From Isca to Excester*. Oxford, Oxbow, 27–44.
Rippon, S., and N. Holbrook (eds.) (2021). *Roman and medieval Exeter and their hinterlands: From Isca to Excester*. Oxford, Oxbow.
Rivet, A. L. F., and C. Smith (1979). *The place-names of Roman Britain*. London, Batsford.
Rogers, A. (2016). 'The development of towns'. In M. Millett, L. Revell, and A. Moore (eds.), 741–66.
Roller, D. W. (2018). *A historical and topographical guide to the geography of Strabo*. Cambridge, Cambridge University Press.
Roman Inscriptions of Britain. https://romaninscriptionsofbritain.org/.
Romer, F. E. (1998). *Pomponius Mela's description of the world*. Ann Arbor, University of Michigan Press.
Romm, J. S. (1992). *The edges of the earth in ancient thought*. Princeton, NJ, Princeton University Press.
Romm, J. S. (2014). *Dying every day: Seneca at the court of Nero*. New York, Random House.
Roncaglia, C. (2019). 'Claudius' houseboat'. *Greece and Rome* 66(1), 61–70.
Rose, C. B. (1990). '"Princes" and barbarians on the Ara Pacis'. *American Journal of Archaeology* 94(3), 453–67.
Rothe, U. (2020). *The toga and Roman identity*. London, Bloomsbury.
Roymans, N. (2014). 'The Batavians between Germania and Rome'. In M. A. Janković, V. D. Mihajlović, and S. Babić (eds.), *The edges of the Roman world*. Newcastle upon Tyne, Cambridge Scholars, 232–50.
Roymans, N. (2018). 'A Roman massacre in the far north'. In M. Fernández-Götz and N. Roymans (eds.) , 167–81.
Roymans, N., and M. Fernández-Götz (2019). 'Re-considering the Roman conquest'. *Journal of Roman Archaeology* 32, 415–20.
Rutledge, S. (2012). *Ancient Rome as a museum*. Oxford, Oxford University Press.
Sailor, D. (2008). *Writing and empire in Tacitus*. Cambridge, Cambridge University Press.
Salway, P. (1981). *Roman Britain*. Oxford, Clarendon Press.
Sande, S. (2015). 'The "barbarian princes" in the Ara Pacis procession'. *Acta ad archaeologiam et artium historiam pertinentia* 280, 7–46.
Sauer, E. W. (2000). 'Alchester, a Claudian vexillation fortress'. *Archaeological Journal* 157, 1–78.
Sauer, E. W. (2005). 'Inscriptions from Alchester'. *Britannia* 36, 101–33.
Schörner, G. (2009). 'Rom jenseits der Grenze: Klientelkönigreiche und der impact of empire'. In O. Hekster and T. Kaizer (eds.), *Frontiers in the Roman World*. Boston, Brill, 113–32.
Schulz, V. (2019). *Deconstructing imperial representations*. Boston, Leiden.
Score, V. (2011). *Hoards, hounds and helmets: A conquest-period ritual site at Hallaton, Leicestershire*. Leicester, University of Leicester Archaeological Services.

Scott, E. (2018). 'Polyandry in Late Iron Age and Roman Britain'. Eleanor Scott Archaeology. https://eleanorscottarchaeology.com/els-archaeology-blog/2018/3/6/polyandry-in-late-iron-age-and-roman-britain-myth-or-reality.

Scott, M. (2003). *Boudica: Dreaming the eagle*. London, Bantam.

Seller, W. C., and R. J. Yeatman (1930). *1066 and all that*. London, Methuen.

Serban, M. (2009). 'Trajan's bridge over the Danube'. *International Journal of Nautical Archaeology* 38(2), 331–42.

Sharples, N. (2010). *Social relations in later prehistory*. Oxford, Oxford University Press.

Sharples, N. (2014). 'Are the developed hillforts of Southern England urban?' In M. Fernández-Götz, H. Wendling, and K. Winger (eds.), *Paths to Complexity*. Oxford, Oxbow, 224–32.

Shotter, D. (2009). 'Why did the Romans invade Scotland?'. In D. J. Breeze, L. M. Thoms, and D. W. Hall (eds.), 15–9.

Shumate, N. (2006). *Nation, empire, decline*. London, Duckworth.

Smith, A., M. Allen, T. Brindle, and M. Fulford (2016). *New visions of the countryside of Roman Britain*. Vol. 1. *The rural settlement of Roman Britain*. Britannia Monograph Series 29. London, Society for the Promotion of Roman Studies.

Smith, G. (2018). 'Hillforts and hut groups of north-west Wales'. *Internet Archaeology* 48. doi.org/10.11141/ia.48.6.

Smith, I. G. (2015). 'A chronology for Agricola'. *Zeitschrift für Alte Geschichte* 64(2), 156–204.

Smith, R. R. R. (2013). *The marble reliefs from the Julio-Claudian Sebasteion, Aphrodisias VI*. Darmstadt, Phillipp von Zarbern.

Sparey-Green, C. (2015). '*Inungi delectus*—The recruitment of Britons in the Roman army during the conquest'. In S. T. Roselaar (ed.), *Processes of cultural change and integration in the Roman world*. Leiden, Brill, 106–35.

Speed, J. (1632). *The history of Great Britaine under the conquest of ye Romans, Saxons, Danes and Normans* (1611). London, John Sunbury and Georg Humble.

Stafford, E. (2012). *Herakles*. London, Routledge.

Stewart, D., P. Cheetham, and M. Russell (2020). 'A magnetometry survey of the Second Augustan legionary fortress at Lake Farm, Dorset'. *Britannia* 51, 307–87.

Stewart, P. C. N. (1995). 'Inventing *Britannia*'. *Britannia* 26, 1–10.

Strobel, K. (1986). 'Zur Rekonstruktion der Laufbahn des C. Velius Rufus'. *Zeitschrift für Papyrologie und Epigraphik* 64, 265–86.

Strong, D. E. (1968). 'The monument'. In B. Cunliffe (ed.), *Fifth report on the excavations of the Roman fort at Richborough, Kent*. London, Society of Antiquaries, 40–73.

Symonds, M. (2015). 'The curious incident of fortlets in the Pennines'. In D. J. Breeze, R. H. Jones, and I. A. Oltean (eds.), *Understanding Roman frontiers*. Edinburgh, John Donald, 82–100.

Symonds, M. (2018a). *Protecting the Roman empire*. Cambridge, Cambridge University Press.

Symonds, M. (2018b). 'A composite coastal cordon on Exmoor?' *Britannia* 49, 53–77.

Symonds, M. (2020a). 'Fords and the frontier: Waging counter-mobility on Hadrian's Wall'. *Antiquity* 94, 92–109.

Symonds, M. (2020b). 'Putting the wall into Hadrian's Wall'. *Journal of Roman Archaeology* 33, 752–8.

Symonds, M., and D. J. P. Mason (eds.) (2009). *Frontiers of knowledge: A research framework for Hadrian's Wall*. Vol. 1. Durham, Durham County Council.

Tacoma, L. E., T. Ivleva, and D. J. Breeze (2016). 'Lost along the way'. *Britannia* 47, 31–42.

Taylor, A., C. Falys, A. P. Fitzpatrick, and M. Giles (2020). 'Farewell to arms: The North Bersted warrior burial'. *British Archaeology* 171, 16–23.

Taylor, A., A. Weale, and S. Ford (2014). *Bronze Age, Iron Age and Roman landscapes of the coastal plain, and a Late Iron Age warrior burial at North Bersted, Bognor Regis, West Sussex*. Monograph 19. Reading, Thames Valley Archaeological Services.

Thomas, E. (2007). *Monumentality and the Roman empire*. Oxford, Oxford University Press.

Thompson, F. H. (1983). 'Excavations at Bigberry, Near Canterbury, 1978–80'. *Antiquaries Journal* 63, 237–78.

Todd, M. (1981). *Roman Britain, 55 BC–AD 400*. London, Fontana.

Todd, M. (2004). 'The Claudian conquest and its consequences'. In M. Todd (ed.), 42–59.

Todd, M. (2007). *Roman mining in Somerset: Charterhouse on Mendip*. Exeter, Mint Press.

Todd, M. (ed.) (2004). *A companion to Roman Britain*. Oxford, Blackwell.

Tomlin, R. S. O. (2003). 'The girl in question'. *Britannia* 34, 41–51.

Tomlin, R. S. O. (2013). 'Inscriptions'. *Britannia*, 44, 381–96.

Tomlin, R. S. O. (2016). *Roman London's first voices*. London, Museum of London.

Tomlin, R. S. O. (2018). *Britannia Romana: Roman inscriptions and Roman Britain*. Philadelphia, Oxbow.

Tomlin, R. S. O. (2020). 'Inscriptions'. *Britannia* 50, 495–524.

van Driel-Murray, C. (1994). 'A question of gender in a military context'. *Helinium* 34(2), 342–62.

Wacher, J. (1995). *The towns of Roman Britain*. 2nd ed. London, Routledge.

Wallace, L., and A. Mullen (2019). 'Landscape, monumentality and expression of group identities in Iron Age and Roman East Kent'. *Britannia* 50, 75–108.

Walton, P., and S. Moorhead (2016). 'Coinage and the economy'. In M. Millett, L. Revell, and A. Moore (eds.), 834–49.

Webley, L. (2015). 'Rethinking Iron Age connections across the Channel and North Sea'. In H. Anderson-Whymark, D. Garrow, and F. Sturt (eds.), *Continental connections*. Oxford, Oxbow, 122–44.

Webster, P. (2003). 'An early fort at Caerwent?' In T. Wilson (ed.), 214–20.

White, R. (2018). 'Fortresses, forts, and the impact of the Roman army in the West Midlands'. In R. White and M. Hodder (eds.), 15–33.

White, R., and P. Barker (1998). *Wroxeter: Life and death of a Roman city*. Stroud, Tempus.

White, R., and M. Hodder (eds.) (2018). *Clash of cultures? The Romano-British period in the West Midlands*. Oxford, Oxbow.

Williams, J. H. (ed.) (2007). *The archaeology of Kent to AD 800*. Woodbridge, Boydell Press/Kent County Council.

Williams, J. H. C. (1999). 'Septimius Severus and Sol, Carausius and Oceanus'. *Numismatics Chronicle* 159, 307–13.

Williams, J. H. C. (2000). 'The silver coins from East Anglia attributed to King Prasutagus of the Iceni'. *Numismatics Chronicle* 160, 276–81.

Williams, J. H. C. (2005). 'Coinage and identity in pre-conquest Britain, 50 BC–AD 50'. In C. Howgego, V. Heuchert, and A. Burnett (eds.), *Coinage and identity in the Roman provinces*. Oxford, Oxford University Press, 69–78.

Williams, J. H. C. (2007). 'New light on Latin in pre-conquest Britain'. *Britannia* 38, 1–11.

Willis, S. (2007). 'Sea, coast, estuary and land in Iron Age Britain'. In C. Haselgrove and T. Moore (eds.), 107–29.

Wilmott, T. (2008). 'The vallum'. In P. Bidwell (ed.), *Understanding Hadrian's Wall*. Kendal, Titus Wilson, 119–28.

Wilmott, T. (2012). *Richborough and Reculver*. London, English Heritage.

Wilson, P. (ed.) (2003). *The archaeology of Roman towns*. Oxford, Oxbow.

Wilson, P. (2009). 'Holding the line?' In D. J. Breeze, L. M. Thoms, and D. W. Hall (eds.), 8–14.

Woodman, A. J. (ed.) (2010). *The Cambridge companion to Tacitus*. Cambridge, Cambridge University Press.

Woodman, A. J. (2014). 'Introduction, commentary'. In Tacitus, *Tacitus Agricola*. Cambridge, Cambridge University Press, 1–37.

Woolliscroft, D. (2009). '79 AD and all that: When did the Romans reach Perthshire?' In D. J. Breeze, L. M. Thoms, and D. W. Hall (eds.), 33–8.

Zant, J. (2009). *The Carlisle Millennium Project, excavations in Carlisle 1998–2001*. Vol 1. *Stratigraphy*. Lancaster, Lancaster Imprints.

INDEX

For the benefit of digital users, indexed terms that span two pages (e.g., 52–53) may, on occasion, appear on only one of those pages.

Figures are indicated by *f* following the page number